GREGORY PECK

A Charmed Life

Lynn Haney

CARROLL & GRAF PUBLISHERS
NEW YORK

GREGORY PECK
A Charmed Life

Carroll & Graf Publishers
An Imprint of Avalon Publishing Group Inc.
245 West 17th Street
11th Floor
New York, NY 10011

AVALON
publishing group incorporated

Copyright © 2003 by Lynn Haney

First Carroll & Graf edition 2004

Library of Congress Cataloging-in-Publication Data is available.

ISBN: 0-7867-1473-5

Printed in the United States of America
Distributed by Publishers Group West

Contents

For John

CHAPTER ONE

Rising Star

'Success so big and so speedy never happened to anybody anywhere, not even in Hollywood, not even to Garbo and Gable.'

Colliers Magazine, December 1945

'Who the hell is Gregory Peck?' Leland Hayward barked into the telephone. The hottest talent agent in Hollywood was pressing his New York office for a quick rundown on a rising Broadway actor. The year was 1942 and talent scouts had been circling the young man.

Hayward could see the name Gregory Peck listed in his company's roster of 150 performers and writers, but who the devil was he? He needed an answer fast. Ordinarily, Hayward was too busy making million-dollar deals for his high-flying clients, such as Henry Fonda, Greta Garbo, Judy Garland and Fred Astaire, to bother about newcomers. But in the case of Peck, he was making an exception. An excitement was building about the actor. In fact, at that moment, Sam Goldwyn was holding on another of Hayward's phone lines. The movie titan wanted to sign Peck to a seven-year contract. Leland decided to wing it until he got all the facts.

'I'm willing to go to $1,000 a week,' Goldwyn offered.

'Make it $3,000,' Hayward blithely retorted.

Both men excelled at the art of bluffing, but Hayward had the edge. Known far and wide as 'The Toscanini of the Telephone,' he cajoled, charmed and manipulated whoever happened to be on the other end of the conversation. His daughter Brooke Hayward reminisced in *Haywire*, a memoir of her magical but doomed family: 'He was happiest when he was conducting business on his office sofa with three or four telephones at hand, his head deep in a cushion at one end and his feet comfortably crossed at the other.'

Samuel Goldwyn (originally Schmuel Gelbfisz – his name meant Goldfish but when he merged with the Selwyn Brothers to create the Goldwyn studio, he kept the name for himself) was Hollywood's major independent producer. Besides earning fame as a filmmaker, he was known for his memorable sayings: 'It's more than magnificent, it's mediocre'; 'You've got to take the bull by the teeth'; and 'God makes stars. It's up to the producers to find them.'

When Hayward heard back from New York about Peck, he became even more curious. The actor was described as 27 years old, almost 6 foot 3 inches, 170 pounds and darkly handsome. His gaunt physique and bushy eyebrows suggested a young Abe Lincoln – only sexier. And what a voice! Deep, resonant and compelling, it could reach all the way to the back row of the orchestra and the rear row of the balcony. Talent? Nothing earth-shattering. Still, he was clearly intelligent and ambitious. Plus, he possessed charisma – that elusive star quality.

Then came the choicest morsel of all. Gregory Peck had a bad sacroiliac. The actor was 4-F – a term for unfit for combat – which disqualified him from military service.

Now there was bait Hayward could dangle in front of the studio bosses. With the Second World War raging, the moguls were in a tight squeeze. The best of Hollywood's male stars were heeding the call to fight. Clark Gable, Tyrone Power, Jimmy Stewart, Henry Fonda, Robert Montgomery, Robert Taylor and Douglas Fairbanks Jr were all climbing into uniforms. So the studio heads were desperate to find any reasonable-looking young man with a decent profile who knew a thing or two about acting.

Scour the provinces! The producers exhorted their talent scouts. Haunt summer stock companies. Suffer through high school plays. Above all, lay siege to Broadway. Take a seat up front. If a performer shows promise, then inquire about his draft status. If he happens to be 4-F, throw a net over him and haul him back alive. Or at least get the name of his agent.

To find out more about the promising Mr Peck, Leland Hayward telephoned the actor directly. 'The studios want to get a look at you,' he rasped, in a voice filled with intensity. 'So come on out. I'll front you the money for the trip.'

Greg didn't jump at the offer. For one thing he was a ruminator, given to chewing over decisions. Also, he was shy. The prospect of parading himself in front of the power princes of Hollywood made him extremely nervous. But there was more to it. To get a clearer idea of his state of mind at this point in time, let's take a brief look back at where he came from and where he thought he was going.

To begin with, Greg wasn't born to the limelight. In fact he sort of stumbled into acting. He started out in La Jolla, California, an exquisite seaside community on the outskirts of San Diego. While today La Jolla is known as an affluent town populated by entrepreneurs, scientists and retirees, back then it was unsophisticated, slightly bohemian and quite remote. The feel of the place was much like Macomb, Alabama, which was the fictional hometown of his signature character, Atticus Finch, in *To Kill a Mockingbird* (1962).

In La Jolla, the rich knew the poor, the young knew the old and everybody knew everybody else's business. Springing as Greg did from what used to be called a 'broken home,' he emerged emotionally battered, but also freed from the constraints of hovering parents. He learned early to fend for himself. But his horizons were woefully limited. For a while he thought he'd like to be a truck driver. In fact, he showed a real knack for careening a red Union oilrig about town. Then – as would happen many times in his remarkable life – a woman gave him a push at just the right time. In this case, his girlfriend Betty Clardy urged him to knuckle down and study. So he traveled up north to Berkeley and majored in English. There, he caught the acting bug. Gripped by the fever, he finished his last exam and hightailed it for New York.

'Luck' is a word Greg often used in describing what happened next. He liked to portray himself as fortune's darling. Perhaps it was his way of making up for the embarrassments and economic setbacks he weathered growing up. Or maybe he wanted to propitiate the gods. In any case, when he came East, he not only *was* lucky but he showed a talent for *creating* luck, plunking himself down in auspicious circumstances.

In this respect, he was not alone. As *New Yorker* writer E B White noted in an essay about the city:

The residents of Manhattan are to a large extent strangers who have pulled up stakes somewhere and come to town, seeking sanctuary or fulfillment or some greater or lesser grail. The capacity to make such dubious gifts is a mysterious quality of New York. It can destroy an individual, or it can fulfill him, depending a good deal on luck. No one should come to New York to live unless he is willing to be lucky.

In Manhattan, he landed a two-year scholarship to the prestigious Neighborhood Playhouse. So his tuition was covered. The rest was up to him. Schooled by adversity, he proved adept at the hand-to-mouth existence of the aspiring actor. He sold his blood, ate at the Automat (later claiming it served 'the best eggs and bacon in New York'), and even occasionally camped out in Central Park. In those long ago years before terrorism and heightened security, a man of modest means could store his belongings in a locker at Grand Central Station and join the hobos snoozing under the stars.

'But it didn't seem like a hardship because it was such an adventure,' Greg recalled. 'We didn't have the money to attend the plays and would wait until people came out to smoke a cigarette after the first act. We would mingle with them, then go into the theater and look for empty seats, so I saw the second and third act of practically everything on Broadway.' Years later, he told journalist Pete Hamill: 'I was never hungrier and maybe never happier.'

The intoxication of the thespian life made it all worthwhile. At the Neighborhood Playhouse, he found himself smack dab in the middle of tremendous theatrical energy and ideas, talent and glamour. Sanford Meisner, the school's director, came out of the Group Theater, which revolutionized American acting in the 1930s with psychologically truthful performances in which the characters' inner lives resonated underneath the dialogue, creating an emotional realism that electrified critics and audiences. Greg's classmates included Tony Randall, Eli Wallach and Efrem Zimbalist Jr. Meisner subsequently trained Joanne Woodward, Diane Keaton, Robert Duvall and Grace Kelly.

Three times a week, he took movement class from Martha Graham. She was 45 years old and at the peak of her career as a pioneer of modern dance. 'In the prime of her prime,' Greg remembered years later, still awed by her. 'Her discipline was unyielding,' said Greg. 'With her somewhat vague concept of true art, you could never fully understand what she was talking about.' A *monstre sacré*, a geyser of emotions, she was not a woman to cross. If angered, she was known to rip a phone off the wall. 'The first thing you noticed was the face,' wrote Terry Teachout in *Time* magazine, 'a dead white mask of anguish with black holes for eyes, a curt slash of red for a mouth and cheekbones as high as the sky.'

Part of Graham's class involved rigorous stretching exercises. Though wooden in movement even then, Greg was nonetheless eager to please. An excruciating exercise for him was to put his legs together straight out in front of him and then put his head on his knees. He looked around and saw the girls in the class were stretching like rubber bands while the boys were more rigid. Graham stuck her knee in his back and said: 'Come on, Gregory, you can do it.' There was a loud snap.

The following morning he was in such agony he couldn't move. A doctor's examination revealed he had a slipped disc. Greg spent weeks undergoing various forms of therapy and treatment by osteopaths and other spinal specialists until he got back on his feet. But the sacroiliac problem was chronic.

Although he never saw battle, Greg's life was no picnic. Heroes went to war. Any guy who was 4-F was either scorned or pitied. To earn his stripes as an actor, he submitted himself to a tough apprenticeship treading the boards in summer stock and in touring companies. The whole time he was learning, learning. One can't ignore the role dedication played in his fate. What Greg lacked in depth of talent, he made up for in tenacity. Veteran actor Helen Hayes maintained: 'Only a true actor with a deep-seated compulsion is going to stick out the struggle that goes with being in the theater. It's brutal, it's worse than a Marine boot camp.'

Still, the road got to him. Long train rides, cast iron sandwiches and battery acid coffee. He was lonely, riddled with insecurity about his future and often at a loose end. Enter Greta Konen. She was the hairdresser to Katharine Cornell, star of Guthrie McClintic's touring theater company. Some biographers have upgraded her position to secretary to Cornell, but 'That's wrong,' said Greg. 'She was her hairdresser and a darn good hairdresser, too. She could even produce those complicated eighteenth- and nineteenth-century hair-dos.' Vivacious, optimistic, divorced, and five years older than Greg, she contrasted sharply with him in looks and personality. True to her Finnish heritage, she possessed cornsilk blonde hair, light skin, and wide cheekbones. A tiny woman, she stood only as high as the top button of his jacket. Although he towered over her – both physically and intellectually – it was little Greta ('cute as a Christmas tree ornament' people said) who shored up his shaky self-confidence and teased him out of his black Irish moods. When the touring company landed in San Francisco and the city went dark with a wartime blackout on 8 December 1941, following the Japanese attack on Pearl Harbor on the 7th, Greg proposed to Greta.

Her steadfast belief in his acting ability proved to be a lifeline for him. When Greg landed the lead in Emlyn Williams' play *The Morning Star* in 1942, a critic of the Philadelphia tryout carped: 'Mr Peck looks more like a wax dummy in a tailor shop than an actor headed for Broadway.' Crushed, Greg clung to Greta. She rehearsed his eight lines with him over and over again until, she admitted, 'I thought I'd scream.' But when he opened on the Great White Way – as Broadway became known for the street's bright lights – he received reviews so full of praise the talent scouts came courting.

Morning Star didn't fare as well as Greg. The play opened on 14 September 1942 and folded in October 1942. Finding himself 'between engagements' as they say in show business, Greg decided to throw his customary caution to the winds and go ahead with the wedding. 'Comes a time when a man just has to get married,' he explained. Another spur to tying the knot was Greta's refusal to sleep with Greg – even though she'd been married before – until after they made their relationship legal. While in New York she was staying in her brother Paul's $14-a-month small walk-up on East 39th Street that had two bedrooms and a shared kitchen with another apartment. Paul allowed Greg to stay at the apartment but Greta refused to share her bedroom until they were married.

Years later, Greg said he wed Greta simply because they were thrown together. True, propinquity played its part. But the fact remained that Greg was determined to stabilize their relationship. As with many of his generation, the Great Depression and the uncertainties of the Second World War created a deep yearning for security. Marriage offered a shelter from what Franklin D Roosevelt called 'the winds of change and the hurricane of disaster'.

Greta came from a loving family of Finns. 'My parents had a country house and a city house,' Greta said, explaining the dramatic circumstance of her birth in Finland. On a frigid day on 25 January 1911, during her mother's eighth month of pregnancy, Mrs Kukkonen (later Americanized to Konen) went into labor while returning by train from their country place to Helsinki. Greta was born in the railroad station. Marveled Greta, 'It was as cold as it could get and I was naked.'

Her parents emigrated from Helsinki when she was two years old. They settled in Jersey City, where her father, a watchmaker, worked for Tiffany's. After his death, her mother remarried and they now lived on a large farm in the Halsey Valley, located in the Finger Lakes region of New York State. To a young man from a bitterly split family, Greta's home ties represented wholesomeness. Besides, they wouldn't starve. Greta brought home a steady paycheck of $60 a week with her hairdressing job.

Even by the wartime standards of the early 1940s, the nuptials were extremely impromptu. Greg and Greta invited a ragtag group of friends to a Yankees game, the 1942 World Series, New York Yankees vs the St Louis Cardinals. (The Cardinals, Greg's mother's hometown team, were young, hungry and daring. They ran every grounder, dove for every ball, and took every extra base on their way to victory. They also won the Series.) Following the game, the gang repaired to the Palm restaurant on Third Avenue and feasted on $5 steaks. Wildly expensive. 'Ah, but what *steak*,' Greg recalled with relish. Then they paid a visit to Christ Church United Methodist on 61st Street and Park Avenue. There, a casually dressed minister named J Gordon Chamberlain, agreed to perform the service at short notice. (Now 89 and still writing articles and occasionally teaching, Reverend Chamberlain says, 'I was just four years out of the seminary and much was new to me.') The vows were exchanged at 9.20 p.m. in the men's lounge that was located in the path to the WC. Greg recalled: 'It was in the lounge where the men's club meets. We wanted it informal, not in the church. The minister was one of those regular guys – didn't wear his collar backwards or anything.' (Greg was raised as a Catholic but since Greta was divorced, getting married in the Catholic Church was out of the question.) Although the only relative who attended was Greta's brother Paul, her mother sent them a lace tablecloth she made herself.

The newlyweds remained with Paul for a spell in his apartment. Then, when Greg started getting $200-a-week paychecks for performing in his next play, *The Willow and I*, which opened on Broadway on 10 December 1942, they rented a one-bedroom, one-sitting-room apartment at The Townhouse on Lexington Avenue for $200 a month. When *Willow* folded after a brief run, the bills started piling up. Peck hated being in debt. Growing up with a father who lost his pharmacy business to bankruptcy, the actor knew what that kind of defeat did to a man.

Of all the people sending him late notices, none extended credit with more graciousness than Dr J Y Pokress – 'dentist to the stars.' He sawed, hacked, chopped and whittled some of the best teeth on Broadway. Greg owed him $1,400 for sprucing up his smile. Shy, stagestuck and an ardent theater-goer, Pokress was said to be the inspiration for Ben Stark, the timid dentist who develops a reckless desire for his receptionist during one steamy New York summer in Clifford Odets' Depression era tale *Rocket to the Moon*.

Around this time, Leland Hayward contacted Greg urging him to come West. Greg wasn't sure what to do. Hollywood was barracuda country! And given Filmland's obsession with appearances, he might be just another handsome face. While in New York, he was hitting his stride, developing solid theater credentials. He wanted to stay long enough to prove his talent, make his place, and achieve something. He figured it was just a matter of time before he would be getting parts in plays with longer runs.

But maybe he wouldn't. His Broadway plays were of short duration. Doubt and insecurity haunted him. 'When am I going to work again . . . if ever?' Greg recalled, 'I felt I was going up a one-way street into a blind alley. If I didn't make it, what in God's name would I do with myself?'

Another caveat. Theater folk didn't regard Hollywood as a step up. Legitimate thespians often dismissed film acting with contempt. Stolid British actor Cedric Hardwicke, who played with Greg in *The Keys of the Kingdom* (1944), reflected: 'I believe that God felt sorry for actors, so He created Hollywood to give them a place in the sun and a swimming pool. The price they had to pay was to surrender their talent.'

With Greg, it was not so much snobbery as fear. The year before, he had flunked a screen test commissioned by none other than David O Selznick, the legendary producer of *Gone With the Wind* (1939). Selznick took one look at the test and fired off a memo to Kay Brown, his East Coast representative: 'I don't see what we could do with Gregory Peck . . . He photographs like Abe Lincoln, but if he has a great personality, I don't think it comes through in these tests.'

It's ironic to think that Gregory Peck, later headlined as 'The Most Handsome Man in the World', possessed a face that once caused seasoned professionals to shake their heads. But such was the case. Even his mentor, Katharine Cornell, who regularly fed Greg roles, confessed to French actor Jean Pierre Aumont: 'Poor Greg! I like him a lot but he'll never make a picture to save his life. One of his ears is larger than the other.'

In the jargon of the industry, Greg didn't possess 'bullet-proof camera angles'. Seen at a distance on the stage, he cut quite a figure with his great height complemented by shoulders so broad they looked padded. Up close, his features were large, irregular and gaunt. He had three perpendicular lines across his forehead and two perpendicular valleys in his cheeks. Still, the profile was vintage matinée idol and there was no denying he was darkly handsome in a morose sort of way. A few years later – after the world took notice of Greg – George Burns' clever wife Gracie analyzed his magic: 'It's just eyes, nose and mouth. But what an assembly job!'

Finally, Greg said 'yes' to Leland's offer. The money looked too good and, besides, Hayward never accepted 'no' from anyone. Aside from his own concerns, Greg was determined to give his wife the best. He vowed: 'As soon as I'm in the chips, I'm going to buy

Greta a mink coat and then I'm going to get me a house on a hill and raise a flock of kids.'

So the Pecks embarked for Los Angeles. Hayward put them up for ten days in a suite at the Beverly Hills Hotel on Sunset Boulevard. Then, as now, the hotel was a gathering place for visiting royalty and Hollywood's crème de la crème.

Greg took to Hayward right off the bat. Most people did. Attractive and dashing with an air both haggard and elegant, Hayward stood out as an anomaly in the cut-throat world of Hollywood agents. He wore white flannel trousers and linen underwear and was the first Filmland executive to decorate his office with antiques. In his forties in the 1940s, his features were delicate, with a prominent nose and piercing blue eyes set off by an enthusiastic smile. His crew-cut gray hair gave him, according to *Life* magazine: 'the aspect of an elderly Yale freshman.'

'He could sell the proverbial snowball to the Eskimos,' claimed Henry Fonda. Director William Wyler swore he 'just charmed the birds off the trees, the money out of the coffers, and ladies into their beds.' Leland's ex-girlfriend Katharine Hepburn – also a client – pronounced him 'the most wonderful man in the world'. In her gushy style, she later wrote that with Leland 'nothing was a problem. There were solutions to everything. Joy was the constant mood. Everything was like a delightful surprise.'

The studios wined and dined the Pecks and sent Greta little presents of candy and roses. In the daytime, she was free to bask on a chaise longue beside the hotel's fabled pool sipping exotic drinks. (The cabana area would be featured in the 1957 movie, *Designing Woman*, starring Gregory Peck and Lauren Bacall.)

The mock paradise of Beverly Hills suited her just fine. At 32 and with one marriage already behind her, Greta was primed for the next stage in her life. She had seen enough of seedy living while touring the country as Katharine Cornell's hairdresser. Now here was a chance to live a smart, luxurious lifestyle where the perfect climate provided a healthy place to raise children. Like Greg, Greta yearned to start a family.

Meanwhile, Greg was getting a lightning tour of the major studios. It was the Golden Age of movies and each movie empire was turning out 70 or 80 films a year. 'Studios had faces then,' said the brilliant director Billy Wilder. 'They had their own style. They could bring you blindfolded into a movie house and you opened [your eyes] and looked up and you knew, "Hey, this is an RKO picture. This is an MGM picture."'

Greg got a kick out of walking the Paramount lot. He said, 'I was thrilled to stand there and watch people work.' Resembling a country club, the studio was steeped in history. Here is where giants such as D W Griffith, Cecil B DeMille, Joseph Von Sternberg and Preston Sturges made movies that featured stars such as Mary Pickford, Clara Bow, Gary Cooper, Bing Crosby and Marlene Dietrich. Had he a crystal ball in his pocket, he would have known that in 1953, this studio would release one of his own all-time smash hits, *Roman Holiday*, with Audrey Hepburn.

For many, Paramount best represented that great juncture of romance, glamour and illusion that typified the legendary studios of the past. Inside its gates, magic was created on a daily basis. Diehard fantasy lovers found it preferable to the real thing outside. Famed director Ernst Lubitsch once said: 'I've been to Paris, France, and I've been to Paris, Paramount. Paris, Paramount, is better.'

Being repressed, and needing the mask of a theatrical role to reveal true feelings, Greg was fascinated by the ruthless, bawdy and daring studio bosses. Not only did these men lead hurly-burly lives; they also had a way with words. Sometimes mangled, but, none-theless, a way. People delighted in quoting their snappy phrases – even if they had never actually said what was ascribed to them.

Here's a sampling. Darryl Zanuck: 'For God's sake, don't say "yes" until I'm finished talking.' Louis B Mayer: 'The number one book of the ages was written by a committee, and it was called the Bible.' Harry Cohen: 'I don't have ulcers, I give them.' Jack Warner: 'I would rather take a 50-mile hike than crawl through a book.' But in the *bon mots* department, nobody rivaled Sam Goldwyn. 'A verbal contract isn't worth the paper it's printed on.' 'I had a great idea this morning, but I didn't like it.' 'You've got to take the bitter with the sour.' 'Gentlemen, include me out.' 'I'd hire the devil himself if he'd write me a good story.' Finally, there was a command ascribed to just about every major producer in town: 'Never let that bastard back in here – unless we need him!'

The despotic studio chiefs ran their huge factories with contract players, and writers and directors constantly assigned, reassigned, and substituted. Since it took several years to groom a talent such as Gregory Peck, it was in the best interests of the studios to hang on to an actor until he matured. As one executive put it: 'We are the only company whose assets all walk out the gate at night.' To lock in their talent, the studio bosses pressured actors into signing seven-year contracts; it was the maximum number of years the law allowed and the terms invariably worked in the producers' favor. Some of those in bondage compared the studios to luxurious slave quarters in which they wore golden shackles.

Of all the moguls, none was as powerful, notorious or feared as Louis B Mayer. Numerous myths, which Mayer cherished and cultivated, surrounded the man whose sobriquets ran from 'Mister Movies' to 'that son-of-a-bitch, LB'. The stars in his stable had to submit to his histrionics and conniving if they wanted to survive.

The experience of German-born star Luise Rainer is but one example. She won the Academy Award for best actress in *The Great Ziegfeld* in 1936 and for *The Good Earth* in 1937. Rather than helping her career, her double Oscar success meant she was offered poor films that needed a star to give them a boost. And because she was tied into a contract with MGM, she had no choice in which movies she made. She grew so frustrated that she famously walked out on the contract, which prompted Louis B Mayer to threaten: 'We made you and we can kill you.'

Imagine if you will the setting in which Greg's encounter with Louis B Mayer took place. The actor was ushered through huge walnut doors into the producer's office. There he beheld a 60-foot-long plush white carpet leading to a desk that was white leather and crescent-shaped. Quipped Sam Goldwyn: 'You needed an automobile to reach his desk.' There sat Mayer, a chubby little man with beady eyes, rimless glasses on a chain and the dimpled hands of a cardinal.

The mogul was seated between a map of the world and two flags. Behind him, like some gigantic crest, was a window with a commanding view of the grounds surrounding the studio. These cardboard landscapes held wonders such as a Swiss village, the Chicago underworld and the canals of Venice.

'Initially, he used the fatherly approach with me,' recalled Greg, 'pointing out, quite emotionally, how he had sired the careers of actors like Mickey Rooney, Robert Taylor and Judy Garland. When I declined to budge, he shifted his campaign to an attack against the legitimate theater, demeaning my career in it in the process.

'Noting that this wasn't getting results, Mayer, as if programmed, took still another tack. He pulled out a handkerchief and began to cry, deeply saddened by my ingratitude that wouldn't allow him to make me the biggest movie star of all time.'

Greg stood his ground, but Mayer still wasn't ready to concede defeat. 'His final ploy was to depict my refusal as an offense to motherhood, the American flag and family decency. Big fat tears continued to roll down his cheeks and fell off his chin.' Then, seeing that Peck would not relent, he shooed him out the door.

'My God, what a performance,' Greg said to Hayward.

The agent laughed. 'He does that every day. He loves to cry.'

Greg kept the memory of his encounter with Mayer vivid in his mind. It was a story he retold hundreds of times in the course of his long career. For him, it was a defining moment. Greg was shrewd enough to realize that the moguls were going to lose their grip on actors. But Greg also proved something vitally important to himself. In the teeth of Mayer's formidable powers of persuasion, bullying and contemptuousness, he did not capitulate. Even though he was unsure of his abilities as an actor, he nonetheless summoned the courage not to sign on the dotted line. It was a signal both to Mayer and to himself that no matter what the future held, he was going to be his own man.

Hayward was left to smooth things over with Mayer. 'As a matter of fact,' said Hayward, 'one of the biggest feuds in years developed between me and Metro, particularly between myself and L B Mayer, because they weren't able to sign Peck then and there.' Time healed the breach, but it never became, in Hayward's words 'a passionate love affair.'

Having resisted the snares of Mayer and the other studio bosses, Greg finally agreed to do a movie with top screenwriter Casey Robinson. Robinson endeared himself to Greg because he didn't give him the usual sign-with-me-and-I'll-make-you-a-star line. He told him that in his opinion he *was* a star. He offered him the principal role in *Days of Glory* to be produced by RKO studios, and a contract of $1,000 a week that didn't tie him down to a seven-year term. Said Greg, 'I thought *that* was a hell of a lot of money.' And it left Greg free of the bondage of the exclusive actor–producer arrangement.

Described by film critic Richard Corliss as 'the master of the art – or craft – of adaptation,' Robinson scripted such memorable literary and theatrical adaptations as *Captain Blood* (1935), *Four Daughters* (1938), *Dark Victory* (1939), *Now, Voyager* (1941), and *Kings Row* (1942). Because he preferred to remain faithful to his source material, Robinson was much admired by the authors whose works he brought to the screen.

So, in late summer of 1943, Greg and Greta made the move to sunny California. First they camped in the Monterey Motor Court off Sunset Boulevard because wartime made housing scarce. Then they rented a pink house high up in the Hollywood Hills.

In *Days of Glory* (1944), Robinson cast Peck as the leader of a band of Russian guerillas fighting the Nazis in the Second World War. His leading lady was Robinson's fiancée Tamara Toumanova. She was an internationally acclaimed ballet star who, legend had it, was born on a Russian train heading for Paris. At the time, her parents were fleeing the Bolshevik Revolution. Although she had performed with a number of highly regarded troupes including Balanchine's Ballets Russes de Monte Carlo, Toumanova also wanted a crack at a movie career.

Though a beauty, she came across as a shade fulsome in the department of facial expressions, accustomed as she was to project-ing a balletic character across the footlights. Still, speaking in the tones of her native Russia, she at least *sounded* Slavic. Greg opened his mouth and out popped his deep, resonant and quintessentially American accent. The effect was deeply jarring.

In an effort to get Greg to sound proletarian and not over-project, director Jacques Tourneur urged him to 'Common it up.

Project. Common it up.' The microphone was only 2 feet over the actor's nose and it was doing all the projecting he needed.

For Greg, the learning process was excruciating. Theatrical and screen acting differed considerably. 'The camera can read your thoughts,' explained Greg. 'You cannot get away with vocal prowess. You have to almost, somehow, become the role and think what the character thinks and feel the emotions he truly would feel in a set of given circumstances.'

Despite his best effort, Greg's stony composure rendered his character's defending of Mother Russia dubious. To compound the problem, his laconic style and gloomy mien were comically at odds with his Resistance character's ardent words. 'Nina Nichova, where do you come from? Your eyes are so wonderful as a forgotten dream.'

One afternoon, Greg was standing on the RKO sound stage, when a tall, thin, elegant woman with cold blue eyes and a ridiculous hat approached him. She looked him over from head to withers and exclaimed in a brisk staccato voice: 'Golly! How I wish I owned a piece of you!'

It was Hedda Hopper, top gossip columnist for the *Los Angeles Times*. Undoubtedly she had heard about the studios' keen interest in him and she wanted to scoop her rival, Louella Parsons. These two middle-aged harpies had the power to make or break careers. Studio chiefs and stars alike feared their bitchy pens and sharp tongues. Refusing to give one of these journalists the lowdown on a romance, marriage, divorce or impending birth meant banishment from her column or – worse – vindictive, poisonous reprisals. (Hopper's Beverly Hills mansion was known as 'the house that fear built.') Stars engaged in heated debates about which gossip columnist was the most dangerous. Ray Milland cast his ballot for Hopper. Calling her 'an unmitigated bitch,' he maintained, 'She was venomous, vicious, a pathological liar, and quite stupid.'

Over the years only a handful of celebrities – Garbo, Hepburn, Brando – consistently refused to cooperate with these two women. And a *very* few struck back. One was Joan Bennett, who starred opposite Greg in *The Macomber Affair*, released in 1947. She recalled, 'Hedda Hopper had been taking pot shots at me in her column for years. I finally got fed up and I had a skunk shipped to her house. Later, she wrote that she christened it Joan. A columnist always got the last word.'

At this point in time, Greg wasn't unduly concerned with Hedda Hopper – or any other columnist for that matter. He wasn't sure if Hollywood was just a quick phase in his life. And the release of *Days of Glory* didn't reassure him. It failed to make a thorough run of even the second-string houses. With his perfectionism, Greg beat up on himself more than the most virulent critic; in fact, he was all for dropping the movie business then and there and 'crawling back penitently' to Broadway and the theater. But his pride wouldn't let him. Neither would Greta. She had found her home.

In the meantime, Darryl Zanuck, the short, cocky, arrogant and ruthless founder of Twentieth Century Fox, was in desperate need of Greg. In 1943, after testing 40 actors including Spencer Tracy and Franchot Tone and even considering Gene Kelly, he was still casting about for someone to play the lead role in *The Keys of the Kingdom*, the story of a Catholic missionary priest living in China. The character of Father Chisholm ranges in appearance from age 18 to 82. With his surefire instinct for what moviegoers wanted, Zanuck knew Greg would be right for the role.

This time, Greg's visage, voice and frame fit the role perfectly. So did his background. As a lonely boy in his early teens studying at an austere Catholic boarding school, he once dreamed of becoming a priest. And although he played a celibate, his gifts as a heartthrob showed through. Director John M Stahl was forced to close the set because chorus girls from a musical picture nearby spent so much time watching Greg, it was decided they were 'adding more body than soul' to *The Kingdom*.

Critical praise ran high. The *New York World Telegram* said: 'There have been intimations of his forceful talents on the stage and screen. Nevertheless there is astonishment awaiting everyone who sees *The Keys of the Kingdom*, with this fledgling actor tossing in one of the soundest and most intelligently presented performances of the year . . .' Greg lapped up the praise, but it was the shrewd analysis of Leland Hayward that stuck in his mind. His agent said candidly: 'I think you were wonderful in the film, but I don't think you'll ever develop the facility to play just anything. You will always have to have the right material or you will sink like a stone.'

With *The Keys of the Kingdom*, Greg received his first Academy Award nomination. It won him a $25,000 bonus from the Fox studio – and it catapulted him to fame. Suddenly, people previously regarded as sane were scrambling and snarling and begging for a part of him. It was a 1944 Klondike gold rush. Lauded Louella Parsons: 'You couldn't go to a party without hearing the buzz about this wonder man's rugged handsomeness, his thin height, his magical speaking voice.'

Hayward had a field day touting his client as the hottest property in Hollywood. But when it got down to the nitty-gritty of the contracts, Greg once again proved obstinate. He was showing his inner resolve; the tensile strength beneath the gentlemanly surface he exhibited. Before signing, he insisted on clauses permitting him half time on Broadway (something unheard-of for a movie beginner) and he refused to be locked into any one studio. Still, fearful that his popularity wouldn't last, he let himself in for enough work to keep him hopelessly busy in the studios for a solid seven years. His commitments went like this: four pictures for Fox, four with David O Selznick, four with MGM, and two with Casey Robinson at RKO. These commitments were made in 1944. More commitments followed. According to *Time* magazine: 'When the moguls were through shuffling around their pieces of Mr Peck, he was the most owned and least available leading man in Hollywood, and one of the most valuable.'

During this time, Hayward's wife, the highly gifted and temperamental actress Margaret Sullavan, was pressuring him to give up his talent agency for Broadway production. She hated the agency business. Her opposition was voiced with an electric intensity worthy of her best stage and screen acting. 'Flesh peddler' she'd shout when he reached for the phone.

Largely at her insistence, he sold the agency in 1945 at a substantial profit to Dr Jules Stein's Music Corporation of America to join the more prestigious realm of Broadway producers. For his first attempt, Hayward chose John Hersey's *A Bell for Adano*, enlisting Greg as one of the play's investors. 'I used to borrow money,' Greg marveled. 'Now I'm lending it.' The play opened on 6 December 1944 at the Cort Theater.

Upon departure from LA, Hayward left Greg with a sterling piece of advice. He urged him to make movies with extremely popular women stars and gain exposure to their vast audiences. Peck's next movie fit the bill. For *The Valley of Decision*, he was teamed with a titian-haired Irish beauty named Greer Garson.

Though mostly forgotten today, Greer Garson was a discovery of Louis B Mayer, who carefully nurtured her career, presenting her as the epitome of the MGM star. Garson played stiff-upper-lip types in numerous 'weepies'. Her films included *Goodbye Mr Chips* (1939), which won rave reviews and garnered her first nomination as Best Actress, *Random Harvest* (1942) and *Mrs Miniver* (1942), a role for which she would be forever known.

In addition to Garson, *The Valley of Decision* cast included a number of other top Hollywood actors: Donald Crisp, Lionel Barrymore, Gladys Cooper, and Jessica Tandy.

The Valley of Decision is the story of a colleen (Garson) who becomes a servant in a wealthy Pittsburgh industrialist's home and spends the rest of her life there – as a maid and then married to the son (Peck). Not a great film, but Greg acquitted himself admirably as the scion of a steel-mill fortune. Dressed to the nines, he looked every inch the patrician. Nobody was more pleased than Greta, who despaired over his lack of interest in clothes. She perhaps ignited Greg's ire by confessing her frustration to a fan magazine: 'He sometimes wears the same shirt for a month . . . He never wants to comb his hair – and he has a bad habit of leaving his clothes around until you pick them up in self-defense.'

Greg was determined to wring every last drop of wisdom out of the veteran stars on the picture. His number-one teacher was Greer Garson. She showed him the difference between genuine movie stars and all other film actors. True movie stars are always worth watching, no matter how lousy the picture. Garson loved the camera as much as the lens loved her. She was like a reverse voyeur, ravishing the camera. Her power was inescapable. She beamed her way into the audience's hearts and minds. Greg recalled: 'When I viewed the rushes I saw how every time I was in a scene with Greer, her face was the only thing you saw. It shone like a luminous moon floating in the center of the screen, and I was just a rather dim figure next to her.'

When Greta watched the movie, she had a different perspective: 'It's really a shock to see your husband making love to someone else – in front of thousands of people.'

The Valley of Decision was a box-office hit. Greg garnered more glowing reviews. *Newsweek* enthused: 'Gregory Peck impersonates the intense young man with both the authority and the romantic appeal the role requires . . . [he] is established as one of Hollywood's outstanding leading men.' The *New York Times* concurred: 'Gregory Peck is quietly commanding as the best of the Scott boys.' *Variety* also saluted him: 'He had the personality and ability to hold attention in any scene.'

Now that Greg was a star, the Pecks were invited everywhere. There was a party in Hollywood every night. The magnificent houses would be thrown open, revealing fine rooms with master-pieces on the walls, vivid people laughing and flirting or dancing to the latest tunes.

Much of the Hollywood social life revolved around the studio heads. Jack Warner gave parties at his Beverly Hills estate with huge buffets around the swimming pool, Darryl Zanuck hosted croquet games on his lawn or parties at the beach, and David O Selznick entertained lavishly with his famous Sunday night dinners.

With her natural exuberance, Greta loved dressing up and gliding into a brightly lit room on Greg's arm. What a feeling it was to sit on somebody's sofa and watch the door open and a cornucopia of famous faces she had known from childhood sweep in and sometimes walk straight up to her husband.

But women swamped Greg. As his wife, Greta was relegated to the position of appendage. At one gathering, a female sat herself down on the arm of Greg's chair and started to come on to him. Greta fumed. 'I was so damn mad there for a minute, I thought I'd hit her.' Upon reflection, she decided: 'I should remember a movie star isn't supposed to have a wife.'

For his part, Greg preferred entertaining at home and his will prevailed. Poker, gin rummy and records stacked high on the phonograph provided the ingredients for a night of fun with their boisterous crowd. While in later years (and with another wife), a gathering *chez* Gregory Peck meant exquisite French cuisine and the finest wine, in the 1940s it was steaks on the grill barbecued by the host himself. Over at the bar, the hooch flowed freely. In those heady days, drinking was considered an American sport, red-blooded, even romantic. Humphrey Bogart boasted: 'I don't trust any bastard who doesn't drink.' A large man like Greg could metabolize great quantities of alcohol to no apparent detriment. In fact, he was applauded for his 'hollow legs'. Pint-sized Greta had to be careful. Alcohol works faster on women. What's more, she was in her fertile years. In fact, a baby was expected to arrive in June 1944.

Fatherhood! Greg was jubilant. As the time drew near, his compulsivity took hold and he laid out plans for the Blessed Event like a general responsible for a military operation. No detail was to be left to chance. He drew a map with five routes from home to hospital and then made practice runs to determine which road was fastest. In anticipation of the child's homecoming, he sanitized the carpets, walls and furniture. It's a wonder the floorboards didn't give way under the weight of all the baby books he purchased.

And once Greg set eyes on his son Jonathan, he became as awestruck as any new father. Greta recalled: 'Always, between two people, there are moments that one of them will never forget. For me, it's that time when I saw Greg standing scared and white, holding our just-born son Jonathan in his arms, and afraid to breathe.' After they took the baby home, Greg studied Jonathan and sighed: 'I just hope he doesn't get gangly and bony like I was. Gee, how I used to envy those big-muscled Tarzans on the beach – they got all the girls in sight.'

With the baby home, Greg paid attention to every detail. Greta remembered: 'The housekeeper told me that Greg made his father take his shoes off before he'd let him set foot in the nursery.'

Even with a new baby, Greg couldn't slow down. He was hooked on the movie life. Each morning he had the fascinating studio crowd waiting for him. His colleagues were talented, witty and charming. But it was an ephemeral world – and his place in it wasn't secure. 'The life span of a movie star is comparatively short,' claimed Spencer Tracy. 'We're something like the common housefly.' While the length of Tracy's career belied that crack, Greg had no guarantees that he would be allowed to stick around beyond the first flush of his fame. The pressure was building. Soon the war would be over and the established actors would be returning home. What's more, there were a lot of new people coming up, good-looking and young. If he didn't maximize every opportunity that came his way, he could slip back to obscurity.

Consumed with his career, Greg expected Greta to be in service to his monomania and relentless discipline. Mealtimes, social life and baby schedule had to be worked around his priorities. Yes, it was selfish. All artists are self-centered. If they aren't ruthless with their energy and time, they won't fulfill their promise and they'll be overtaken by the competition.

Still, the long hours and his fragile ego made Greg tense, withdrawn and angry. Greta took the brunt of it. He raged. She raged. It was a contentious household. 'Both of us have quick tempers,' Greta admitted, 'and an argument can get going a mile a minute even before we know what it's about.'

Despite their ups and downs, Greg loved Greta and regarded her as his staunchest ally. On weeknights, she listened patiently while he recited his lines for the next day's shoot. When he went to bed, the stress of his career took its toll in fitful sleep but he could count on her to be there beside him. 'Greta helped me,' he later recalled, 'not to beat my brains out.' Frequently depressed, he experienced 'moments that others might describe as a nervous breakdown.'

To gear up for another day's work Greg adopted a peculiar morning ritual. He admitted to Mary Morris of *PM* magazine he gulped down a raw egg floating in sherry. (Eye openers were not unusual in Hollywood. W C Fields started each day with two double martinis before breakfast. When someone suggested he try water, the gravel-voiced, bulbous-nosed curmudgeon scowled, 'Fish fuck in it!')

Prodding Greg about his sherry-egg concoction, Morris asked: 'What's the point?'

'It's quick – booming, boom,' he said. Then he added: 'Never had time to spend on breakfast and, besides, I get up feeling fuzzy, can't face real eating for several hours.'

Greg's next film, *Spellbound* (1945), promised him enough adrenaline-pumping excitement to make sherry superfluous. Conceived as a psychological thriller, it portrays a romance between an amnesiac (Peck) and a frosty, generally unbending psychiatrist (Ingrid Bergman).

Spellbound brought together a formidable constellation of talent. The producer was two-time Oscar-winner David O Selznick, who had been undergoing psychoanalysis at the time and even hired his shrink as technical advisor. To direct, Selznick selected Alfred Hitchcock, who had made *Rebecca* (1940) for him and was already cementing his reputation as the Master of Suspense. To do the screenwriting, he chose Ben Hecht. A facile and prolific storyteller who completed most scripts in two weeks, never more than eight, Hecht was generally believed to be the highest-paid screenwriter of his day. He claimed: 'The job of turning good writers into movie hacks is the producer's chief task.' To create dream sequences that would be both psychologically astute and visually mesmerizing, Selznick hired the surrealist painter Salvador Dalí. All in all, *Spellbound* was going to be as innovative a production as Hollywood had ever seen.

In the movie, Ingrid Bergman is convincing as the intense iceberg psychiatrist, Dr Constance Peterson, who is sexually awakened by Greg as her institute's new chief, Dr Anthony Edwardes. She finds herself embroiled in a murder mystery revolving about him. An imposter suffering from amnesia, Greg is everybody's prime suspect. But through a combination of love, psychological technique, and persistence, Bergman cracks his amnesia and solves the crime.

The picture includes some beautiful scenes. One of them is the first meeting between Gregory and Bergman clearly love at first sight. For such a scene to work, it's important that the male and female leads are attracted to each other. In real life when two appealing people meet the moment is not so charged with titillating expectation. They just meet, and the moment usually passes. But people in films carry another aura around with them. A film costing millions can depend on the chemistry between two people who will be spending every waking hour together for at least three or four months. Selznick and Hitchcock must have been heartened to witness the sexual heat building between their co-stars. Hitchcock once quipped: 'All love scenes started on the set are continued in the dressing room after the day's shooting is done. *Without exception.*'

Bergman was then 29 and in full bloom. Tall, fresh-faced and fun-loving, she didn't need ever-flattering lighting, the make-up people hiding imperfect skin, or a hairdresser to make her hair look sexy. Already the recipient of an Oscar for *Gaslight* in 1944, she could project an image of purity and pristine magic.

When Greg met her, he was not only struck by her beauty but he also picked up on her lively sense of humor. To break the ice he joked about how his multiple studio contracts had prepared him for *Spellbound*. 'You know I am perfectly cast as the guy with a split personality, because I am split four ways – between David Selznick, RKO, Twentieth Century Fox and International.'

At first Bergman wasn't happy about playing opposite a leading man who was slightly younger than she was, but once they started rehearsing it was obvious they were simpatico. Ingrid loved to woo, and charm, and win over her leading men. She knew that an actress can only be fertile if she renews herself. And there is no more fruitful source of this than the enchanting exploration of another human being, particularly one as virile as Gregory Peck.

For Greg, Bergman was not only one of the world's most beautiful women; she was also a mentor, extending a helping hand at a time when he sorely needed it. Much more experienced about acting before the camera, she aided him in accessing his deeply repressed emotions. As her character says in the movie: 'We are bundles of inhibitions.'

The intense sexual magnetism between the leading actors raised eyebrows on the set. After all, the stars each had a spouse at home. According to one cast member: 'Ingrid and Peck came in late and disheveled, and there was a lot of speculation.' All Greg would admit to was, 'I loved her.' When pressed for details, he'd back off saying, 'I don't talk about things like that.'

Peck was fortunate to have an ally like Bergman as he stumbled – sometimes quite literally – through the film. One of the pivotal scenes in *Spellbound* required Greg to follow Ingrid Bergman on skis down a steep snow-covered slope. He didn't ski at all and Bergman, though Swedish, was a rank beginner. For long shots, Hitchcock used doubles. But there were a number of scenes requiring medium shots and close-ups.

To solve the problem, carpenters constructed a 40-foot-high slope made of gypsum and cornflakes (sprayed white). All Greg and Bergman had to do was stay vertical while the camera focused on them. The close-ups were shot in front of a rear projection screen showing lofty mountains and crisp clean snow. Greg had to stay in character as the confused amnesiac shouting loudly enough to alarm the audience and to convince his psychiatrist that he was really becoming unhinged and about to kill her, and ski into a clump of mattresses.

Despite tremendous effort, Greg couldn't get the hang of skiing, thus forcing Hitchcock to re-shoot the scene several times. 'The memory is painful to me – even now,' Greg confessed years later. 'I fell down sideways, forward, on my rear – and every possible way – before I actually managed to stay up for the 40-foot run. You can imagine my relief when I got to the bottom.'

Greg's relationship with Alfred Hitchcock was tricky. Hitchcock once said: 'My favorite is the actor who can do nothing well. By that I mean one who has presence, authority and can attract attention without actually doing anything.' His deft timing and sharp, imaginative camera work could do the rest. He also expected them to have developed a persona that was immediately recognizable to the audience. (Cary Grant is an excellent example of a Hitchcock actor.)

Greg, an alumnus of the Neighborhood Playhouse and a disciple of the Stanislavsky or 'Method' school of acting, was somewhat disdainful of Hitchcock's 'clever shell games'. At the same time, he was doing everything he could to meet Hitchcock's high expectations. 'I felt I needed a good deal of direction,' Peck said, 'but when he asked for assistance, Hitchcock wasn't forthcoming. 'My dear boy,' he replied in answer to a question about motivation, 'I couldn't care less what you're thinking. Just let your face drain of all expression.'

Despite Hitchcock's lack of specific acting pointers, Greg found him clever and ingenious. 'He was full of jokes and quips and puns,' Greg recalled. 'I always thought of him a little bit as an overweight English schoolboy with some obvious complexes but with this uncanny talent for building suspense and holding an audience in the palm of his hand.'

The Pecks entertained the Hitchcocks and the invitations were returned. A connoisseur of food and drink, Hitchcock regarded Greg as a bumpkin. Because he found it pitiable that Greg didn't know about good wines, he sent him a case of 12 vintage bottles including Montrachet and Lafite-Rothschild with instructions attached to each bottle explaining the kinds of food to serve them with. Greg drank the whole case and tossed out the labels.

David O Selznick liked to say: 'Nothing in Hollywood is permanent. Once photographed, life here is ended.' And so it went for the romance of the two *Spellbound* stars. When the film wrapped in mid October 1944, Bergman lost interest in Greg. Her love 'em and leave 'em attitude had been established with other leading men. Gary Cooper, with whom she made two movies, *For Whom the Bell Tolls* (1943) and *Saratoga Trunk* (1945), complained out loud about being spurned. 'In my whole life I never had a woman so much in love with me as Ingrid was,' Cooper said years later. 'The day after the picture ended I couldn't get her on the phone.'

Greg never griped about Bergman's fickleness. He saw the relationship for what it was – a romance of the moment. The important thing for him was to preserve their friendship. On his way up, he needed to forge lasting bonds with his more successful colleagues. So he portrayed his intimacy with Bergman – physical or psychological – as the beginning of a lifelong bond. Over the years, he tossed his 'Swedish rose' bouquets of admiration and she responded with complimentary statements praising his skills as an actor and his worth as a man. From a career standpoint, it was a smart strategy. Domestically, it probably didn't play so well.

Selznick, with his genius for ballyhoo, ran adverts for *Spellbound* hinting at both horror and sex: 'Will he kiss me or kill me?' 'Irresistible their love! Inescapable their fears.' One graphic poster showed Greg with his arms wrapped around Bergman but with a straight razor in one hand. *Spellbound*'s box-office success was staggering. In the first week at New York's Astor Theater, for example, it grossed $60,000, breaking all records – even those of *Gone With the Wind.*

Selznick was floored by the reaction to Greg. 'We could not keep the audience quiet from the time his name came on the screen until we had 'shushed' them through three or four sequels, and stopped all the dames from oohing and aahing and gurgling.'

Now Greg's face was familiar to millions. Every fan publication either featured him on its cover, or ran a special article about him, or both. His mail averaged 3,000 letters a week. Men wanted to go out and have a couple of drinks with the star. Mothers and daughters fantasized about Gregory Peck making love to them. The mother of Venezuelan athlete Iginia Boccalandro saw Greg skiing in *Spellbound* and insisted her daughter take up the sport. Iginia competed in cross-country skiing, switched to the luge, and at 37 became Venezuela's first Winter Olympian. Jazz musician Mike Melvoin remembers that when he was a boy in the 1940s, his mother became so infatuated with Greg she announced to her son: 'I'm going to change your middle name to Gregory.' He pleaded: 'Don't do it Ma! Then I'll be MGM.'

This kind of adulation was so new to him that Greg hadn't yet built up his trademark shield of dignified reserve. In later years, he became fiercely protective of his private life, adopting Humphrey Bogart's position that 'All you owe the public is a good performance.' But in the 1940s, he didn't have a public front. He was who he was – a rough diamond. When he was asked to pose for a picture, he said to the photographer: 'Just tell me which pose you want. I've got two. You want me frownin' and gloomin', or laughin' and scratchin'?'

Similarly, when a journalist questioned him about his income, he didn't dodge the question. 'Why, sure I'll tell,' he replied, like a kid queried about his allowance. 'I made $125,000 last year, and we've got $8,000 left.'

Callow though he was, Greg was learning fast. One of his smartest moves was to endear himself to the gossip columnists. To all intents and purposes, they ran the town. Greg understood their power and handled them with kid gloves. It showed the lengths he would go to further his career.

'Today, it's hard to understand the power of these two women in Hollywood,' said Celeste Holm, who won an Oscar for her appearance in *Gentleman's Agreement* (1947) with Gregory Peck. 'At one time Louella invited me for lunch at Romanoff's, and before we left, every star, producer, director and agent had come to our table and verbally kissed her rear end.'

The majority of stars played the humiliating game of flattery with Hedda Hopper and Louella Parsons, figuring it was far less troublesome having them with them than against. Greg followed this path, but he did so in his inimitable fashion. He beguiled the viper-tongued women with his simplicity, humor and normalcy. (In a hotbed of neuroses like Hollywood, normal is exotic.)

Like a loyal nephew, he treated each woman as though she was his favorite auntie in whom he was confiding the exciting details of his private life and the films in which he was involved. By playing this role, he brought out their gallant and softhearted sides. They responded by protecting his reputation – for the most part. Of the two, Greg favored Parsons.

Parsons wrote a daily column for the newspapers owned by William Randolph Hearst (the apparent inspiration for Orson Welles' classic 1941 movie, *Citizen Kane*). Her flagship was the *Los Angeles Examiner*. She also produced movie reviews and Sunday supplement features, and hosted a successful radio show called *Hollywood Hotel* on which Greg appeared as a guest star.

Parsons was short, dumpy and doughty with large brown eyes and a carefully cultivated scatterbrained style that proved very useful as she flitted from celebrity to celebrity. She never forgot a thing and never forgave anyone who crossed her. 'Louella Parsons is stronger than Samson,' claimed Sam Goldwyn. 'He needed two columns to bring the house down. Louella can do it with one.'

Fortunately for Parsons, she was married to a fun-loving Irishman named Harry 'Docky' Martin. He was a popular Beverly Hills proctologist – whom the stars affectionately nicknamed 'Old Velvet Finger'. The studios relied on him for treating venereal diseases and performing abortions. In a community renowned for fornication, he was in high demand. Through Docky, Parsons had a line to all the testing laboratories in town and could tell if an actress or an actor's wife was expecting (she twice announced Greta was pregnant before Greg had been given the word).

Now, it's one thing to beguile a news hen and it's something else entirely to work them up into a frenzy. Unwittingly – or wittingly – Greg had just such an effect on a slightly less well-known Hollywood columnist named Sheilah Graham. She was a pretty British chorus girl turned reporter who had been the mistress of F Scott Fitzgerald in the late 1930s. Fitzgerald, a not-so-recovering alcoholic was out in Hollywood doing screenwriting to pay for his wife Zelda's confinement to a mental hospital and his daughter Scottie's Vassar tuition. Graham truly loved Fitzgerald and even wrote a book about their tender and tortured romance called *Beloved Infidel.* It eventually became a movie starring Deborah Kerr and – who else? – Gregory Peck. But Fitzgerald wasn't much of a lover. In fact, Graham admitted she never saw him naked. He died in 1940 and, though she grieved many years for him, she was, well, horny. So when Greg hit town, her fantasy life kicked into overdrive.

In her lusty memoir, *A State of Heat,* she writes: '. . . now, driving to the studios, driving back home, when I read the trade papers, when I ate, all of the time, I thought about sex, mainly imagining myself in the arms of Gregory Peck, who always flirted with me. He narrowed his eyes and looked meaningfully at me through the slits while I asked him questions. I became confused and forgot what I was saying. I would almost have an orgasm. Just imagining Gregory Peck making love to me was enough to turn my loins into warm liquid.'

The Pecks were now able to afford a house on Mulholland Drive, high above the golden pastures of Hollywood. On a clear day, Greg could see Santa Catalina Island where he used to camp out in a tent with his father. They had arrived. 'Mulholland is a phenomenon of Los Angeles,' wrote David Thompson in his essay about the celebrated road, 'both an idealized spectacle and a place from which to survey the classic city of visibility. Even as you drive, the panorama turns into a model for grace and dread.' He added: 'The road is like a location in a film, chosen and dressed for its magnificent vantage and for the juxtaposition of inane civilization and a dangerous wilderness.'

The Pecks' home was situated atop a steep ridge above Mulholland. In those days, the ridges and canyons off the drive were sparsely inhabited with film folk; yet alive with rattlesnakes, deer and coyote. The air was balmy, but the light raw and cruel; a light for young people.

Driving back from the studio, Greg would grip the wheel of his second-hand jalopy (the Second World War meant there were few new cars), fixing his eyes straight ahead. Mulholland was so serpentine and strewn with crumbling rock and chaparral at every curve that sometimes cars skidded off the road and toppled over the edge. Just like the hardboiled bosses at the dream factories, the cliffs were not forgiving to people on the way down.

Once in the door, Greg liked nothing better than to duck into the nursery and wrap his long arms around baby Jonathan. Then he'd take a romp with another beloved member of his family – Perry, a 150-pound white Alsatian police dog. He took delight in teaching Perry tricks and the dog proved a quick learner. He slept outside, making the perfect watchdog.

Having never had a real home growing up, Greg considered the little gray Mulholland house a landmark. Though modest by Filmland standards, it nonetheless provided the fan magazines with a bucolic backdrop in which to present Greg and Greta as one of Hollywood's happiest couples. Hand in hand they cavorted about their property in supposedly casual photographs. Of course, the magazine layouts were carefully staged. One picture shows the Pecks on top of their house supposedly cleaning the roof. Greta is wearing a fetching romper outfit and her hair looks like it's just been set at the beauty parlor. In another, she's sporting high heels to skip across the grass. Still, there was a glow about them. They seemed like two kids tickled no end by all the good things coming their way.

What the pictures *didn't* capture was the changing balance in their relationship. Greg and Greta had started out on an equal footing. He was a struggling actor and she was the pretty hairdresser to the star of the company. Now, Greg's name blazed across the marquees of theaters from sea to shining sea and as far away as Europe, Asia and Australia. Greta, whose support had been so crucial to him when he was practically an unknown, was receding into the role of an admiring fan holding on to his coattails as his star rose higher and higher.

Home was the one place where Greg had privacy. Nobody was watching him. He sought sanctuary in gardening, playing the piano (badly, he admitted) and reading, little by little adding to his collection of books about his hero Abraham Lincoln. Like Honest Abe, Greg could project an image of simplicity, but he was actually a complex man. Just as Greg had to make his Faustian bargains in order to survive in Hollywood, Lincoln had to undergo inner struggles of conscience to get elected. As Greg said, '. . . no purely innocent country bumpkin becomes president of the United States.'

In a poignant interview with a Washington journalist named Frederick C Orthman, Greg confessed: 'My wife and I just sit and stare at each other. It happened to us, and here we are with this income. Fabulous, I think, is the word – and we don't know exactly what to do about it. The thing that really gets us is the fact that I never really did amount to much on the stage . . . then this happened to us. I don't know exactly how it happened, but needless to say, I'm grateful. I might also add that I am stunned.'

Greg's early days in Hollywood were indeed remarkable. More astonishing still, the mid-1940s marked only the beginning of a film career that would span over half a century and comprise more than 50 movies. Where did this bashful, gangly boy from La Jolla get the drive to keep going for so long? How did he manage to keep his head straight while living amidst the hedonistic denizens of modern day Sodom and Gomorrah? What was his secret? For clues, let's journey back to his childhood.

CHAPTER TWO

Early Days

'In those days, La Jolla was a kind of paradise by the sea for kids . . . but my folks were divorced when I was very young and instead of growing up in this idyllic little town, I was bounced around quite a bit.'

Gregory Peck

On 5 April 1916, a strapping 10-pound baby boy struggled out of the womb of a terribly frightened young woman. It was a home birth and the mother of the infant was built too small to expel him without enduring enormous pain. Such was the entrance of Gregory Peck on to the stage of life.

After the torturous labor, his mother Bernice, a dazzling beauty of 21, vowed to her 29-year-old husband: 'I never want to have a child again!' And true to her resolute nature, she didn't. Greg was her only offspring.

Being 'a foolish young girl' as she described herself, Bernice – known as Bunny – was determined that her one child would be special. First off, he must have a name that would set him apart from the Johns, Toms, Harrys or Michaels of this world. And because she had trained as a telephone operator, she consulted the phone book. Out leapt 'Eldred'.

To Greg, the name was an albatross he was forced to carry through childhood and adolescence. He loathed being called Eldred. There wasn't even a nickname for it. So he used it at school and in other situations where it was required. Otherwise, he let people know, in his clear and distinct voice, that he preferred to be called by his middle name, Gregory, or Greg for short. Years later, Greg lamented to social critic Cleveland Amory: 'I kept that damn name Eldred until I was 21. Now, that's what I call filial piety.'

Gregory suited him fine. It was his father's name, one of many bonds he would share with his tall, dark-haired, athletic dad. From Gregory Sr the boy also acquired a sly sense of humor and an immutable code of decency – backed up by good old Irish Catholic guilt. Another legacy from his father was the Celtic relish for engaging in lively chat and spinning yarns. As Oscar Wilde said of his fellow countrymen: 'We are the greatest talkers since the Greeks.'

Although Greg's bond with his mother was less strong, he had her to thank for his imaginative energy, his love of beauty and his charisma. Bunny had the magic. She was giddy, attractive and slightly unconventional. With her slim figure, ideally suited for the post-First World War woman, she could carry off the short skirts, rolled-down stockings, and short 'bobbed' hair then coming into style. And, who knows? If the cards had fallen differently, with her pizzazz, she might have been a success in show business.

Gregory Peck Sr came from Rochester, New York. His mother was an Irish immigrant and his father was of English descent. He cherished his Irish ancestry and would pass this appreciation on to his son Greg. The pride of the family lineage was Gregory Sr's first cousin, Thomas Ashe, a hero of the Irish Rebellion of 1916.

A schoolteacher in County Kerry, Thomas Ashe became active in the Irish Republican Brotherhood. During the 1916 Easter Rising Ashe commanded the Fingal Battalion of Volunteers who took Ashbourne, County Meath. The Ashbourne ambush was the only Republican military success during the Easter Rising. The Fingal Battalion demolished a railway bridge, and captured Swords, Donabate and Garristown. They also took the Royal Irish Constabulary barracks in Ashbourne for six hours, during which 11 RIC (Royal Irish Constabulary) men were killed and more than 20 were wounded. The Fingal Battalion only lost two men, with five wounded.

The following year Ashe was arrested and sentenced to a court martial. While detained, he joined a hunger strike. The prison guards retaliated by taking away the prisoners' bedding and shoes. All requests to Ashe to end the hunger strike were met with a firm resolve. 'No! They have branded me a criminal. Even though I do die, I die in good cause.'

Then the authorities began forcible feeding. On 23 September 1917, while the feeding tube was being inserted it pierced Ashe's lung and he collapsed. He died of heart and lung failure on 25 September in the Mater Hospital. Playwright Sean O'Casey wrote a poem for the fallen patriot titled, 'Lament for Tom Ashe.' It begins: 'The wild mountain glens are now silent . . . '

Without a doubt, Greg's Irish stock was strong. In 1884, at the age of 20, his grandmother Catherine Ashe emigrated from Ireland, settled with relatives in Rochester, New York, and then married Samuel Peck. Catherine gave birth to Gregory Peck Sr on 3 August 1886. When the baby was 11 months old, Samuel died of diphtheria. Catherine returned with her son to Ireland, traveling in steerage. Family members met the boat in Cork and escorted them to Aniscaul, near Dingle in County Kerry – home of the Ashe clan. They remained there for ten years, long enough for the son to develop a lifelong Irish brogue. He hurled out words with a superfluous quantity of breath, saying *broadher, widher, stor-rum, far-um*, and *ladders* for letters.

The two returned to the United States. The resilient Mrs Peck became a traveling saleswoman of ladies' corsets and bloomers, succeeding well enough to buy a 16-flat apartment building in San Diego, California, and put her son through the University of Michigan where he earned a degree in pharmacology. (Almost a century later Greg established a scholarship for aspiring pharmacists at the University in his father's name.) She married a second time to a man named James Gilpen.

Gregory Sr moved to La Jolla, a suburb of San Diego. There, he worked for a year at H L Setchel's Drug Store on Girard Avenue. Then, in 1910 Catherine gave him $10,000 to buy the business.

Gregory became known to the residents of the seaside town of La Jolla, California, simply as 'Doc' Peck. His drugstore featured 'pure chemical compounds' and an 'up-to-date' soda fountain. If a man got drunk and embroiled in a fight leaving him with a black eye, he could count on Doc Peck to apply leeches to the wound. The pharmacist kept the leeches on a shelf where they would fascinate the town's children. The creepy bloodsuckers had three jaws, each with about a hundred teeth.

La Jolla was set like a jewel on the California coast. Legally it was just the northwest corner of San Diego, but it developed in peaceful isolation as a compact village because the northwest passage from San Diego was long and devious around La Jolla's commanding Soledad Mountain.

The cliffs at La Jolla rose from more than 350 feet at Black's Beach on the north to 40-foot gentle bluffs at the sheltered Cove near the center of town. Residents loved the sound of the sea, breaking against the cliffs, surging up the beaches and swirling in the caves. 'Sometimes it was merely a faintly heard presence,' recalled Greg's contemporary, Norma Newman Hacker, 'but when there was a storm and the waves crashed against the coastline, everyone would bundle up against the cold and go down to stand and watch the spray as it flew up from the face of the cliffs and flung itself back on the land.'

In calmer weather, seals could be heard barking and seen sporting themselves. Even whales passed by each year on their migration to Baja, California, and its protected bays and estuaries. Sometimes in the summer one could stand at the top of the cliff and see a spotted leopard shark playing in the transparent shallows below.

The streets in La Jolla began at the sea or followed the contours of the shore. After dinner, people walked the streets – whole families of them. The smells of La Jolla at night were unforgettable: all the garden flower odors were released upon the evening breeze. They mingled with the aroma of sage and low-growing chaparral from Mt Soledad. One could ride horseback up La Jolla Canyon on to the mesa above, and in and around the eucalyptus trees near the 'Bughouse,' as the locals called the newly created Scripps Institute of Oceanography.

In 1915, Greg's mother Bernice Ayres, age 20, traveled from her hometown of St Louis, Missouri to La Jolla for the wedding of her sister Myrtle to Charlie Rannells, the Railway Express agent. Her mother, Kate, was already there, having moved in with Myrtle after her own husband, John Dagget Ayres, died on 9 February 1912. John had worked on and off as a railroad detective and as keeper of the boats at Creve Coeur Lake in St Louis.

Charlie Rannells introduced Doc Peck to 'Bunny', proclaiming he was 'the most eligible bachelor in town.' And, indeed, he was quite a catch. A handsome, tautly muscular man of 28, he had coal-black hair, an aquiline nose and a generous mouth. He was popular with his clients, captained the local basketball team and played in the town band.

For a genial but non-adventurous man such as Doc, Bunny Ayres represented excitement. She radiated a glow that pulled all eyes toward her and made her stand out in a crowd. Her face was fine-featured; eyes glinting with mischief, her small head surrounded by an aureole of curly blond hair. Bunny bubbled with life and with stories from the boisterous, rowdy city of St Louis. It was the birthplace of Ragtime – among the happiest and most infectious music the world has ever heard. Bunny and Doc began courting. However, it later proved to be a case of opposites attracting with a romantic setting triumphing over good judgment. As Greg's cousin, Bernice Rannells, explained: 'There wasn't much else to do in La Jolla, so she married Gregory Peck.'

To please her fiancé, Bunny converted to Catholicism and their wedding took place on 4 June 1915 in the splendid setting of St Louis Catholic Cathedral. The Cathedral's unique design combined a Romanesque architecture exterior with a wondrous Byzantine style in the interior. In 1912 masons began installing mosaics depicting key figures in Judeo-Christian history. The project grew to become the largest mosaic collection in the world.

On the night the couple returned to La Jolla, Doc brought his bride to the bungalow he had built for her for $4,000. It was a red wood, board and batten house, the dominant style of California architecture in the area. There weren't any street addresses at the time. Houses had identifying names such as Sans Souci, Green Dragon and Bide-A-Wee, Silver Palm and Hardbiscuit Heaven. Theirs was called La-Lo-O-Mi.

As darkness fell, he looked out the window to see a rowdy group of locals, led by Bunny's brother-in-law Charlie Rannells, banging on pots, pans and washboards while pistols were shot in the air and firecrackers set off. Doc quickly realized they were the victims of a small-town initiation process called a 'Charivari' or 'belling of the bride.' It was a boisterous, mock-serenade to newlyweds designed to welcome them to the community and add excitement to their wedding night. The dignified pharmacist pleaded with them to go home. Instead, the revelers kidnapped and bundled Bunny and Doc into separate cars and took them for joy rides. It was not an auspicious beginning to their life together in La Jolla.

The new Mrs Peck found it difficult establishing a place for herself in such a sweetly simple community with a population of less than 2,000. The *La Jolla Journal*, the town's first newspaper, had just started printing two years before she arrived. Electricity had come to town in 1911. But the locals had a low regard for progress. Many of the good citizens of La Jolla wanted to keep with gas kerosene and candles, but too many people were having stove blowups. When the gas company tried to run a line down Columbus Street, people fought it with picks and shovels – but the gas company won.

In June 1917, an ordinance was passed making it unlawful for anyone over ten years of age to appear on the street, except in the vicinity of the Cove, without covering for the entire body except the hands, feet and head. It was not vigorously enforced, but it was one of those aspects of small-town life that made it very different from Bunny's native St Louis.

She also had to deal with the fact that there was just one of everything: grocery, grain store, hardware store, notions boutique and sweet shop. As for the one drugstore, owned by Doc Peck, it was in deep trouble.

Doc proved to be an inept manager of the store's finances. He never sent bills. Most of his customers were 'on the tab', and he was too easygoing and softhearted to pursue them or check on an accountant when money was missing. The accountant embezzled $10,000. Years later, Greg asked his father: 'Why didn't you go to a bank and ask for a loan?' Chagrined, Doc admitted he was too ashamed and embarrassed. These traits became ingrained in Greg's character. At the same time, his dad's experience made him resolve to be shrewd about money. After conquering Hollywood and seeing money roll in, Greg sought out the best advisors and invested his fortune wisely.

The demise of the Pecks' marriage was messy and full of bitter disclosures on Bunny's part. In filing for divorce on 3 February

1921, Bunny accused her husband of hurling profanities at her and hitting her on two occasions. She alleged he frequently threatened little Greg, saying he would 'knock the hell out of him.' Bunny further claimed that in October 1917 she suffered from an attack of appendicitis, but Doc refused to send for a doctor until two days later when the appendix burst.

Hearing the complaints, Superior Court judge C N Andrews issued a restraining order against her husband. Then, after Doc pleaded with her to take him back, she withdrew the petition for divorce. The reconciliation lasted until 19 July and the couple were divorced on 30 July 1921.

Greg never went into the specifics of his parents' divorce except to say that money and the differences in their ages was the reason the marriage didn't work. Of course, he was too young to have known what actually transpired. Even if he may have learned more facts at a later date, he chose not to disclose them. When Gary Fishgall was in the process of writing a biography of Greg, he wrote to the actor (Fishgall never met with Greg, nor did he talk with him on the phone) and asked him specifically about the recorded legal accusations of Gregory Sr abusing his spouse and son. Greg responded in a letter to Fishgall: 'Nothing like that ever happened.' It was 'impossible. If you knew my dad, it is impossible.'

The court ordered Doc to pay $30 per month in alimony and $20 per month in child support. In 1922, Bunny moved back to St Louis and found work as a telephone operator. Six-year-old Greg followed on after her. His father took him to the train station in San Diego and tipped the Pullman porter $10 to look after him.

Cast a glance at any six-year-old nearby and imagine the anguish experienced by Greg when he said farewell to his father. He didn't know when he would see him again. The youngster boarded the train, and traveled two and a half days alone. He crossed half the continental United States, sleeping two nights without a familiar face to read him a goodnight story or soothe his anxieties. In St Louis, his mother was waiting at the train station.

Years later, when *Cosmopolitan* magazine interviewed Greg, he said: 'I don't care to talk about my childhood because it was so sad.' His cousin Bernice Rannells, who grew up with Greg and whose family looked after him, took umbrage at that remark. 'He had the most wonderful childhood,' she insisted. Certainly, he didn't grow up in abject poverty, nor was he raised by non-family members. Yet, one is left with the impression that the trauma he experienced at the time of his parents' divorce and the upheaval that followed triggered a longstanding depression – which never left him. A picture of Greg in 1922 shows a frightened child in a sailor suit, his hands gripped tightly around his knees as his father gently holds him.

Bunny took Greg to a shabby boarding house at 4715A Washington Street. He recalled the place as 'straight out of Tennessee Williams', with a wild assortment of down-at-the-heel characters. 'I remember the landlady had red hair,' said Greg who compared her to Tallulah Bankhead.

Some landlady! Tallulah Bankhead was a supremely gifted actress of the 1920s and 1930s who during the course of her career appeared in more than 50 plays and 20 movies. However, her most entertaining and spectacular role was herself. She drank too much and talked too much and turned cartwheels when the whim seized her. As Brendan Gill noted in *Tallulah* (1972), his pictorial biography of the star: 'The violent scatological energy of her speech and the celebrated speed and frequency with which she shucked off her clothes and prowled about naked, long after her body had grown ugly with age, were intended to convey an impression of untrammeled emotional freedom . . .'

For the twice-a-week poker nights at the boarding house, Greg swooshed gin in the bathtub. Then he mixed it with lemonade and sold it to the residents at a nickel a glass. He also shined their shoes. During the day, he joined the landlady's son, who was just a little older than he, in selling newspapers on the street corner half a block away, where the trolley cars stopped.

In the early 1920s St Louis was a rowdy wonderland, a magnet for the hard-muscled dockworkers who labored on steamboats and for pleasure-starved salesmen in town on business. The decade was starting to roar with jazz, flappers, flasks, rumble seats, and raccoon coats. Streets such as Chestnut and Market were honeycombed with barrel houses – called honky-tonks – serving 10¢ shots of liquor, gambling joints, and brothels boasting beautiful women of mixed blood, making St Louis an inland rival of New York's Tenderloin and San Francisco's Barbary Coast. There was an almost wholesome air about the place. Girls solicited on bicycles, riding the streets in broad daylight, advertising their charms by letting the wind sweep up their skirts.

Despite the local color, Greg was in a vulnerable position for a six-year-old boy who has been taken away from his father and out of school. But the manner in which he chose to recall those times indicates that he was a survivor early on. He had the ability to adapt to the ramshackle lifestyle, developing spunk and the beginnings of a work ethic. He also got material for a good story that he told and retold once he became famous. Maybe the St Louis chapter of his childhood didn't happen exactly as he remembered it, but he showed he could stand back and extract humor from the situation. Also, he was with his mother who possessed guts and a zest for life. It rubbed off.

After about six months in St Louis, Bunny took Greg for a brief stay in San Francisco where her brother Ben, who worked as a trolley car motorman, lived. Once again, she found it too tough to raise her son alone on her meager income. So she returned to La Jolla where she rented a redwood bungalow at 7453 High Avenue for her mother, Greg and herself. Bunny worked briefly as a waitress in a tearoom earning $25 a month. She enrolled young Greg in the La Jolla Elementary School, and tried unsuccessfully to reconcile her differences with Doc Peck.

Alas, La Jolla still appeared backward to Bunny. Most of the roads weren't paved and during the rainy season the wide expanse of mud was so formidable that children such as her son were asked to wade to school in their bare feet, carrying their shoes, stockings, books and a towel. The first few minutes of the school day were spent cleaning up.

When the first sidewalks were laid, a faction of the villagers refused to walk on them. They said they made their bare feet sore, and prophesied they would ruin the town. But change was in the air, and the protests were overruled. Bunny's niece and namesake,

Bernice Rannells remembered: 'About once a week, my mother gave me a nickel and I would go down and walk across the street when they were paving Girard Avenue, and I couldn't get across the street because all the cement was being poured, so I stayed on the corner and just yelled, "Mr Tetless." He came across and brought me an ice cream cone.'

Not being suited for full-time motherhood and sorely missing the big-city lights, Bunny left young Greg in the care of her mother and moved to Los Angeles. There she worked as a telephone operator for an advertising agency. At this point, Doc was working nights in San Diego as a pharmacist for Ferris and Ferris. He didn't have the time to look after a young child. However, he faithfully visited every Thursday.

Grandmother Kate Ayres was a gentle widow who had once been quite pretty, but now looked older than her years. Although she was not physically active enough to play with young Greg, she had a great deal of love in her heart and he remembered her with the utmost tenderness. More important, Charlie and Myrtle Rannells lived nearby with their children Warren (whom they called Stretch), Catherine, Bernice and Myrtle Adele. Greg could enjoy the company of relatives close to his age.

Greg's three years with Grandmother Kate represented the happiest in his childhood. 'I actually lived in a house when I was little which was called the Silver Pine, for the obvious reason that we have a silver pine tree in the yard . . . I have such wonderful memories of La Jolla as a kid. It was a wonderful combination of bohemian West Coast artistic little enclave and some very practical, pragmatic people who ran the stores and brought produce into town . . . I had an uncle, through marriage, Nathan Rannells, who was the postmaster whenever there was a Democrat in the White House. And when there was not, he was not.'

On Sundays, Grandmother Kate and Greg joined Myrtle and Charlie Rannells and their family for Sunday service at St James Episcopal Church. The group would then make their way back to the Rannells' house to prepare for Sunday dinner. Uncle Charlie, who had been a silver-miner in his youth and was an earthy man, would doff his Sunday best suit and head for the chicken coop.

He'd grab a bird by the neck and swing it around and around until its head popped off.

The scene was not lost on Greg. 'I was lucky to have seen and experienced just that bit of the Old West,' he later said. 'It gave me a connection with those rougher, self-reliant, hearty characters I was later to play in Western film.' (Charlie's son Stretch became Greg's model for the lubricious rascal Lewt in *Duel in the Sun* (1947).)

Kate Ayres did not keep close tabs on her charge. This meant Greg was free to experience the joys of small-town life. It was sweet compensation for being the child of absent parents. 'I don't think it hindered my growth or gave me complexes,' Greg said, reflecting on the years from seven to ten he spent with his grandmother. 'Instead, it was the best possible way to grow up, something like Tom Sawyer and his Aunt Polly. My grandmother was a lot more lenient than my parents would have been.'

It wasn't the best way to go through childhood, but Greg chose to see it that way. He never wanted to be considered a victim. Yet, perhaps as a reaction to being bounced around by his parents, he grew up to be controlling about situations – anticipating the worst became second nature – and persnickety about his possessions. He insisted on a fixed spot where he could keep familiar and loved things.

Greg had little money living with his grandmother, but neither did most of the other kids. There was always something to do if you just used a little imagination. 'I knew everybody,' said Greg. 'I'd go on my bike anywhere in town and be among friends and feel perfectly safe. We played games with home base under the corner street lamp and Run Sheep Run. We built tree houses and we'd climb into spare tires and roll down the street. It was just like *To Kill a Mockingbird*.'

Halloween was always a special occasion. The adults built big bonfires; the children paraded in their costumes, and competed for prizes. But Fourth of July was best of all, particularly 4 July 1924. It was the celebration of the arrival of the electric railway complete with luxurious glassed-in cars. The *La Jolla Journal* reported 25,000 people came for the 'smoothly run' event. There were picnickers galore and little trains were busily puffing in and out for hours bringing visitors. In the afternoon, there was a real cakewalk at the pavilion. And at night, there were fireworks on the raft down by the Cove and a few that twinkled along the shoreline.

Greg loved watching his father march with the band and the Civil War veterans in the Fourth of July parade. Among the white-haired veterans shaking with infirmities was Grandfather Rannells, the father of Greg's Uncle Charlie and Uncle Nathan. He was a lean, leathery, clear-eyed old man whom Greg remembered as 'a solid nineteenth-century character who had led a very exciting life.'

'I'm very grateful for the contacts I had with him and had with others of that era,' Greg said. 'They gave me a great respect for the past and they made me realize how close the past really is. Because of them history has never seemed remote to me.'

The Civil War – America's greatest, deadliest, bloodiest drama – was 'a fairly recent memory then,' said Greg, and seeing the old men proudly marching fuelled his interest in his hero Abraham Lincoln. Even before growing up to resemble Lincoln, he identified with him. By age twelve, Greg had memorized the Gettysburg Address. Here was an ordinary man who went from a log cabin to the White House; here was the representative man, transformed into the extraordinary by both his belief in principle and the demands of history. 'Lincoln is the ideal American,' Greg said years later. 'A native genius, cast up out of a very ordinary heritage . . . the great American saga and legend from start to finish.'

Though he was a voracious reader who took out his first library card at the age of six Greg was a middling student. He did not form close bonds with his teachers and he kept himself aloof from his classmates. He explained: 'I was alone a lot as a kid and a kid who spends a lot of time on his own simply has no habit of having fun or of conversation at home, of doing things together.'

Greg was a pleaser. When his grandmother gave him a pair of high-button shoes, he was mortified because none of the other children sported anything so old-fashioned, but he suffered in silence. 'I used to hide my feet as much as possible, and the only thing I noticed about a schoolmate was his footwear. My grandmother had meant to please me, so I couldn't let on how much I hated those shoes. I wore them for what seemed years – until they were completely worn out.' He was learning also that if your place in the family is not secure, it's best to express gratitude.

Like any actor, Greg vividly recalls the first time he faced a live audience. It was the La Jolla Elementary School's fifth-grade production of the ancient legend of Pandora's Box. 'As I recall, I was resplendent in a green velvet vest. I was the one who opened the box.' What he remembered most about the production, however, were his co-stars: 'They were three of the most beautiful girls I'd ever seen. I wanted to marry all of them.'

From the beginning, acting was his therapy. 'I suppose part of my fondness for it was that I could be someone else. My real personality had always been held back. Who knows why? I didn't have a very warm childhood, I guess.'

Fortunately Grandmother Kate shared Greg's love of books and drama. In the evenings before he went to bed, she would take out the family Bible, a repository of the births, deaths, marriages and baptisms in the Ayres clan. She'd read to him and he was fascinated '. . . not so much with the lessons in doctrines, but with the wonderful stories and tales of adventure and mayhem.' He credits the Bible with giving him a good sense of theatrics. 'It fed my love of storytelling and legends and drama and sacrifice and suffering and exultation. The Bible is full of strong emotions, and you have to bring strong emotions into storytelling, to be able to use them as needed.'

One day Greg was walking home from school and a black and brown mongrel with a bit of Airedale in its blood appeared beside him. 'I happened to have a left-over sandwich in my lunch pail,' remembered the actor. 'He looked hungry. And after I fed him, he followed me home. Never did find out where he came from.' He named him Bud and loved him with all his heart.

Whenever his father came to visit, Greg would persuade him to take Bud with them to the country. When they came upon a deserted strip of road, Bud would be allowed to race his father's car going '30 miles an hour' and often winning.

Like other La Jolla youngsters, Greg lived for the summers. His Uncle Charlie operated a feed and grain store and owned a big barn, built sometime in the 1880s. Along with his cousins, Greg whiled away many an afternoon talking and dreaming under its sprawling roof. 'There was a big hayloft and it was cool and dark, a great place to hide away from everyone.'

With La Jolla's superb Mediterranean climate, life revolved around the beach. The Cove was protected from the waves by rock formations and an outstretched arm (Alligator Head) of land on the southern edge. Here is where the children often took their brown-bag lunches and passed the day. Greg and his friends would swim out to the raft and sit, letting their legs dangle into the cool water, or they would swim to 'the reef,' a slab of rough rock, pitted by chitins and smoothed by the feet of generations of bathers, that rose from the bottom to within 4 or 5 feet from the surface, depending on the tide. The boys liked to wrench abs (abalones) with a tire iron from the underwater reefs out between the Cove and the Caves. They would also spend hours exploring the beautiful tidal pools (now almost extinct) and learning about marine life.

'The kids I played with were like myself,' recalled Greg, 'interested in sailing.' One summer he built a boat with his next-door neighbor Johnny Buchanan. They bought a blueprint and warped their own lumber, carefully shaping and fitting each piece. The project appealed to Greg's dogged persistence and his attention to detail. He was willing to work endlessly on the undertaking, making sure everything was perfect. 'The result turned out to be quite a boat, and for some time I could think of no occupation so absorbing as boat-building.'

Like Jem and Scout in *To Kill A Mockingbird*, Greg was discovering there was an undercurrent of evil amidst the quotidian joys of La Jolla. It was a white Anglo-Saxon community that Greg remembered as 'unthinking.' People who looked different, such as the colorful gypsies who wandered through town and told people's fortunes and the Chinese and Mexicans who built the houses, were marginalized. The term 'nigger' was commonly used. In 1923, when a black family rented a house on the outskirts of town, the Ku Klux Klan burned a cross on Mt Soledad.

'None of us youngsters knew what it was all about,' said Greg. 'But even with the sheets we could recognize some of the hot bloods of the town. They made quite an impression on us.

'I was told later they were trying to impress a family of colored folks. They were domestics, and I expect they wanted to be closer to their work. I don't know if they were frightened. But I know I was. The scene has stuck in my memory ever since.'

Started after the Civil War, the KKK experienced resurgence in the 1920s. Members of the terrorist KKK presented themselves as defenders of the white against the black, of Gentile against Jew, and of Protestant against Catholic. They thus traded on the newly inflamed fears of credulous small-towners in places like La Jolla. Their message appealed to ordinary men with an infantile love of hocus-pocus and a lust for secret adventure. By setting a cross ablaze in the night, they aroused fears of burning houses, beatings and sometimes lynching.

When Greg grew older he was able to appreciate the immense power of movies as propaganda. As Darryl Zanuck liked to say: 'The movies are the greatest political fact in the world today.' In the case of the KKK, the organization benefited greatly from D W Griffith's *The Birth of a Nation* (1915). This controversial, explicitly racist movie set up a major censorship battle over its vicious, extremist depiction of African Americans. Nonetheless, the film was a huge box-office moneymaker, raking in $18 million by the start of the talkies. It was the most profitable film for over two decades, until Walt Disney's *Snow White and the Seven Dwarfs* (1937).

What made this astonishing success possible? Several factors. A wave of immigration from Southern and Eastern Europe troubled 'old stock' Americans. Then there was the experience of the First World War, in which '100 per cent Americanism' was enforced by vigilante groups and by the government, armed with the Espionage and Sedition Act. Following that, the Bolshevik Revolution inaugurated a Red scare that brought a frantic search for 'agitators' to arrest or deport. These tensions were felt in La Jolla. With the opening of two movie houses, the residents were being given the opportunity to see popular films such as *The Birth of a Nation* and some sympathized with its message.

When Greg turned eight, he lost some of his innocence. Eight 'was a bad year for me,' the actor noted. 'I discovered there was no Santa Claus, no Easter Bunny and Bud was kidnapped.'

Greg learned of the disappearance of his dog after spending a blissful vacation with his father camping on Santa Catalina Island off the California coast. They took the steamer over to the 21-mile-long island and roughed it for a week. A gathering spot for the privileged few who fled by yacht from the urban sprawl, the island was a forest sanctuary where buffalo roamed the interior. It was also open to campers who didn't mind living without running water. Greg and his father climbed the mountain trails overlooking the Pacific and fished for hours from the beach.

When they returned to La Jolla, Grandmother Kate told Greg that Bud had been kidnapped. In actuality, Bud was disposed of because his barking riled the neighbors. Since Doc could not face telling his son that Bud had to go, he arranged with Kate to have the dog disappear. Greg never found out if the dog was put to sleep or given away. It was a deeply hurtful experience. Reflecting on the incident he said: 'For the next 40 years I always took a second look at every black and brown mongrel I saw.'

The charms of La Jolla was not lost on the early filmmakers. One day Greg stood behind a rope at the Cove and watched a crew shooting silent movie actors as they cavorted in the sand. He remembered: 'They all had orange paint on their faces and black lips and black eye shadow – certainly they weren't like any people I'd ever met in La Jolla.' The star, Lew Cody, had made his mark as a suave, roguish leading man, with a few villain roles on the side. Sporting white flannels and a panama hat, he brandished a long cigarette holder, occasionally darting it playfully under the skirts of bathing beauties in the cast.

The Granada Theater, seating 712, was opened on 25 March 1925. Grandmother Kate saw to it that Greg received a solid film education. 'We went to the picture show two or three times a week,' said Greg. 'We didn't care what was showing.' They even increased the church attendance in several denominations because sometimes there was a movie after the service.

Although films were still silent, cinematography in particular had reached a level of exquisite sophistication, bestowing an artistic patina on even the most banal of plots and exaggerated pantomime. Movie stars (a designation coined in the previous decade) were becoming increasingly popular. In watching the 'flickers', Greg was allowing the films and the stars to shape his imagination, give him some glimpse of adulthood and a sense of worlds beyond small-town La Jolla. Radio did not come close to having the power over people's lives that the movies did.

One night Kate took Greg to see Lon Chaney, the legendary chameleon known as 'the man of a thousand faces', in *The Phantom of the Opera* (1925). Chaney was a master who crafted some of the most grotesque physical portrayals of human misery on film. The actor was already a superstar at the time, like John Gilbert, Douglas Fairbanks and Harold Lloyd, much of his success due to his title role in *The Hunchback of Notre Dame* (1923). Chaney became an artist through direct contact with disability; both parents were deaf, causing him to develop a repertoire of facial and body tics and gestures to communicate with them. This experience led him to create compelling performances in a number of scary roles in which he was required to be legless, armless or otherwise deformed.

In *The Phantom of the Opera* Chaney managed to be repulsive and sympathetic at the same time. The story takes place in Paris in the late nineteenth century and concerns a young opera singer who hears the voice of a mysterious man in her dressing room. He promises to make her a famous opera star provided she never removes his mask.

The movie maintains a creepy atmosphere throughout, leading up to the famous unmasking of the phantom. At this point, Chaney created a pantomime closely akin to dance. He moved with singular grace. He put down his heels and swiveled around facing the heroine.

'She snatched his mask off,' remembered Greg, 'and he turned his head to a close-up. He had no face, practically. God, my hair stood on end! I think my grandmother's hair stood on end, too. I was positively stunned. After the picture we walked home, and I held my grandmother's hand all the way. It wasn't until we got halfway home that I realized she was as frightened as I was. We walked right down the middle of the street, which had eucalyptus trees on each side. We were terrified of the dark sidewalks.' Kate let him sleep in her bed that night.

By 1926, Bunny had remarried and moved to San Francisco. Her new husband was a traveling salesman named Joseph Maysuch, formerly Masucci. She did not invite her son to live with them; she wanted to travel with her husband. 'Since she hadn't stuck with the first husband, she was doubly determined to stick with her second,' Greg said, adding, 'Italian men seem to need a lot of looking after.' But then, so do boys. In any case, it was presented to Greg as a *fait accompli*. 'There wasn't much communication in my family,' Greg recalled. 'I can't remember ever sitting around the table discussing things.' Now he was about to be taken away from his beloved La Jolla and required to live at a school he would later describe as run by 'tough Irish nuns and ROTC (Reserve Officers' Training Corps) drill instructors.'

CHAPTER THREE

Growing Up

'If anybody was least likely to succeed Greg was definitely it. He would be the last person I would've thought would make it.'
Richard Lustig, Gregory Peck's classmate,
San Diego High School, 1933

After romping about barefoot in La Jolla, Greg had a hard time adjusting to the confinement of St John's Military School, where he was sent in 1927. Fronting on noisy West Washington Boulevard in a drab section of Los Angeles, the three-story main building – formerly an orphanage – was a forbidding affair that reeked with the smell of wax.

Under the watchful eyes of the stern but kind Sisters of Mercy and the iron-jawed First World War veterans they hired to turn the boys into fit cadets, Greg was leading a highly structured life. Reveille woke him at 6 a.m. Then he was expected to rise and stand at attention. The boys shined their shoes every day, 'like little robots,' Greg remembered. They prayed before and after meals, before and after classes. Dinner was at 6.30 p.m.; taps at 9 p.m. 'We were marching and praying all day long,' he recalled, 'from the time we woke up until the time we went to bed at night, they had us hemmed in.'

Cadets were permitted off the grounds on Sundays and one weekend per month. For the two-night furloughs, Greg caught the trolley to Los Angeles' Union Station, then traveled south by train to San Diego. At his father's place, he was to witness a sad spectacle. Doc Peck was caring for his terminally ill mother. The invincible Catherine Ashe, who had raised Doc alone by selling ladies' undergarments, was now dying of uterine cancer.

Greg, who was 11, sat by her bedside – a helpless witness to her suffering, unable to ease her pain and powerless to heal her. He saw and smelled it all, the bouts of nausea and the peculiar odor emitted by terminal cancer patients, the wasted countenance and the weakened voice emitting pitiful groans. Catherine died on 19 May 1928, but the memory of her excruciating last days never left Greg. 'I remember strength and an almost stoic way of dying,' he said years later, 'except for the groaning which I can hear to this day.' In the 1960s he honored her through his tireless work for the American Cancer Society.

When he wasn't staying with his father, Greg spent his furlough weekend in La Jolla where he camped on Uncle Charlie and Aunt Myrtle's living-room couch. Their daughter, Bernice, three years younger than Greg, recalled, 'He'd come in real cute in his military suit and say, "I've got to get out of these things." Then he'd go swimming and zoom around town.'

St John's provided a sense of order to Greg's chaotic childhood, yet he deeply resented being placed there. He remembered the institution as largely attended by the children of divorced parents who, 'out of guilt and uncertainty,' sent their offspring there for discipline. In reality, Doc and Bunny may well have felt they were giving their son a leg up in life. St John's had opened two years before Greg's arrival and its mission was to provide an excellent education for pre-adolescent boys from working-class, often troubled families. The school maintained a selective admissions policy and took only bright boys with promise.

Dramatics weren't stressed at St John's; still, the school nurtured Greg's thespian instincts. An actor lives off what he has stored up in the way of impressions and experiences. And what could be more dramatic than daily mass – particularly when it was recited in Latin – and students such as Greg had a chance to be altar boys. 'I got very thoroughly indoctrinated,' Greg said later. Three days a week, he went to the sacristy, laid out the priest's garments and poured the sacramental wine. Then he would put on his black altar-boy robe with white lace and assist the priest during the service. Greg memorized the entire Latin mass. 'I knew the whole routine by heart,' he said, 'when to ring the bells, when to swing the incense burner, and somehow I took to that.'

Producer Martin Scorsese, a friend of Greg's, has drawn heavily on his Catholic boyhood for film inspiration. He notes: 'The church and the movie house both are places for people to come together and share a common experience. I believe there is spirituality in films, even if it's not one that can supplant faith. I have found over the years that many films address themselves to the spiritual side of man's nature, from Griffith's *Intolerance* (1916) to John Ford's *The Grapes of Wrath* (1940) to Hitchcock's *Vertigo* (1958) to Kubrick's *2001* (1968) and so many more . . . It's as if movies answer an ancient quest for the common unconscious. To fulfill a spiritual need that people have to share a common memory.'

The indelible mark of Catholicism was being pressed into Greg's mind and heart. Prior to enrolling in St John's, he hadn't given much thought to sin. Now, he was learning the fine points of mortal and venial transgressions. Sin produced blemishes on the soul that could keep him out of Heaven, put him in Purgatory for years, or, God forbid, hurl him into Hell forever. Prayer was a safeguard against sin. In fact, the nuns commanded memorization of prayers under pain of humiliation at the business end of a ruler. Plus, they expected their charges to be brave, charitable, obedient, respectful, and pure in thought, word and deed.

He longed for his chums in La Jolla. They didn't have to polish their shoes or worry about sin; they could lark around shooting spitballs, passing notes, making fun of teachers, and generally having a good time. Yet it is characteristic of Greg that he didn't rebel at St John's. Instead, he suppressed his disappointment at being parked there by his family and made the most of it. He began to idolize his spiritual advisor, Father Timothy Crowley, and even considered becoming a priest.

Perhaps without realizing it, Greg absorbed the activist philosophy of the Sisters of Mercy. While these nuns were academically narrow, they were fiercely committed to social justice. The order, established in Dublin in 1831, had a history of caring for the less fortunate – and they infused their students with this fervor. (One huge stain blots their record on human rights. Sisters of Mercy ran at least three of Ireland's infamous Magdalene Laundries. In these barbaric institutions, which were under the auspicious of several Catholic religious orders, the mentally infirm, victims of rape or incest, or girls who were potentially promiscuous were locked away and forced to atone for their sins by washing the dirty linen of the Catholic clergy.) The Sisters of Mercy's founder, Catherine McAuley, was a stylish, cultured woman whose personality and adventures were the stuff of Hollywood. (Her life would have made a great movie starring Greer Garson.) An Irish artist of the time described McAuley as 'remarkably well made, attentive to good grooming and conservative in her dress.' She 'lived in what is usually called good style . . . went into society.'

Catherine McCauley's gentle manner masked her radicalism. She had a passion for the plight of the poor and spent her time in the slums of Dublin, a commitment that won her loyal friends. When she was 40, she inherited a fortune from a childless couple that she had befriended. With the money she established the Sisters of Mercy as a community of 'walking nuns' who would live outside convent walls. Their mission was to introduce Catholic education and healthcare to immigrants in poverty-stricken communities throughout the world. When they arrived in the United States in 1854, they lived in whatever space was available, sometimes in stables, railway cars and quarantine or 'pest' houses. At the same time, they nursed victims of cholera, earthquakes and floods. In some towns, anti-Catholic feeling ran rather high and they were driven out.

Putting down roots in Los Angeles, the good sisters opened orphanages, shelters for working girls, hospitals and a tubercular sanitarium. Their purpose in founding St John's was to develop future Catholic leaders out of a select group of boys. These students would be given a solid education in the importance of activism on behalf of social justice. Irish culture permeated the school. Athletic teams were named 'The Shamrocks'. Embracing the culture, Greg took 'Patrick' for his confirmation name.

According to biographer Michael Freedland, Greg's best friend at St John's was Augustine Mackessy, a recent Irish immigrant and the undisputed hero of the school, who came over to the United States after his father, a Dublin policeman, had been killed by a bomb thrown by Eamon de Valera himself.

On Sundays Greg and his school chums liked to hop on a trolley to see a movie, often going from one film to another. 'We really went overboard about them,' Greg recalled.

Hollywood in the 1920s was a land of enchantment. Here were wildly talented directors (such as King Vidor, William Wellman and Raoul Walsh – all of whom would eventually work with Greg), legendary stars and classic films. In the sanctuary of the movie house, Greg could see people on the screen who were more beautiful and fascinating than mortals leading ordinary lives. It was his kind of world.

In the mid-1920s, Hollywood made the transition from silent to talking films. The idea was met with opposition in some quarters. Studio boss H M Warner cracked: 'Who the hell wants to hear actors talk?' D W Griffith, the film pioneer often referred to as the 'father of the movies', protested: 'It will never be possible to synchronize the voice with the pictures.' Screenwriter and director Joseph Mankiewicz said later: 'I can remember vividly how tough it was on actors and actresses when the silent pictures gave way to talkies. That microphone was a nemesis – if you didn't record well, you were finished. There was a fire one day at Paramount, and Clara Bow ran out screaming, "I hope to Christ it was the sound stages."'

Greg thrilled to *The Jazz Singer* (1927) starring Al Jolson at the exotic Egyptian Theater. It was the legendary first talkie that is in fact silent with several sound musical sequences. In it, Jolson sings a full-throated rendition of 'Dirty Hands, Dirty Face', then he raises his hands and stops the audience's applause, speaking his first words on the screen and some of the most famous lines of dialogue in film history: 'Wait a minute! Wait a minute! You ain't heard nothin' yet! Wait a minute, I tell ya. You ain't heard nothin'! Do you wanna hear "Toot, Toot, Tootsie"!? All right, hold on, hold on.' *The Jazz Singer* is the story of Cantor Oland's son going into show business over the objections of his father. The conflict paralleled Greg's own later experience with Doc Peck, who disapproved of his son becoming an actor.

Another unforgettable event for Greg was being present at the opening of Mann's Chinese Theater in 1927 where Cecil B DeMille's *King of Kings* premiered. Greg recalled: 'The ushers were dressed in Chinese Mandarin garb, the carpets were a foot thick, the air was perfumed with Chinese incense, and along with the movie, a biblical epoch, there was a magnificent stage show.' Years later, when Mann's had become the most famous movie theater in the world and the forecourt boasted the imprint of Hollywood legends such as Jimmy Durante's nose, Harpo Marx's harp and Betty Grable's legs, Greg was invited to put his handprint in the cement in front of the theater. The experience didn't come close to matching the joy of being there when the theater first opened.

The movies he watched in the first days of the talkies made a profound impression on him. Greg explained: 'I'd never seen any live theater, and I was watching these great actors – who could speak so well – playing out dramas and comedies and eventually Westerns and adventure stories, and it was just a revelation.'

Rowdy newspaperman Ben Hecht (screenwriter for *Spellbound)* arrived in Hollywood in 1925. He marveled at the city's endless possibilities, seeing Filmland not as a child like Greg but through adult eyes. In his memoir *A Child of the Century* (1954), he recounts how producers were greedy for talent, 'any kind of talent, from geese trainers to writers and actors.' Hecht contends his nerves were alive to its hawker's cry an hour after he left the train:

> Hungry actors leaped from hall bedrooms to terraced mansions. Writers and newspapermen who had hoboed their way West begin hiring butlers and laying down wine cellars. Talent, talent, who had talent for anything – for beating a drum, diving off a roof, writing a joke, walking on his hands? Who could think up a story, any kind of story? Who knew how to write it down? And who had Ego? That was the leading hot cake – Ego or a pair of jiggling boobies under morning-glory eyes. Prosperity chased them all. New stars were being hatched daily, and new world-famous directors and producers were popping daily out of shoeboxes.

Greg's forays into this world stayed with him. Meanwhile, at St John's he was developing a bulldog tenacity that impressed the nuns, priests and veteran military officers. He was promoted to Cadet Captain Peck and was given the responsibility of whipping 60 of the youngest students, aged from eight to ten, into shape. 'I shouted at them like Erich von Stroheim,' he recalled, acknowledging that his martinet tendencies were evident even then. 'God knows what I did to the psyches of those poor little kids. But having put the fear of God, the Pope and the school chaplain into them, we won the gold medal for drill.'

Greg gorged on books, reading everything from Zane Grey to Walter Scott, and as the editor of the school's monthly newspaper, *The Bugle Call*, he developed a keen writing skill. Obedient and dutiful, he also proved adept at winning the support of teachers and other adults.

The pressure to be a 'good Catholic boy' points up the limiting quality of this impressionable period of his education and proved to be a liability in some of the roles he played as an actor. It encouraged a self-imposed constipation, a rigidity of posture that translated into conventional heroics rather than the go-for-broke intensity we see in actors like Marlon Brando and James Cagney that really strikes a nerve. Still, St John's imbued him with sensitivity to the social importance of authority figures and a high regard for persistence, which enabled him to stretch his modest talent to the limit. Recalled Greg: 'One of the things that you didn't do there was quit anything once you'd started. You went to the finish.'

By the spring of 1930 Greg had completed ninth grade at St John's and was ready to graduate. Decked out in his gray-blue military uniform for a photograph, he looks composed yet somewhat melancholy. Upon graduation, it was decided he should live with his father. Since he knew few young people in the port city of San Diego, it wasn't going to be easy. Father and son shared a box-like bungalow next to the apartment house his grandmother had owned located on Broadway Street in Golden Hill, a lower middle-class part of town. Doc still worked nights at Ferris and Ferris drugstore at Fifth and Market – for years the only 24-hour pharmacy in San Diego County.

They saw each other mostly at breakfast in what Greg called 'a barren household.' Then Greg would catch the trolley for a school made up of gray granite structures with ivy crawling up the front that were designed to resemble the buildings at West Point.

When Greg entered San Diego High School in the fall of 1930, the confidence gained at St John's quickly eroded. He had worked diligently to create an identity at the Military School and now it was stripped from him. Also, he missed the support of a structured routine. There was no polishing brass, no marching drills, no mass in the morning. He kept fairly much to himself, feeling depressed and sleeping a lot. One classmate remembered him as an 'angular, painfully shy, rail of a boy.' Another said he was 'not impressive in any way – not anyone you ever heard about.' His mediocre report cards included a D in geometry.

He was too caught up in the quagmire of adolescence to take much notice of world or local events. But in the early 1930s, everybody listened to the radio. The news was desperate. Across the land there were bread lines, soup kitchens, uncontrolled floods, devastating droughts, migrant workers moving north and west, general despair. As Americans tried to come to grips with the Great Depression, they avidly followed the fireside radio chats of their newly elected President, Franklin D Roosevelt. He assured his countrymen they 'had nothing to fear, but fear itself.' Roosevelt was creating his 'New Deal' with many programs meant to bring immediate relief to the needy and recovery to the economy. He set up a federal agency to provide the states with funds to feed the hungry. Legislation was passed to aid farmers and homeowners in danger of losing their property because they could not keep up mortgage payments. The Civilian Conservation Corps was organized, providing jobs for unemployed young men in forest conservation and road construction work. 'I have no expectation of making a hit every time I come to bat,' Roosevelt liked to say. 'What I seek is the highest possible batting average.'

Though his father was a 'Hoover Republican,' Greg instinctively sympathized with Franklin D Roosevelt. In fact, the President became one of his heroes. Unlike Doc Peck, FDR was an optimist. He was an interesting choice for Greg's hero in other respects as well. FDR could put up a show of being frivolous when in actuality he was dead serious. And when the chips were down, his strength showed through. Before becoming crippled with polio, he was debonair and somewhat thoughtless and arrogant.

Polio toughened him. Then he became courageous, polite and generous.

Some nights Greg would go by Ferris and Ferris on Market Street to see his father. The Stingaree district was located south of the pharmacy; it was comprised of several blocks of bawdy houses, gin joints and gambling halls. The habitués of this neighborhood would come into the drugstore revealing a world quite different from pristine La Jolla.

Greg may well have witnessed some of the racial prejudice that was condoned – even encouraged – in establishments like Ferris and Ferris. One night in 1936 a black boy walked into the drugstore and sat down at the soda fountain. Instead of waiting on him, the white employee behind the counter threatened to beat him up. 'We don't serve no blacks in here . . .' he yelled. Even when an officer intervened, the employee continued to make threats.

Greg missed his mother, whom he saw rarely now, and yearned for a warm family life. His ache for happiness was palpable. 'I was lonely, withdrawn, full of self-doubt,' he admitted. He vividly recalled the Christmas of 1931 when he was 15. He spent it shooting baskets at a local athletic club. Then he went to a movie. Afterwards he wandered home in time for his father to wake up and take him to dinner at a local café. Just as he had done with the bleak stretch he passed with Bunny in St Louis when he was six, Greg stepped outside the experience and looked at it as a story. 'I've often thought it would make a nice little scene in a film,' he said one time in recounting the incident. 'If I were producing it, I would want a young Tony Perkins or James Dean in the role in his hometown with nothing else to do one Christmas Day.'

New Year's was better. Father and son had a tradition of driving to Pasadena for the Rose Bowl parade and football game on New Year's Day. They'd watch the colorful floats sail down Pasadena's Colorado Boulevard and bask in the clear and sunny Southern California skies while most of the nation was in the throes of the winter chill. Then it was on to the big game and eating hot dogs. Sadly, Doc was no longer alive in 1988 when his 71-year-old son presided over the 99th Rose Bowl parade.

Greg's inhibitions held him hostage in many ways. He joined the glee club of Walter (Pop) Reyer but still held back. 'If you could hit a few notes, you were in. I tried never to be heard.' Once he entered a set of lyrics in a contest to select a new school song. Greg remembered: 'Each student was to sing his song in front of the glee club. When my turn came, I froze. I was just too shy to get up in front of all those people and sing. Naturally, my song lost.' He did manage to land a role in the all-male variety show called *Boys' High Jinx*.

Doc strongly believed his son should be involved in sports and encouraged him in that direction, but Greg was paralyzed by bashfulness. 'My first hero was a football player on the school team . . . I was too shy to speak to him, but I used to watch him, admire everything he did, and glow over his triumphs.'

Finally Greg went out for football. His brush with greatness came in the B-team tryouts of 'The Cavers' as the team was known. He told Welton Jones of the *San Diego Union-Tribune*: 'We had great football teams then. The quarterback was Cotton Warburton, about 165 pounds, swift, elusive, later a famous star at USC. In a scrimmage one day, he was coming right at me. I closed my eyes, threw myself toward him and got hit with his knee as he went by. Though stunned, I scrambled to my feet and was proud ever after.' He also joined the San Diego Rowing Club.

Despite his shyness, Greg was developing resiliency and independence. 'By the time I was 15, I realized I was going to have to look after myself – I was pretty much on my own as for education, money, and my future.'

Schoolwork was the least of his concerns. Though he lugged bags of books home from the library, his intellectual curiosity wasn't fully awakened. For example, when Albert Einstein came to San Diego and drove past the high school, the students lined the curbside. Greg joined them but he had no idea why Einstein was famous and didn't bother to ask.

About the age of 17, nature took a hand. He shot up from 5 feet 4 inches to 6 feet 2 inches. 'I grew like an asparagus – and looked like one too.' Maybe so, but he was an eye-catching asparagus. His appeal was not lost on girls.

Greg screwed up his courage and asked a classmate named Harriet for a date. He saw her as an almost unobtainable beauty and since he had never had a date before, he was both thrilled and terrified that she accepted. Reminisced Greg: 'What I remember most about the night is a ten-minute wait with her father while she was getting ready. I had supposed that like my father he was interested in sports, so I had boned up on all the latest scores in preparation. It turned out that he didn't care at all about them. It was a dreadful wait.'

One failure in high school gnawed at Greg for years to come. In 1933, he was passed over for the lead in *Oh Wilbur*, the senior class play. Three decades after graduating, Greg returned to San Diego. He was in town for the local premier of *To Kill A Mockingbird* (1962), the film that won him an Oscar. Walking into the Spreckles Theater lobby, he spotted a familiar face. Pointing a finger at this gentleman, he exclaimed: 'YOU! *You* are the one who beat me out for the lead in the senior play!'

The man to whom Greg's finger was pointed was Richard Lustig, a San Diego accountant. Robust in build with bushy sideburns, Lustig said he honestly didn't remember competing with Greg for the lead. However, he did recall him as 'very shy, a tall, bashful, gawky guy – very awkward in his movements. He was all voice and no body.' And did the success of his classmate surprise Lustig? Did it ever! 'I think the whole class was stunned.'

Greg graduated on 16 June 1933 in a class of about 450 students. In the fall of that year he enrolled at San Diego State Teachers College. (The institution dropped the name Teachers in 1935 and became known as San Diego State University.) He took the standard courses for a freshman, but for an elective took speech class from Professor Paul Pfaaf. There he made an acting debut of sorts: 'In speech class, I was assigned to recite a selection from Eugene O'Neill's *Emperor Jones*, and without realizing what I was doing, I acted it out.' Seeing talent, Pfaaf encouraged Greg to pursue acting, at least in college.

In April 1934 Greg turned 18. Like many boys growing up in Southern California, he ventured across the border to Tijuana for a rite of passage. Here, a youth walked down the main drag, Avenida Revolucion, passing beggars, shoeless tattered children, con men, whores and beaten up wrecks of cars. A sewer-like stench traveled on the thick breeze and challenged the olfactory sense, but it also carried with it the delicious scent of onions, pepper, charred meat and fish. The air vibrated with yelling and screaming from the balcony bars. Entering a darkened restaurant, a traveler like Greg was invited to quaff down Mexican beer (colloquially known as buzzard piss) and watch ancient porno flicks. Some of the cruder establishments featured live stage shows involving naked women and donkeys. Afterwards, the local prostitutes introduced themselves and let it be known they were available to clear up any mysteries a young man might have about sex. The Sisters of Mercy at St John's would have called Tijuana 'an occasion of sin.'

Despite this, the principles of social justice learned at St John's did prevail. When Clifford Odets' smash hit play *Awake and Sing!* came to town, Greg was determined to see it. Written in 1934, it established Odets as the defining American playwright of the 1930s and the champion of the underprivileged. Filled with tragedy and hope, *Awake and Sing!* chronicles the struggles of the Berger family in the Bronx. It's funny and heartbreaking as they cope with survival and grasp for dreams in the Depression era.

That spring Greg started to wonder what he wanted to do with his life and dropped out of school. He drove a truck for Union 76. 'I was a good driver, I liked it, I was proud of that. I knew I was somebody, rolling that big trailer around town.'

With his $125-a-month salary, he bought himself a Ford Roadster. He was very proud of his car – a blue model with wire wheels, a white canvas top and a rumble seat. With he-man truck and a convertible, it's no wonder he soon had a girlfriend. Her name was Betty Clardy. Her two brothers were friends of Greg.

With Betty, he experienced the joy of falling in love for the first time. And he started to feel good about himself and his physical appearance. Fortunately, his handsomeness, deep voice, and height developed at the end of adolescence rather than earlier. While as an adult Greg certainly had his share of vanity, he never regarded his looks as his stock in trade.

At work his boss, Mr Tilson, was giving him more responsibility. He was allowed to start driving the huge trucks that carry 5,000 gallons of gasoline from one end of San Diego to the other. He was also a night watchman. His boss told him: 'I've been watching you. You could be a plant manager one day – like me.' Greg thanked him, but he also knew his boss was getting only $350 a month. It was a wake-up call to think about his future.

Betty Clardy's family took him under their wing. They were Irish Americans and Greg fit right into their home life. This was fortunate since he was once again experiencing domestic upheaval. Doc Peck planned to marry again, this time to Harriet Harrington, a conservative Protestant from Denver. Greg didn't get along with her and for her part she was wary of the tall, stubborn, brooding 18-year-old. Exacerbating the situation, her mother planned to moved into the Peck household. So, once again Greg didn't feel he had a place he could really call home.

Betty Clardy turns out to be an unsung heroine. (When he talked about her after he became famous, Greg changed her name to Kathie Moore to spare her embarrassment. She's now deceased.) She encouraged him to set his sights higher. Now fueled by the desire to leave home, he returned to San Diego State and took his classes seriously. In the evenings, he studied at the Clardys' dining room table. The work began to pay off. Recalled Greg: 'For the first time I got As and Bs.' With a dramatic improvement in his scholastic average, he gained admission to the prestigious University of California at Berkeley.

Greg's moving away and his subsequent breakup with Betty were a harbinger of his split with his future wife Greta. Both women gave him the belief in himself to make a leap forward. And in doing so, he left them behind. Greg mused about Betty: 'I often wonder if just about every successful man doesn't have behind him a first love who is primarily responsible for his success.'

In the fall of 1936, Greg walked though the green-filigreed arch at the entrance to the University of California at Berkeley and entered a whole new world. He looked around the hillside campus with its streams, stunning architecture, groves of trees and spectacular views of San Francisco Bay and he knew he was where he wanted to be. Yet it wasn't the geographic setting that stirred his mind and heart as much as the whirlwind of intellectual, political and artistic possibilities spinning around him. 'I don't know what the hell would have happened to me if I hadn't gone to Berkeley,' said Greg, 'for I see my life before that time as not going anywhere.'

Although Bunny and her husband Joe Maysuch had an apartment nearby in San Francisco, Greg lived in boarding houses during his three years at Berkeley. Tuition for a full 15-credit course load was $26. Thinking back to 1936, Greg said: 'It was a very good year for college boys without independent means.' He was required to pay for his books and supplies, room and board. Doc sent him pin money as did Bunny. But it wasn't enough, so Greg became a one-armed paperhanger doing anything and everything.

With three of the other students he became a janitor in an apartment house, trading those chores for a free room. Alas, sometimes he overslept, incurring the wrath of the occupants for failing to turn on the hot-water heater, at 4.30 a.m. At another point, he bunked on a cot in the attic of a boarding house. During sports events, he parked cars for the fans. He charged them $2, yet never mentioned that the lot was a mile from the stadium. For free meals, he worked as a 'hasher' for the Alpha Gamma Delta sorority house on Haste Street. 'The girls were a bunch of dogs,' Greg told a reporter. 'They'd put on records and dance with each other.' Nonetheless, the gig kept his belly full – an imperative because Greg was a junior member of Berkeley's first-rate varsity team.

No longer so withdrawn, he started to get to know people and was included in social events. 'One of the things I loved about Cal was the eccentrics. The professors who served turkey hash and red wine with string quartets at home on Sunday evenings,' Greg recalled with relish. 'There was "Bull" Durham, an English professor who loved to recite Shakespeare. He spent a semester getting in shape, then took a sabbatical and married Judith Anderson. He returned looking just terrible but still married. Not for long, though . . .'

The high 1930s were a particularly exciting time to be at Berkeley. The campus reverberated with the tension, vitality and crosscurrents of America's hard times. The Great Depression was still a scourge upon the land. Millions of families, with their savings exhausted, were living not far from the edge of starvation. Among students and professors, the prevailing sentiment was one of tremendous sympathy for the underdog. In classrooms, dormitories, parties and public plazas the air was filled with lively discussions about Bonus Marchers, the bloody miners' strikes in Kentucky, the Southern Agrarians, the John Reed Club, and the massive May Day parades.

Berkeley then as now had a reputation for pushing the envelope, bringing issues to the forefront; a sounding board, before the same issues gained momentum in other parts of the country; free speech exercised with passion and intensity. 'It woke me up and made me a human being,' Greg said of his Berkeley experience.

Though he enrolled as a pre-med student at Doc's urging and 'liked the *idea* of becoming a doctor,' Greg floundered in his physics, chemistry and biology courses. His mind lacked the grounded precision for those kinds of courses. Later he quipped: 'The best thing I did for the medical profession was not to become a doctor.'

Switching his major to literature, he studied English and American writers, as well as the French, Greeks and Russians in translation. He also took history and political science, and even psychology and anthropology. At the same time, he became interested in the arts, in the graphic arts and in music.

He'd take out books by the bagful from the library, read late at night and in between classes in the day. Books were the solution to his life. He lived along with the authors of the great novels, transported by the light of their stories. It helped him understand the drama of his own life.

He liked Marcel Proust, Anthony Trollope, Thomas Hardy, Joseph Conrad and satirist Ambrose Bierce. (Little did he imagine that one day he would be portraying Bierce in *Old Gringo* (1989) opposite Jane Fonda.)

Greg's roommates, both engineering students, teased him about burying his nose in Hardy or Shakespeare. 'What do you call *that*, majoring in bullshit?' Greg countered. 'This is good stuff. It's going to come in handy someday.' In his classes, there was much discussion about contemporary writers, Theodore Dreiser, F Scott Fitzgerald, Allen Tate, Clifford Odets, and others – who in the phrase of the time, 'went Left' in search of a more just social order. Greg thought of becoming a writer himself. With his formidable tenacity, he could easily have found work as an investigative reporter. In fiction, he may not have faired so well. His writing showed clarity, grace and precision, but it lacked the visceral intensity that a fiction writer needs to compel the attention of the reader.

The 1930s were made for writers, many of whom felt they were living in history. A perfect example is the signature play of the era, *Waiting for Lefty*, written by Clifford Odets and directed by a young Elia Kazan. It was inspired by what Odets read about the New York taxicab drivers' strike of 1934. *Lefty* opened in 1935 and stunned the audience because it was such an expression of the times. Swept up in the fervor of the performance, the crowd participated in the actors' lines, especially the concluding call to 'STRIKE!'

The sense of upheaval and social collapse would be expressed in many novels of the era, most directly in Dos Passos's *The Big Money* (1936), where everybody and everything goes to pieces, but also with the end of Fitzgerald's *Tender Is The Night* (1933) and in the Key West chapters of Hemingway's *To Have and Have Not* (1937).

Students like Greg, who were reading politically conscious writers, felt anger, a need for social change and a hunger for comradeship. They wanted to surrender their middle-class identities and join the common effort to make a better world. This was the dream in their shining young eyes.

On Sprawl Plaza, the hub of Berkeley, volunteers would cluster around a recruiting table for the Abraham Lincoln Brigade. Students were signing up to go off and fight in the Spanish Civil War (1936–39), a cause that evoked fierce passions. Greg was sorely tempted to join their ranks, but he decided to postpone the decision until after graduation. By then, it was too late; but in any case, it wasn't in his nature to throw caution to the winds in such a dramatic fashion. Still, the conflict was very much in his consciousness during his college years.

The Spanish Civil War was a turning point in world history, the dress rehearsal for the Second World War; the moment, signposted by Picasso's *Guernica*, when civilization began its slow relapse into barbarism and the new dark ages. A worldwide outcry was raised when, for the first time in history, a civilian population was bombed from the air and an entire town was destroyed.

Though largely forgotten by Americans now, the Abraham Lincoln Brigade – organized by Communists – was a group of 2,800 American volunteers who took up arms to defend the Spanish Republic against a military rebellion led by General Franco and aided by Hitler and Mussolini. To the Abraham Lincoln Brigade, which fought from 1937 through 1938, the defense of the Republic represented the last hope of stopping the spread of international fascism. The Lincolns came from all walks of life, all regions of the country, and included seamen, students, the unemployed, miners, fur workers, lumberjacks, teachers, salesmen, athletes, dancers and artists. They established the first racially integrated military unit in US history and were the first to be led by a black commander.

The members of the Brigade were great romantic figures to idealistic young men such as Greg. He could follow their adventures in news reports by such writers as Ernest Hemingway, Martha Gellhorn and Lillian Hellman who helped strengthen anti-fascist opinion in the United States. He could read about luminaries rallying for the cause by raising money for medical aid to the Spanish Republicans. Such participants as Albert Einstein, Dorothy Parker, Gene Kelly, Paul Robeson, Helen Keller and Gypsy Rose Lee reflected the wide base of support for the Republicans.

If Greg had quit college and headed for Spain, his life would surely have turned out very differently. Those who did go experienced a rude surprise when they returned in 1939 after Madrid fell to Franco. Instead of being greeted by any of the usual pomp and circumstance that meets soldiers upon their home-coming, they were met by the police waiting to arrest them as they stepped off the boat.

Little in the way of experience was ever lost on Greg. The romance and the tragedy of the Spanish Civil War stayed with him. In 1964, in partnership with Fred Zinnemann, he co-produced and starred in a film about the war called *Behold A Pale Horse*. Though Greg received enthusiastic reviews in his role as an anti-fascist hero, the movie was panned. Lamented Greg: 'It lacked passion and that's a big lack.'

When Greg was in his seventies, he returned to the Berkeley campus to show the students clips from his movie career. He told the standing-room-only audience that Berkeley represented 'the three happiest years of my life.' Only a glutton for punishment could make that statement, but then, people who row usually are.

Crew played a big part in Greg's first two years at Berkeley. He was rowing 18 miles a day on the Oakland Estuary under the tutelage of Berkeley's legendary coach Ky Ebright. He led Berkeley crews to Olympic gold medals in 1928, 1932 and 1948, a record unequaled by any crew coach in the world. 'There are no stars in crew, we all had to work together,' said Jack Collins, who rowed with Greg in 1937 and 1938, and said he was just one of the guys.

'It's the most grueling sport known in college,' asserted Greg, who, although he never rose above the ranks of junior varsity, credited rowing for teaching him rhythm, harmony and discipline as well as the capacity to go beyond his limits. 'It's a sport where strong men faint as they go over the finish line because they have spent every last ounce of their strength and consciousness. Your chest feels like cement, your legs feel like rubber, your mind is numb, your back feels broken but you learn never to give up.'

The oarsmen put in terribly long hours, often showing up at the Berkeley boathouse at 6 a.m. for pre-class practices. Both physically and psychologically, Greg and his crew buddies were different from their classmates. They had to be able to endure pain in order to turn themselves into exceptional competitors.

Greg learned the glory is in the team, not the individual. Rowing proved to be excellent training for the collaborative work of filmmaking. No picture can get off the ground without the synergy of the actor, director, producer and other members of the crew. Similarly, a boat does not have 'swing' unless everyone is putting out in exact measure, and because of that, and only because of that, there is the possibility of true trust among oarsmen.

Greg was often chosen to 'stroke' the boat – that is, sit in the first seat and set the pace the seven other oarsmen would follow. A great stroke is mostly a fighter and racer, someone who loves going into battle and always thinks that he can win. For Greg, it helped instill confidence in himself, a belief that when the race came down to a short distance between his boat and another one, he, as the stroke, would be able to make the difference between winning and losing.

Rowing is a tremendous discipline for developing concentration, a skill that became a hallmark of Greg's approach to acting. The sport permits ordinary and not particularly talented men to reach beyond themselves. 'The key is not God-given,' writes David Halberstam in *The Amateurs*, a classic on rowing. 'It's in the rowers themselves.'

Then, too, for someone like Greg who tended to repress his emotions, rowing was an outlet. What better way to exorcise anger than through hard rowing. Yet, perhaps more than anything, it touched his sense of beauty. He relished the feel of the boat, all the oars in the water together when the synchronization was almost perfect. In moments like that, the boat seemed to lift right out of the water. George Pocock, a legend in the sport, once said: 'It's a great art, is rowing. It's the finest art there is. It's a symphony of motion. And when you're rowing well, why it's nearing perfection – and when you reach perfection you're touching the divine. It touches the you of you which is your soul.'

In 1938, as stroke of the third boat, Greg traveled to the annual Poughkeepsie Regatta in New York. His manner of transportation is a testimony to his grit. Coach Ebright issued free train tickets for team members in the first two boats; everybody else was on their own. Knowing the university also reserved a baggage car for the racing shells, Greg hopped aboard as a stowaway.

At the time the Poughkeepsie Regatta was considered the 'World Series of Racing.' Teams were drawn to it because it was so popular among spectators, and because the Poughkeepsie course was considered the best straight 4-mile stretch of water available in the country.

Although the competition wasn't a triumph for Berkeley, Greg had the satisfaction of seeing the first man he ever voted for – Franklin D Roosevelt – in the flesh. The President was staying at 'Springwood', his home in nearby Hyde Park and came to watch the race. It saddened Greg to see his hero diminished by illness and confined to a wheelchair.

With the competition completed, each team member was given a Pullman ticket home and $75 spending money. Setting out with crewmate Frank Lawrence, Greg traded the train ticket for more money and went off to see New York City. They would do the town and sleep in Central Park. 'I liked jazz,' explained Greg, 'and we hit all the spots along 52nd Street, Red Nichols and His Five Pennies for instance, then we went to Harlem and caught drummer Chick Webb, then on to Greenwich Village for more music.' He also went to his first Broadway show; it was Joshua Logan's first production, *I Married an Angel* starring Vera Zorina. A ballet dancer by training, Zorina burst upon national consciousness the year before starring in the 1938 film *The Goldwyn Follies* in which her husband choreographer George Balanchine made use of her outright sex appeal as well as her arabesques when he cast her as a nymph in a wet, clinging tunic, rising out of a pool. Greg remembered: 'I went mad for Vera Zorina. Like a dream.'

Returned to campus for his senior year, Greg was thus primed for the moment that would change life. He was galloping down the sidewalk wearing his navy blue rowing sweater with the gold varsity C on the front when he heard the penetrating voice of Edwin Duerr. The esteemed director of the Little Theater, who was known around campus for presenting plays of high professional quality, had wisps of hair under his tweed hat and thick glasses.

'Hey you,' Duerr called. 'I wanna big guy for my new play.'

'What play?' asked Greg.

'For *Moby Dick*,' replied the Professor. 'I have a short, fat Ahab and I need a tall, skinny Starbuck.' It happened he was planning to present the play on 17 November 1938. 'Will you do it?'

Greg didn't even pause to think about it. He was well aware of Duerr's reputation. *Moby Dick* would be a change of pace from the director's usual fare. Most at home in twentieth-century theater, Duerr gave the campus an opportunity to see excellent productions of modern plays during the Depression, when few companies toured. Under his direction, the campus mounted a production of the English language premiere of Jean Giradoux's *Intermezzo*, the world premiere of Robinson Jeffers' *Tower Beyond Tragedy*, Maxwell Anderson's *Elizabeth the Queen*, and many others. Duerr's Mask and Dagger Revues were eagerly awaited each year, and, under his sponsorship, student writers, directors and actors received a thorough, if informal, training in all aspects of the theater.

Moby Dick was one of the Thalian Society workshop plays that were staged weekly on the campus. Greg was thrilled to be given the chance to act, but the thought of facing an audience made him so nervous he wanted to 'disappear down a hole and come up in Mexico.'

Before *Moby Dick*, Greg made his debut on the Wheeler Auditorium stage on 28 October 1938, as the lead in *Rain from Heaven* by S N Behrman, which originally opened on Broadway in 1934. Behrman was known for his sophisticated comedies, which often attempted to probe the consciences of the wealthy and privileged. Greg played Rand Elderidge, a Lindbergh-like explorer, innocent and waiting to be duped by the Nazis. In rehearsals, the nervous neophyte rattled the prop teacup so badly that it had to be taped to the saucer. His fellow thespians felt he was playing out of his depth. Ken Tobey, who would go on to fame as a star of science fiction movies, was particularly scathing. He suggested that the theater group should get rid of people 'who can neither speak nor act. I mean, of course, Mr Peck.'

Despite his less than auspicious start in show business, Greg saw that he had found his way into a unique and special world. 'It was hard for me to communicate with people,' he later remembered. 'So I tried to reach out to that audience – to try to make contact with them, to try to make friends with them and to tell them a story that I wanted to tell.' Offstage, he was enjoying the company of young women, especially while walking them home after rehearsals. 'I felt for the first time that I was making conversation with my kind of people.'

In *Anna Christie*, which was presented on 17 and 18 March 1939, he played the young sailor Matt Burke who is saved in a storm by Anna, a prostitute with whom he falls in love. The reviews were mixed and included a scathing one from the *Daily Californian*: 'Eldred Peck . . . almost endangered the success of the production with his exhibition of inexperienced acting technique. Lack of restraint was his chief fault. There was almost no variation in his gestures or voice, so that he never accomplished the difficult transformation from swashbuckling seaman to a changed man who had experienced a genuine emotion.' Greg agreed with the review.

'I was lousy,' he admitted. 'It did something to me. It made me sore. You can call it a challenge if you like.'

Just when he needed it, he got a boost. George Marion, the actor who played Chris, Anna's father, in *Anna Christie* in the original New York production of the 1922 Pulitzer Prize winner, sat in the audience of the Berkeley production. He then met with and read parts of the play with the cast. Afterwards, he talked with Greg and encouraged him to pursue his career in the East, to aim for Broadway. Greg needed an encouraging word because he had been skirting the edges of the drama crowd at Berkeley. The student actors took themselves very seriously. They didn't consider Greg talented enough to really be one of them.

Then a Berkeley alumnus showed him the way. Crahan Denton, who would later play the leader of the lynch mob in *To Kill a Mockingbird* (1962), had blazed a path for a legion of young actors migrating from the Little Theater of Berkeley to New York. In 1938, he enrolled in the Neighborhood Playhouse and he thus served as a role model for Greg.

Living close by in San Francisco, Bunny attended his performances and cheered him enthusiastically. She also endorsed his plan to take off for New York and train as an actor. Meanwhile, down in San Diego, Doc (who by now had become a father again to a son named Donald) had dreamed of Greg becoming a doctor and was appalled that he wanted to be an actor. Fussing with makeup and exhibitionism was for females. Grown men didn't dodge the hard work of life by playacting in a fantasy world shrouded with fake options. He warned his son: 'You'll be ridiculed. You'll be sorry. You'll have missed your chance to learn a profession or a trade. You'll be broke at 35 and you'll end up borrowing from me. Don't do it.' But it was too late. Greg was stage-struck.

In the spring of 1939, Greg headed for the train station after his last exam at Berkeley – where his diploma would list his name as Eldred Peck – and, with $160 and a letter of introduction in his pocket, he took a coach seat on the Twentieth Century Limited to New York. Somewhere over the Rockies or maybe the Great Plains, he jettisoned 'Eldred' forever. Gregory Peck, the actor, stepped off the train in Manhattan.

CHAPTER FOUR

Call of the Stage

'He was the most gorgeous creature I'd ever seen in my life.'
Lauren Bacall upon meeting Gregory Peck

A visitor to the 1939 World's Fair may have noticed a tall young man clad in a white coat, aviator glasses and a flying helmet standing in front of the Meteor Speedway. He is haranguing the crowd, urging them to try the Speedway, a carnival ride imported from Belgium consisting of caterpillar cars on long arms that climb the wooden walls of a bowl. 'Step this way, folks, for the ride of a lifetime!' he hollers. 'Just 25¢. It's a mile a minute and a thrill a second!'

The barker – called a 'talker' by the cognoscenti – was none other than Gregory Peck. Enduring the sweltering summer heat, he was fumbling through his first theatrical job. 'Twelve people could get in the contraption,' explained Greg. 'It'd crawl up the wall and hang almost upside down.' As the cars accelerated faster and faster, the customers shrieked with fear and delight, praying to survive 'the wall of death.'

Alternating with a professional talker, a Cockney named Buck Boochester, Greg worked 12-hour days, one half hour on and one half hour off, noon to midnight. The pay was $25 per week.

Boochester taught Greg to single out any guy who had a girl on his arm. They had someone to impress; they'd be an easy mark. So, endangering the rich, dark voice that would be his trademark, Greg delivered his spiel at the top of his lungs: 'Hey, Buddy, ya' got any sportin' blood in your veins? Give that girl a R-E-A-L thrill! Step right in and climb the walls of the bowl. Come on, brother, defy the laws of gravity!'

What was our future Academy Award winner doing in a place like this? Well, it wasn't his first choice. Like most actors, he felt the magnetic, powerful and overwhelming pull of Broadway. But before he could grace the Great White Way, he had to survive and get some training. So, to keep the wolf from the door, he made use of an entrée his stepfather, Joe Maysuch had given him and called on Mr J W Shillam who owned the Meteor Speedway concession at the Fair. Then Greg talked himself into this 'off-Broadway' gig. Alas, it was quite a distance from the Great White Way – in Flushing Meadows, Queens, to be exact.

Greg traveled an hour by subway from his $6-a-week room on West 110th Street near Columbia University, to the site in Queens that had once been a swampy landfill known as the Corona Dumps. In 1939, in the teeth of an arming Europe, these 1,200 ignominious acres had been transformed into an architectural wonderland gleaming with cities and civilizations of the future. The colossal New York World's Fair beckoned all comers with its extravaganza of fireworks, exhibitions and country fair gaiety.

Greg loved the razzmatazz. In the Amusement Park, he could see the Frozen Alive Girl, the Penguin Village, Jungle Land and Little Miracle Town – a collection of performing little people (then ungraciously called midgets). There was a winter sports resort with punctual snowstorms and there was Billy Rose's Aquacade, which featured Eleanor Holm and Johnny Weissmuller of Tarzan fame swimming in waltz time. The impresario ignored his own advice: 'Never invest in anything that eats or needs painting.' The Aquacade was a true spectacle, a Broadway musical in swimsuits complete with hundreds of swimmers, divers, singing and special effects.

Or Greg could enter Salvador Dalí's Surrealist Fun House. Paying 25¢ at the Dalí Pavillion, Greg entered a fish-head box-office and passed between a pair of parted, gartered female legs. There he beheld a dream – a tank filled with topless swimmers known as 'Living Liquid Ladies.' He also encountered a mummified cow, some rubber telephones and a piano keyboard painted on a woman's torso.

With wit and cunning, Greg teamed with Boochester to bring in extra income by charging spectators a dime to climb the steps of the scaffolding holding up the bowl. At the top they were rewarded with a commanding view of Norman Bel Geddes' Crystal Lassies (near-naked dancers gyrating within a mirrored octagon). Word got around and business picked up.

'It was the lowest rung of show business,' Greg said of his World's Fair job, but it allowed him access to other worlds. 'I made friends with the Pin-headed Boy from Yucatan. And the Lindy dancers.'

His tenure was short. 'At the end of the month, I had a voice like a gravel mixer,' Greg recalled. To save his pipes, he took a job as a $40-per-week guide at Rockefeller Center on Sixth Avenue in Manhattan. He also applied for and received a two-year scholarship to the Neighborhood Playhouse, a prestigious drama school that was renown for its avant-garde approach to acting. Classes were to start in the fall.

To sell himself as a guide for the summer, Greg claimed to be a New York native. He even purchased a map of the area and studied it. Still, he couldn't quite remember if the Bronx was up and the Battery down – or vice versa. After escorting a group of tourists through Radio City Music Hall (where one day he fell asleep and let the tour-goers watch the whole show instead of their allotted ten minutes), he'd take them to the roof of the building. There, with his sketchy grasp of local geography, he'd point out the landmarks. Motioning towards the New Jersey Palisades, for example, he'd announce with a flourish: 'There's Brooklyn over there.'

In his own sly way, Greg also managed to draw the crowd's attention to the cause of a certain man embraced by young liberals such as himself. 'I used to give 'em big talks about those wonderful murals – all about progress of industry in America. You know the Rockefeller stuff. When they were training us they implied it would be good if we wove in a little propaganda, a happy glow. But if anybody ever asked me I was ready with the story of the Rivera murals that never got put up.'

Greg was alluding to the Mexican muralist Diego Rivera's battle with Nelson Rockefeller over the walls of Rockefeller Center. In 1933 the Rockefeller brothers commissioned Rivera to paint a mural on the wall of the RCA building. 'Man at the Crossroads' was to depict the social, political, industrial and scientific possibilities of the twentieth century. In the painting, Rivera included a scene of a giant May Day demonstration of workers marching with red banners. Included was a clear portrait of Lenin in the demonstration. When Nelson Rockefeller asked Rivera to substitute an unknown, Rivera refused to yield and the whole affair became a cause célèbre. Around midnight on 9 February 1934, the painting was removed from the wall and smashed. Rivera's patrons in the United States boycotted him and he was blacklisted.

When classes started at the Neighborhood Playhouse on 3 October 1939, Greg found himself in a fascinating new environment. He had a direct link to all the big names in show business. New York was the center of theatrical glamour. Ruled by a handful of writers, stars and producers, it was the prime source of energy, ideas and talent. Through his teachers and the people he was meeting, he was being plugged directly into the excitement.

The school was located at 16 West 46th Street where it remained for nearly 20 years. (It is currently located at 340 East 54th Street.) Founded in 1928 by Alice and Irene Lewisohn and Rita Wallach Morgenthau, the school offered a two-year program led by a formidable roster of teachers.

Alice Lewisohn traveled abroad extensively, recruiting lecturers and teachers and collecting music and costumes. Her sister Irene worked actively with Rita Morgenthau on maintaining and strengthening the faculty. The students were carefully chosen for talent and character; a good percentage received working fellowships. The curriculum included dancing, music applied to movement, voice, acting, literature of the drama, psychology of place, design, costume and stage direction.

The school was located on the second floor. It had dark, interconnecting rooms, and the students had to go through the boys' lavatory to reach Martha Graham's dance studio. Sassy dancer, Anna Sokolow always flushed the toilet by way of salutation.

Laura Elliot taught voice. She had been a singer of some note but had forsaken an opera career to concentrate her time and talents on groups of working artists. She was coaching several theater and opera stars when she joined the staff of the Playhouse. Of Laura Elliot, Martha Graham's assistant Dorothy Bird said: 'She was a very strong lady. She used to pull out her hair in exasperation while teaching. She was so frustrated by us she had a bald spot from pulling.'

Elliot had a distinct teaching style in that she focused on movement and voice together – on movement in relation to music, that is, total simultaneous expression in the body: vocal, visual, invisible. She was intent on freeing the personality.

Rita Morganthau sat in on many of the dance classes. She had a little, short body and she would sit with her knees wide apart, wearing stout shoes and she would nod in total approval no matter what Graham happened to be up to. One day she shared her philosophy about the school with Bird: 'Now, Dorothy,' she said, 'I want you to understand we're not in business to find pretty blond girls and handsome boys and put them on Broadway. We're in the theater business as opposed to the Broadway business. I want you to know the one with the glasses who is knock-kneed and has buck teeth is probably the playwright. And that one, the gangly one who is too tall and poorly coordinated, is going to do the lighting. This one's going to be the stage manager. That one's going to be, maybe, a star. Maybe the others will be in the theater. Maybe they'll just love the theater. *You're* not going to decide what they're going to do. You just throw everything you have like grain to chickens. *Your* job is to give everything that's in your heart and in your experience. Give out.'

Sanford Meisner, the school's director, assumed his position in 1935 and held it for 56 years. Sandy, as his loyal followers called him, came from the enormously influential generation of acting teachers that also included Lee Strasberg, Stella Adler and Robert Lewis.

Acting has been called the revenge of the shy person. This adage held true for Greg as well as for Sandy Meisner who started out as an actor. Reflecting on his lonely childhood, Meisner said: 'When I went to school . . . I lived in a state of isolation as if I was some kind of moral leper, because my parents, who were good people but not too bright, told me that if it hadn't been for me, they wouldn't have had to go to the country, where my younger brother got sick, and from which illness he died. The guilt of this tragedy haunted me. In my childhood I rarely had friends. I lived, as I'm afraid I still do, in a world of fantasy.'

Meisner was a member of the Group Theater, actors who believed in acting as a means of promoting social change. Their productions included *Awake and Sing!*, *The Young Go First*, *Men in White* and *Gold Eagle Guy*. Although the Group dispersed at the end of the 1930s, its philosophy had a strong impact on Hollywood and, also, in the creation of the Actors' Studio.

Like other veterans of the Group Theater, Meisner adapted and refined the 'Method' approach to acting to suit his particular philosophy. The Method was a system of vocal, physical and emotional exercises initiated in Russia by Konstantin Stanislavsky, which encouraged the actor to use his psyche and subconscious in preparing for a role.

The essential and rather simple technique consists of recalling the circumstances – physical and personal – surrounding an intensely emotional experience in the actor's past. Elia Kazan, who directed Greg in *Gentleman's Agreement* (1947), explained it this way: 'It is the same as when we accidentally hear a tune we may have heard at a stormy or an ecstatic moment in our lives, and find, to our surprise, that we are re-experiencing the emotion we felt then, feeling ecstasy again or rage and the impulse to kill.'

The Meisner Technique focused on actors becoming aware of their emotions through daydreaming and imagination. Once he is aware of his emotional resources, the theory goes, then the actor can awaken, by self-stimulation, a great number of intense feelings, and these emotions are the material of his art. Arthur Miller said he could tell Meisner-trained actors, because they were honest and simple and didn't lay on complications that weren't necessary. They communicated emotions they really felt. They gave you a sense of life.

Opponents of the Method – of which there are legions – believe it encourages actors to be self-indulgent, to forget the character in pursuit of behavioral motivation, and that it does not prepare actors to play classics. Stereotypically, opponents contend, the Method actor is mannered to the point of unintelligibility.

As Greg would find out when he migrated to Hollywood, the Method was scoffed at and lampooned by many acting veterans.

James Cagney dismissed it with contempt: 'You don't psych yourself up for these things, you do them.' Before rehearsals for *Major Barbara* (1941), Charles Laughton cornered fellow actor Eli Wallach and barked, 'I don't want any of that Stanislavsky shit from you.' And Humphrey Bogart had two rules for playing with Method actors: '1. Let them improvise to their heart's content and just wait for your cue; and 2. Don't ever play an eating scene with them, because they spit all over you.'

The Method requires that an actor, in preparing for a role, delve not only into the character's life in the play, but also, far more importantly, into the character's life before the curtain rises. Tony Randall, who was Greg's vintage at the Neighborhood Playhouse, recalled that Meisner taught them that the character they were playing had a background – a history – that his life didn't begin when he walked on the stage. 'It was up to each actor to create his character's biography – a back story – that brought him up to the point where he walked on the stage.'

For Greg, who had steadfastly resisted opening up the Pandora's Box of his childhood wounds, this introspective approach to acting provided salutary benefits; it enabled him to release his pent-up emotions while taking on the personality of the character he was portraying. He developed the capacity to use everything that had happened in his life, such as the painful absence of his mother while he was growing up and the heartbreaking disappearance of his dog Bud, to create the character he was working on. He learned to dig in the dark cave of his subconscious and root out every experience he had ever had.

Greg embraced Meisner's ideas. He focused on the mental and emotional processes that go on beneath the words, contending, 'What's underneath the words is more important than the words themselves because what's underneath produces the external effect.' Nevertheless, he still suffered from stage fright even in small groups. He'd break out in sweats, develop rapid shallow breathing and feel faint.

In class, he was learning for the first time to share pieces of his life and, in the process, reveal his secret self. During one improvisational exercise, a girl in the group suddenly stood up and pointed her finger at Greg. 'I know, you be a priest, Greg, and I'll confess to you.' The idea brought approving ripples from the others. Thus he earned the nickname 'Father Peck'. The group sensed he was someone trustworthy, a sympathetic listener who could keep a confidence. It was a role he would play not only in *The Keys of the Kingdom* (1944), but also with troubled and unhappy friends such as Ava Gardner, Frank Sinatra and Cary Grant. In the scandal-strewn world of Hollywood, he found his niche as father confessor.

Three times a week, Greg took a movement class from Martha Graham. He regarded her as one of the most provocative minds he ever encountered. She was far from the first dancer to toss out her toe shoes and break ballet conventions with modern dance, but her technique – the fierce pelvic contractions, the rugged 'floor work' – caught on, becoming the cornerstone of post-war modern dance.

She was also a tempestuous innovator and an unrelenting task-master, who would sacrifice everything – love, friendship, money – for the sake of her art. She knew how to use her power to entrance the opposite sex. And although most of the men had no thought of anything physical with her, they nevertheless sensed the overtones and responded with electric excitement and eagerness. Among these was playwright Horton Foote, a modest, unassuming, charm-ing Texan who wrote the screenplay for *To Kill a Mockingbird*. At one point in his youth he collaborated with Martha Graham on a production at the Neighborhood Playhouse. In telling about his first meeting with her, he said: 'She made you feel as if you could take on the world . . . I've never been so charmed in my life. She acted as though it were a great privilege to work with me. With me! Imagine! . . . She could have had anything I had . . . I've never fallen so totally for anybody in my life. On what level I still don't know. If she had said, "Walk across the desert in bare feet on burning coals," I'd have said, "Indeed, I will." . . . And if she had said, "Come tonight and bring your pajamas and don't bore me," . . . I would have loved it, I think. I think I would have . . . I might have been a little frightened of that.'

Greg, in his early 20s at the time, remembered her as a voluptuous woman with a strong sensuality. 'She didn't have a sense of humor,' said Greg, 'but there were compensations in her richness, inner womanliness, and in her passion. She was not funny – she was something else. She was also a disciplinarian – determined, firm, demanding. It wasn't playtime.' Greg once asked Graham if he had moved properly. She icily responded: 'Tears are running down the inside of my cheeks.'

The idea was not to turn the students into dancers, but to use dance to make them better actors. One of the most difficult, and for Greg most embarrassing, projects that Graham's students were required to do was choreograph a piece of 32 bars of music that they chose. 'If you've never created original movement before,' said Greg, 'it's as if you were in deep water and didn't know how to swim.'

Greg's concept was a factory line – inspired by Charlie Chaplin in *Modern Times* (1936). He had harsh, mechanical gestures. 'It was horrible,' he admitted. Still, in the long run it proved to be an invaluable experience for him. To get up and do the assignment gave him courage. It helped his stage presence. He learned to use his body in acting as a matter of choreographing his own movement as he went along, so that each movement helped to reveal the character. It benefited him when he was acting in Westerns such as *Yellow Sky* (1949) and *The Gunfighter* (1950) because he always found himself almost subconsciously moving in a way that would complement the cinematography – the way he walked, the way he got out the words.

It was during one of her classes that Graham permanently injured his spine. Graham told Greg to put his legs out front and his head on his knees. And then she placed her knee against his back and pushed. The snapping sound was so loud that the other students heard it.

'I had ruptured a disk in my lower back,' said Greg. 'The school sent me to an orthopedic specialist who just put me in an old-fashioned canvas strap which I wore for two or three years and gradually the condition began to remedy itself, though off and on, it bothered me all my life.'

Despite the injury, Greg always spoke well of Graham as he did of his other teachers at the Playhouse. Being in the circle of such highly gifted people had an enormous effect on him. Bound by ties of temperament and congeniality, he emulated them and, figuratively speaking, developed more backbone. He would not be someone for whom life called the shots.

Those were great days for Greg, even though money was hard to come by. Of course, the standard of living was quite different back then. A trolley ride cost 10¢, a room at the Plaza $7.50. His scholarship provided him with a small amount of cash each month. Sometimes he turned to the school's patrons, Rita Morgathau and Irene Lewisohn. 'I was often broke,' recalled Greg, 'and once in a while I would go upstairs to their rather stylish, old-fashioned offices with pictures and nice furniture, and I'd borrow ten or twenty dollars.' Plus, he picked up some modeling gigs. He appeared in the 1940 Montgomery Ward catalog in dozens of assorted guises: tennis player, business executive and more casually dressed camper. When things got desperate, he sold his blood.

For lodging Greg often doubled up with Ken Tobey, fellow Berkeley grad – and previous nemesis – who was equally destitute; they usually lived in basement rooms. At one time, Greg rented an apartment on 54th Street between Fifth and Sixth Avenues for $6 a week. During good weather, when they couldn't spring for rent, they'd deposit their belongings in a locker at Grand Central Station and sleep in Central Park. Even when they were living apart, they often got together for breakfast at Nedicks for the Nine-Cent Special. The street corner joint was best known for its hot dog on a butter-toasted split-top roll washed down with an orange drink. When they walked in they not only smelled toasting bread, but the hot dogs as well.

For dinner they feasted at the Automat, the 'in' spot for the fiscally challenged and a gathering place for the acting crowd. By popping 20¢ in a slot and flicking his wrist, Greg could purchase spaghetti and three vegetables or he could enjoy such mouth-watering delicacies as Macaroni and Cheese, Boston Baked Beans, Chicken Pot Pie and Rice Pudding. As Lorraine B Diehl explains in her book *The Automat,* eating at a restaurant with self-serving vending machines rather than waitresses, and Art Deco architecture instead of stuffy dining rooms was an unforgettable experience. Asserts Diehl: 'By the peak of its popularity – from the Great

Depression to the post-war years – the Automat was more than an inexpensive place to buy a good meal: it was a culinary treasure, a technical marvel, and an emblem of the times.'

More typically, Greg and Tobey dined in their quarters. One celebrated evening, Greg arrived at Tobey's room with 17¢ in his pocket.

'Don't flaunt your wealth before my starving face,' Tobey told Greg.

'Have you checked your cupboard?' asked Greg.

A minute search revealed one half-box of buckwheat flour in which there were no trespassers from the animal kingdom. 'Muffins,' announced Ken. 'I'm celebrated for my secret recipe.'

While Tobey was measuring out the buckwheat, Greg took his 17¢ to the neighborhood delicatessen and bought two eggs and a quart of milk. One egg and a portion of the milk was added to make the batter, the rest of the milk was divided between two glasses, and the remaining egg was scrambled. Something proved to be wrong with the oven, which hadn't been used much, so that the outer rim of the muffins formed a horsehide casing, whereas the interior was still viscid. However, the boys ate the muffins, diligently shared out their portions of the scrambled egg, and drank their milk in simple gratitude.

Clothes – or lack of them – presented another problem. Greg was greatly heartened when he received a box from one of his California relatives. Inside was a note saying, 'I've grown too hefty around the perimeter to get into this, so decided to forward it to you in hope that you can derive some good from it.' Neatly wrapped in tissue was a handsome gray flannel suit boasting such niceties as hand-picked detail, leather buttons, and pleated trousers. Greg, beaming, slid into the coat. Slowly his delight turned sour. His arms extended from the sleeves for 3 lonely inches, and if he had taken a deep breath, the back would have split from collar to vent.

In 1939, a beguiling sketch by legendary caricaturist Al Hirschfield appeared in the drama section of the *New York Times*. It showed patrons of the Barter Theater in Abington, Virginia, lined up to watch a play. They were holding produce or livestock in their hands ready to hand them over in lieu of tickets. Greg may have seen the illustration. In any case, he certainly heard the clarion call of the Barter Theater's founder, Robert Porterfield, coaxing New York actors to head south for summer stock. Porterfield exhorted them: 'It's better to eat in Virginia than starve in New York.'

The Barter Theater had a short, interesting history. Back in 1933 – the nadir of the Depression – Robert Porterfield was one among thousands of struggling actors trying to keep body and soul together. He was working as an elevator operator in New York after the touring Shakespearean Company to which he belonged folded. Suddenly, he was hit with a brainstorm.

He figured that with actors out of work and hungry and residents of southwest Virginia in need of good theater, why not combine the two. The residents could feed the performers and the actors could give them ideas, laughter and music. So food items were used in exchange for theater. When Barter opened, comedian Fred Allen quipped: 'Along about Labor Day, if Bob wants to tell whether he's had a successful season, he just weighs the actors.'

The box-office had to contend with some interesting scenarios. One man tried to stuff a dead rattlesnake through the ticket window. The frightened ticket seller didn't want to accept it, but the man talked her into it with the argument that the paper said they were going to accept anything good to eat and that 'rattlers is good vittles.' Another man brought a cow, milked the cow to the required ticket value, sent the animal home and proceeded to enjoy the show he had purchased. Greg remembered, 'Someone brought a live pig and got a season ticket.' The local barber brought his clippers, combs and razor and gave haircuts to the actors for admission. Others brought corn, pickles, preserves, bacon, apples and cakes to barter for their tickets.

Actors weren't the only ones to receive payment in edibles. Early on, the custom was established to pay the playwrights their royalty fees in Virginia hams. Claire Booth Luce was the recipient of a ham for the rights to *The Women* (1936) as were playwrights Noel Coward, Tennessee Williams and Thornton Wilder. One exception was George Bernard Shaw, a vegetarian, who bartered the rights to his plays for fresh spinach.

This 'crazy idea' of Robert Porterfield turned out to be just crazy enough to be successful. He was able to secure so much publicity and cooperation in the fledgling theater primarily because it was such a great scheme and, secondly, because of his own personal charm and enthusiasm. He was the quintessential Renaissance man, one part Southern gentleman, one part hustler, one part actor and one part Madison Avenue advertising genius.

Since it sounded like excellent training and a change of cuisine from Nedicks and the Automat, Greg and Ken Tobey applied to be members of the Barter Theater's summer stock company. Ever the competitor, Greg set his sights on winning a scholarship. At the audition, he jumped up on stage and did a speech from *Saturday's Children* (1924) a play by Maxwell Anderson that examines the marital problems of a young couple. The *New York Times* reported that he won the scholarship along with classmate Evelyn Fargo (of Fargo, North Dakota). Dorothy Stickney, who was starring at the Empire in the enormously popular *Life With Father* (1939), was the one to select the scholarship winners.

Greg's enthusiasm was dampened when he was told his first job would be to drive the theater truck, loaded with the sets, props and lighting equipment for a comedy called *Button Button* (1940) to a school hall in Big Stone Gap, Virginia.

However, just the day before setting off, the leading actor had fallen ill and so a script was thrust in Greg's hands and he was told to do the part. In only 24 hours, he had to learn the whole play and, at the same time, drive the truck. And there was no time for rehearsal.

Chugging across country, he did his best to commit the play's lines to memory. Making his entrance in *Button Button,* his mind went blank. Tobey sat in the wings feeding lines to him. 'It was a complete disaster,' said Greg. 'We got the second and third acts mixed up and I kept giving the wrong cues to the other person. Still, we got through it all and the audience never noticed the difference.'

Usually the plays were produced at the town hall on a stage that once saw both John Wilkes Booth and Sarah Bernhardt. In addition to acting, the cast also did the production work of the company, lugging cables, wiring sets, and, in Greg's case, driving the bus or trucks to theaters across the state; tough work for actors subsisting on bartered food. Greg recalled eating spinach 'until I though it would come out my ears.' Already thin, he began to lose weight.

Greg played in at least five shows during the summer of 1940. Porterfield later recalled in his memoirs: 'Repertory offers the greatest challenge possible to an actor's development, and I found tremendous joy in watching an actor like Greg Peck mellow like wine from the experience of playing a piece of comic trivia like *Button Button* one night and electrifying audiences with his portrayal of Judah in *Family Portrait* the next.'

In the spring of 1941 the graduating class of the Neighborhood Playhouse put on a play titled *The Chief Thing* by Nicholas Evreinhoff. Greg played a con man decked out in a moustache and brandishing a cigarette. Members of the New York theater establishment were invited to attend what was known as a commencement performance.

In the audience that day was famed Broadway producer Guthrie McClintic. He ran a theatrical touring company in conjunction with his wife Katharine Cornell. She was a huge talent who was often referred to as the First Lady of American Theater.

A dazzling theatrical presence, Katharine Cornell was one of the two most famous and successful actresses in America at the time (the other being Helen Hayes). With McClintic, she toured from coast to coast and was known throughout the length and breadth of the country. From their first production together, *The Green Hat* in 1925, they proved to be a successful team, with such productions as *The Barretts of Wimpole Street* (1931), *Saint Joan* (1936) and *Candida* (1937); now they were mounting a production of *The Doctor's Dilemma*. Cornell was often able to carry a weak pro-duction on the basis of her strong voice, expressive face, and acting style. McClintic's vigilant and canny management of her career provided Cornell with everything she needed to function perfectly. He had staged all her performances and produced many of them. This kind of arrangement enabled her to carry out her work freely and hold her own against stage competitors such as Helen Hayes and Jane Cowl. The sexual aspect of their marriage may not have been of great importance, as it often isn't in these kinds of union, because so much energy passed into the work. The celebrated couple had recently garnered enthusiastic publicity for proving 'the road is not dead.' They had taken their repertory company on a tour of 75 cities, giving 225 performances and covering 17,000 miles.

The day after the Neighborhood Playhouse commencement performance, following tradition, Greg and the other graduates assembled at the Playhouse to wait for calls from producers. It was a very tense room.

The moment of truth had arrived. Acting school days were done. All the techniques they had so painfully acquired; all that palaver about 'level of emotion' and 'playing in depth' and the superb technical training of the Meisner Technique might not mean a damn thing. It's personal chemistry that matters. Your instrument is *you* and not the skill. Your face, your body and your personality is what sells. No acting teacher can give you the magic. That occurred at the instant of conception. As playwright and author of *Peter Pan*, J M Barrie said, it's like charm in a woman: 'If you have it, you don't need to have anything else; and if you don't have it, it doesn't much matter what else you have.'

Greg was just as scared as everyone else; two obsessed, passionate, exultant, despairing years were suddenly up. The Neighborhood Playhouse, with its immersion in the murky waters of one's own psyche, would now be behind him. The world where teachers were gods suddenly dwarfed. The world outside was the real one.

Where did he want to work? Who would have him? If he didn't find work, what would he do? He liked to work; he needed to work. He couldn't feel like an actor unless he was working. Was his father right in calling his theatrical infatuation 'a false errand'? Doc continued to urge him to forget about the grubby rewards the theater offered and get a solid profession.

And then it happened. Everything changed. Greg was standing near the receptionist's desk when a call came through from Guthrie McClintic for the director of the school. 'It's about you,' whispered the receptionist who overheard part of the conversation.

'And that's all I needed to know,' said Greg, recalling the event years later. 'I took off – I knew where his office was – I took off, ran down four flights, ran half a block across 46th Street to Sixth Avenue. I ran four blocks up Sixth Avenue to 50th Street, plunged into the RKO building. There was an open elevator, pushed the button for the eighth floor, rocketed up there, walked through the door.'

McClintic was still talking on the phone to Meisner. Seeing the speedy and now breathless Greg, the producer launched into a fit of laughing and coughing, finally sliding off the chair, on to the floor and gasped, 'You've got the job.'

Greg found himself staring at a man of medium height, with a light complexion, a well-shaped head and a fine brow; he had the friendliest eyes in the world.

With that, Greg signed a contract to appear in the road company of a George Bernard Shaw comedy, *The Doctor's Dilemma*, which was just closing its run on Broadway. Since the tour would not start until the fall, Greg turned to summer stock.

Sanford Meisner was co-director at the Suffern County Theater just north of New York and gave Greg a part in *The Male Animal*, written by James Thurber and Elliot Nugent in 1939, as 'Nutsy' Miller, the bandleader. For $25 per week, Greg was acting with Uta Hagen and José Ferrer. In August 1941, Greg appeared with Diana Barrymore in the musical comedy *Captain Jinks* at the White Plains Theater. Like a good trouper, he also 'croaked out a couple of songs.' He received good reviews, bad reviews and so-so reviews.

Greg made the most of his straw-hat summer. He was laying the groundwork for a Broadway career by building friendships and seeing that his name got around. So it wasn't surprising when Maynard Morris of the prestigious Leland Hayward agency approached him with an offer of representation. He assumed that since Morris worked in the New York office of the firm, he would find him roles in Manhattan theaters. As it happened, Morris put Greg's name down on the agency's client roster and that list was being studied not just by New York theater people but also by producers and talent scouts stalking the hinterlands for new leading men to fill in for screen actors who had joined the forces fighting in the Second World War.

In September 1941, *The Doctor's Dilemma*, a light satire on the medical profession, opened at the Foster Theater on Walnut Street in Philadelphia. Oh, how Greg loved the City of Brotherly Love!

While he would describe the good thing that happened to him there as a stroke of luck, it was also an occasion where preparation met opportunity.

Greg's job amounted to eight lines in the third act. He played the role of Mr Danby, an art gallery attendant. Understandably, he was nervous and thrilled to be sharing the stage with Katharine Cornell. Anyone who came close to her was electrified by her presence. French actor Jean Pierre Aumont and playwright Henri Bernstein, both of who came into her life shortly after Greg did, found her remarkable. Remembered Aumont: 'At 40 there was more of the peasant about her than of the actress. Nothing affected or artificial; but something warm and robust, like the scent of hay. Her handshake was solid, she had a clear and hearty laugh, and she looked you straight in the eye when she talked.' Bernstein rhapsodized: 'She's merely the greatest actress in America, that's all. You can tell Sarah Bernhardt and Helen Hayes to start packing. She can play *any*thing. She has the brow of an intellectual, the eyes of a saint, and the mouth of a whore . . . '

The show's opening coincided with the 25th wedding anniversary of Katharine Cornell and Guthrie McClintic. The Lunts, Dorothy Gish, Joan Fontaine, Diana Barrymore and other stage luminaries came down from New York, and some pre-curtain champagne flowed, at least enough so that Cornell 'dried' at the beginning of the last act.

The star made her entrance, walked directly to Greg, opened her mouth and said nothing. 'Her eyes seemed to start spinning,' said Greg. 'She had forgotten her lines. I turned my head upstage and whispered her first two or three words. It just happened instinctively; she picked them up immediately. At the party afterwards, she kissed me and introduced me to everyone as the man who saved her life.'

Philadelphia provided the setting for another dramatic moment in Greg's life. It was there, on 8 September 1941, he met Greta Konen. She was Katharine Cornell's hairdresser, a former art student, who had also attended cosmetology school. Pert and blond, Greta seemed to burst with life and vitality.

Actually, Greta spotted Greg from the wings, a vantage point she was destined to hold throughout their relationship. Recalled

Greta: 'The first time I saw him, backstage in Philadelphia, I sneaked a look at the call board to see who he was. Gregory Peck – hmm, he certainly picked a fine stage name for himself, I thought – but somehow it seemed to fit him. I never knew it was his own until I met his parents some months later and found out he wasn't a full-blooded Indian as he told me the first time I went out with him.'

When the tour hit Boston, Greg took Greta to the Merry Go Round Bar. There he pretended to be a palm reader so he could hold her hand. And of course he got away with it. As well as the sexual attraction, they were drawn to each other for other reasons. Greta was divorced after a five-year marriage to businessman Charles Rice whom she married at 18. She saw in Greg, a few years her junior, someone who wasn't cynical about romance and love. He had the right values. He'd make a good father.

For Greg, Greta was his good magic, his talisman for success. She penetrated his shy shell. She coaxed and eased him up and out of his solitary hole. All she had to do was look at him and he knew she believed in his worth. She pledged herself to his cause from the beginning. 'I just knew he was going to make it,' she said.

As *The Doctor's Dilemma* touring company zigzagged across the country playing in cities and towns, Greg and Greta became increasingly infatuated with each other. They plunged quickly, eagerly into an intimate relationship. Their bond was cemented by the confinement of the tour and their positions near the bottom of the company's hierarchy. While the important actors were put up in top hotels, they had to make do with standard rooms.

The road as it existed then was a hard, grueling life for actors. The body, the mind, the nerves had to be able to take punishment. Small-town inns with creaking doors and sheets gray with age; the sense of termites eating away the very floors under their feet. The towns start to look alike. In most instances, the actor's path restricts itself to three points – the station, the hotel, the theater.

Greg remembered: 'Well, like anything else, if the people are fun you have a good time – you become a little family, you eat together and you have your little jokes. But this company was full of English actors. So Greta and I had a proletariat club with a wonderful guy named Lester Ampolsk, the comedian whose job at the moment was selling souvenir booklets in the lobby. We stayed in hotels — Greta earned $60 week, I got $50 and Lester had about $35. Our entertainment after a performance was to chip in on a bottle and go back to one of the rooms and play rummy.'

In San Francisco, Bunny and Joe Maysuch welcomed them with open arms. The San Francisco *Chronicle* sang hosannas about the Berkeley boy hobnobbing with Katharine Cornell. The Rannells cousins from La Jolla boarded a Greyhound and arrived at the Curran Theater where Greg had left passes for them to see *The Doctor's Dilemma*. Afterwards, he took his cousins to the Brown Derby. The young people stayed up until 2 a.m. eating scrambled eggs and bacon. 'I loved him with all my heart,' recalled his cousin Bernice 50 years later. 'He was so good.' And when exquisitely beautiful San Francisco went dark that December night in a blackout, Greg proposed to Greta. Could life be any better?

The play closed in San Francisco, but the company stayed there, because Cornell wanted to rehearse her next vehicle in the city. This was *Rose Burke*, a translation of a French play by Henri Bernstein that had been playing with success on the Champs Elysées before the Nazis moved in. Although there was no part for Greg, McClintic kept him employed as assistant stage manager for the touring company. He also used him as understudy to two actors in the cast, Jean Pierre Aument and Philip Merival. It was in this capacity that Peck received what he considered to be his best theatrical experience.

Cornell preferred props when rehearsing. Though dressed in street clothes, should the part require a hoop skirt, a train, or some article of clothing to which she was unaccustomed, she had the equivalent constructed for rehearsals, attaching it over her street clothes.

The long stretches rehearsing opposite Katharine Cornell confirmed for him that he indeed belonged on the same stage with distinguished professionals. And being in close proximity to her, he was surprised to learn she was shy, and had never fully conquered stage fright. 'I used to see her backstage, before her entrances, keyed up and trembling, and then sweep on stage and take command, projecting self-assurance, grace, nobility.'

In early 1942, *Rose Burke* played Portland, Seattle, Toronto and Detroit but stopped short of Broadway. Back in New York, Greg went through another road tour show taking the juvenile lead in *Punch and Julia* by George Baston which ran for two weeks in May in 1942, starring Jane Cowl. When it flopped, he decided to seriously set his sights on Broadway. But no offers were forthcoming, so he did summer stock at the Cape Playhouse in Dennis, Massachusetts.

The brainchild of Californian Raymond Moore, the Cape Playhouse was housed in a nineteenth-century former Unitarian Meeting House fronting on Old Kings Highway. His vision was to have a smart, sophisticated summer theater, which would bring Broadway to Cape Cod. To this day the original pews, now with cushions, serve as seats. Over the years, Moore attracted big-name stars such as Bette Davis (who first worked as an usher), Gertrude Lawrence, Lana Turner, Ginger Rogers, Humphrey Bogart, Tallulah Bankhead, Helen Hayes, Julie Harris and Paulette Goddard.

Greg played in *The Circle* with Daren Morley; *Rebound* with Ruth Chatterton; *You Can't Take It With You* with Fred Stone and *The Duenna* with Jimmy Savo. Guthrie McClintic had a house nearby in Martha's Vineyard and one day in mid-summer of 1942 he sent for Greg.

Nestled among the dunes, the McClintic house was situated beyond the two headwaters, West Chop and East Chop. Thus McClintic and Cornell called their beach house Chip Chop. A Chop means a point of land with a light on it and that is what Chip Chop was – a point of land from which, out at sea, could be seen the light of the McClintic summer home.

Arriving, Greg approached a frame house (really three houses strung together), with broad and conspicuous white stone chimneys. Walking inside, he found airy rooms, uncrowded and spacious. One room, the room with the grand piano, contained two fireplaces, a ping pong table and a real Bavarian tile stove. Chip Chop had every convenience except a telephone.

McClintic had a great surprise – the script of *The Morning Star,* a big hit in London running ten months there with writer Emlyn

Williams as the star. Would Greg be interested in playing the lead on Broadway? Would he! Later he called Greta. This would make him rich enough to get married. 'Do you hear wedding bells?' asked Greg. 'I do.'

The action of *The Morning Star* was set in London during the Nazi bombings of the city. Greg's part was that of a 'sensitive' young medical student who has a breakdown, and, unable to continue his studies, takes up with a prostitute (to be played by Wendy Barrie in her stage debut). Greg and Barrie would be the only Americans in an otherwise all-British cast, which included Gladys Cooper, Rhys Williams, Brenda Forbes, Jill Esmond and Nicolas Joy. During rehearsals, McClintic focused on Greg's voice, helping him to master theatrical projection.

McClintic's direction was poised, kindly, quiet. No swearing, pacing back and forth, ranting, whipping the actors with sarcasm. Wearing a sweater and smoking incessantly, he sat at a table to the left of the stage giving directions.

Greg's classmate, Tony Randall also worked with McClintic on several productions. He said: 'McClintic wasn't an exceptionally good director but it didn't matter. He loved actors and the theater. He was stage-struck – more than anyone I've ever known. He was there at every performance, unlike most directors, whom you never see again after opening night. Guthrie would sit backstage on the floor just listening to the play, often weeping, and in between the matinée and the evening performance he'd often go to sleep right there. Many actors gave their career-best performance for him simply because he loved them so much.'

The Morning Star was scheduled to open on Broadway on 14 September 1942. The preview in Philadelphia had gone badly with one critic comparing Greg's acting skills to that of a waxwork dummy. As a result, Greg frantically rehearsed with Greta. She loosened him up and helped him to stop being so solemn. Still, as the performance approached, Greg developed a case of the shakes. There was no escape unless the theater burned down. If he blew his Broadway debut, then what would become of him?

In the wings of the Morosco Theater, he stood rooted to the spot, paralyzed with fear. 'The critics then – Wolcott Gibbs of the

New Yorker, George Jean Nathan, Brooks Atkinson, Richard Watts Jr – were called Murderer's Row. There were seven daily papers in New York then. Boy, did I ever want to burrow through the cement in my dressing room and head for Mexico.'

Another time he reflected, 'You can die up there and say, "Call it all off, give 'em their money back and let 'em go home," or you can collect yourself and do it. The instinct for self-preservation takes over.'

Once he made his entrance, heaven was on his side. The feared reviewers panned the play, but praised Greg. Said the *New Yorker*: '[*The Morning Star*] is another account of the behavior of London civilians under the bombs, and, like its several predecessors, it is a dismal mélange of too casual heroism, inflated rhetoric, and invincibly pawky humor.' John Mason Brown of *The World Telegram* detected shades of Gary Cooper in Greg: 'a remarkable young actor, sensitive, intelligent, and expert, and an uncommon type.' And the *New York Times* concurred: 'As her wayward son, Gregory Peck plays with considerable skill.'

The play closed after 24 performances. Greg and Greta got married. Then Greg spent two futile months looking for work. In the meantime, his father kept urging him to get a real job. Finally, he landed the lead in *The Willow and I*. Barbara O'Neil and Martha Scott were his leading ladies. The production itself met with mixed notices, but New York critics continued to praise him. The *New York Daily Mirror* chimed: 'Gregory Peck, New York's new matinée idol, is excellent as Dr Todd and his son, Kirkland Todd. Young Peck is good-looking and he's a first-rate actor. That's quite a combination.' The *New York News* agreed: '[Peck] is by way of becoming, I strongly believe, one of our most popular leading men both here and on the coast. He has poise, good looks, a splendid voice, and a compelling sympathy.' Though the play only lasted 28 performances, Greg was well on his way to becoming a star.

So there it was. He had achieved his dream – a quintessentially American dream. In only three years, Gregory Peck had gone from a nobody to a headliner on Broadway with his name in lights. Frequently wracked with terror and despair, often hungry, often broke, he stuck to his rifles. He survived through determination and a protean ability to grow with each new experience. His success was all the sweeter for the ordeals he suffered in achieving it. Even the announcement that *The Morning Star* was closing after only a month hadn't stopped him from running out and buying a marriage license.

The finger of fate beckoned him to Hollywood. Talent scouts had seen *The Morning Star* and *The Willow and I*. In short order, in early 1943, Leyland Hayward whisked Greg out to Los Angeles where he fought off the advances of the big studio bosses such as Louis B Mayer. If he committed to a seven-year contract, he could be locked into B-movies and still required to pay Leland Hayward ten per cent of his earnings.

Greg felt torn. Broadway was the world he loved. He believed in the healing power of the theater, a place to come together and take refuge. It was his second-chance family. Plus, it had a vitality the movies could never match. 'The most distinctive characteristic of the theater is simply that it's alive,' said noted composer Richard Rodgers. 'A play can't be put into a can like a movie to be taken out and shown without change. Theater exists only when there are real people on both sides of the footlights, with audiences and actors providing mutual stimulation. No two performances or audiences are exactly alike; it is this unpredictability that makes the stage a unique art form.'

One producer wouldn't take 'no' for an answer. Casey Robinson was after Peck to sign for his movie *Days of Glory* (1944). A highly respected screenwriter, he now had plans to set up his own independent production company – an animal that, like independent actors, was a rare species in 1942.

Their relationship began when Greg debuted on Broadway with *Morning Star*. Robinson came to Greg's dressing room. Accompanying Robinson was Hal Wallace, with whom Robinson had been working at Warner Brothers. Wallace had previously offered Greg a deal but – like the others – it had been an exclusive contract for seven years' labor for Warner Brothers. Greg had rejected it just as firmly as the others.

Robinson's offer was different: four pictures in four years, and since he reckoned it would only take ten weeks to make a picture,

Greg could do what he liked in the other 42 weeks of the year. He could go back to Broadway or, if the Hollywood madness took root, he could make pictures for other people. The offer seemed not just tempting, but realistic. It was also a way to pay the overdue rent on his apartment. So Greg closed the deal with Robinson. However, before relocating to the West Coast, he insisted on accepting the lead in an Irwin Shaw play called *Sons and Soldiers.* The cast included Geraldine Fitzgerald and Karl Malden.

Shaw was a crackerjack storyteller. Excelling at the short story with the skill to create unforgettable characters, he produced such literary gems as *Girls in Their Summer Dresses* and *The Eighty Yard Run.* These earned him a place up with John Cheever, John O'Hara and J D Salinger as a master of the form. His first play, *Bury the Dead,* an anti-war story in which six soldiers killed in battle rise up, was produced in 1936 as his screenplay *The Big Game.* He worked constantly in the late 1930s producing books and magazine articles, but when the Second World War aroused his patriotic ardor, he took off for Africa to drive an ambulance *à la* Hemingway. In his wake, he left his play *Sons and Soldiers,* which badly needed to be shaped and trimmed.

Aware of the play's problems and knowing he would be paid only $400 per week, Greg nonetheless snapped up the contract. He would have given his eye teeth to work under Max Reinhardt, the *Sons and Soldiers* director. Short and stocky with extraordinary cobalt-blue eyes, Reinhardt was a golden name theater people uttered with reverence.

Viennese by origin and trained as an actor, Reinhardt became one of the most influential and original producers in the world. He created a flashy-yet-real style, which even his competitors had difficulty replicating. Today he is still studied in great detail in theater classes; his methods and techniques are copied by professional directors. To him, the theater was a place for display, for spectacle and magic. Using the plays of Shakespeare, stretching all the possibilities of light and stage, he was a master of gigantic productions and a genius of the mob scene. When the Nazis came to power in Germany, Reinhardt fled to the United States where, in 1934, he founded an acting school and theater workshop in

Hollywood. He had left behind him his home, his treasures, virtually everything but his self-respect and prodigious talent. By the time Reinhardt took on the job of directing *Sons and Soldiers*, he was in his late sixties and had lost most of his once considerable physical strength.

In rehearsal, the play's problems became glaringly evident. To complicate matters, Shaw left his wife with strict instructions that not one word of dialogue was to be cut in his absence. Since there wasn't any way to contact an ambulance driver 5,000 miles away, the play was left uncut.

Greg played a small-town American boy, who, against the wishes of his parents, goes off to join the army. In one scene, he had to argue with his mother and father, shout, cry, and jump out of a window. It required a highly charged emotional performance and Greg, who in life was the consummate dutiful son, wasn't sure he could get through it. Whenever he came to the difficult part, he would feel his chest muscles tightening. Worse still, his performance was having an effect on the other actors. 'I murdered it.' He confessed. 'I couldn't fight off my nervousness and apprehension in doing that scene and as we were getting rather close to the opening night I had to fake it.'

Finally, Reinhardt stopped the proceedings from the orchestra pit, where he was watching rehearsals. Because of his frail condition, he usually stayed put. When he had directions to give to his players, he would send his assistant, Louis Jarvis, to discuss the matter. But this time, he shuffled slowly and deliberately all the way up the stairway on the side of the stage and took Greg off in a corner.

It wasn't a comfortable moment; Greg, 6 foot 2 inches, being held by the sleeve by a slightly portly, 5-foot-4-inch director with the most astonishing cobalt-blue eyes, who was gently chastising him.

Reinhardt whispered in his German accent: 'You know, I can see you're not happy, and I've been wondering what to say to you. Well, there's one thing I can say. We must remember how lucky we are in the show business because we can go on playing "let's pretend" all our lives, whereas most people have to stop when they are through being children. Look at me, and my age. I'm still pretending, and don't you think it's fun?'

'Oh yes,' said Greg. 'I love it.'

'Well,' replied Reinhardt. 'You must put yourself in the corner just offstage and then you must send the player – or child if you will – out on to the stage to playact. So let's pretend . . . '

'It was,' Greg recalled, 'a great breakthrough. It enabled me to throw off my self-consciousness. You have to be willing to make a damn fool of yourself and be horrible and embarrassing before getting it right. I think there must be a lot of people around who would be good actors if they were able to overcome that fear, or the fear of fear.'

Given its structural problems, *Sons and Soldiers* was the sort of drama that needed almost unanimous critical approval in order to attract a sufficient audience; when the unanimity was not forthcoming, neither were the ticket buyers. The show opened on 4 March 1943 and closed after 22 performances. Reinhardt suffered a stroke and died on 31 October at New York's Gladstone Hotel.

For Greg, there wasn't time to dwell on *Sons and Soldiers*. Soon he and Greta would be boarding the Twentieth Century Limited for the long trip to Los Angeles. The prospect of being able to take home $1,000 was something to relish, even in anticipation. Money generates its own kind of excitement. Looking forward to it created an ambience of gaiety and merriment in Greg and Greta's lives. They were a little intoxicated with the anticipation of the great changes to come, good changes most of them. Still, Greg would lose one thing that he would never regain. Gone forever were his footloose days as a carefree bohemian. From now on, people would watch his every step.

CHAPTER FIVE

Tinseltown

'Hollywood is wonderful. Anyone who doesn't like it is either crazy or sober.'

Raymond Chandler, detective novelist and screenwriter

Now residing in the magical land in the sun, Greg plunged into a crazy work schedule. It was a frantic, erratic montage of ups and downs, ins and outs, as he struggled to find his feet. Far from looking down his nose at film acting, Greg only hoped to be good enough. 'My training was telescoped,' he remembered. 'I had to pay attention. It was survival of the fittest.'

Days of Glory came and went in the bat of an eye. Screenwriter and producer Casey Robinson intended it to be a sophisticated film about a group of Russians who join together to resist the invasion of their country by the Nazis. What he got was a curious hybrid, caught between the trappings of the theater and the trajectory of the realistic war movie. It was made for RKO Pictures, a studio that never achieved the peaks of MGM, Paramount or Warner Brothers. With the war on, a popular crack went: 'In case of an air raid, go directly to RKO: they haven't had a hit in years.'

Cast as a Russian guerilla, Greg, with his clean-cut features and Yankee speech inflection, proved jarringly out of sync with the role. To play the romantic lead opposite Greg, Robinson cast his fiancée, Tamara Toumanova, a former star of the Moscow ballet, who was also a novice to the film world. Fortunately, the director, Jacques Tourneur didn't have a problem with it. 'It was a pleasure for me,' he recalled, 'because I did with them everything I wanted, exactly as with clay.'

Days of Glory wrapped in early November 1943. After viewing the rough cut, Greg decided to skip the finished film. 'I got a feeling I was amateurish,' he said. 'Why should I see the picture and prove it.' Then he added defensively, 'I just came out to pick up ten grand and go back to New York.' In actuality, he dreaded the trek back East. With a forgettable movie under his belt, he'd be just one more actor who had made the three-day train journey to the West Coast to no avail. In fact, there was a saying on Broadway about the experience of having to 'schlep' one's possessions back on the eastbound train: 'Never buy anything in Hollywood that you can't put on the Chief.'

Fortunately, there was someone else who saw the rushes and understood the newcomer's potential. It was none other than the tough, cigar-smoking, lecherous and supremely gifted head of Twentieth Century Fox, Darryl Zanuck. He'd watched Greg in *Morning Star* on Broadway and found him an interesting type.

Zanuck was in the midst of casting for *The Keys of the Kingdom* in 1943, a film adaptation of A J Cronin's best-selling novel about a nineteenth-century Scottish priest named Father Chisholm who finds himself in the line of fire during the Chinese civil war. The *New Republic* described it as 'an adventure and travel story packed with melodramatic action.' Zanuck had already tested 40 actors for the part but couldn't find a good fit. Then he saw Greg in an early cut of *Days of Glory*. Like the priests at St John's Military who encouraged their spiritually inclined student from La Jolla to pursue a religious vocation, and the girl at the Neighborhood Playhouse who inspired the moniker Father Peck, Zanuck knew he'd found his Father Chisholm.

'I fell in love with the part,' Greg said after reading Cronin's novel. Still, he stubbornly refused to sign a seven-year contract with Zanuck. So, to preserve Greg's autonomy and at the same time satisfy Zanuck, Leland Hayward worked out an arrangement in which Greg agreed to a four-picture deal with Twentieth Century Fox with a salary of $750 a week.

The hardiest and longest-lived of the mighty moguls, Zanuck was a small man with prominent white teeth, a tanned face and ferret-like eyes. He spoke in a voice several decibels too loud for the size of the room and the nearness of his listeners. He moved around as he talked, flexing a polo mallet with a shortened stick – an exercise to strengthen the wrist and forearm. He had started out at Warner

Brothers where he'd risen meteorically from dialogue writer for *Rin-Tin-Tin* to executive head of the studio. After making a few movies for MGM, he started a new company, Twentieth Century Pictures, which later became Twentieth Century Fox.

Zanuck's most talked-about personal trait was his avid sexual appetite. In this regard, Gregory Peck was lucky to be an actor not an actress. 'If you were not sexually operational, forget your career,' remembered Joan Crawford. '. . . I went over to Fox, for one of my late films, and when I was ushered into his office he promptly opened a desk drawer and took out a genuine gold casting of his genitals. I must admit he was admirably hung, but I couldn't help wondering what sort of so-called "obligations" had hung over the ladies at Twentieth over the years.'

When Greg met Zanuck, the producer looked him straight in the eye and vowed, 'I'm never going to ask you to make a picture you don't want to make. You can rely on me.' Could he? Greg wondered.

Despite winning the coveted Father Chisholm role, Greg was plagued with self-doubts. Calling himself lucky was not just a way of deflecting envy, he still didn't believe he deserved the breaks coming his way. He confided to Mary Morris of *PM* magazine: 'If it weren't for the shortage of leading men, a place like Twentieth Century Fox wouldn't have been interested in me – think of it, they'd lost Henry Fonda, Victor Mature, Tyrone Power, Richard Green and John Payne.' Similarly, those up-and-coming actors who were drafted and fought in the Second World War lost momentum.

Irrepressible Leland Hayward spread the word that Darryl Zanuck wanted Greg for a key role in an important film. So indefatigable, so insuperably optimistic was he, people figured Greg must really be something special. As his daughter Brooke Hayward recounts, he'd wire people to warn them he was about to call or call them to warn them he was about to wire them. Anything to get a prospect worked up. Sometimes he mapped out deals in a high-pitched frenzy while reclining with his feet draped over the top of his sofa and other times he'd be the archetypal mogul in his office. With one haunch parked on a desk corner, he dazzled his listener with his contagious enthusiasm about Gregory Peck.

Ballyhoo paid off. The major studios were falling over themselves to sign Greg. Louis B Mayer agreed to a nonexclusive contract for Greg to make four films for MGM over the next five years, starting with the salary of $750 a week on the first film, with a flat salary of $45,000 for the second, and $55,000 for the third and $65,000 for the fourth. David O Selznick now kicked himself for not signing Greg after his early screen test, and he managed to buy half the contract Greg had with Casey Robinson. After Greg signed his four-picture deal with the producer, Kay Brown, who first brought Greg to Selznick's attention, recalled: 'It cost David about four times what he would've had to pay originally.' In essence, Hayward had succeeded in getting Zanuck, Selznick and Mayer to agree to signing Greg for four films at each studio. This was before *Days of Glory* was even released.

Thus Greg became the first actor to embark on a successful movie career without the usual exclusive studio contract, a trend that was followed by Burt Lancaster, Kirk Douglas and Charlton Heston, eventually leading to the complete breakdown of the studios' star system. His head swam in the confusion of all these contractual complications, but Hayward told him to let the agency worry about that.

The next thing Greg knew, Hayward was selling his agency to Music Corporation of America (MCA) and moving East to produce Broadway plays. Jules Stein, founder of MCA, recalled that when they bought the agency in 1944, Hayward's clients turned out to be the firm's most important ones. 'He overshadowed everybody in the business . . . I was flabbergasted to think that he had so many important people – not only performers, but writers and directors – he had the best cross-section of artists in the whole field.'

Although delighted to have Greg as one of its clients, MCA found itself with the headache of trying to unravel his tangled contracts. This unenviable task was handed to George Chasin by his boss Lew Wasserman, who told him: 'If you do nothing else for the next six months, make yourself Gregory Peck's agent because he's going to be a very, very big and important star. Just devote yourself to him.'

At this point Greg made a modest investment in Hayward's first Broadway play, *A Bell for Adano*. It signaled the direction he would take with his finances. *Adano* opened with a bang. The play made Hayward an overnight success as a Broadway producer. Greg not only received a return on his investment, but it strengthened his bond with Hayward, whose keen instincts were invaluable.

As he walked on the set of *The Keys of the Kingdom*, Greg knew he had to prove himself. With *Days of Glory* about to be released – and aware it would probably be panned – he needed to show the producers nipping at his heels that he could, indeed, act for the screen. (On 16 June 1944 *Days of Glory* made an embarrassingly brief appearance in the theaters. It failed miserably with the critics. Bosley Crowther of the *New York Times* summed up the consensus of many about the male lead: 'Gregory Peck comes recommended with the Gary Cooper angularity and a face somewhat like that modest gentleman's, but his acting is equally stiff.')

Just strolling around the Twentieth Century Fox lot proved tremendously exciting for a newcomer, somewhat like Greg's old stomping ground, The New York World's Fair. The studio buildings, executive offices, cutting rooms, fire department, casting office and the huge towering sound stages seemed like a miniature city, and everywhere the streets teemed with cowboys, Indians, Southern gentlemen, soldiers, policemen, troupes of dancers and Hawaiian show girls, jungles, sections of Venice, New York's streets and what passed for a medieval castle and a lake with a large schooner and native canoes on it. Inside the buildings, state of the art equipment hummed day and night. As drama critic and editor George Jean Nathan so aptly described it: 'Ten million dollars' worth of intricate and ingenious machinery functioning elaborately to put skin on baloney.'

Zanuck had actors, writers, directors, producers, all the creative talent and labor that was required to produce a motion picture, signed to exclusive long-term contracts to work for the studio. All he had to do was run his finger down the list of talent under contract to Fox – a list he always kept pressed firmly on the top of his desk beneath a heavy sheet of glass – and deftly put together all the elements necessary to make a movie.

He presided over his crazy wonderland like the ringmaster in a circus. He was inclined to dress in riding britches and boots. Perpetually in motion, he compensated for his slight physical stature by keeping in such good trim that few men twice his size possessed his strength and endurance. He could arm wrestle a world-champion boxer and beat him (as he did several times with Jack Dempsey). He could perform on the high wire, the vaulting horse, and the trapeze to well-nigh professional standards.

Perhaps another compensation for his diminutive size was his over-sized imagination. 'Ignore the facts,' actress Ruth Gordon liked to say, and this might have served as Zanuck's slogan. He could overcome the highest obstacles in service to his imagination. For example, in producing battle movies during the Second World War, Zanuck found himself with enough actors to play the good guys but was desperately short of those to play the bad guys. According to actor Sheriden Morley, Central Casting couldn't rustle up the requisite Germans or Japanese. So Zanuck figured it would be all right to use other foreigners in the role so long as they did not look too American.

Thus, he concluded, for one particularly turgid war film he was making, that in the absence of the genuine Japanese – who were mainly now to be found in California internment camps – the entire Tokyo War Cabinet could be played by Englishmen. He figured that American audiences would be better able to detect by their voices that they were un-American and therefore likely to be 'baddies'. Accordingly, Basil Rathbone, Nigel Bruce, Aubrey Smith, Cedric Hardwicke and Ronald Coleman were summoned to make-up at 5 a.m. one morning. Dedicated technicians spent the next five hours endowing them with Japanese characteristics, and they were then assembled around a replica of the Cabinet table in Tokyo.

'When I came out here,' recalled Greg, 'Fox was making 65 features a year, and the others were making about that many. The parking lot was full. All the sound stages were busy. In those days, when they didn't have the competition of television, I think they were more apt to say yes to something a little cockeyed.'

The screenplay for *The Keys of the Kingdom* was originally written by Nunnally Johnson for David O Selznick. When the rights were sold to Zanuck's office, the scripting and production went to Joseph L Mankiewicz. Starting out as a newspaper man, Nunnally Johnson went on to distinguish himself as a playwright, screenwriter and movie producer. Upon meeting Greg, he surmised that the actor wasn't very bright simply because he didn't say much in an atmosphere of sparkling conversations. Later he realized in Greg's case, still waters ran deep. Johnson said of Zanuck: 'He had a kind of tough, stubborn faith. If you believed in your project, by God, he would see that it got made. There weren't many men who could produce a script and recognize a good one, but he could.'

Principal photography for *The Keys of the Kingdom* got underway on 15 November 1943. It was shot in three months entirely on the studio lot. Greg came to the set the first day knowing the script from the opening scene to the final fade-out. With a few acting friends he had already played out the role so that he not only had perfected the lines and memorized the cues, but he had the whole personality of Father Chisholm deeply engraved in his psyche. Still, his idea of a priest came from the provincial, narrowly educated immigrant Irish clerics who oversaw his spiritual training at St John's Military School. He couldn't quite grasp how Father Chisholm broke through to the Chinese.

Fortunately, Fox, like other studios, relied heavily on consultants, offering employment to large numbers of people with a great variety of skills – all in the service of manufacturing dreams. In Peck's case, they brought in Father Albert O'Hara, a Jesuit priest who had spent several years as a missionary in China and spoke the language fluently. Renowned for their scholarship in every conceivable field as well as for being saintly (41 saints and 285 blesseds), the Jesuits had been sending missionaries to China since 1583. The order was very receptive to the customs and values of the Chinese civilization. They took the daring step in China of trying to integrate Confucian values and Chinese cultural traditions with the Gospel message.

In Father O'Hara, Greg saw 'that grave courtesy and respect for each person as an individual.' The two became close friends and correspondents until the priest's death in Taiwan. Over the years Greg served as a stalwart fundraiser for the priest's missions. And the input of Father O'Hara on Greg's characterization worked well enough to impress the author of the novel – no mean task. A J Cronin marveled: 'I just can't understand how any actor could so well catch the clumsiness in the beauty of Father Chisholm's character.'

As the pre-film publicity machine for *The Keys of the Kingdom* got underway, Greg's 4-F draft status presented a major problem. In newspaper photographs and at weekly newsreels shown at the movies, Americans saw brave GIs getting their legs, arms and heads shot off. These boys were defeating tyranny, freeing oppressed people. So why was a healthy-looking physical specimen like Gregory Peck sitting out the war? Zanuck was not about to let the public know Greg suffered an injury in anything as 'sissified' as a dancing class, so he put out a release explaining that the very masculine actor injured his back while starring on Berkeley's rowing team.

The fudging on Greg's résumé was standard procedure at the studios. In his autobiography *The Moon's a Balloon*, David Niven recalled being called in by Jock Lawrence, the head of publicity at MGM. The discussion went as follows:

'Mother?'

'French.'

'Good, we can use that. Father?'

'Killed in the war.'

'Great! What rank?'

'Lieutenant.'

'Jesus, that's terrible. We'd better make him a general.' A general he became.

Although he was undoubtedly aware of Zanuck's dark side, Greg – ever conscious of building his own long career – accepted the tycoon's famously vulgar personality and recognized him as an artiste among businessmen. Of the Hollywood creative studio heads, Zanuck lasted the longest. At the end of his career, he had close to 1,000 movies to his credit; he painstakingly crafted (working at an extraordinary level of detail) an unprecedented string of noteworthy, and unusually successful, films, from *All About Eve* (1950) to *The Grapes of Wrath* (1940) and *How Green Was My Valley* (1941).

Greg, who counted organization among the cardinal virtues, admired Zanuck's efficiency and his uncanny instincts. Zanuck led script conferences to improve story lines, characterizations, and sequences of action, and he frequently dictated new scenes for the writers to fill out. His personal energy and acumen were expressed in his constant exhortation to make the scripts as concise as possible and to move the action along quickly. If the script didn't do it, Zanuck, who supervised postproduction equally closely, would re-cut the film accordingly. He believed action – even if wrong — was sometimes better than no action at all.

Rather than being put off by a hard taskmaster with rough edges, Greg did his best to ensure the two of them would have a long working relationship. And since Greg stayed in the game so long, he saw the advantages of this connection trickle down to the next generation.

During a break in filming, Greg recalled noticing a youngster, about eight years old, with tousled hair and dirty sneakers, hanging around the shoeshine stand and helping himself to a Coca-Cola. 'Who's that kid?' He wondered out loud.

'That kid is going to grow up to be your boss. His name is Dickie Zanuck,' was the prophetic retort. When Greg returned to Fox in the 1960s to film *The Chairman*, Richard Zanuck Jr greeted him warmly.

With a $3 million price tag, *The Keys of the Kingdom* did not earn back its costs. Nonetheless, it vaulted Greg to the top ranks of Hollywood's male heroes. He earned his first Best Actor Oscar nomination, yet he would lose that award to Ray Milland for *The Lost Weekend*. Though Greg earned just $750 a week for his starring role, Zanuck gave him a $25,000 bonus for the Oscar nomination.

With the release of *The Keys of the Kingdom* Greg burst through on to the public consciousness. The role of Father Chisholm established him as a man of honor and deep spirituality. 'I was beyond good guy,' he recalled. 'I was a walking saint.'

The Keys of the Kingdom has not held up as well as many other films in Peck's repertoire. Viewing it years later, critic Pauline Kael derisively tagged it 'Hollywood at its most virtuous.' About Greg, she carped: 'His saintliness comes across as lack of imagination –

utter sterility.' Then she added: 'This is perhaps the most dignified and sexless performance ever given by a rising male star.'

Maybe so, but in 1944 thousands of women found Greg irresistible. Fan mail poured in from females hell-bent on defrocking him. 'Please let me spend a night with you,' wrote an ardent female. 'You can do what you will with me.' Ever the gentleman, Greg instructed his secretary to write each one a polite note saying: 'Sorry, I'm all booked up.'

Hollywood had its own social hierarchy, a rigorously observed caste system. It wasn't noticeable in the daytime, when stars and extras worked side by side in the studios. But at night, social life was rigidly structured according to the weekly salary checks. The stars invited stars, or producers, directors and writers. Ticket to admission: success. Said Hedda Hopper: 'Our town worships success, the bitch goddess whose smile hides a taste for blood.'

A good pretext for a party was somebody's return from overseas service. In 1945 Greg and Greta lined up at one shindig for a picture of a glowing Ronald Reagan with his wife Jane Wyman celebrating his safe return from the war. Of those times, Greta said: 'It was grand. I bought clothes like crazy. I'm the saving kind by nature. It's the Finn in me, I guess. But Greg said I had to get clothes and he gave me the nicest mink coat.' Thriving on people, Greta found these occasions thrilling.

Greg didn't enjoy big splashy parties. He liked picnics with Greta and long walks in the woods near their home. 'It was absolutely wonderful out there then,' recalled Greg's friend Harry Carey, Jr. 'Anybody who was anybody lived there. Robert Taylor lived just up the road. So did Jean Arthur, and John Charles Thomas, the great baritone. Shirley Temple and her handsome husband, John Agar, were just a mile away – and so was Joan Crawford, Gary Cooper, Claude Rains and Pat O'Brien. On Tigertail Road, you could see Henry Fonda with little Jane riding behind him on his tractor as he plowed his land. Gregory Peck was up on the hill, and Rex Harrison and Lilli Palmer live further up on Mandeville Canyon.' When the couple entertained, Greg preferred backyard barbecues and raucous drinking sessions with his buddies, Robert Mitchum and Burl Ives.

During the mid-1940s, Burl Ives was best known as a wandering minstrel. Due to tax problems, he found it expedient not to have a fixed address. He would travel from town to town, and sometimes from house to house, singing ribald ballads in his distinctive voice. He popularized songs such as 'Foggy Foggy Dew', 'Blue-tailed Fly', 'I Know an Old Lady' and 'Big Rock Candy Mountain'.

One weekend he came for a Saturday night party at the Peck's and slept most of the following Sunday in time to take part in a slightly less raucous gathering in the evening. Greg had to report at the studio at 7.30 Monday morning. When he returned, Ives was still there, curled up on the carpet, looking, Greg recalled, like a beached whale. Ives left on Tuesday.

The verbal jousting and parrying at elegant Hollywood parties tested Greg's reticent nature. Not one to whom conversation came naturally, he paused frequently between sentences to think out what he was going to say. Most of the time he keep his comments to a bare minimum. A friend suggested it was because he was terrified of the community's smart set. Peck didn't want to fall victim to the snare of trying to say something scintillating and having it fall flat. He admitted, 'When I get mixed up with Nunnally Johnson or Herman Mankiewicz or Ben Hecht, I am struck dumb.' Katharine Hepburn, who suffered from the same problem, commented: 'I think many actors are very shy, but they have a strong urge to express themselves or to hide behind the characters they play.'

But at the same time, Greg relished the intellectual stimulation of rubbing shoulders with talented people – and listening hard to what they had to say. In the 1940s, Hollywood parties boasted an abundant supply of the avant-garde. Ambitious hostesses gathered artists, writers, designers, and, of course, directors and actors about them in their fabulous houses. You seldom saw anybody at their gatherings who wasn't a star in his field. The rooms rang with knowledgeable talk about paintings, design, sculpture, collecting antiques, owning thoroughbreds – and Peck was absorbing it and would later bring the information to bear on his own lifestyle.

As a hedge against gatherings he would have preferred to skip, Greg tried to arrange it so the couple would be the last to arrive and the first to leave. Tinseltown affairs had a way of getting out of hand: somebody jumping in the pool; men tossing punches at each other; an actor's wife and girlfriend squabbling; strangers meeting and disappearing together; stray guests falling asleep on couches and leaving at daylight. Lord knows, Greg loved merriment and the opportunity to hoist a few, but he was learning the price of prominence. If he got blitzed and made a spectacle, the story would take on a life of its own.

For some bashes it was wise to leave hat and coat in the car. That way you could exit at a reasonable hour without calling attention to yourself. George Sanders, a British actor known for playing both leading men and suave cads, followed this rule and often made his way swiftly upstairs and escaped through the bathroom window. He claimed: 'I got to know a lot of bathrooms like that; the best was undoubtedly Greer Garson's. It was all done in pink marble, and had a huge glass wall, which opened on to a private garden. It was the biggest production for the smallest audience that Hollywood ever achieved.'

Yet, when it came to the legendary names, Greg was happy to stick around. 'I certainly admired the big stars,' he said. 'They were not stars for no reason, you know. They were stars because they were so damn interesting.'

One evening in 1946, Gary Cooper sidled up to Greg and introduced himself. Cooper was 44 years old, still handsome, but the early sensuality of his face had been replaced by a weathered, granite appearance, accentuated by iron-gray hair. He walked slowly, spoke deliberately and was in full possession of his unassailable dignity.

By the time Greg met him, Gary Cooper had been in films for 20 years, a star for 16, and among the top box-office attractions for 10. Some of his movies were the best ever made. He was a folk hero, an American symbol to be cherished almost as much as apple pie and motherhood. As Carl Sandburg put it, Cooper was 'One of the most beloved illiterates this country has ever known.'

'How many movies have you made?' Cooper asked.

'Two,' Greg responded.

'How'd they turn out?'

'One good, one bad.'

'You're ahead of the game,' Cooper replied. Then he said, 'Don't worry if you get a few flops. You'll be lucky if you have two good movies out of every five.'

Good advice. But Greg may well have asked himself: Do I want to turn out like Gary Cooper? The film icon was a cautionary tale both professionally and personally.

Certainly there was much for Greg to admire in Cooper's screen image. The quintessential strong, silent type, he performed exciting deeds and left the talking to his admirers. He could make a moral choice seem a matter of real immediate moment.

Cooper's explanation for his success was: 'To get folks to like you, I figured you sort of had to be their ideal. I don't mean a handsome knight riding a white horse, but a fellow who answered the description of a right guy.'

Greg liked the idea of that kind of public adulation, but he also wanted to be taken seriously. His idols were Barry Fitzgerald, James Cagney, Humphrey Bogart, Spencer Tracy and Walter Huston. These men took risks to stretch their talents and they refused to be pigeonholed.

Cooper's success – like that of Cary Grant and Clark Gable – sprang from his looks, personality and animal magnetism. The public assumed he didn't work at his acting. For his part, Cooper downplayed the discipline and perfectionism required to play himself. If complimented for a serious role, such as his Academy Award winning *Sergeant York* (1941), he'd dismiss the praise with an endearing excuse: 'It's a cinch. I just learn my lines and try not to bump into the furniture.' At the same time, many of those in the movie business reinforced the image of Cooper as an uncomplicated natural. Director King Vidor said: 'He got a reputation as a great actor just by thinking hard about his next line.' Playing opposite him in *Cloak and Dagger* (1946), Lilli Palmer recounted: 'Cooper could deliver a long speech on camera while rummaging in his pocket for a cigarette, continue talking while he fiddled with matches, pause for moment of what looked like intense concentration, pick up where he left off, put the matches away, rub his nose, and go on talking as if the camera didn't exist.'

The major studios deliberately set about creating a distinctive public style for each star. Such perception played a large part in Cooper being cast in roles in the latter part of his career that made him look like a caricature of himself; the same held true for Jimmy Stewart and John Wayne.

Greg may also have been put off by the tawdry stories about Cooper's tumultuous love affairs. At a time in his own life when he was struggling to build a good marriage with Greta while fending off the advances of eager women, he knew he could easily find himself the target of unfavorable publicity. Some paramours don't know when to keep quiet, such as Cooper's girlfriend, Clara Bow, who combined awesome vitality with childlike vulnerability. 'I like him very much,' she assured the press corps. 'He always lets me take my dog in the tub when he gives me my bath in the morning.'

CHAPTER SIX

Leading Ladies

'I'll tell you about these men. They were monsters and pirates
and bastards right down to the bottom of their feet, but they
loved *movies*. They loved *making* movies, they loved *seeing*
movies and they protected the people who worked for them.'
Director Richard Brooks on the Hollywood moguls

Greg's next film was shot at Metro-Goldwyn-Mayer (MGM), a
place where talent, enthusiasm and virtually limitless financial
support made almost anything possible. The studio, which looked
like an academy with Georgian columns and a Georgian façade, was
known as 'The Tiffany of the business' and boasted 'More Stars
Than There Are in Heaven.' MGM was not only the premier movie
factory; it was very much a city unto itself.

Eventually, MGM's Culver City property covered six lots,
encompassing 180 acres. All the filmmaking trades – make-up, art
direction, set and property construction, special effects and
publicity – reached new heights at MGM. The studio's stated goal
of turning out a film a week was seldom met, but it often managed
three releases a month.

In the studio commissary, Greg sometimes caught sight of Louis
B Mayer, the man who had cried when he turned down his contract
offer. Now Greg watched the most powerful and feared mogul of
them all sitting with his employees eating chicken soup. Here was a
man who knew how to develop stars. He cared, was formidably
organized, and treated the stars well – as long as they stayed in line.
Canadian actor Walter Pigeon who specialized in distinguished and
gentlemanly roles recalled: 'I was like a kept woman during my 21
years at MGM. Hollywood was like an expensive, beautifully run
club. You didn't need to carry money. Your face was your credit
card – all over the world.'

Mayer exercised all the passions fiercely. He could love and he could hate. He could help you or hurt you badly. Greg spoke well of Mayer and made sure he stayed on the producer's good side – without getting mowed over. He noted: 'I think Mayer gained a great respect for me as a result of my haggling with him, because over the years to come he never once held it against me.'

Biographer Bosley Crowther took a darker view of the tycoon, calling him 'a man whose tapeworm ego had to be fed by driving activity, ruthless use of power, and adventures with beautiful women.' Director Jules Dessin was leery of Mayer's expansive paternalism. 'To me, Louis B Mayer's arm around your shoulder meant his hand was closer to your throat.'

For psychological reasons as well as career expediency, Greg viewed Mayer in a good light – just as he did Zanuck. He didn't look up to these tyrants as models of integrity the way he did his father, but he saw them as blazing successes. They were romantic devils; men who loved the movies and had the balls to reach out and grab what they wanted. While his father resigned himself to working nights in a drugstore he didn't own, these men survived, prevailed and flourished.

Greg soon learned that, unlike Zanuck, Mayer rarely interfered with film production. At the same time, he was vitally interested in everything that concerned his people: their politics, their lovers, whom they should or should not romance, how they worked, their habits, their lifestyles, and even the color of their hair. He was a rabid Republican, and made political shorts to be shown in the Loew's theaters. He was also a profoundly sentimental man who disliked realism in movies, press releases and police reports alike.

When a drunken Clark Gable drove around a curve too fast one day in 1933 and struck a pedestrian, killing her instantly, Mayer actually got an MGM executive to take the rap. He had a cozy relationship with the Los Angeles DA and knew where to send the money that kept things out of the newspapers.

In *The Valley of Decision*, Greg was playing opposite Greer Garson, a personal find of Mayer's who was then considered one of the brightest stars in the MGM galaxy. Garson was a witty Celtic beauty with an ineffable presence and enormous drive. She got her start on the stage and rose to prominence in the 1930s and 1940s, playing noble women in films such as *Goodbye, Mr Chips* (1939), *Pride and Prejudice* (1940) and *Random Harvest* (1942). But it was her portrayal as a steadfast, loving *Mrs Miniver* in the 1942 movie that won her an Oscar – her only win out of an impressive six nominations – and made her one of the most beloved actresses of her generation. (Her Oscar acceptance speech took up so much time, the audience began to wonder if it was going to run longer than the movie itself.)

Greg knew he had to do a respectable job for Mayer or he might find himself relegated to B-movies. When it came to actors, Mayer's standards were very high and he was not overly impressed with newcomers like Gregory Peck. He once told British actor Robert Morley that the cinema had given precisely one great artist to the world: 'Greta Garbo . . . unless you count that damn Mouse.'

Versatile in both comedy and drama, Greer's popularity had begun to slip about the time *The Valley of Decision* was being filmed. Also, she was keenly aware of being eight years older than her co-star. At about the time they met, she snapped at a photographer who was shooting her: 'You're not photographing me as well as you used to.'

'Well, I'm ten years older,' the photographer replied diplomatically.

Greg found her 'a bit of an Irish cut-up, radiant, funny, bracing, and smart.' He called her Big Red and they got along fabulously.

On the home front, Greg was a spectator in a heartwarming domestic drama – the birth of his first child. On 20 July 1944, while he was filming at Culver City, Greta went into labor. He was called to the hospital and after several hours he heard a nurse announce over the loudspeaker: 'Mr Peck, your son wants to speak to you.' He shouted 'Yippee!' When the nurse came into the room to take him to see his baby boy, he told her, 'The Yankees have found themselves another pitcher.' The Pecks already had a name chosen: Jonathan.

'A family name?' asked a reporter.

'Oh, no, indeed,' Greg answered in his 'ah, shucks' way. 'We found it in a book of 3,500 names, and it seems to fit him.'

Much to Greta's disappointment, there was little time for Greg to enjoy his baby son straightaway as he still had a film to finish. And he was continuing to make a good impression on industry insiders. *Valley of Decision* director Tay Garnett enthused: 'Peck has everything it takes to be a megastar. He has the looks, the personality, the poise and the control, and a magnificent voice.'

By osmosis, Greg was strengthening his mindset as a real trouper. It was a quality he admired tremendously in great character actors such as Lionel Barrymore. Greg never forgot one afternoon during the filming of *The Valley of Decision* that Barrymore was going all out during a rehearsal. He was working from a wheelchair (he had a bad heart), and it was a strike-breaking scene outside a steel mill in Pittsburgh. 'He was on the picket line and he had a scene where he had to shout and go into a tirade, and he did this in rehearsal. Tay Garnett, came up and said, "Lionel, please! You don't have to do that in rehearsal. I don't want you to have a heart attack." And Barrymore said, "Who gives a damn!"'

Of the old-timers, few would hold as high a place in Greg's regard as Walter Huston (father of John Huston). The gravel-voiced character actor was in his early 60s and down to playing loveable old rogues by the time Greg got to know him, but for years Huston enjoyed success both on the New York stage and in films such as *Abraham Lincoln* (1930), *Dodsworth* (1936), The *Maltese Falcon* (1941) and *The Treasure of the Sierra Madre* (1948). He liked to say, 'Hell, I ain't paid to make good lines sound good. I'm paid to make bad ones sound good.' As Greg sat with him during filming breaks on the set of *Duel in the Sun* (1946) the two men swapped stories about boxing and baseball. Huston also shared some nuggets of advice such as: 'Give 'em a good show, and always travel first class.'

When Huston died in 1950 at the age of 66, Spencer Tracy praised him in a rousing eulogy: 'Two Americans have won the Nobel Prize for literature. It's no accident that when you mention Sinclair Lewis or Eugene O'Neill you think of Walter Huston. He helped them tell their stories better than anyone else. He gave more color to their lines; he gave more drive to their action. He turned guts into a good word. He filled in with 45 years of the best playing you'll ever see. It was the works – singing, dancing, Shakespeare. Call your shot. Huston could do it.' That was the sort of career Greg hoped to have for himself.

The fact that Greg was working so much and spending so little time off the set added tension to the marital home. But Greg was like a miner, bidding a metaphorical goodbye to the daylight and the outside world for the duration. Even when the cast broke for lunch on the set, he was consumed with talking shop with his colleagues. In years to come, Greg would regret the large chunks of time he spent away from his family, especially Jonathan.

The Keys of the Kingdom was set to premiere in New York on 28 December 1944 and the Pecks ventured East for the occasion. Jonathan stayed home. 'He'd just be a nuisance,' Greg explained to a reporter who wondered why the couple wasn't taking the baby along to visit Greta's mother. Relaxing at the Waldorf Astoria, the couple couldn't suppress their glee in comparing their plush rooms with the fifth-floor, shared kitchen walk-up that was their last New York address.

The luxury hotel setting appealed to Greg's emerging appreciation of the finer things in life. 'There must have been aristocrats somewhere back in my family history,' he joked. Indeed, the simple guy who sported flannel-checked shirts, and barbecued humble burgers, was developing a strong aesthetic taste.

The Waldorf Astoria was a 1930s Art Deco masterpiece occupying an entire city block between 49th and 50th Streets. Greg could bathe in a marble bathroom, sink his feet into a soft red carpet, stroll along Peacock Alley and dine in the Empire Room. This was the hotel for royalty, show business and US Presidents. Decorations were executed by noted artists: the murals in the Sert Room were by José Maria Sert; the rug (*The Wheel of Life*) and the paintings in the main foyer were by Louis Rigal; the murals in the Starlight Roof Garden by Victor White. Thereafter, whenever he visited New York, Greg occupied one of the Waldorf's residential suites.

At the film's opening, the New York press corps turned out in full force. Greg and Greta were whisked up to the theater in a white limousine accompanied by a four-motorcycle police escort. The scene was a blur of jewels, furs, celebrities, critics and jittery nerves.

Looking up, Greg was confronted with a 54-foot billboard featuring his portrait. 'It stretched for half a block,' he recalled, 'and the impact on me was not lost, let alone on the people it was meant to attract.'

Next came *Spellbound* – and Ingrid. It was a suspense thriller with psychoanalytic content about an amnesiac John Ballantine (Peck) and a Freudian psychologist Dr Constance Peterson (Bergman). Greg was at a disadvantage having to play a none-too-plausible character in what is, despite the film's status as a minor classic, an overripe piece of melodrama. The film is really a showpiece for Bergman, who is on camera nearly every second of the movie's 111 minutes. Producer, David O Selznick originally wanted Joseph Cotton, Dorothy McGuire and Paul Lukas for S*pellbound*, but now it is difficult to imagine the film without Bergman, Greg, and, for tops, Salvador Dalí designing the dream sequence.

Greg had heard a great deal about Selznick's sharp, impulsive mind and his daring promotional escapades. The producer's résumé included such memorable films as *King Kong* (1933), *Dinner at Eight* (1933), *Anna Karenina* (1935), *A Star is Born* (1937), *Rebecca* (1940) and of course, *Gone With the Wind* (1939). He had a keen eye for a worthwhile project and new talent, but when he became obsessed with a project or person, he tended to go over-board and his judgment often erred. He would find himself in trouble with his bankers in spite of the fact that he was able to turn out pictures that ran up fantastic grosses at the box-office.

Selznick and other major independents such as Sam Goldwyn and Walt Disney were in a class by themselves. While the big studios emphasized efficiency and productivity, these intrepid men produced only a few high-cost, high-yield pictures annually. They turned out prestige pictures that often tested the economic constraints and the creative limits of the system. But the so-called 'independents' were closely tied to the studio system, and especially to the integrated majors. The independents needed the system for its resources and theaters, while the system needed them to cultivate the 'high-end' of the market and to keep the first-run theaters stocked with quality product – an obvious benefit to the majors since they took a sizeable exhibitor's fee on these releases.

If Greg weren't a fan of larger than life personalities, he might have been exasperated with David O Selznick. The most fabulous and unpredictable of the independent filmmakers, Selznick was arrogant, rude, desperately insecure and wildly self-destructive. He was also a hot-tempered slave-driver, a sloppy satyr, a meddler and a poor sport when the joke was on him. But Greg chose not to dwell on his shortcomings. Of all the Hollywood tycoons, Selznick was the one with whom he socialized most.

Being around Selznick meant observing the producer's romantic life at close range. When *Spellbound* went into production, Selznick's wife was the princess of the kingdom, Irene Mayer, daughter of Louis B. (Years earlier when Selznick had married the iron-willed Irene, screenwriters Charles MacArthur and Charles Lederer composed a cruel ditty which began: 'Someone had to marry Irene Mayer, someone had to have the guts to lay her . . . '.) But the producer was in the midst of separating from Irene because he had fallen crazy in love with a young beauty, Jennifer Jones. Determined to present her to the public as a great actress, he would make Jones Greg's co-star in the upcoming *Duel in the Sun* (1946).

Jones, recently divorced from actor Robert Walker, was half in love and half repulsed by Selznick. The producer was far from gorgeous. Tall, shaggy in appearance, with black, curly hair turning white, thick-lensed spectacles, tie awry and cigarette ash on his sleeve, Selznick nonetheless lured Jennifer with two great aphrodisiacs: money and power.

For his part, Selznick was so captivated by the 'the big-eyed girl' (as he referred to Jennifer in one of his famous memos) that it was endangering his precarious mental balance. She would become his obsession and he would spend the rest of his life nurturing her career. Greg recalled, 'Selznick was so ambitious, so extravagant, such a big spoiled kid, so talented, so undisciplined. He made *Gone With the Wind*, which everybody seemed to think was the greatest picture ever made. So he was riding on that fame.'

The movie *Spellbound* came about through Selznick's interest in psychiatry. He was a man divided into three. He submitted himself to analysis because of his confusion over leaving Irene, falling in love with Jennifer Jones, and being excessively involved in work. His fascination with psychiatric treatment led him to purchase the novel *The House of Dr Edwardes* (1927) by Francis Beeding, which he gave to Ben Hecht to transcribe for the screen. (Hecht was also in analysis at the time, and he and Selznick often compared their experiences.) Alfred Hitchcock was asked to direct.

For many critics, then and now, *Spellbound*'s treatment of psychoanalysis – a theme woven into its narrative of a fraught love affair between a repressed analyst and a potentially psychotic amnesiac – has been dismissed as obvious, even grating, and merely an inferior template of ideas that would later reappear in *Vertigo* (1946) and elsewhere.

Searching for surreal imagery, Hitchcock persuaded Selznick to have Salvador Dalí create a dream sequence; though the artist made hundreds of sketches, only a fragment of his efforts made it to the screen.

Hitchcock told New Wave director François Truffaut: 'I was determined to break with the traditional way of handling dream sequences through a blurred and hazy screen. I asked Selznick if he could get Dalí to work with us and he agreed, though I think he didn't really understand my reasons for wanting Dalí. He probably thought I wanted his collaboration for publicity purposes. The real reason was that I wanted to convey the dreams with great visual sharpness and clarity, sharper than the film itself. I wanted Dalí because of the architectural sharpness of his work . . . But Dalí had some strange ideas; he wanted a statue to crack like a shell falling apart, with ants crawling all over it, and underneath, there would be Ingrid Bergman, covered by the ants! It just wasn't possible.'

Dalí composed more than a hundred sketches and five paintings to be filmed (at $1,000 a clip). According to Bergman's account of the visual effects in the movie: 'It opened with 400 human eyes glaring down at [Greg] from black velvet drapes. Then a pair of pliers fifteen times taller than Peck chased him up the side of a pyramid.'

By the 1940s, Salvador Dalí had become a darling of American high society. Celebrities such as Jack Warner and Helena Rubinstein gave him commissions for portraits. His artworks became a popular trademark and, besides painting, he pursued other avenues, such as jewelry and clothing designs for Coco Chanel. He attracted the attention of the media by playing the role of a surrealist clown. Reporters knew they could count on him for a snappy quote such as: 'Each morning when I awake, I experience again a supreme pleasure – that of being Salvador Dalí.' Perhaps he came by his hubris from his mother who boasted of baby Salvadore, 'Even his pee is golden.' In any case, he made a lot of money and was contemptuously nicknamed Avida Dollars (greedy for dollars) by Surrealist André Breton.

For shrinks, Los Angeles was the land of opportunity. Leo Rangell, a psychiatrist who arrived in the Movie Mecca in 1946 found the residents possessed a fascinating mix of great ambition, visibility, exhibitionism, cultism, and exciting and eccentric ideas.

To no one's surprise, a mutual infatuation developed between moviemakers and psychiatrists. Mary Romm, the colorful 'Queen of Couch Canyon,' parlayed her role as David O Selznick's personal analyst into a plum assignment as his advisor on *Spellbound*. The producers evangelized psychoanalysis and led the way in making the Freudian-led science – with all its contemporary offshoots – an integral part of American life. Quipped Nunnally Johnson: 'As long as Hollywood stands, no freeborn American need surrender to an inferiority complex. It is the greatest boon to psychiatrists since sex. Hollywood never gets the credit due to it.'

Both Hitchcock and Hecht were familiar enough with the topic to exploit it in the service of the real subject: romance. In preparation, the writer and director toured mental hospitals in Connecticut and New York, then focused on the psychiatric ward at Bellevue Hospital in New York City. The Hitchcock–Hecht collaboration was a fruitful one. The two men shared an interest in the darker passages of the human mind.

Greg benefited from Bergman's strong relationship with Hitch-cock. She knew what Hitchcock wanted and she also had another advantage. The 300-pound, cherub-faced, pot-bellied director liked to flirt with her. With his combination of jollity and edginess, he played up to Bergman in a sort of seduction. And she responded to his mixture of humor and authority with her own charm. Years later, he would murmer, 'Ah, Ingrid. So beautiful, so *stupid*.' Their relaxed relationship made it easier for Greg to loosen up.

'Now Ingrid, for instance, is so straight – so strictly on the square about everything she does – it's practically painful,' said Greg. 'She has a terrific sense of truth that it causes her great embarrassment if she has to do anything theatrical, or overly emotional. That's one reason I like her so much. Her acting also followed clean classic lines I guess – I get tense if I have to *emote*.'

But Greg was bewildered by the man who had perfected himself as a machine for making movies with a clearly laid out plan in his mind. (Hitchcock contended: 'In a good movie, the sound could go off and the audience would still have a perfectly clear idea of what was going on.')

Greg recalled: 'Hitchcock is like an architect in this manner; he never starts to wreck the building until he has drawn up the perfect plan so that when he begins there is very little that can go wrong. His preparations are meticulous. He needs to be able to place actors into this plan, and he is always at his best with technical actors – that is, actors like Cary Grant who have an accomplished technique of producing effects. Grant worked very hard on his technique and it's very facile, something he can just turn on.

'With him, given his long record of success, you don't quarrel. You do it his way. I don't think I was at my most effective with him – not because I didn't like him as a director, but because I was not quite flexible enough, nor indeed professional enough yet – it was quite early in my film career – to do everything he wanted and needed and at the same time provide my own inner truth. Because it's quite possible to act the other way about, from the externals *in*. Many, many great actors do this. But I wasn't experienced enough to do that.'

Even for seasoned actors, finding themselves in the arms of someone they don't know well can feel awkward. Not to mention that a dozen strangers are watching your every move with interest because, as cameramen or electricians or prop men, they are being paid to do so. For this reason, passionate love scenes in front of the camera are anything but passionate, particularly in close-up. There you are lying lip to lip, while the cameramen complains, 'I can see nothing but noses. Can't you move your face a bit to the right?'

To make things tougher for Greg, Selznick was also concerned about the close-ups, worrying if the glamour standards were being upheld. He dispatched a memo to Hitchcock stating: 'Peck's beard is still showing a little too heavy . . . I can't understand this as I understand he is now shaving three times a day . . . I don't want to lose the quality of his face . . . but perhaps a different kind of powder and more of it is indicated . . . Also the wave in his hair should be changed to make him look more attractive.'

Together Greg and Bergman created their own universe and it was one in which he felt safe. Locked inside those thick, windowless, soundproofed walls that so completely shut out the rest of the world, he could let down the barriers. At home with Greta, he had to negotiate his way through a real relationship and that was becoming more and more difficult for him. Since his parents had never really been able to talk to each other, he lacked the template for domestic communication. Playing a role with Ingrid, he felt comfortable and, at the same time, more alive. Hitchcock liked to say, 'Drama is life with the dull bits left out.' And Greg was finding acting in a drama much more exciting than quotidian family life. Romance is fun. Marriage is a lot of work.

As for Bergman, she was always honest about her priorities and number one was her professional goals. Bergman told author Mike Munn: 'Greg was a very handsome man – very sexy. It was difficult not to be attracted to him.' Certainly this was true, but, at another time, Bergman made a comment that encapsulated her relationships: 'I'm only interested in two kinds of people, those who can amuse me and those who can further my career.'

While *Spellbound* was in the works, Selznick returned one day from a meeting with psychiatrist Mary Romm to find Bergman's husband, Peter Lindstrom, had been waiting for him in his office. Lindstrom was concerned about his wife's extramarital imagination.

Instead of commiserating with the beleaguered husband, Selznick shared an insight he had gleaned from his shrink. 'You'll understand this,' he said to Lindstrom. 'I have a problem with Irene. I found this other girl, whom I love. It was terribly hard on me. How could I explain this to Irene and to myself? So I went to this woman psychiatrist. I paid her double her fee. She gave me a scientific explanation why I had to leave my wife. I wanted you to know there is a scientific basis!'

Like Greg, Bergman took great pleasure in the sheer business of making a film. She worked compulsively, making sure every detail, every gesture, every inflection of her screen character was just right. He operated the same way and they had much to talk about. Plus, he found, in contrast to her sophisticated professionalism, she had a charming naturalness, which he prized in a woman. Like Greg, she was not one to reflect on her own psyche. She coped with anxiety by 'getting herself three or four ice-cream sodas by way of dessert' and by falling in love.

Hitchcock waved off *Spellbound* as 'just another manhunt story wrapped up in pseudo psychoanalysis.' And esteemed critic James Agee dismissed its treatment of psychiatry as lightweight, maintaining it contained 'just enough of the Id as could be displayed in Bergdorf Goodman's window.' Other critics dismissed the whole psychoanalysis business as one of Hitchcock's 'McGuffins', a device giving impetus to the plot but having little significance in itself.

The film opened on 1 November 1945 at New York's Astor Theater and became an immediate commercial hit. It had cost $2 million to make, quite a considerable sum for 1944, and it recouped $7.9 million on its first release. It brought Ingrid Bergman a 'Best Actress Performance' from the New York Film Critics' Circle, although it was for *The Bells of St Mary's* (1945) that she won an Oscar nomination that year. *Spellbound*'s Oscar nominations were for Michael Chekhov as Best Supporting Actor, for Hitchcock's direction, for Miklos Rozsa's superb score, and for the film itself – of them only Rozsa won. Peck got just $50,000, but the role continued his streak of triumphs.

After *Spellbound*, Bergman went on to make *Notorious* (1946) with Hitchcock. By that time, they were good friends and, according to Bergman and Hitchcock's biographer Donald Spoto, the actress confessed to Hitchcock that she was trying to get over a wrenching affair with the photographer Robert Capa. According to Spoto, the two sat down for what turned into a 'boozy afternoon' of reflection.

During the talk, the ever-observant Hitchcock saw in Bergman's features, according to Spoto, 'a somewhat forlorn look and noted the absence of her usual ebullient good humor.' Bergman's evident distraction Hitchcock rightly took for emotional turmoil. Certainly he had his own emotions to hold in check since he had fallen in love with Bergman and she had graciously declined his attentions.

Then, 'as Hitchcock poured hefty drinks for them,' Bergman confessed to her old friend 'she was in love with Robert Capa . . . [and] saw no hope for the fulfillment of that love.' Hitchcock listened sympathetically to the whole story, finally quoting a little speech from *Spellbound*: 'It is very sad to love and lose somebody. But in a while you will forget and you will take up the threads of your life where you left off not long ago. And you will work hard. There is lots of happiness in working hard – maybe the most.'

As for Greg and Bergman, they stayed friends through thick and thin. Greg put Ingrid up in his pantheon of all-time favorite leading ladies – along with Ava Gardner and Audrey Hepburn – no mean feat considering that Peck played in 60 movies.

CHAPTER SEVEN

Animal Magnetism

'I thought of the guy in *Duel in the Sun* as a kind of rascal, a kind of spoiled kid of a cattle baron being given everything he wants. I didn't see me as evil.'

Gregory Peck, speaking about his role as
Lewt McCanles in *Duel in the Sun*

Back when *Duel in the Sun* was just a gleam in David O Selznick's eye, his thought was to make a modest Western showcasing his mistress, Jennifer Jones. By the time the producer finished, *Duel in the Sun* was just about the most super-duper-Technicolor ever made. Nicknamed 'Lust in the Dust' and 'Hump in the Sump' (a sump is a pool where water is collected), it ended up costing over $5 million (which the film easily earned back), employing a huge cast and crew and taking an amazing 18 months to shoot. The movie's unhealthy eroticism and flaming bad taste astonished Americans who associated Selznick's name with family classics and love stories. Nonetheless, the dark sexuality and touch of obsession is exactly what moviegoers enjoyed the most.

Greg watched from the inside as the producer became completely consumed with the project. 'I knew Selznick was consciously putting on a Selznick Western,' said Greg, 'pumping it full of showmanship with an outsized cast and an enormous production, and I knew that he was intent on making Jones a great star, creating a movie that would overtake his wildly successful *Gone With the Wind*.'

A nervy, ambitious actress, Jennifer Jones made a big hit with the public as a virginal young woman in *The Song of Bernadette* (1943) a role that won her an Oscar. Selznick was her Pygmalion, who had seized upon her raw talent and good looks and turned her into the saintly Bernadette. Subsequently, he insisted she never be typecast, but always show versatility and range. So in *Duel*, he cast her as the libidinous Pearl Chavez, 'a full-blossomed woman built by the devil to drive men crazy.'

Greg, aka Father Chisholm, seemed an unlikely choice for the male lead. Lewt McCanles was a rapist, a forger, a killer, a liar, a thoroughly rotten no-good – but with a certain likeability. Selznick, however, loved to toss the public a surprise, just as he was doing with Jones. He charted the popularity curves of Clark Gable and John Garfield and found that at that point in their career in which they played a 'bad-boy' part, their audience appeal soared.

Greg rejoiced in his character's lubricious wickedness. 'I never enjoyed any role better than I did *Duel in the Sun*,' he told Hedda Hopper. 'You know, after my first pictures, I got the mantle of nobility flung around my shoulders. I didn't like it. But I'm gradually breaking that concept down. And I think *Duel* will finish it off. In that character, I don't have one redeeming quality, but he has a whale of a good time. Does everything any man would want to do. Oh yes, he gets killed in the end, but that just lasts a minute. He sure enjoys himself while he has life.'

From the outset, Selznick's impact on the film went far beyond the mere financing and administration of production. Famous for his relentless memos, Selznick managed to rattle off hundreds during the course of *Duel in the Sun*. To him, a memo was a weapon – a creative outlet and a way of making sure his orders were followed. He boasted: 'The difference between me and other producers is that I am interested in the thousands and thousands of details that go into the making of a film. It is the sum total of all these things that either makes a great picture or destroys it.'

Selznick wrote the script for *Duel*, based on the novel by Niven Busch. It's about the collision of the Old West – set in Squaw's Head Rock – with the new, pitting wide-open spaces, hot-blooded outlaws and passionate resistance to railroads, civil authority and common decency. Beginning among giant rocks drenched in a blood-red sunset, with the velvet-voiced Orson Welles intoning the searing legend of doomed Pearl Chavez and her demon lover Lewt, *Duel* never strays far from lush romance, spiced with a dash of sadomasochism. Selznick fleshed out his concept with a huge cast including Lionel Barrymore, Walter Huston, Harry Carey, Herbert Marshall, Charles Bickford, and Butterfly McQueen.

Orphaned Pearl comes to live at Spanish Bit Ranch, where frail Laura Belle McCanles (Lillian Gish) tries to make a lady of her, despite her questionable origins and insistent voluptuousness. Pearl, the underdog, is torn between good and evil brothers, the reasonable, forward-looking, repressed Jesse (Joseph Cotton) and the unprincipled, spoilt Lewt, dividing a stormy household ruled by Sen McCanles (Lionel Barrymore). Pearl and Lewt are both victims of impulsive sensuality arising from their isolation.

Duel was a film noir – a genre that regularly had an interest in erotic violence and in vindicating a notorious woman. Pearl's famous ride out to exterminate Lewt anticipates the revenge cycle of Westerns. Fortunately, everyone in the movie seems to believe the story line, which makes for a fun ride in spite of the sadistic scenes and the downright hokiness of the plot.

To direct *Duel in the Sun*, Selznick enlisted King Vidor – one of the few directors with the logistical know-how to handle such a sprawling film. A highly respected Hollywood figure, King Vidor was a superior movie craftsman, who started out making amateur movies in his hometown of Galveston, Texas. At MGM Vidor would direct his greatest films. His rise to super-director status began with *The Big Parade* (1925), starring John Gilbert and Renée Adorée; *La Bohème* (1926), starring John Gilbert and Lillian Gish; and the groundbreaking masterpiece of one ordinary man's life, *The Crowd* (1928) starring James Murray and Eleanor Boardman. He also created *Hallelujah* (1929), the first motion picture by a major studio with an all-black cast, headed by Daniel L Haynes and Nina Mae McKinney.

Vidor believed the movie director has a voice, a powerful and articulate sounding board, and he should use it well. He wrote: 'The story in every man's heart is human progress. I believe that every one of us knows that his major job on earth is to make some contribution, no matter how small, to this inexorable movement of human progress. The march of man as I see it is not from the cradle to the grave. It is instead, from the animal or physical to the spiritual.'

Yet, Vidor was no moralist when it came to the opposite sex. So it is unlikely the movie's erotic theme bothered him. Leatrice Gilbert Fountain, daughter of actor John Gilbert, was a starlet in Hollywood and had the opportunity to observe Vidor in action: 'He was a talented filmmaker, but he went through women like Kleenex . . . He used them, was ruthless and went on to the next.'

Going to work for Selznick, Vidor thought he was prepared for anything. As he recounts in his autobiography *A Tree is a Tree* (1953) at one time he lived across the street from the producer and he had ample opportunity to observe Selznick's quirks. 'At first I used to be awakened in the middle of the night by the arrival of machine guns and other odd sounds,' remembered Vidor. 'It seems that Mr Selznick had a private projection room in his house and he often ran films at the hour he was known to have started many other projects – midnight. Two or three full-length pictures would carry him well into the early morning hours. Selznick does everything at unconventional hours. He breakfasts at lunchtime or later; he sleeps when others are working; he works while they sleep – a sort of one-man revolution against conformity.'

Selznick was a 'big thought' person who didn't waste time on penny-pinching. If he wanted an actor, nothing would stop him until he had the performer under contract. The part Walter Huston played was scheduled for four days. Huston's minimum salary for a picture at the time was $40,000 and his agent refused to make any concessions because of the brevity of the engagement. Selznick agreed to the sum but made certain that he could spread the work over ten weeks if he wanted. When Walter Huston finished in *Duel in the Sun*, Selznick had used up his ten weeks and was paying him overtime salary because the engagement had run over the specified time called for in the contract.

As the Sin Killer in *Duel in the Sun*, Huston spouts some delicious lines, such as: 'Pearl, you're curved in the flesh of temptation. Resistance is gonna be a darn sight harder for you than for females protected by the shape of sows. Yes siree, Bob. You gotta sweeten yourself with prayer. Pray till you sweat, and you'll save yourself from eternal hell-fire.'

Legendary Lillian Gish proved to be another source of inspiration. (By the time she died, her career spanned films from 1912 to 1987.) Way back in 1927, she told Sidney Sutherland, who interviewed her for *Liberty* magazine: 'You see we are in such a strange business out here. We of the screen are more intimately known to the public than any other men or women who ever lived. More people see our faces in one night than saw Napoleon in all his 52 years. We excite the emotions of our audiences; we incite their sympathy or dislike or laughter every evening; they know us by our given names or our surnames or our nicknames. Anything that happens to us is of obvious interest.'

Before shooting started for *Duel*, Greg was told: 'You'll have to jump over a horse's rear end and land in the saddle while it's in full gallop.' Not a small challenge for a man with a bad back. Greg signed on at a riding stable and trained for three solid weeks. He also mastered rope tricks and wore cowboy costumes from dawn until dusk to get used to the feel of Levi's, a close hugging shirt, and high, cowpoke heels.

Dice, a flashy black and white pinto colt spotted at a rodeo by a talent scout, was selected to carry Greg. The horse was known for its extraordinary ability to 'track' exactly in its own tracks. This is hard for a horse to do but very important to the filmmaker who must set his cameras and lights perfectly. When Dice was working on a scene, the trainer would walk him along the path that he was to follow. Once they were ready to film, Dice was turned loose and cued for the speed they wanted. Greg and Dice proved adept enough for the actor to ride his mount into a nightclub and rear it over the heads of the diners.

Shooting began on 1 March 1945 at a location near Tucson. Almost immediately, Selznick's over-active imagination and lack of discipline got the better of him. Preliminary sketches of ranch houses and streets were set aside and new ones were ordered. Episodes were added; beginnings and ends of scenes were changed; and previous estimates for cattle, cowboys, and cavalry had to be revised accordingly. Experts were called in as consultants on Western folklore, dancing and customs. Everything that had ever happened west of the Rocky Mountains was considered for the script.

Meanwhile, Selznick's obsession with Jones was building to the point where he was driving everyone crazy. Morning, noon and night, he was present, redirecting the actors, the cameras, and even the lighting. There were strict orders on the set that not a single scene was to be photographed, and not even a single angle of a single scene, until he had been consulted on the lighting, the setup, and the actors. By his own admission, 'ninety-nine times out of a hundred' he felt something had to be changed.

As filming progressed, Selznick's behavior kept Jones in a state of mild hysteria. She had to get up every morning at 6 a.m. to apply Indian make-up, which also took a couple of hours at night to get off, so that in effect she was working 15-hour days for the better part of a year. This ongoing tension made her extremely enervated. She clawed, screamed and hit Greg as she performed at the extreme of her emotional range. Claimed Ginger Rogers: 'She chewed him up and ate him for breakfast.' Still, it was Jones's smoldering intensity that somehow goaded the laconic Greg to come alive as the hell-raising Lewt.

Charles Bickford who was cast as Sam Pierce, a gentle straw boss who is in love with Pearl, also kept Greg on his toes.

'I had to draw on Charlie Bickford – and shoot him dead. There was just one small problem . . . he was a faster draw.'

'Every time we shot the scene, Charlie plugged me first. The director kept pleading with me to draw a little faster. "I'm drawing as fast as I can," I told him. So he turned to Charlie and instructed him to let me beat him to the draw.'

' "But," Charlie growled, "It wouldn't look right – let Peck go and practice." '

'So we had to shoot the scene nine times before I outdrew him and he fell over "dead." After the ninth take, the director shouted, "Print that" – and I could hear the relief in his voice.'

Jones was desperately unhappy and almost certainly feeling guilty over the breakup of her marriage to actor Robert Walker. The two had met at the American Academy of Dramatic Arts. In love and excited about their career, they married in 1939 and together headed for Hollywood, where Jones began her screen career that same year playing leads in minor action films. She attracted the attention of David O Selznick who signed her to a long-term contract and groomed her for stardom. Robert Walker staged a modest ascent as the boy-next-door type of leading man with an ingratiating smile in such productions as *See Here Private Hargrove* (1944) and *The Clock* (1945). Selznick's determination to possess Jones broke up her marriage and exacerbated Walker's deeply rooted mental problems.

Partly because the script was being rewritten on a daily basis by Selznick and partly because the censors were eager to see it, people from the Breen office (the production code administration) had to be on the set. Selznick was continually at loggerheads with them, causing a slowdown in production. Their script concerns included costuming (too much exposure of breasts), kissing, positioning (get Pearl off the bed), and incest. The dialogue also distressed the censors. Orders came back to omit lines such as 'I get that kind of service from my studs' and 'I want to lie where you are softest.' Much of Walter Huston's praying as the Sin Killer was cut after protests against his parody of prayer. Jennifer Jones had taken dancing lessons and performed a sexy dance by the sump, but the censors insisted it be cut. Editors were hired to remove the sump dance from over 300 plates – and have every outtake burned. As Greg recalls, the film was certainly tame by today's standards: 'We'd imply that hanky-panky was going on, but we didn't show it.'

In the midst of production, a strike was called at the studio. As a result of this dispute, Selznick suspended work on *Duel in the Sun*. So Greg traveled to Florida and went to work on *The Yearling*, making all its exterior shots. Among a cast of illustrious players – Lionel Barrymore, Lillian Gish, Joseph Cotton, Walter Huston – Greg was the only one to keep on working. As soon as the strike was over, Greg jumped back into *Duel*.

In the bloody climax of the film, outlaw Lewt is trying to make his getaway to Mexico when he is engaged in a gory gun duel with the vengeful Pearl. She then crawls to him up a jagged cliff to be reunited with her lover for one final embrace before their deaths – 'one of those chunks of theatrics', the *New York Times* said, 'that ranks with Liza crossing the ice.'

Their final moments, among those red rocks, provide as orgiastic a finale as you could ask for in a 1940s film. Still, Selznick clamored for sexier orchestration. 'That's not fucking music,' he yelled at Dimitri Tiomkin who wrote the score. Angered, Tiomkin shot back: 'Mr Selznick. You fuck your way and I'll fuck mine. That's fucking music!'

King Vidor, concerned with Jones's safety, wanted to protect her body in these final scenes with insulated padding, but Selznick would have none of it. Jennifer would be inhibited, he said. So Vidor shot the scene as it was.

The result was that by the time the sequence was finally completed to Selznick's satisfaction, Jones's arms and stomach were covered with bloodied bruises; and Selznick was beaming at having secured such magnificent footage. Everybody thought it odd, but it wasn't the only such instance. Selznick drove Jones to excesses of 'primitive passion,' in the words of the film's foreword, as if a man possessed. Vidor even swore that during some of the heated love scenes between Jones and Greg, he could hear Selznick panting in the background.

Annoyed with Selznick's relentless intrusions, Vidor controlled himself until 10 August 1945, when he was busy trying to direct the shoot-out between Pearl and Lewt. Selznick, judging the latest of many takes to be insufficiently dramatic, took the liberty of dashing stage blood over the actors. 'You can take this picture and shove it up your ass,' Vidor told him. It happened that the desert road stretched 8 miles westward without a bend. The whole *Duel* company, including the perspiring Selznick and the blood-spattered Jones, watched in silence as Vidor's black limousine sped toward the horizon, growing smaller and smaller until it disappeared into a distant row of hills. 'Well, that's all for today,' said Selznick.

He simply replaced Vidor with William Dieterle (Vidor automatically got the screen credit) and finished the film, months behind schedule and more than $1 million over budget. It cost a record of $4,575,000 to make.

When the picture was previewed, Vidor saw that the episode in which Greg blew up a freight train, killing the engineer, was distasteful to the audience, destroying what little sympathy they had for the character. He decided to make one last plea.

He found Selznick shaving himself in the bathroom. He used every conceivable argument against the scene. Aside from the bad taste, he pointed out that when Lewt sang 'I've been working on the railroad,' as he rode away from the scene of destruction, nothing he could do thereafter would restore him to the good grace of the audience.

Selznick went on shaving. Presently he turned to Vidor and said: 'I want to make Lewt the worst son of a bitch that's ever been seen on a motion picture screen, and I believe the train wreck scene will help me prove my point.'

Greg counted the scene among his favorites. He talked jocosely about out-heeling Satan and out-Laurencing Olivier. Recalling watching the train blow up from a distance, and then riding off singing, he said: 'Well, at that moment I just kind of imitated a cousin of mine (Warren Rannells) who was a beautiful rascal, a black sheep in the family but likeable. He was called Stretch – is no longer with us, but he wouldn't mind me saying that. I'm sure.' And there was never any indication on Greg's part that he worried the public would be repulsed seeing him as the swaggering, feral Lewt. Even years later, recollection of the role brought a smile to his face: 'I'm a murderer, a rapist, a passer of bad checks. And at the end my old pappy, Lionel Barrymore, in a wheelchair, looks after me affectionately and says, "What a boy, what a boy!"'

With characteristic gusto, Selznick set about publicizing *Duel in the Sun*. His ideas were original – sometimes bizarre – and they worked. The scam he devised with Paul MacNamara, his longtime publicity man, to publicize *Duel* was a classic. He obtained lists of names of bartenders in cities and towns all over the country, then hired teams of workers to sit down and write – by hand – thousands of letters, addressing each bartender by his first name:

Hi Charlie,
Well I made it. I'm out here in California finally, and it sure is everything they said it was. The sun shines just about every day. They got palm trees all right, and my sister even has a

swimming pool in her back yard. I'm staying with her. We go down to the beach at a place called Santa Monica just about every Saturday or Sunday for a swim in the Pacific Ocean and sometimes downtown to take in a picture. There's sure a lot of things to see and do here. One of the things I liked best was getting to go out to one of the movie lots and actually see them making a movie. It was called *Duel in the Sun*, with Jennifer Jones. Boy is she an eyeful! It's a Western, but not like any Western you ever saw. It's got a surprise ending. They told me what it was, but said I shouldn't tell, so I won't – but it's sure going to be one of the best pictures of all times.

Well Charlie, I got to go now. Say hi to all the gang there for me will you? Hope to see you soon.

Your old buddy, Joe

Naturally, the bartender would show this letter to the regulars at the bar, and they would try to decide who 'Joe' was.

No slouch, Paul MacNamara contributed schemes of his own. He called Walter Winchell, a columnist for the *New York Times*, and persuaded him to run this item: 'Paul MacNamara at Hollywood Selznick Studios has been given $1 million for promotion ideas of his new picture, *Duel in the Sun*. Anybody with an idea call MacNamara. Don't call me.'

MacNamara was in heaven: the phones rang off the wall. He paid $1 for ideas that would reach 1,000 people and $10 if it reached 100,000. About 10,000 ideas were submitted, and 100 were purchased; maximum money, $1,000; minimum result, public furore.

Another of his ideas was to release 5,000 weather balloons announcing the film, one of which contained the number of the winning horse in the Kentucky Derby. The winning balloon was recovered from the top of a high-tension wire in Ohio with MacNamara and Lloyd's of London holding their breath.

By January 1946, ads were a daily fixture in the trade papers. Five million book versions of the movie were distributed along with T-shirts, light bulbs, lollipops, sunflower seeds, and 'Sun' stickers. Tie-ins were made with the circus and with rum drinks called the 'Sun cocktail.'

Life magazine called these gambits the 'most expensive and flamboyant publicity campaign ever generated in Hollywood.' The cover for the sheet music of 'Got to Get Me Somebody to Love' showed Greg and Jones lying in the hay, with him laughing and her teasing him with a flower.

Marathon editing sessions got the film out for its 30 December premiere at the Egyptian Theater in Los Angeles, just in time to qualify for the Oscars. Jennifer's ex-husband Robert Walker and his longtime pal Jim Hennigan went to see *Duel in the Sun* at the Egyptian. Walker was stunned by what he saw. Sickened. After leaving the theater, the two men went up the street to Musso and Frank's restaurant, but Walker couldn't eat a thing. Hennigan recalled him saying bitterly, 'That bastard, that goddamn bastard.' Then Walker clutched his hands to his head and let out a piercing shriek: '*David Selznick!*' Hennigan concluded: 'I think that eventually he'd have been able to accept Jennifer's leaving him for another man – a handsome man, say, like Gregory Peck – because of his own deep-rooted inferiority about his physical appearance, but what he couldn't accept was that a girl he had worshiped, the mother of his children, could have left him solely to gratify her own blind ambition.' Certainly Selznick's drive to possess Jennifer Jones contributed to the deterioration of Robert Walker's already poor state of mind that would lead eventually to his sudden death from drugs and alcohol in 1952.

Los Angeles saw the 138-minute *Duel in the Sun* and word spread. The picture would not open in the rest of the country until the spring of 1947. Greg was on hand at the Birmingham Hospital in Los Angeles to see 2,000 injured veterans watch the film. The rehabilitation premiere had all the trappings of a Hollywood opening and Greg made the rounds shaking hands.

Hedda Hopper was outraged by the movie. She reared up in the *Los Angeles Times*: '*Duel in the Sun* is sex rampant. Jennifer Jones as Pearl Chavez is no Bernadette. Gregory Peck as Lewt McCanles is no Father Chisholm. But these two are hotter than a gunman's pistol.'

The bishop of Los Angeles forbade Catholics from seeing *Duel*, and it was censored in Memphis and Philadelphia and run out of Hartford.

For Selznick, this was a serious matter. The Roman Catholic Church, through its agency, the National Legion of Decency, dominated the American film censorship scene in the 1930s and 1940s. The National Legion of Decency was formed in 1934 to combat immoral movies. People took a pledge, in church, against bad movies. They pledged not only never to go to any morally objectionable movie, but never even to go to any movie theater that had ever shown a morally objectionable film. The Legion claimed membership of over 11 million Americans – about one moviegoer in 12 – and had the power to bring moguls such as David O Selznick to their knees.

There was also, of course, the volatile notoriety of Selznick and Jones themselves. Playing on her performance in *The Song of Bernadette*, the media had a field day with headlines such as 'From Saint to Sinner in Just Three Years!'

Selznick needn't have worried too much. Often when a parish priest ranted against a movie, it aroused the curiosity of his parishioners sufficiently for them to rush out to see it.

As the tempest over *Duel* mounted, Representative John Rankin (Democrat in Mississippi and a longtime enemy of Hollywood) felt compelled to bring the matter before Congress. He took the floor and read a letter from Lloyd T Binford, head of motion picture censorship in Memphis, Tennessee: 'This production contains all the inequities of the foulest human dross. It is sadism at its deepest level. It is the fleshpots of the Pharaohs, modernized and filled to overflowing. It is a barbaric symphony of passion and hatred, spilling from a blood-tinted screen. It is mental and physical putrefaction.'

Meanwhile, Selznick had formed his own release company, cutting distribution costs by 60 per cent. He also had the idea – novel for the time – of opening the picture in many theaters simultaneously, a way of cleaning up quickly and outflanking bad reviews.

Though many critics panned the film, their reviews are a joy to read as minor masterpieces of sarcastic wit that *Duel*'s publicity campaign had virtually begged for. Here's a selection:

It cannot be said that in putting together his hymn to the West Mr. Selznick has stinted on anything. He has provided actors enough for a dozen movies, horses enough to equip every milk route in the country, and clichés enough to make his film an imposing example of specious vacuity.

When a single movie offers murder, rape, attempted fratricide, train-wrecking, fisticuffs, singing, dancing, drunkenness, religion, war, prostitution, fancy equitation and sacred and profane love, all in 135 minutes, the fact that it has neither taste nor art is not likely to deter the unsqueamish.

Life magazine

Whenever night falls in the course of *Duel in the Sun*, the faces of the gentlemen in the picture turn blue. This is the most interesting aspect of this Technicolor saga of the old days in Texas, which was written, produced, and furiously ballyhooed by David O. Selznick, a man who doesn't believe in hiding his light under anything smaller than the celestial concave. I have no idea whether Mr. Selznick intended the males in his film to take on a Surrealist hue in his nocturnal scenes, but the fact that they do provides a lively contrast between them and the heroine, played by Jennifer Jones, whose fiery complexion might lead you to suspect that the makeup man had been baking her in a kiln for several weeks before the film was shot.

The New Yorker

. . . There are some hot scenes, not counting how that girl wraps herself around every doorway and wall she encounters; and the end, when the dying Pearl claws her way through half an acre of opalescent hills to reach her no-good lover whom she has accurately and repeatedly shot, is very affecting.

Shirley O'Hara, *The New Republic*

. . . if only the dramatics were up to the technical style. But they're not. Nor are the performances, which are strangely uneven – all of them. The best and most consistent is that of Mr. Peck, who makes of the renegade brother a credibly vicious and lawless character . . .

Bosley Crowther, *The New York Times*

The only notable acting is that done by Gregory Peck. As the lecher at Spanish Bit he is eminently convincing. This is a picture that will enrapture many persons, and I don't want to spoil their fun. But don't mistake it for a good movie just because it's a big movie.

Bradford F Swan *The Providence Journal*

The releasing company's campaign, abetted by the censorship publicity, was followed by a crafty use of saturation booking. The film opened simultaneously in 300 theaters, a merchandising milestone for the motion picture industry. With grosses of $11,300,000 *Duel in the Sun* finished third for the year behind *Song of the South* and *The Best Years of Our Lives*.

Jennifer Jones and Lillian Gish earned Oscar nominations for Best Actress, which went to Olivia de Havilland for *To Each His Own* and Best Supporting Actress, which went to Anne Baxter for *The Razor's Edge*. In 1979, King Vidor received his only Oscar, an honorary one presented by Audrey Hepburn.

The bond Greg forged with Selznick during *Spellbound* and *Duel in the Sun* continued for years to come, despite their very different styles and values. Patricia Neal recalled having dinner with Greg, Greta and David Selznick in New York in 1945 when she was starring in her first Broadway play, *Another Part of the Forest*, by Lillian Hellman. 'Mr Peck was gracious and charming and such a perfect gentleman that he convinced me that tales I had heard about Hollywood were false. Mr Selznick proved that everything I heard about Hollywood was true. He got very drunk, told me how much he loved Jennifer Jones, and then tried to get me into bed.' Neal became so livid she almost kicked Selznick down the stairs. (Jones married Selznick in Genoa, Italy, on 13 July 1949.)

Greg, the team player, put up with Selznick's antics and when complimented on his role in *Duel*, he tossed the bouquet to his leading lady. 'Jennifer Jones was one of the main reasons I loved this part. I had never worked with her before, but had admired her work on screen.'

Thirty-eight years after they made the movie together, Greg and Jones were at an Academy Award reception. Jones, radiant in a gold lamé dress, was standing talking to Greg when he noticed a man staring at them. Greg invited him over and introduced him to the actress. The man, a Spanish director, said: 'Forgive me for staring. The first movie I ever saw was *Duel in the Sun*. I flew from Madrid and arrived in the United States today for the first time. On my first visit I win the Academy Award, and now I see that Pearl and Lewt are still together. What a wonderful country the United States is!'

While shooting *Duel in the Sun*, Greg also made *The Yearling* (1946), a Pulitzer Prize winning tale about a lonely boy who adopts and is adopted by an orphaned fawn during the post-Civil War period. The two films were in various stages of production for periods of more than a year each and their overlapping schedules caused Greg to go back and forth between them. Both pictures were complex in construction, requiring extended periods on location, and were plagued with problems.

The Yearling's author, Marjorie Kinnan Rawlings, was just the sort of bohemian character who intrigued Greg. She wrote on old upright typewriters in her sprawling farmhouse – a Royal on the screened porch and an L C Smith & Corona Silent on a night stand in her bedroom. Day and night she pounded away while drinking coffee and liquor, and chain-smoking unfiltered Lucky Strikes. *The Yearling*, as well as her other stories, helped put Florida on the map – and herself as well. Rawlings' home became a popular stopping-off place for literati such as F Scott Fitzgerald and Ernest Hemingway who appreciated the gin swirling in the bathtub and the red roses floating in the toilet bowl. Rawlings had lived through several attempts to turn her book into a movie and she wasn't sure about Peck's fitness for the part. 'You'll like him,' A J Cronin, author of the novel *The Keys of the Kingdom*, assured her: 'He's a nice boy.'

Kids and animals were favorite themes during the 1940s, featured in such films as *Lassie Come Home* (1943), *My Friend Flicka* (1943), *National Velvet* (1944) and *The Red Pony* (1949). Claude Jarman, who played the boy in the movie, was one of the 12,000 children who auditioned for the part.

MGM had taken an assembly line approach to the deer 'character' – they had 24 at various stages of growth – but such forethought could not offset the delays brought about by rain, heat and insects. Nature stalled the shooting while perpetuating the growth of the deer, bears, bobcats, raccoons, foxes and squirrels. It took 72 takes to film a scene featuring the fawn. Not receptive to training, the creature kept disappearing from the shot while the actors delivered their dialogue. Over the two days it took to get the single scene, director Clarence Brown paid more attention to the fawn than he did to the actors. After the film was finished, he said: 'Never again. You have to direct a fawn or a stock of corn to understand my problems.'

A great amount of effort was spent on difficult locations in the Florida Everglades, resulting in much spoiled footage and a later decision to re-shoot on the sound stages at MGM. Acknowledging 'it was the most difficult film to make', Greg added that the pressure and tension were eased by Jane Wyman's 'plucky humor.'

Funny and formidable, Jane Wyman was one of the great stars of the time. She was also a moody person, temperamental, ambitious, restless and seeking. Like Greg, she learned early how to be a survivor, and she cultivated that trait as she made her way to the top. After working up from bit parts at Warner Brothers playing leggy, wise-cracking cuties in low-budget films, she finally got some respect as an actress for *The Lost Weekend* (1945). With the release of *The Yearling* she received an Oscar nomination and, finally, with *Johnny Belinda* (1948), a tender portrayal of a deaf-mute farm girl, she won the Oscar in 1948. As Jane's career peaked with *Johnny Belinda*, her second marriage, to Ronald Reagan, was slipping. When Greg asked her about the divorce, she said: 'I couldn't stand to watch *Kings Row* [1942] one more time.'

The location was wrapped in February 1946 and the rest of the film shot in the luxury of MGM's Culver City studio. About this time, the Pecks were invited to their first formal party – and Greta was galvanized. She had to figure out a way to get casually dressing Greg into a dinner jacket. Finally, in exasperation, she took the tailor down to *The Yearling* set, where she made Greg stand still between scenes for a fitting. The suit turned out fine, but her next challenge was trying to buy him a white collar. 'I finally showed up at the studio with two, one too small and one too large. When I finally got him dressed, wearing the big collar as the lesser of two evils, we were late to the dinner party and Greg said: "See, everybody's too busy to notice what I'm wearing."'

Concurrently, David O Selznick was doing retakes for *Duel in the Sun*, and Greg found himself going from one studio to the other. 'I'd get out of my Southern cracker overalls in my Southern accent and put on a cowboy suit and slide into my Texas drawl. I really enjoyed it, actually. It was frantic and fun.' It was interesting for Greg because each film required him to be completely different in character: solid, decent and kindly for *The Yearling*, and crude and lascivious for *Duel in the Sun*.

After the films finished, the Pecks rented a place at Lake Arrowhead, an hour's drive from Los Angeles, near a place leased by Ronald Reagan and Jane Wyman. Greg took two months off and put on 20 pounds. He recalled: 'It was the first vacation I had since hitting Hollywood and for the initial two weeks I went for it. I did nothing but walk around and I filled out a lot, which I needed, for I was still only 185 pounds for my 6 foot 3. But by the beginning of the third week I began to get restless and by the eighth week I was stir crazy. The truth is I can't stay away from acting. I'm really all ham and I'm never so happy as when facing a camera or an audience.'

The Yearling was released in the winter of 1946 to good reception from critics and moviegoers. On 23 January 1947 it began a long run in New York City at Radio City Music Hall. It earned several Oscar nominations including Greg and Wyman for Best Actor and Best Actress. The *New York Times* praised its vitality, zest and sensitivity. When *Time* criticized the Technicolor as too brilliant, Rawlings wrote them that the 'too blue sky' and 'too bright sand' were made by God and not by MGM. But she admitted to friends that only the superb, sensitive acting of Gregory Peck and Jane Wyman made them acceptable to her as Penny and Ma Baxter, for 'Penny was a little runty man and Ma was as big as a barn.'

In the summer of 1946, when he finished *The Yearling* and *Duel in the Sun*, Greg ventured east to the Cape Playhouse for a brief return to the stage. In part, it was a gesture to express gratitude for the early training he'd received under director Arthur Sircom and also because he wanted to portray Christy Mahon in J M Singe's *Playboy of the Western World*. Greg chose the classic Irish play as a vehicle because he admired the work and he was attracted to the challenge of achieving an Irish brogue. Some of the critics who came to see the play were not convinced he completely conquered the accent, but Greg was undaunted by the bad reviews. 'I stuck my neck out and that's what happened,' he told an interviewer. 'I really care, though. I got what I came for. I wanted to try something I hadn't done before. I did. And I feel better for it and I think I'll go back to Hollywood and do better work because of it . . . I think it's good to do things the hard way once in a while.'

CHAPTER EIGHT

Ungentlemanly Behavior

'You can take all the sincerity in Hollywood, place it in the navel of a fruit fly and still have room enough for three caraway seeds and a producer's heart.'

Fred Allen

In 1946, Greg still owed one more film to Casey Robinson, the screenwriter-producer who brought him to Hollywood in the first place. Greg, the omnivorous reader, suggested they make a movie based on a short story by Ernest Hemingway called 'The Short Happy Life of Francis Macomber.' A bitter tale of big-game hunting and marital infidelity, it portrays a cuckolded and cowardly American on safari who regains his manly courage in time for his wife to shoot him in the back of the head. Robinson liked the idea. Then he asked: 'Who should direct it?'

Greg replied, 'How about Zoltan Korda?'

Intriguing choice. A one-time cavalry officer, Zoltan Korda started working in films as a cameraman, then an editor before becoming a director with London Films, run by his brother Alexander Korda. Stubborn and headstrong about his liberal/socialist ideals, he often clashed with the more successful Alexander who, despite being born in Hungary, was a proud supporter of the British Empire.

Zoltan Korda's name undoubtedly popped into Greg's head because the director had made a number of entertaining, exotic adventure movies with African themes. He directed *Elephant Boy* (1937) (collaborating with Robert Flaherty), *The Four Feathers* (1939) and *Jungle Book* (1942) as well as *Shahara* (1943) filmed with Humphrey Bogart in the deserts of California. Zoli, as he was called, liked India and Africa as much as he liked tales of high adventure. He was also known as a genuinely gifted director who could goad a strong performance out of an undistinguished actor.

Now, Zoli was a tough customer. Mercurial, bitter, suspicious and eccentric, he had earned his place on the Mount Rushmore of difficult directors. For starters, he hated noise, chatter, conversation, fuss, fixed mealtimes, shopping, in-laws and the opinions of women. He was so sensitive to noise, he refused to have celery or toast served at the table. Once in a restaurant, he reached across a table to throttle a young woman who was eating melba toast after he had warned her to stop.

Teaming up with Seymour Bennett, Robinson adapted 'The Short Happy Life of Francis Macomber' into a solid screenplay. What makes the movie work is its nasty story, and Robinson's excellent and correct interpretation of it. The Hemingway mood, macho and misogynist, and misanthropic more than anything else, is caught to such perfection one might almost suspect that he was technical advisor. (He definitely *wasn't* as we shall see.)

In the film, a wealthy couple (Robert Preston, Joan Bennett) arrive in East Africa ostensibly for a safari vacation but it soon becomes apparent that they are ill-matched and resentful of each other's failings. Their safari guide (Peck), attempting to conduct things professionally, becomes an unwilling spectator to their petty arguments and vicious insults. But as the party treks through the jungle in search of game, the true personalities of the warring couple emerge, playing havoc with Greg's sympathies and his growing interest in the beautiful wife.

The story actually centers on Robert Preston as Francis Macomber, a paranoid tycoon and hunter whose courage is in question. Greg as Robert Wilson is hired by Macomber to guard him on a hunt, during which Macomber has to overcome his cowardice to establish his manhood. As the hard-bitten white hunter, Greg provides the romantic interest with Joan Bennett as Margaret Macomber.

The Macomber Affair marked Robert Preston's return from the army; his best films, including his stunning success in *The Music Man* (1962), lay ahead. He was known as a sturdy, capable performer who always seemed to end up in the second lead position.

Unlike Greg, he was neither wildly in demand in Hollywood nor hamstrung by contract obligations. So, like Greg, he was free to mix making movies with playing on Broadway. Growing his talent in front of a live audience paid off big for Preston; he came into his own as Harold Hill in *The Music Man*. As the gifted con artist who sells the gullible residents of River City on the virtues of a student band, he was a smash hit in both the stage and screen versions.

On the other hand, lovely Joan Bennett didn't give a fig about developing her talent. A divorced single mother when she started out, she acted in movies to pay the bills. Appearing with such stars as Ronald Coleman and Spencer Tracy in the 1930s, she was known as an undeniably beautiful but frequently vapid leading lady who was blossoming into a more interesting actress. She made her finest films in the 1940s with director Fritz Lang, *Man Hunt* (1941), *Woman in the Window* (1944) and *Scarlet Street* (1945), becoming the queen of femmes fatales. *The Macomber Affair* enhanced her reputation as an actress of note. Unfortunately, in December 1951 producer Walter Wanger (by then her husband of 11 years) shot her agent in a jealous rage; the resulting scandal virtually ended Bennett's film career. Looking back, she said: 'I don't think much of the films I made, but being a movie star was something I liked very much.'

As shooting got underway, Greg and Zoltan Korda developed a good rapport. Greg remembered: 'He could be bad-tempered but not to me; he liked me and I liked him. He was one of my favorite directors.'

The principal target of Korda's ferocious anger was the film's co-producer, Benedict Bogeaus, a flashy Chicago real estate dealer who was trying his hand in the movies. According to Greg, Bogeaus bedecked himself in gold jewelry and expensively tailored suits and was 'always moving in a cloud of cologne.'

At this point, everybody knew 'The Short Happy Life of Francis Macomber' was too long a title to fit on a movie marquee. So, what would make a catchy, shorter one? Since the film crew had a buffalo under construction made of rubber and hair, looking very lifelike and costing $30,000, novelist Graham Greene suggested that they call the film 'The Rubba Buffalo'.

Then Benedict Bogeaus had a brainwave. One morning, he burst on the set calling: 'Zoli, Zoli, I've found it. Get this – Congo!'

According to biographer Michael Freedland a deathly silence descended on the company, as the director reached into his back pocket, pulled out a switch knife, clicked a button and jabbed the blade against Bogeaus's rib cage. As he began twisting it, he sneered at the producer: 'Stupid son of a bitch. You come on my sound stage again and I'll cut out your liver!'

Location shooting is rife with temptations for actors – and *The Macomber Affair* was no exception. Much of the praised visual realism of the film came from background footage shot in Africa and the creation of a credible camp setting on the studio backlot. But Korda insisted they not shoot exterior scenes on the studio grounds, and he took his crew and cast off to the Mexican border in the northern part of Baja. Greg found himself bouncing over rough Mexican terrain while firing his rifle at nothing; the attacking beast would be matted in during the editing. When shooting ended for the day, Greg was faced with boredom and missing Jonathan, as well as Greta who was pregnant again. The nights got mighty lonely.

Greg recalled, 'We were there for about six weeks, 80 men, only two women – Joan Bennett and the hairdresser. We were all going kinda stir crazy.'

Every evening on location Bennett went to bed at 8.30, as did her hairdresser, who shared the bungalow. The men, said Greg, had 'one big stag party every night. Zoltan Korda sensibly avoided these parties we had – he went to bed at 10. Sometimes some of the crew drove 80 miles to Tijuana to take advantage of whores and bars.' The road to Tijuana was so terrible they called it 'dead man's highway.' The group descended on a scruffy bar and joined the local band in roughhousing, drinking tequila and playing poker.

Greg, Preston and the whole crew, minus Zoltan Korda, stayed up till sunrise getting more and more sloshed. Then someone said, 'The cars are leaving for the location in 20 minutes.' The gang stripped, swam, drank as much black coffee as possible and climbed into the cars for the long trek back to the film location. Ever the pro, Greg was sober and ready to shoot at 8.30 a.m.

To please the censors, the final moments of the movie had to be changed. For five-sixths of the action, the story and dialogue was pure Hemingway. In Hemingway's story, the hunter and the killer wife simply go their own ways. But the tale of the sexually frustrated wife (Bennett) who shoots her husband (Preston) and gets clear away with it, had to be altered for the censors to make it seem that she got her just deserts.

All this would have been easy enough, if only Hemingway could have been found. At his Cuban hideout, he refused to answer the telephone or to reply to telegrams. Greg recalled: 'We appealed to Hemingway to write the new ending himself. We appealed by letter, by telephone, by telegraph. Nothing! Total silence!'

'Ernest sold his books to the movies,' Mary Hemingway explained, 'then he paid absolutely no attention whatsoever to what they did with them. He made no effort to influence them in any way . . . his theory being that whatever he might try to do it wouldn't be effective anyhow.'

As for Hemingway, he offered this advice to authors. 'Let me tell you about writing for films. You finish your book. Now, you know where the California State line is? Well, you drive right up to that line, take your manuscript and pitch it across. First, let them toss the money over. *Then* you throw it over, pick up the money and get the hell out of there.'

Finally, the studio had no option but to produce its own ending. Bennett goes to jail, but the audience knows that somewhere in a Nairobi white hunter's bar, Greg will be waiting for her.

The studio's advertising department dreamed up tantalizing ads for the film: 'Gregory Peck makes that Hemingway kind of love to Joan Bennett! . . . After the biggest game of all – a woman! On the hunt he took two things as they came – the charge of a snarling lion – the fury of a fear-crazed coward – the lips of a love-crazed woman – cruelty and yearning – of such things was their love made.'

The ending irritated many reviewers. A typical reaction came from *Herald Tribune*'s Otis Guernsey Jr, who wrote, '. . . the whole thing ends up in the air, a model of motives and excuses.' However, the film pleased literary-minded critics who then and now regarded it as the best adaptation of Hemingway's work.

After *The Macomber Affair*, Greg took a breather and helped Greta prepare for the arrival of a new baby. Having made so many dry runs when Jonathan was expected, Greg knew the 15 miles from their Coldwater Canyon home to the hospital by heart. About 4 a.m., when Greta went into labor, he handled the chauffeuring task with aplomb. He recalled: 'I took the wheel, calm and collected, which comes from being an old hand at that sort of thing.'

Sailing into the waiting room with an air of authority, he found about eight other expectant fathers. He recalled they were 'a collection of sad sacks . . . Collars askew, whiskers on their chins, knee-deep in old cigarette butts – some of them had been there all night. I couldn't help feel superior when, after just one long hour, the nurse called out my name and said, "It's a boy!" Darned if I didn't feel those other fellows had something to learn about efficiency.'

Stephen Joseph Peck weighed in at 7 pounds 6 ounces. Greg brought a large camera complete with lights and other equipment for photographing the baby and Greta. Because of regulations at the time, he could only photograph Stephen through the glass window of the hospital's nursery.

Greta relished the pampering. 'I tried to think it was because I was such a pleasant patient that the nurses liked to do things for me. But I couldn't help noticing that the extra attention always began just a few minutes before visiting hours.'

Good fortune blew Greg's way when Darryl Zanuck asked him to star in *Gentleman's Agreement*, a film about a magazine writer who poses as a Jew in order to experience and expose anti-Semitism in America. Screenwriter Arthur Laurents later described *Gentleman's Agreement* as 'the movie that says you better be nice to a Jew because he might turn out to be a gentile.'

Seen in the light of all that has happened since, *Gentleman's Agreement* seems a mild assault on snobbism as practiced against Jews at suburban white-collar clubs. But when it first appeared in 1947, it was hailed as a brave and outspoken denunciation of bigotry in the enclaves of establishment America.

It posed the question: what happens when a successful member of the middle-class community of a fashionable town applies to join a local club that has an unwritten ban against blacks and Jews? Everyone thinks he is WASP (White Anglo-Saxon Protestant), but he turns out to be Jewish. The title of the film was taken from the concept of the unwritten 'gentleman's agreement' that keep religious prejudices alive in every area of life.

Cary Grant refused the role because he contended he was Jewish and he thought he looked Jewish. He maintained: 'The public won't believe my portrayal of a gentile trying to pass himself off as a Jew.' After that, Greg's agent, George Chasin, told him it would be too risky. 'This is going to hang around your neck,' Chasin said. 'People are going to think you're a Jew for the rest of your career.' Greg rejected this advice because he was impressed with the quality of the script and he felt it was the right thing to do. 'I know it's good to get the subject out in the open,' he contended. 'Entertainment is all right, but entertainment with an idea behind it is much more important. It's time the industry took a stand on a lot of things; instead of hanging on the tail of public opinion, we should be leading it.'

Darryl Zanuck harbored a burning desire to make a breakthrough film. In the case of a movie about anti-Semitism, he had a personal reason to hand over $75,000 for the rights to Laura Z Hobson's best-selling novel on which the film was based. Although one of the few movie moguls who was *not* Jewish (insiders referred to Fox as the goy studio), he had an experience as a young man starting out in Hollywood in which he was the target of just the kind of anti-Semitism portrayed in the novel.

When one works in the film industry, assumptions are made. How could Zanuck be in the same business as Zukor, Mayer, Cohn and Warner and not be Jewish? Yet, he clearly wasn't. He was born in Nebraska, on the plains, a second-generation middle-class American. It was a white, Episcopalian-Methodist upbringing. Still, when he applied for membership to the exclusive Los Angeles Athletic Club, he was turned down. He learned from an inside source the reason: no Jews. Ignoring the bigoted rules of the club, he persisted and obtained membership. But the incident of his initial rejection and the outrage he felt at the time were never forgotten. Zanuck stashed it away in his fertile brain, and later on, when he had more power, when the climate was more suitable, he used it.

Now, one would think in a town built by Jews – junkmen, cobblers, pelt traders and glove salesmen – who had fled the shtetls, the ghettos where Jews were confined in Eastern Europe, in search of something better, that prejudice would not be tolerated. Not so. One day Zanuck was confronted by a group of powerful Hollywood Jews – Sam Goldwyn among them – who pressured him not to make the film. 'We're doing fine,' they argued. 'Why stir up trouble?'

Their opposition ignored the prejudice around them. For example, no Hollywood star could have a Jewish name. Princeton, Dartmouth and other colleges supported Jewish quotas. On the floor of the House of Representatives, Republican John Rankin called radio commentator Walter Winchell a 'kike.' This attack triggered a standing ovation. The prejudice was then both cruel and pervasive.

Still, the fact remained Zanuck wasn't a Jew and vulnerable to the particular kind of prejudice the studio bosses were coming up against. The studio bosses had to get their films approved by Joseph Breen, a professional Catholic who was the driving force behind the Motion Picture Production Code that censored the content and image of Hollywood films. According to Mick LaSalle, author of *Complicated Women: Sex and Power in Pre-Code Hollywood* (2001), Breen was an anti-Semite, who repeatedly called Jews 'lice' and 'the scum of the earth.' In various letters and memos, Breen referred to Jews as 'a dirty, filthy lot,' 'a foul bunch, crazed with sex . . . and ignorant in all matters having to do with sound morals,' and 'simply a vile bunch of people with no respect for anything but the making of money.'

At the end of the meeting with the Hollywood Jews who sought to advise him, Zanuck told them to mind their own business. He was equally adamant with Catholics who opposed the film because the female lead was divorced, yet romantically involved with the hero.

And if Zanuck was to get away with that, the movie just had to be a box-office success, because he knew that if he failed with this one, his Board of Directors would refuse to give him a second chance with another. He pointed out that *Gentleman's Agreement* represented a double challenge to him: 'the subject on one side and the utter necessity for an exciting lively drama on the other side.'

The tale of intolerance told in *Gentleman's Agreement* is built on a simple premise about living in someone else's skin. It's the story of Phil Green (Peck), a non-Jewish magazine writer who assumes a Jewish identity for six months to gather material, write a series of articles, and better understand discrimination and anti-Semitism. The primary setting is New York City at the end of the Second World War. Green has moved to Manhattan from California, taking a staff job at *Smith's Weekly* magazine. At first he is stumped by the assignment he's given to write a long story on anti-Semitism. Then – flash! – Christian that he is, he'll simply pretend to be Jewish like his best friend Dave Goldman (John Garfield) and see what happens.

At work, only his editor, John Minify (Albert Dekker) knows about the ruse. Although *Smith's* has a decidedly liberal slant, Green quickly discovers an undercurrent of religious discrimination in the office. He is told he's 'too sensitive' or 'too pushy' or 'that way'. Only the rag's spunky women's editor Anne Dettrey (Celeste Holm) treats him like one of the gang. Even Green's secretary, Miss Wales (June Havoc), is overtly anti-Semitic – and she is Jewish.

Worse perhaps is Minify's niece Kathy (Dorothy McGuire). Green falls for her immediately and they get engaged. Turns out Kathy suggested the anti-Semitism series to Minify. Yet she owns a comfy weekend cottage on her sister's (Jane Wyatt) large property in Darien, Connecticut – and respects the 'Gentleman's Agreement' that keeps Jews out. She is a moral waffler.

With his characteristic efficiency, Zanuck set about assembling the *Gentleman's Agreement* team. He chose Method-driven Elia Kazan to direct and Moss Hart, one of America's top playwrights, to do the screenplay. Hart wrote his first play as a teenage office boy working for producer/manager Augustus Pitou. His big break came when he collaborated with George S Kaufman on the hit comedy *Once in a Lifetime*. However, Hart's screenplay for

Gentleman's Agreement does not show him at the top of his game; the dialogue sounds as if it were written for the stage and the message about anti-Semitism is delivered in a too self-righteous fashion.

The two other leading stars in the movie – Dorothy McGuire and John Garfield – quickly became good friends of Greg as the production got underway. McGuire arrived in Hollywood from Broadway and stayed on to play vulnerable, intelligent and steadfast women. John Garfield's star rose during the Depression era movies. There was an attractive roughness about his persona combined with a social conscience that matched those difficult times. Celeste Holm was a talented actress from stage on her way to becoming a major dramatic film star and a superb comedian.

Elia Kazan – known as Gadge – began the film with a bias against Greg. And working on the movie didn't change his opinion. He was disappointed with the casting of Greg, seeing him as the quintessential WASP (White Anglo-Saxon Protestant). And then when they began to work together, he was sorry to realize that even with his Sanford Meisner training, Greg couldn't go deep enough. As a result, concluded Kazan, the film didn't have 'the intimate experience of someone who has been through the bitter and humiliating experience.'

Greg tried to get in Kazan's good graces at the time, and, since then, he always spoke well of him. 'Not only does he rehearse more than most directors,' said Greg, 'but we'd get together in his trailer to break down and analyze the script ahead of time, just like in the theater. And the man is fairly loaded with ideas . . .'. Yet, when Kazan tried to get him to punch the wall in frustration *à la* Brando or Newman, Peck just couldn't do it. They never worked together after *Gentleman's Agreement*.

Kazan preferred working with John Garfield who was cast as an explicitly Jewish character for the first time in his career. Garfield played Green's childhood friend, Dave Goldman, who arrives to enlighten the journalist's journey into the heart of anti-Semitism.

Born Jacob Julies Garfinkle, John Garfield changed his name when he signed a contract with Warner Brothers. He took a supporting role in *Gentleman's Agreement* because he believed so strongly in the film's purpose – to expose anti-Semitism. 'He had a smoldering, somber, troubled, street-guy kind of presence that was incredibly attractive,' said actress Lee Grant.

After the picture was released, Kazan concluded that Garfield was 'experientially right for his role.' Of the actors involved in the film, he thought him 'the best of the lot . . . with a maturity he hadn't shown before. When he finally appeared on the screen, halfway through the action, it was a relief.'

Dean Stockwell – who specialized in 'sensitive child' roles – gave a winning performance as Greg's young son. Yet he has few happy memories of making the film. To evoke tears from Stockwell for a crying scene, Kazan urged him to concentrate on a puppy dying. 'I didn't want to think of dead puppies, for Christ's sake,' said Stockwell. 'And I got the idea that Gregory Peck didn't like working with a kid. You know that old axiom in Hollywood, "avoid working with kids or dogs." For that reason I didn't feel much warmth from him.'

Scenes for the movie were shot on location in Darien, Connecticut. It had been a sought-after residential community since the turn-of-the-century. The town was only 38 miles east of Manhattan, about an hour by train from midtown. A suburban paradise, it boasted rolling hills, substantial houses and exclusive clubs – beach clubs, hunt clubs, yacht clubs, tennis clubs and golf clubs.

In Darien, 'gentleman's agreements' between landowners excluding Jews from buying property were securely in place until well into the 1950s. But the enclave welcomed the film stars, and the *Darien Review* reported:

Hollywood came to Darien on Monday when the tall, handsome Gregory Peck and slender and pretty Dorothy McGuire enacted a scene at the Darien railroad station. Elia Kazan, who directed *Boomerang* (1927), which was filmed in Stamford recently, was in charge of the proceedings. The scene is a minor one for the film *Gentleman's Agreement*, a story of real estate dealings.

In March 1986, *New England Monthly* published an article titled 'The Town as Private Club' by Richard Todd who had grown up in Darien. He wrote: 'It would be an error to think of Darien solely in terms of its clubs, yet club life symbolizes the town, and indeed the town itself is a kind of club. Success may be a journey, but for many, Darien is a destination. It is a place that like a club seems to have honorific powers; it affirms one's sense of self.'

He found that while the practice of 'gentleman's agreement' had died out, there were few Jewish residents. The town had 12 churches but no temples. 'This is a game reserve for the white and the wealthy,' Diana Barnard, managing editor of the *Darien News-Review*, told Todd. 'Thank God for *Gentleman's Agreement* and all the filmmakers and writers and artists who have taken a stand against intolerance.'

Journalist Kinny Littlefield grew up in Darien and felt she had lived 'gentleman's agreement' her whole young life: 'With "Gentleman's Agreement", my hometown made the movies – in a sad and embarrassing way.'

'Of course,' said Kinny Littlefield, 'if you were casting a preachy sort you couldn't do better than Gregory Peck . . . Moody, bitchy, given to smug self-righteousness – Peck makes the perfect neurotic-compulsive journalist, just as he made the perfect obsessive-compulsive Captain Ahab in *Moby Dick*.'

Cautious about public reaction, Fox kept the lid on the film with only the barest description of its content: 'Now it comes to the screen with nothing left unsaid, with no emotion unstirred.' On the other hand, a Fox press release provides the link between bigotry in America and the Jewish experience at the hands of the Nazis: 'Phil finds prejudice cropping up fast. Flicks here and flicks there are the insult constantly on the nerves. No yellow arm bands, no marked park benches, no Gestapo, no torture chambers – just a flicks here and flicks there.'

The studio needn't have worried. When *Gentleman's Agreement* was eventually shown, it became not only one of the big box-office hits of the year, but proved to be a prestige success as well, and the Academy of Motion Picture Arts and Sciences members recognized that fact by awarding it several Oscars. Greg and Dorothy McGuire both lost in the Best Actor and Best Actress category but there were three wins – Best Picture, Best Supporting Actress (Celeste Holm) and best director (Elia Kazan). (Holm refused to remain at the same salary at Fox since her option called for a raise. Zanuck broke the contract. Then, according to Holm, 'he called every other studio and said he had fired me because I was too difficult to work with.') The *Hollywood Reporter* called *Gentleman's Agreement* 'the most spellbinding story ever put on celluloid.'

Surprisingly, years later Kazan had trouble remembering it: '[In] Hollywood, it was a producer's game. I've been wondering why the store of my memory on *Gentleman's Agreement* is so bare. Although Darryl carried off the Oscar for best picture and I for direction, there is very little I have to say about how it was made. A model of big-studio production, it was perfect of its kind, which means it had no face, only *faces*, those in a group photograph: the faces of Darryl Zanuck and Twentieth Century Fox's department heads. The production was perfectly managed by Zanuck, with an energy that never relaxed and a determination that on every shooting day he'd get the best out of everyone working.'

If the principal character had been played by someone less clean-cut and Caucasian than Greg, reasoned Kazan, the problem presented by the movie might have been more honestly and frankly confronted. He found Greg 'sober, worthy, no way mysterious, completely straight, no surprises.'

Gentleman's Agreement became a landmark film about the evils of anti-Semitism. It helped establish Greg in the public mind as a stand-up person who was not afraid to fight for his beliefs. In later years, the actor recalled the movie with pride and conviction. 'We felt we were brave pioneers exploring anti-Semitism in the United States – today, it seems a little dated.'

According to people close to Greg, the prejudice exposed by the film took a personal tone. Many 'exclusive' clubs in the Los Angeles area, clubs that did not admit Jews, blackballed him because they felt so threatened by the film. For many years they would not permit Greg to be invited to functions at their facilities. In the 1960s and afterwards these same clubs did extend invitations to Greg, but he returned the favors of the late 1940s and 1950s and declined to attend.

Ironically, in 1947 when Greg was making *Gentleman's Agreement*, he also chose to invest his talents and energy in a playhouse based in his birthplace, La Jolla – a town that actively excluded Jews. La Jolla's anti-Semitism in housing goes back to the 1920s when Greg was growing up there. Isabelle Baresch, a resident of La Jolla since 1910, said restrictive covenants became obvious when the town experienced a miniature land boom in the 1920s and developers began construction of La Jolla Shores in 1926. That development restricted ownership to people of Caucasian blood.

Prior to 1948 when the Supreme Court made restrictive racial covenants illegal, the covenants were common in the village. They ruled out 'any persons whose blood is not entirely that of the Caucasian race . . . either as owner, lessee, licensee, tenant or in any other capacity than that of servant or employee.'

After 1948, in the years when the La Jolla Playhouse flourished, new tactics were created to enforce anti-Semitism. A 'gentleman's agreement' was put in place. In an article in *Los Angeles Times West Magazine*, Roger Rapoport described the green card system used by local realtors. 'If the realtor felt a prospective buyer was undesirable he put "positive" on the slip. If he was desirable he wrote "negative". This slip was passed among realtors. Property owners colluded with the system. If they did not wish to sell to Jews they would leave their porch lights on in the daytime so that real estate agents would know not to show that property to any Jewish clients.'

Alice Craig Greene, a resident of a nearby town, decided to investigate for herself and posed as a prospective buyer who 'preferred restricted property,' implying anti-Semitism on her part. The real estate agents she spoke to were open and reassuring about their discrimination policies. They proudly explained how 'a kind of gentleman's agreement had taken the place of legal restrictions.' She called ten real estate agents. They referred to the objects of their discrimination as people who were 'unpleasant in that line,' the 'Semitic race,' 'this menace,' or simply 'Them.'

A surviving rumor (denied by Greg) asserted that when La Jolla Playhouse players held cast parties at the La Jolla Beach and

Tennis Club, Jewish cast members were not allowed to attend. For his part, Greg was concerned that his actors would conduct themselves in an upright fashion. He marched into a tailor shop and told the owners: 'If any actor leaves town without paying his bill, let me know.'

Greg had dreams of building a theater overlooking the sea to give film actors like himself the opportunity of performing in front of a live audience. To Greg's way of thinking, the British system was vastly superior. 'Laurence Olivier is making a picture in the daytime, and in the evening he does *Richard III* on the stage and somehow manages to do a big part in *Peer Gynt* – it must be playing in a theater next door. That's wonderful. We should work like that in this country.'

And he wanted to re-establish his connection with the town that had nurtured him in his childhood. So, he conceived the idea of the La Jolla Playhouse. That way, he could grow his acting talent and, at the same time, go home again. With David O Selznick's financing (in providing the funds, he called Greg 'a maniac about the stage'), he joined with Joseph Cotton, Jennifer Jones, Dorothy McGuire and Mel Ferrer to get the Playhouse underway.

Greg felt a sense of urgency about his career. This was his strongest motivation for establishing the Playhouse. Though cast in one hit movie after another, he feared he was losing valuable ground and he was ever mindful of the competition. Each year there were thousands of newcomers, ready to do anything to get a role. When a reporter asked about Broadway, Greg sounded exasperated. 'The stage, yes, when I get through these commitments.' But he knew that wouldn't happen for at least three years.

Greg knew that 'wonderful' and 'excellent' were weak words in a town where everything is spoken of in superlatives. He lamented: 'Hollywood is a vacuum in which criticism doesn't exist. The only way you can get an honest opinion is in front of an audience that pays to see you.' John Barrymore expressed the same sentiment years earlier when he wrote off Filmland as 'the flatulent cave of the winds.' Actors live in a cocoon of praise. They never meet the people who don't like them. Without audience feedback, it was hard for an actor to know if he was any good or not. At the same time, Greg was keenly aware that men whom he looked up to such as Alfred Hitchcock and Elia Kazan didn't consider him an actor of the first rank. Even King Vidor gave him only a backhanded compliment when asked about Greg's performance in *Duel in the Sun*, saying: 'He was better in this than anything else I've seen him do.'

During breaks in the shooting of *Gentleman's Agreement*, Greg discussed the idea for the La Jolla Playhouse with Dorothy McGuire and they got the ball rolling. He knew she also bemoaned the fact that her film contracts did not allow her time to return to Broadway. So they formulated the idea for what would be known as the Actors Company, which would enlist the services of well-known stars in revivals of hit shows, the same format that had been so successful at Santa Barbara's Lobero Theater six years before.

The actors at the La Jolla Playhouse were paid $55 a week plus hotel accommodation and two meals a day. The tone changed somewhat when Jennifer Jones, an Oscar winner for *The Song of Bernadette* and engaged at that time to Selznick, came to do *Serena Blandish*, a play by S N Behrman, from the novel *A Lady of Quality* by Enid Bagnold. She arrived with luxury trailer and butler, chauffeur and maid, plus a wardrobe designer and acting coach – the famous Constance Collier, who also played a major role.

The town's leading hotel, La Valencia, a huge and venerable Spanish-style building, contained suites luxurious enough to satisfy the demands of the cream of California society, as well as movie stars, and its small single rooms were moderately enough priced to solve the featured players' housing problems. A striking gold mosaic-tiled tower atop the hotel had presided over Prospect Street since Greg's childhood when the beachfront homes were just cottages. In the 1930s, stars such as Greta Garbo, Charlie Chaplin and Lillian Gish found the hotel an ideal hideaway. The tower was used as a lookout for enemy planes during the Second World War. The 'Playhouse' itself was the large and comfortable high school auditorium.

With his tunnel vision, Greg focused on getting the Playhouse underway. He was coming back a success; the small-town boy raised by his grandmother was now being treated with deference. It was a triumph. Drinking at the Whaling Bar at La Valencia, his two small boys playing at the Bath and Tennis Club, he didn't have time, nor, perhaps, the inclination, to put his beloved small town under a harsh lens and look at its ugly legacy of prejudice.

Greg quickly learned that you must be forgiven your triumphs by those who stayed behind. And you must hang on every word said to you lest you appear 'uppity.' And you must ask questions before they are asked of you. 'How many kids do you have?' He would inquire before anybody could bring it up. As long as people talked about themselves to him, they thought he was great and had not changed one bit for the worse.

The Whaling Bar was the social nexus of the early Playhouse years. Greg put in more than his share of late nights at the bar, which constituted one of his all time favorite haunts. Then he'd make the long drive back to Los Angeles, catch a few hours' sleep and report to the set at 6 or 7 a.m. 'Yeah, well, I don't know how the hell we did it,' he reminisced years later. 'We were young. It's the only explanation.'

Greg and Mel Ferrer often drove down to La Jolla together to help with new plays and encourage the actors and crew. On one occasion the two of them were putting on the play *Command Decision* which called for a couple of fliers to walk onstage at the end of the last act, and Greg and Ferrer agreed to do the walk-ons the final night.

Ferrer recalled: 'About halfway down the coast, I asked Greg what we'd do for Air Force uniforms and he said, "Forget it. I already picked up the costumes." We arrived to find the play already in progress. Then we went into a special little dressing room to get into what I thought would be the military uniforms. Instead, Greg got me some outlandish costume and a gorilla suit for himself. You can imagine the surprise of the cast when we walked onstage right on cue, wearing those outfits. Everybody broke up and forgot their lines. And the audience became hysterical.'

Greg functioned as artistic director for the first critical years. He helped choose plays, attended openings and charmed stars into performing at minimum wages. He also acted in three plays during the three years following the Playhouse's opening. When he departed for London in 1951 to film *Captain Horatio Hornblower*, he became less active in the Playhouse. Mel Ferrer and Dorothy McGuire continued it with McGuire's husband, John Swope, taking over management.

Looking back on the rough and tumble early years Greg said: 'It was a lot of fun – and a lot of work. We had only one week to rehearse, so we had to schedule every hour into 20-minute scenes, 40-minute scenes. It was like a railroad schedule. We demanded – no, we couldn't really demand, because they were working for practically nothing – but we fervently requested that everybody learn their lines before they got there. We didn't have time for people to walk around with a book in their hand.'

In 1947 Greg and Greta bought their dream house. It was located at 1700 San Remo Drive in the high reaches of the Pacific Palisades. A choice area for film people, the community offered steep bluffs and dramatic views of the sea. Sticking out into a canyon, their house provided a view of 20 miles in all directions. Innovative for its time, it was designed in the late 1930s by Clifford May, who virtually invented modern ranch style – justified by low, long, one-story houses with sliding glass doors, and concrete slab floors leading directly on to the hard, packed earth to enable people to pass from interior to exterior without stepping down. It was a concept architects called 'ground contact,' and it traced its roots to the Spanish houses in the nineteenth century and old California missions. A drive circled up to the front door, a Clifford May touch that became an instant status symbol when first used.

The house was designed for comfort, with great glass windows open to breathtaking views. Drawing on her Finnish background, Greta took the lead, furnishing it comfortably with blond Scandinavian pieces with splashes of color in the draperies, rugs and paintings. It was an open, frank and sensible house, much like Greta's nature.

When home, Greg gravitated to the den, his preferred retreat. It reflected his personal taste. An upright piano stood in one corner; a glass-top bar upholstered in green leather with matching stools stood in another. (Greg and Greta appeared in *Life* posing for a Pabst Blue Ribbon beer advert at this bar.) The room also contained a leather-covered sofa, rows of bookcases (over 500 volumes on

Lincoln) and a record player with a stack of vinyl next to it – lots of Burl Ives. (Greg's favorite record was Harry the Hipster playing a barrelhouse piano and singing 'Fry Me A Cookie in a Can of Lard.') Some evenings, he hosted poker games in his lair. It was a place for casual entertaining and for family evenings with dogs and kids. Other times, the den served as his private space in which he isolated himself and stretched his mind. Many of his intellectual interests were beyond the ken of his wife.

As he became more sophisticated, Greg was learning to pull up the drawbridge and be more selective about who got close to him. When he first arrived in Hollywood, he and Greta threw Sunday open houses – 'Y'all come!' kind of affairs. Now he was able to make excuses and extricate himself from people who weren't particularly talented or interesting. He'd talk to someone for a few minutes and then send them on their way. He also relied more heavily on his secretary to act as a shield. He considered it 'part of the process of growing up in Hollywood.' Greta remained spontaneous and open. While Greg liked to present himself as something of a handyman around the house, Greta blithely told a reporter: 'He tries, but that's about all. Someone else has to finish the job.'

Despite all the work pressure and the temptations of women and drink, he knew he liked the film colony. He reflected: 'Hollywood has given me essential values more than anything else about living, about my work, my family and the relative importance of things. It's taught me the value of simplicity, of what makes for lasting happiness. This is a place that can throw you or make you. I have long ago stopped believing my own publicity. And the town is still molding me.'

With his bad sacroiliac, Greg appreciated his new home's big swimming pool, rimmed by high glass walls to keep out the winds. He still rode horseback to keep trim – but he was clearly tempting fate. Back in 1946 he was out in the San Fernando Valley at the place of a rancher friend when his horse slipped and pinned down one of his long legs. The bone was broken in three places. He laughed it off: 'I'm not the hero type anyway.'

As soon as the Pecks got settled, they held a surprise fourth birthday party for Jonathan. Greta hired a troop of entertainers.

They staged a small-time aquacade in the pool, complete with the hula dancer on a surfboard. 'I couldn't tell who had the best time – the kids or me,' Greg admitted. He was on hand to see that nobody got lost, strayed or stolen, and when the magician's rabbit scurried down into the canyon, he chased it through the cactus while the kids let out a chorus of cries. He came back scratched and bruised, but he had the rabbit.

By one account, Greg was a hit with the kids in the 'hood. Leslie Epstein, author of numerous novels including *King of the Jews* and *San Remo Drive: A Novel of Memory* and director of the Creative Writing Program at Boston University, was a Pacific Palisades neighbor of the Pecks when he was a child. His father and uncle wrote dozens of films together in the late 1930s and 1940s, including *The Man Who Came to Dinner, Arsenic and Old Lace, Strawberry Blonde, Yankee Doodle Dandy* and *Casablanca*. 'We lived at 1341 San Remo Drive,' said Epstein. 'As I remember it, Gregory Peck lived northward a few blocks up on the same street. As kids we would trick or treat in the neighborhood. Our favorite by a long shot was Gregory Peck's house. More often than not the actor would come to the door himself, kind and genial. I remember once he dropped a big gingerbread man into my Ralph's [supermarket] shopping bag.'

Greg had arrived. In the eyes of the world, he had an attractive adoring wife, two healthy children and a beautiful home. He had received three Oscar nominations. Yet, he couldn't stop striving. Another symbol of success – his picture on the cover of *Time* magazine with a profile inside, clarified how far he had come.

On the plus side, *Time* noted the diversity of Greg's roles and his resistance to typecasting. 'During 1947, cinema addicts watched him as a gentle backcountry father in *The Yearling*, as a lady-killing hunter in *The Macomber Affair*, as lascivious Lewt in *Duel in the Sun*, and as a crusading journalist in *Gentleman's Agreement* – performances which established him as an actor of solidarity and range.'

At the same time, the article gave the readers a candid evaluation of Greg's abilities: 'He has shown no signs of that depth of intuition which would suggest that he will ever become a great actor – as

Olivier, for instance, may become. But he seldom fails to turn in a performance that is honorably beyond the line of movie duty. He is diligent, definitely if quietly talented, intelligent about his work; and he has an obvious capacity for study and for growth. Unless he succumbs to boredom, frustration, wealth, or the hideous difficulties of trying to be both a matinée idol and an honest artist, he is certain to become a thoroughly good actor.'

There it was, in a nutshell. If he worked hard, kept his eye on the ball, he could be 'a thoroughly good actor.' Was that enough for Gregory Peck? He was in his early thirties now and at a point in his professional life when he didn't have to break his neck. But his compelling drive wouldn't let him slow down. He recalled: 'I was like a fire horse breaking out of the barn three times a year to make a movie.' Consumed by ambition, he was about to put himself in peril of losing everything.

CHAPTER NINE

Trouble in Paradise

'But for the grace of God . . . '
Gregory Peck, on escaping the blacklist

In the late 1940s and early 1950s, the Red scare – or Communist witch hunt – hit Hollywood and eventually the whole country. It gave rise to a miasma of fear, hysteria and guilt. Director John Huston, who positioned himself at the vanguard in the fight against this tyranny, recalled it as a period of true national shame. 'There was a Communist under every bed,' Huston recalled, 'and everyone seemed eager to drag him out. It was brother against brother, friend against friend. Innocent people were hustled off to jail. Many lost their jobs – even their lives – simply because they believed in and exercised what they knew to be their Constitutional privileges: freedom of speech and political affiliation.'

Though the movie bosses insisted there was no official roster of those in disfavor, in reality the list of names of those to be barred from employment was privately exchanged among the studio heads. But in June 1950 three former FBI agents and a right-wing television producer, Vincent Harnett, published Red Channels, a pamphlet listing the names of 151 writers, directors and performers who they claimed had been members of subversive organizations before the Second World War, but had not so far been blacklisted. The names had been compiled from FBI files in a detailed analysis of the *Daily Worker*, a newspaper published by the American Communist Party.

The House Un-American Activities Committee (HUAC), headed by Thomas Parnell, sent out a rash of subpoenas, addressed to prominent Hollywood executives, actors, producers and directors, calling for them to testify before the Committee. A procession of 'friendly witnesses' appeared first, who willingly shared hearsay and cast aspersions on the characters of their colleagues. Given total immunity, they demonstrated what some considered true patriotism and others regarded as categorical cowardice; they pointed fingers at their peers, their employees, their families and friends, branding them as Communists, and offering 'evidence' of their transgression.

Greg's friend Burl Ives was one of those named but he agreed to appear before the HUAC and named several former friends, including Pete Seeger, as members of the Communist Party. This enabled him to continue his career in Hollywood and he appeared in *Show Boat* (1954), *East of Eden* (1955), *Cat on a Hot Tin Roof* (1955) and (co-produced by Gregory Peck) *The Big Country* (1958).

Of the 41 witnesses, 19 declared their intention to be 'unfriendly' (to refuse to answer questions about their political affiliations). Of the 19, 11 were directly questioned about their membership to the Communist Party. German émigré playwright Bertolt Brecht left the country after his appearance, leaving just ten – the infamous Hollywood Ten.

To counter what they claimed as reckless attacks by the HUAC, a group of Hollywood liberals led by actor Humphrey Bogart, his wife Lauren Bacall, John Huston, William Wyler, Gene Kelly and others, established the Committee for the First Amendment (CFA). The CFA traveled to Washington to lend support to the Hollywood Ten. However, as the 'unfriendly witnesses' began to respond to their inquisitors with much disdain, and often without a solid grounding in historical facts, the Hollywood stars began to look foolish and to appear as tools of the Communists.

Humphrey Bogart wrote a piece for the March 1948 issue of *Photoplay* magazine entitled 'I'm No Communist,' in which he admitted being 'duped.' His trip to Washington, he said, had been 'ill-advised.' John Garfield wrote a similar article called 'I'm a Sucker for the Left.' Edward G Robinson lamented, 'The Reds Made a Sucker Out of Me.'

The most pathetic attempt to ask the HUAC for mercy was made by Larry Parks. Parks, best known for the lead in *The Al Jolson Story* (1946), pleaded with the Committee on his hands and knees. He named, among others, James Cagney, Sam Jaffe, Sterling Hayden, John Garfield, M D Devine, Madeleine Carroll, Gregory Peck, Humphrey Bogart and Edward G Robinson. It turned out that Greg and Bogart were actually speaking *against* Communism in situations Parks recalled. Parks was blacklisted even after his many attempts not to be. Anyone who opposed the hearings was branded a 'Communist sympathizer' and instantly placed on the blacklist.

Subsequently, Hedda Hopper – giddy Hedda, who boasted of ordering 150 hats a year – and Louella Parsons – who proclaimed her Catholicism to the world with a 10-foot high electrically wired statue of the Virgin Mary on her lawn – took up the banner of the 'Red Baiters' and began taking pot shots at directors, actors and writers. Their right-wing patriotism gathered exuberant, dangerous momentum. Hopper especially, counting Joseph McCarthy and J Edgar Hoover among her good friends, carried on so fiercely and with such a specious lack of knowledge or analytical ability that many conservatives, including John Wayne, urged her to shut up. She ignored him.

Because he was such a big star, Greg received a degree of protection against being placed on the blacklist. Yet, the way he conducted himself at the time of the scourge and the manner in which he related to those who were blacklisted says much about his character. He never kowtowed to the red baiters. He stayed loyal to blacklisted friends. Yet he never took a front position at the barricades; his was not one of the braver stances. Most interesting of all, he refused to throw stones. While studio heads such as Darryl Zanuck and Jack Warner behaved like cowards in the name of patriotism, Greg remained loyal to them. And when Elia Kazan, the brilliant director of *A Streetcar Named Desire* (1951) and *Gentleman's Agreement*, turned stool pigeon and handed over the names of colleagues including Lillian Hellman, Dashiell Hammett, Pamela Miller, Morris Kozlowski, Phoebe Brand and Tony Graber, Greg refused to publicly excoriate him. He could separate the director's character from his enormous contributions to the theater and the movies. And he held to that position for the duration of both his and Kazan's careers.

In his autobiography, *A Life* (1988), Elia Kazan sums up his motivation for betraying friends: 'For years I declared myself an ardent liberal and made all the popular declarations of faith, but the truth was I am like most of you, a bourgeois. I go along disarming people, but when it gets to the crunch, I am revealed to be a person interested only in what most artists are interested in, himself.'

The atmosphere was deeply chilling. Greg watched in anguish as the careers of some of his friends were destroyed. The case of John Garfield was particularly poignant. His distinctly leftist views and staunch support of the working class led to him be labeled a Communist sympathizer by the HUAC. He did not cooperate at the official hearings and suddenly found it difficult to get work. Through he returned briefly to the theater, Garfield did not flourish. At the age of 39 he died of coronary thrombosis, a condition that some have attributed to the stress the Committee placed upon him.

One thing which was always more or less evident was that the hearings were not so much about establishing criminal behavior as getting people to renounce their past – and in some cases their friends. For the most part the Committee already knew the names that it demanded the testifiers should reveal. This symbolic ritual, Victor Navasky called 'degradation ceremonies.' Arthur Miller and Lillian Hellman referred to it as 'an inquisition.' Miller added in *Timebends*, his memoir of the period, 'With the tiniest Communist Party in the world, the United States was behaving as though on the verge of bloody revolution.'

A number of Hollywood directors, screenwriters and actors had joined the Communist Party or contributed funds to its activities during the Depression of the 1930s. Greg was a Democrat with strong sympathy for the underdog and he supported many ultra-liberal causes, but he was not Red or even Pink. It was not in his nature to be that radical. Besides, committed political activism would have taken too much time away from his career.

In 1948 Greg was called before the Red-hunting Fact Finding Committee set up by the California Legislature. He was named for his association with several liberal organizations, along with a host of other stars. His strategy was simply to give them a list of every liberal organization to which he had contributed money, with the letterheads of their stationery, and explain that he made the contributions because he thought they were legitimate organizations. He told the Committee: 'I am not now and never have been associated with any Communist organization or supporters of Communism. I am not a Communist, never was a Communist and have no sympathy with Communist activities.'

The Committee accepted his explanation as coming from someone who, in films and in life, appeared to be a straight shooter. And Greg never deviated from this stance. To one concerned fan he wrote, 'I hold no brief for Communists, but I believe in and will defend their right to act independently within the law. I question whether members of the committee are interested in defending our form of government or whether they are attempting to suppress political opinion at odds with their own.'

Fate works its ironies, however. Hollywood had known its most prosperous year ever in 1946. But as the 1940s drew to a close, the industry began eroding from its very foundation. The Hollywood Purge was draining the industry of some of its best writers such as Dalton Trumbo (who wrote the screenplay for Greg's triumphant *Roman Holiday* using a friend as a front), Ring Lardner Jr, Abraham Polonski, Carl Foreman; directors such as Edward Dmytryk; and actors Marsha Hunt, Gale Sondergaard, Betty Garrett and Anne Revere. It was extinguishing new ideas, sapping fresh blood, and discouraging innovative story treatment. The atmosphere was rank with fear, betrayal and stagnation.

The period of the blacklist continues to fascinate because, as critic Harold Clurman said, it was mostly about conscience. 'How people felt about the whole procedure called "naming names" and how they prioritized morality and conscience vs. their jobs.' Though he wasn't at the front of the barricades, Greg proved true blue.

Keeping his career afloat occupied most of Greg's time. When he had been making *Spellbound*, he was given a gift of a leather binder. From then on he used it to contain his personally annotated script of whatever picture he was working on. And he regarded it as his good-luck charm. He needed all the talismans he could get as he embarked on *The Paradine Case* (1947). Just as with *Spellbound*, it was produced by David O Selznick and directed by Alfred Hitchcock. And Hitchcock wasn't happy with the choice of Greg for the lead. For that matter, Hitchcock resented working with Selznick again, due to the producer's manic obsession with Jennifer Jones.

Still, Hitchcock owed Selznick one more picture before the expiration of their contract. Hitchcock had become a major force in the movie industry. The director's notoriety and his ability to independently create successful films of substance signaled, for many, the rise of the director and the decline of the producer. As for Greg, Selznick knew putting him in another Hitchcock picture wasn't ideal, but he gave him the lead anyway to ensure box-office. Hitchcock was bristling at the continued interference from the producer and was already dreaming of the days ahead on his own.

Hitchcock would have preferred Laurence Olivier or Ronald Colman for the role of Anthony Keane. Greg realized he looked too young for the part: after trying out various moustaches to suitably age himself, he settled for graying his temples. 'I don't think that Gregory Peck can play an English lawyer,' Hitchcock complained.

Although Hitchcock certainly loved murder and suspense he hadn't done many courtroom dramas. *The Paradine Case* provided him with such an opportunity. A beautiful woman, Maddalena Anna Paradine, played by the enchanting Alida Valli, stands accused of murdering her wealthy, blind husband. She enlists the aid of renowned lawyer Anthony Keane (Peck). As they prepare her defense, the chemistry between the two begins to heat up. And as his emotions for Mrs Paradine grow stronger, Keane grows more convinced of her innocence. The case is difficult, however, as the judge (Charles Laughton) is no friend of Keane's; the Queen's Prosecutor, played by the excellent Leo G Carroll, is a serious foe; and only an inspired defense will have any chance of clearing Mrs Paradine.

Selznick had high hopes for Alida Valli whom he had only seen in Italian films and had the impression she had a beautiful face and figure. Otherwise, he bought her 'sight unseen.' He envisioned turning her into a star of Ingrid Bergman magnitude. He even decided to omit her first name from the credits to create a mysterious European aura about her. But when Valli arrived in Hollywood, it was apparent she was in need of a rigorous diet, extensive dental work and English lessons.

Another foreign talent in the film was the French actor Louis Jourdan. He was already under contract to Selznick. As the part was originally written, he was not the right choice by far, but Selznick had an engaging way of changing the script to make it fit any of his contract actors. Hence Louis Jourdan made his US debut and became a very successful performer in America from then on.

Due to Selznick's fiddling with the story, *The Paradine* script could never catch up with the shooting schedule. Each day, Selznick would arrive on the set with newly written scenes for the day's shoot. As Greg recalled: 'This, of course, drove Hitchcock to distraction – Selznick was a totally disorganized but essentially lovable man, while Hitchcock, whose manner was not quite to lovable, was totally organized.' The budget was a generous $4 million, with $70,000 of it going towards an exact replication of the Old Bailey courtroom.

To complicate matters, the Breen censorship office was hard at work shaping the movie to its narrow moral boundaries. Mandated: the design of the prison cell must not include a toilet; indelicate and profane words and phrases must be omitted – such as 'Good God!' and 'Good Lord!' and 'Oh Lord!' and 'God knows'; the word 'smut' must be stricken from the dialogue; and the phrase 'disorderly house,' referring to a sloppy home, must be omitted since it might be taken to mean a house of prostitution. 'Finally,' Breen wrote in a long letter, 'in the scene in the bathroom, it would be advisable to omit any showing of Gregory Peck in the bath, even by suggestion, in order to avoid showing a man and a woman in the bathroom at the same time – even if fully clothed.'

'Mr Selznick could be a slave driver!' remembered Ruth Birch who worked on costumes. 'We used to get memos by the thousands of words! The only time I got a short one was once when I made a goof. He sent me a memo simply saying, "Don't let this happen again."'

Before photography was finished, Selznick had dictated more than 400 memos based on his intense daily involvement in the production, from writing the final script to checking costumes to looking at the rushes each morning. Hitchcock's disinterest in *The Paradine Case* was now an open secret, in spite of Selznick's somewhat reckless allotment of a lavish budget.

Hitchcock was always overtly polite to Greg, sometimes taking him to Chasens with actor Charles Laughton. The restaurant invented the famous Hitchcock fish, a filet of sole with a kind of bread crust over it – something from his childhood. Laughton thought well of Greg and boosted his ego by suggesting to him that with his voice he should play Shakespeare. Greg recalled: 'He was a ham – but a great one.'

Greg was flattered by Laughton's advice, but didn't have the confidence to think that big. He also enjoyed getting to know Louis Jourdan and talking about the Yankees with the legendary Ethel Barrymore. She took delight in prizefighting and swapping stories about Joe Louis, her favorite champion.

The principals of *The Paradine Case* were assembled in a picture montage for a full-page ad inviting magazine readers to try Chesterfield cigarettes; each actor cocked his arm in a jaunty pose as he held the cigarette. Smoking helped sell the picture and the film sold smoking. 'My God, when I was young, that's what made us all smoke,' said director John Frankenheimer who worked with Greg on *I Walk the Line*. '. . . I mean Humphrey Bogart smoked. Barbara Stanwyck smoked. Joan Crawford smoked. Everybody that you admired smoked, so you, as a young person, aspired to smoking.'

The film marked the last time Greg would be formally associated with either Hitchcock or Selznick. The producer disbanded his company in 1948, about the time the film industry began feeling the squeeze from television. Thereafter, Greg spoke well of Selznick even though the horse-trading producer would sell Peck down the river a few years hence.

Through the years Greg learned to his dismay that he would never be done with Alfred Hitchcock. 'I must say I'm getting a little bit sick about questions about Hitchcock,' he groused to a reporter years later. 'Almost every interviewer asks the inevitable question about Hitchcock. "What was he really like?"'

On 13 March 1947 *The Paradine Case* opened to lukewarm reviews. After the film hit the theaters, Hitchcock vented his resentments, not at Selznick, but at the players. 'Actors! I hate the sight of them! Actors are cattle – actresses, too. I tell them I hate the sight of them and they love it, the exhibitionists! Any profession that calls for a man to have to use paint and powder on his face in order to earn a living gives me evil thoughts. Think of it; little bits of powder, little bits of paint on the face of adult men and women so they can pay the rent.'

With Selznick literally out of the picture, and only one film obligated to MGM, Greg set about working off his obligations to Twentieth Century Fox. Alas, his director on the Fox project, a Civil War Western titled *Yellow Sky* (1949), shared Hitchcock's disdain for actors. William 'Wild Bill' Wellman was the kind they don't make anymore. A grizzly old director of the silent era, Wellman had a well-earned reputation for profane sarcasm. By the time Greg met him, he was in the autumnal phase of his colorful career. With scores of movies to his credit, he had successfully transitioned from silents to talkies, and helped pioneer today's cinematic language.

Yellow Sky was the handiwork of writer-producer Lamar Trotti who also scripted the critically acclaimed *Ox-Bow Incident* (1943). This film was another quality realistic Western but with more commercial kick. It was a film in which the Western or horse opera, known in the trade as an 'oater' approached an art form.

Packed with suspense and set in the Wild West during 1867, *Yellow Sky* depicts a confrontation in an Arizona ghost town. Greg plays Stretch, the leader of a gang of bank robbers, who falls for a rambunctious young woman portrayed by Anne Baxter. Richard Widmark holds up his end as the dude.

Wellman was refreshingly roguish. Complex and demanding, with a sailor's vocabulary and a pugilist's social skills, he was even better known for his boisterous personality and his First World War exploits than for his prolific career as a film director. His wild youth, his infidelities and the raucous antics on his movie sets all added to his lure. As a teenager, he was put on probation for car theft and then dropped out of high school to join a professional minor league hockey team. His great dream was to become a flier. However, as his father 'didn't have enough money for me to become a flier in the regular way . . . I went into a war to become a flier.'

In 1917 he left the USA to join the French Foreign Legion. There, he became part of a group called the Lafayette Flying Corps, modeled after the famous Lafayette Escadrille. It was made up of 214 crazy kids. 'We were made the rank of second-class soldier in the French Foreign Legion and got three and a half cents a day. But it was rugged,' recalled Wellman. 'You have an instructor on the ground, but you learn to fly alone, by the seat of your pants! . . . They kicked the hell out of you, until you got your wings . . . But I got through it all right with a broken back, some false teeth, a plate in the roof of my mouth, and some occasional strange noises in my skull!' He was released from the service with the *Croix de Guerre* with full-gold palm leaves and five US citations (which later got him the job of directing the 1927 classic silent *Wings*). After working as a wing-walking stunt pilot, he got into the movies. He started as a mailroom boy at Goldwyn and rose to director in the 1920s.

Wellman's reputation was augmented in the 1930s with such diverse productions as the gangster melodrama *The Public Enemy* (1931), which catapulted James Cagney to stardom, the highly romantic initial version of *A Star is Born* (1937), the satiric *Nothing Sacred* (also 1937) and the rousing Foreign Legion action adventure *Beau Geste* (1939). His reputation was further enhanced in the 1940s with the *Ox-bow Incident* (1943), a superb anti-lynching film despite its technical and logistical flaws.

Among Hollywood insiders, 'Wild Bill' was known to be tough on actors and to have frequent clashes with studio bosses. It's not surprising that much of the Hollywood establishment didn't like him. Irene Selznick referred to him as 'a terror, a shoot-up-the town fellow, trying to be a great big masculine I-don't know-what.'

Aware he was about to start a movie with a man who valued toughness, Greg wanted to be ready. He sized up the part, made sure that no aspect of the role escaped him and mapped out the locations where the film was to be shot. He also set out for Ralph McClutcheon's stables in the San Fernando Valley to pick his own mount. McClutcheon trained movie horses.

One of the horses he tried trotted into a gallop beautifully. But when it went into a turn, it lost its footing because the ground was slippery and went down. It fell so fast Greg didn't have time to get his foot out of the stirrup. As the horse hit the ground, it broke his ankle in three places. An ambulance was called and Greg was taken to Cedars of Lebanon Hospital.

As he waited to be taken to surgery, a nurse who was no spring chicken gave Greg an injection of morphine, but the effect of the morphine altered his perception and his behavior. He reached up from the trolley he lay on, stroked her breasts and told her: 'You have the most beautiful breasts in the world. You are an angel. I love you.'

The nurse didn't miss a beat, chiding him: 'Morphine addicts say that to all the girls.'

Studio officials lost no time in contacting Greg's surgeon, Dr Lee Siegel, and letting him know *Yellow Sky* was an expensive project and Gregory Peck an expensive movie star. Could he please get him back to work soon? Usually a broken ankle takes two months to heal; they wanted him on the set in four weeks.

Greg's ankle was reset, and four weeks later Siegel released him after setting his ankle in a special cast that would allow him to walk, even though it was not fully healed. Consequently, his ankle never did repair properly, and thereafter he had to resort to wearing a support to enable him to run – and he would run only if absolutely necessary. Years later, he admitted: 'It was a stupid thing to do and I've paid for it ever since.'

With Greg's ankle in a cast Wellman shot him for the first few weeks from the knees up or from the right side to keep the cast out of the shot. (Old devil Wellman himself found exaggerating his war injury limp was an excellent way to impress women.)

Undoubtedly, Greg had heard stories about the shenanigans on a Wellman film set; now he was about to experience it first hand. A Wellman set was more often than not witness to fistfights, wild parties and daring stunts (all of which usually involved the director himself). 'Now I used to be pretty wild!' Wellman boasted. 'I always had great troops with me. We played, and we worked; but the minute the bell rang, the sound stage fell silent and you could hear a pin drop on my set. But when I yelled, "Cut. Print." I'm telling you, all hell broke loose. We had wild troops.'

He was also extremely fair, treating members of his crew with the same regard as his stars. Consequently, those who were loyal to him were fiercely so. But many actors disliked his method of bullying a performance out of them. On one occasion he got into a fistfight with Spencer Tracy and on another nearly came to blows with John Wayne.

Wellman admitted: 'As far as actors are concerned, the stars, I haven't been too fortunate with them. I've made pictures with most of them, but I don't think I'd win any popularity awards.

'An actor is a peculiar sort of guy. He's not like you or me. I'm not downgrading them particularly, but they are a different breed. They look in the mirrors all the time. They have to. They have to see what they look like and say lines to themselves. They look at their faces to see which is the best side to be photographed. You know, one of two things has to happen: you've got to fall in love with what are you looking at, or you've got to hate the son of a bitch!'

Greg's tendency to be cautious and to over-worry a part due to his perfectionism wasn't Wellman's way. He was known as a director who worked fast. Not because he was trying to save money, but because he thought fast. He told one producer: 'Look, I can't change my ways. I make mistakes, but I make them fast and cheap. If you want slow and expensive, don't hire me.'

Wellman heard Anne Baxter didn't want to work with Greg. So, during the first scene of the two principals in which they fight, the director took Greg aside and warned: 'Anne Baxter will kick the hell out of you. And when you start that fight, you better look out for yourself and wear something over your balls, because she'll destroy you.'

Wellman quickly learned Greg wasn't much of a pugilist – be it against man or woman. In exasperation, he said: 'Well, you can't fight. Can you kick a football? Well, you're going to have to fight with John Russell, knock him into the water and when his head comes up, kick it like a football.' Reflecting on the film at a later date, Wellman said: 'One of my favorite actors is in that film – Greg Peck. I say that sarcastically. We made a good picture, despite him.'

CHAPTER TEN

Domestic Affairs

'A dignified public front is very important to Greg.'

Greta Peck

Greg was now operating independently, not bound by any studio contract. He could choose his movie roles from the scores of scripts that came his way from producers. 'I work as hard picking a story as I do acting it,' Peck admitted.

When reporters interviewed him, he tried to keep the conversation focused on his work, but if a journalist insisted upon asking about his private life – undoubtedly having heard rumors about his marital problems – Greg devised a clever way to dampen their interest. He'd present himself as irredeemably boring. Here's an example:

'Let's forget the picture for minute,' said an interviewer. 'Tell me about your home. What did you do when you went back to the house last night?'

'Well,' said Peck. 'When I got home I found a piece of plaster that fell off the bathroom wall. So I went down to the cellar and mixed some patching plaster. Then I came upstairs again and patched up the wall. It took me about 20 minutes, I guess. Then I went back downstairs again.'

'Then what?' pursued the newsman. 'Did you go out to a night club? Did any of your screen-star friends drop over? Did you go to a film premier?'

'No,' answered Greg. 'It was getting pretty late by then. So I went to bed.'

Actually, there was much going on at home, and not all of it happy. On 21 April 1948 Greta Peck was involved in a car accident in which she was accused of hit and run. She was navigating Sepulveda Boulevard returning home from her Red Cross volunteer job helping veterans at the Birmingham hospital in Van Nuys. The time was close to midnight and when she rear-ended another car, she kept on driving. Later she told investigators: 'I remember slightly bumping into an automobile . . . I was afraid to stop because it was dark. And a man ran me into the curb, cursed me and took my keys. I had another set of keys, however, and drove the car home.'

Max Usland, a 45-year-old plasterer and the owner of the car she hit, said he chased her two miles to Sunset Boulevard. After grabbing her keys, he took them to the West Los Angeles police station and told the cops she hit his car three times.

Police traced the set of keys and the license number to the Pecks' home on San Remo Drive. There, Officer L M Long reported, he found Greta 'hysterical.' She told the officers that she had taken 'a couple of drinks when I got home to quiet my nerves.' A hearing was held later and Greta was acquitted of the charges. The Uslands subsequently sued the Pecks because Mrs Usland, a passenger in the car, claimed to have suffered injuries to her neck. One can only imagine how this matter sat with Greg.

Whether she had a few drinks before she got into her vehicle or afterwards, the fact remained that both Greg and Greta were imbibing prodigiously. Alcohol was at the very heart of their lives, it was inseparable from the everyday rituals. Unless there was a traffic accident or some other public display, people took scant notice in Hollywood. Greg was not only drinking heavily but also taking Seconal to help get to sleep. It was dulling the edges of his perception and affecting his judgment. Their mutual heavy drinking was a red flag that something was out of kilter in their lives. It was a cry for help.

Greg was spending a great deal of time in La Jolla with the players: moments stolen from his wife and children. When he was around, he was a perfectionist. No picnic to live with! He was intolerant of mistakes, particularly those he made himself. He pushed hard and he could push others equally hard. Flexibility wasn't his strong point. In his mind there was a right way and a wrong way to do something. He set goals for himself and others that were often impossible to reach. He had a surfeit of self-doubt and he invested a great deal of energy into details in order to make sure he could do his best when the moment arose. He believed: 'Constant attention to detail before the cameras all day carries over into the home . . . what you do, think, and feel has to be right.'

An actor's limited power to determine the outcome of a movie was brought home vividly to Greg when he joined the cast of *The Great Sinner* (1949). MGM studios was celebrating its 25th anniversary and set about mounting several Silver Jubilee Productions. The opulence of *The Great Sinner*'s settings and the caliber of its cast clearly indicated that the film was in the high production budget bracket. As usual, the undoing of noble intentions started in the scripting. The story, without credit, is taken from Dostoyevsky's *The Gambler*. Christopher Isherwood, author of *The Berlin Stories* which became the smash hit musical *Cabaret* (1972) created the screenplay, borrowing biographical elements from the Russian novelist's romantic feelings and gambling adventures.

The plot revolves around a serious young man (Peck) who can't resist the lure of the gambling tables. Ava Gardner was cast as the daughter of a Russian general who saves Greg from gambling his life away. Her elaborate period costumes were magnificent, but the film was not. One critic said there was depth to Ava's acting, but no depth in the dialogue.

Directed by Robert Siodmak, it boasted a big-time cast, including Walter Huston, Agnes Moorehead, Ethel Barrymore and Melvyn Douglas – and, of course, Ava. Greg knew right away he'd met a kindred soul. She became his all-time favorite leading lady. Over the years, they made three pictures together. 'When I first worked with her, she was 23, and she was so beautiful she took your breath away. Now, when I look back, Ava is the most beautiful face I've ever seen.' He was not alone in that opinion. Her gaze was dead-on, challenging, and immensely alluring. With her sensuous mouth, prominent cheekbones, green tigress-like eyes, luminous skin and auburn hair, she was animal magnetism personified. Ernest Hemingway pronounced her 'the most beautiful animal in the world.'

In contributing a chapter to her autobiography *Ava* (1990), after Gardner died before she could complete it, Greg reflected: 'What I liked about Ava was that we had so much in common it was like we were young people from the same hometown. We both were products of middle-class, small American towns where everybody knew everybody, and it was on that basis that we struck up an immediate friendship.'

Like Greg, Gardner was caught up in a whirlwind and she didn't know where she was going to land. Her private life was marked by parties, brawls, sprees and bedroom antics and, while Greg was never one of her lovers, he thoroughly enjoyed his role as her confidant.

'Our relationship was and always has been as pals,' Greg wrote. 'I suppose some fellas would say, "Oh, come on, this is one of the most desirable and beautiful women in the world, and you tell me you were just *pals?*" And the answer is yes, that's the truth. You don't make a run at every beautiful girl you meet. It's quite possible for a young man and a young woman in their prime years to be great friends.'

Greg needed Gardner to help liberate him from the prison of his repression. While he kept his emotions locked tightly within his rigid body, she spilled her guts, punctuating her stories with gestures, poignant insights and raucous laughs. He loved her for being so authentic, so utterly herself. Plus, she was very bright, yet very few people could appreciate the fact because her education was so limited. This played a major part in her low self-esteem and shyness. There was a kind of infinite sadness about her, as if everything good that came her way was undeserved. It made her an easy prey for bad relationships.

Recalled actress Arlene Dahl who worked with her at MGM: 'Ava wouldn't even go eat in the commissary because she was so scared to walk in and see Lana Turner and Greer Garson. She said she'd rather crawl under a rug than climb down some stairs at a party.'

MGM swim star Esther Williams recalled: 'I tried to talk with her at the parties at Louis B Mayer's, but if she was a little tipsy she'd say, "You don't want to talk to me, Esther. I'm just trailer trash."'

Beauty may be only skin deep but it's a valuable asset when you're poor. Ava Gardner was destined to be a star by an act of nature.

Looks alone propelled her out of Grabtown, a tiny dot on the map of North Carolina. (Her photograph was spotted in a store window by an MGM talent scout.) On the way out of town, she told her mother: 'I can stay here and be a secretary, or I can go to Hollywood and breathe the same air that Clark Gable breathes.' So the tomboy who liked nothing better than to run barefoot, climb trees and ride around in jalopies with the local boys found herself at MGM. When director George Sidney viewed her screen test, he threw up his hands and rejoiced. 'She can't act. She can't talk. She's terrific.'

Louis B Mayer was determined to mold Gardner into an ideal fantasy creature. He put diction coaches to work on her thick Southern accent. The pros scolded her for cracking her gum and cussing like a stevedore. They made fun of her lack of education. (By the age of 18 the only book she had read to completion was *Gone With the Wind.*) Though paralyzed by shyness and haunted by painful experiences from her childhood, Gardner fought to find her footing amidst the stars and oddballs, frauds and geniuses, tycoons and flesh peddlers.

It wasn't until 1946 that Ava Gardner was discovered by the public, along with another newcomer, Burt Lancaster, in the screen adaptation of Hemingway's *The Killers.* She quickly replaced Rita Hayworth as Hollywood's love goddess and occupied that position until the ascent of Marilyn Monroe in the mid-1950s.

When Greg met Gardner, she was a bird with a broken wing. Although still in her twenties, she had two marriages behind her and had embarked on a stormy relationship with Frank Sinatra. Her first husband was Mickey Rooney. She was only 19 and a virgin when she married him. He was 21 and already a lady-killer. (He boasted his wooing technique combined 'early Neanderthal and late Freud.') He was also an inveterate partygoer who launched Gardner's love affair with booze. When she left him, he turned ugly and threatened to get her back by force. Then he exploited her by publishing graphic descriptions of their sex life.

Her second husband, Artie Shaw, was the swing era jazz genius (Gardner danced to his band as a teenager) who married her as arm candy. 'She was a goddess,' he said. 'I would stare at her, literally stare, in wonder.' But once living with the flesh and blood woman, Shaw zeroed in on faults with the subtlety of a jackhammer. When she was trying to rise in the ranks from cheesecake starlet to legitimate performer, he'd make remarks like 'I know girls who can act circles around you.' Worst of all, he beat her, boasting it was 'an effective method to keep her under control.' After a year of marriage, he dumped her on the pretext she bored him.

Gardner possessed in abundance what Greg lacked (candor, irreverence, knock-your-socks-off humor) and she, in turn, looked to him for the qualities she so sorely needed (spiritual strength, reliability and an educated mind).

Greg could see Gardner's talent was underrated – even by herself. Producers, directors and male co-stars felt threatened by her potent combination of spectacular looks, native intelligence, independence and moxie. This kind of paranoia was articulated years before by Cecil B DeMille when he said: 'Feminine allure is a ruthless tool that has changed the course of civilization.'

Greg took it upon himself to develop Gardner's acting skills. 'I must have told her hundreds of times that she had it in her to be a great actress, that all she needed was a little more courage to attack, to go at a scene with the intention of selling it, of grasping the audience's attention and holding it.'

The weakness of the meandering script of *The Great Sinner*, especially in the length of its ending, was made all the more glaring by Siodmak's direction. Greg and Gardner had a lot of laughs making fun of the director who was a nervous wreck over directing such a 'heavy' picture. A nurse stood at the ready on the set and would periodically jab him in the arm with vitamins or a tran-quilizer, something to keep him from climbing the walls.

'At other times,' recounted Greg, 'with hundreds of people in the casino scene and Melvyn Douglas eyeing me as I'm gambling away and Ava standing there watching me lose my shirt, Bob would really be overcome with the weight of the situation. He was always sitting on the seat attached to the camera crane, and he'd mutter, "Up, up, up", and off he'd go to hide 18 feet above the crowds while he collected his thoughts. And Ava and I would grin at each other and say, "There he goes again!"'

In the period following the filming of *The Great Sinner*, the Pecks' marriage almost reached breaking point. Greg had a tremendous ability to concentrate on one thing at a time and shut out all other concerns. He used this compartmentalized approach in focusing on his movie roles, building a strong base for the La Jolla Playhouse, helping friends such as Ava Gardner find their way in life and, finally, tending to his duties as a family man. On paper, compartmentalization is a highly effective approach to the challenges of daily living. That's on paper. In real life, it often stinks. Spouses, in particular, don't like to be shut out or relegated to the bottom of their mate's list of priorities.

At the beginning of 1949, Greg and Greta had a bitter fight. It was serious enough for Greg to flee the house without telling Greta where he was going. However, their marital drama was picked up by Louella Parson's spy network and shared with her million plus readers. On 21 January she wrote: 'For some days the rumor has been current in Hollywood that Gregory and Greta Peck have reached the breaking point . . . Mrs Peck, who sounded a little vague when I asked if she and Greg had trouble, said: "I hope there is no trouble. I wouldn't like to have anything happen, but I have not heard from Greg in over two days."'

This item was followed several days later with a bulletin from Parsons that came as a total surprise to the runaway actor: 'The Gregory Pecks are expecting a baby!' The article went on to say: 'In the midst of all the rumors that Greg and his wife, Greta, are straining at the matrimonial leash, comes definite news that the Pecks are expecting their third child in June.' She then had the nerve to add: 'I think it is likely that at the time Greg left home he didn't know about the expected baby.'

To cool off from the argument, Greg had flown down to Mazatlan in Mexico and gone deep-sea fishing. After a call from his agent, George Chasin, telling him that Parsons had phoned his office asking for comment on the pregnancy, Greg headed home where Greta confirmed she was pregnant. Greg made his peace with Greta and quickly went into repair mode with Louella Parsons and Hedda Hopper.

Just how much they could damage a career would be seen that

year in the way they alerted the world to the transgressions of Ingrid Bergman. She had been sold to the public as a virginal Swedish beauty who led a happy, healthy home life with her husband Peter Lindstrom and daughter Pia. But Bergman went to Europe in 1949 to make *Stromboli* – and fell in love with her director, Roberto Rossellini. When rumors of a divorce surfaced, this alone sent former fans into a moral frenzy. But when Parsons, affectionately known as 'love's undertaker,' broke the news that Bergman was also expecting Rossellini's child, she not only scooped every other gossip monger in the nation, but signaled Bergman's crucifixion.

The actress married Rossellini soon afterwards, but the harm – in Puritan American eyes – was already done. Banished from Hollywood and from her position as one of the industry's most important (top ten box-office) stars, Bergman – despite being one of the most magnificent screen females in history – did not make an American film again until her award-winning *Anastasia* in 1956, and she did not return to Hollywood until 1969 for *Cactus Flower*.

Some actors gave the gossip columnists the back of their hand. For example, when Kirk Douglas separated from his first wife, Sheilah Graham wrote that the couple's 'alleged' parting was just a publicity gimmick. Infuriated, Douglas broke his usual silence and called her up. 'You cunt! How dare you print that! This is our life. We have two children. And you make it as if we're playing a game.'

Instead of charging the harpies head on, Greg made his Faustian bargains. First, he called on Parsons. It was raining the night he arrived at her house and he was wearing a raincoat curled around his shoulders and an old hat. She took notes and shared their hearthside conversation with her readers in the February 1949 issue of *Photoplay*. She began: 'Don't you believe, for a minute, that the Gregory Peck's marriage is close to the rocks. I *know*, because I have just talked with Greg, in what, I am sure, is the most intimate story he has ever given about his private life.' She then went on to say that Greg blamed himself for the fight. 'We had a quarrel, sure,' he said. 'You know how married people are. They quarrel and battle over trivial things and then comes the big blowup. In our case, it was all my fault. I was nervous and tired. My first thought was, "I'll get out of here, anywhere, just so it is away." So I went fishing down in Mexico.'

Greg gave Parsons one of his rueful, half-quizzical smiles and added: 'You'll never know what a shock it was to read that I had left my wife and that no one knew my whereabouts!' He whistled softly. 'But, I'm glad you printed it. It taught me a real lesson. I'll never go away again without telling Greta where I'm going.'

He stretched his long legs in the general direction of the fire, blazing away cheerfully in her living room. He was dressed in slacks and a soft shirt, looking, according to Parsons, 'as handsome as Lucifer.' Then he popped the question:

'I want to ask you just one thing, Louella. How did you find out that Greta was expecting another baby? I didn't know that myself.'

'Oh, I'm smart that way,' she told him.

'When my agent called and said you had asked him, I was flabbergasted,' Greg admitted. 'Greta hadn't said a word until you phoned.'

'Did you ever stop to think that it might have been Greta's condition at that time that made her difficult?' Parsons suggested.

'But she was not!' he protested quickly. 'It was all my fault. I will tell you why I will never have any really serious trouble with Greta. *I love her and she loves me!*'

He was thoughtful for a moment before going on. 'I hate divorce. I was a child of a broken family. When I was three, my mother and father separated and there was much bitterness. I went from one relative to another, part of the time with my father and part with my mother, accepting, first my mother's religion, and then my father's . . . I've got two wonderful kids, Jonathan, four and a half, and Stephen who is two. Now, maybe, there is a little girl on the way. I don't want them to have that kind of a life, and I can promise you, they won't.'

He finished off these poignant remarks by saying: 'I have gradually been building up a philosophy, Louella, and that is, in order to live happily and fully with others, we must first learn to live with ourselves. If I hadn't been wrong in the first place in squabbling with Greta, there would have been nothing unpleasant to print.'

Then he launched into plans for his next movie, an epic called

Quo Vadis, to be filmed in Italy. 'I figure I'll be finished with the picture in October and then Greta will join me. We will visit her kinfolks in Finland. She's got a lot of relatives over there I have never met and we will descend on them bag and baggage. After that, we'll go on to Sweden and Norway and Paris and London and all the spots that have just been names to us before.'

And how about the children, Parsons wondered. To which, Greg replied: 'No, I don't think we will take the kids along on this first jaunt. I'd like to make this trip just with Greta. The children are too young to get anything out of it, anyway. And to Greta and me it would seem like the honeymoon trip we couldn't afford when we were married.'

'That sounds wonderful,' Parsons said.

'Yep,' he grinned, 'now all I have to do is to talk her into leaving the children!'

One down and one to go! Next he invited Hedda Hopper over to his house in the Pacific Palisades. And, perhaps borrowing a leaf from Parsons, he sat Hopper down in his den in front of *his* fireplace. 'We're a close family here,' he began. 'I'm home a lot and Greta and are around each other all the time. I don't play golf or tennis . . . When I'm not working I'm right here with Greta and the kids 24 hours a day. When I'm working out of town on location, she's with me if it's halfway possible. That's the way we like it. That's the way our whole life ticks.

'Only, sometimes, when two people see too much of each other, some trifle occurs and they take it out on each other, blow their tops, have a spat. That's what happened with us and so I decided to get away for the good of us both for a few days. I packed my bag, hopped in the Lincoln and headed south. Stopped at Del Mar, stayed overnight and got an idea: how about some fishing to relax? I had been tied pretty tight making *Yellow Sky* and then *The Great Sinner* – bang, bang – like that. If I have a hobby it's deep-sea fishing and I've a friend who feels the same way. I gave him a ring; he met me in Tijuana. We hopped a plane to Mazatlan, and – well, I got me a 145-pound marlin swordfish! Then I came back home and things have been fine ever since.'

Quo Vadis, slated to be Greg's next movie, was not exactly part of the Bible, but it was sort of biblical. MGM had been trying for years to get a usable script out of Henry Sienkiewicz's turgid novel about the early Christians. With Dore Schary's encouragement, John Huston had devised what he regarded as 'a modern treatment,' in which Nero was portrayed as a prototype for his 'fellow madman, Adolf Hitler.'

Huston began casting on a grand scale: Greg was cast as the hero and Elizabeth Taylor as the heroine. Huston then went to Europe and started spending money. About $2 million had disappeared by the time the differences between Mayer and Huston brought the production to a halt, and Mayer turned everything over to a man he trusted, Mervyn LeRoy. Greg dropped out because of an eye infection and Elizabeth Taylor had other commitments. Eventually *Quo Vadis* was made and cost $12 million but turned into what Huston called 'another dreadful spectacle, catering to the audience L B thought was there. L B was right; the audience *was* there.'

CHAPTER ELEVEN

The Heart of the Matter

'I've had my ups and downs. There have been times when I
wanted to quit. Times when I hit the bottle. Marital problems.
I've touched most of the bases.'
                                    Gregory Peck to journalist Vernon Scott

Greg's attempts to juggle his work commitments with family life
began to take their toll on his health. In the summer of 1949, while
helping to run the Playhouse in La Jolla, Greg developed heart
spasms. He checked into a hospital but the doctors could find no
physical basis for his condition. He was drinking heavily; frequently
joining his Playhouse colleagues such as Charlton Heston, Ginger
Rogers, Ethel Waters, Vincent Price and Zsa Zsa Gabor at La
Valencia's Whaling Bar. His time with Greta and the boys was
catch-as-catch-can.

   His life was out of control but he wouldn't admit it. He was
determined to keep up the public front of the well-adjusted family
man. About this time, he opined to an interviewer: 'Hollywood is
filled with the most unhappy success stories in the world. Guys and
gals who are making fortunes, being pampered and petted by any
number of people, and basking in the idolatry of movie fans all over
the world still manage to find in this pleasant situation big tears of
sadness, moments of deep depression and that hangdog look that
usually goes with complete failure. Why this happens, I'll never
understand.'

   Fortunately, he was about to embark on a new phase of his career
with a new director, one with whom he would develop his best
relationship. At a time in his life when he sorely needed someone to
give him guidance, Henry King turned up.

   'I think I did my best work with Henry King, who I just seem to
have a good rapport with. Henry was a man's man, warm,

humorous, strong, an expert technician, prepared. He didn't always direct meticulously, in great detail. It's sort of sit back and see what I had to offer, and then he makes little adjustments and changes on what I brought to the part.'

Of all Greg's adventures with the maverick films directors of Hollywood's Classic Era, none made him happier than working with Henry King. He referred to the days under King's direction as 'among the best of my working life.' Of the bond he formed with King, he said: 'It was probably a closer relationship than I have with some of my blood relatives.'

Greg remembered vividly the day in 1949 when Darryl Zanuck introduced him to Henry King. It was in Zanuck's corner office on the second floor at Fox. Zanuck was teaming King with Greg for a Second World War movie called *Twelve O'Clock High* (1950). 'I had been around Twentieth Century Fox about five years by the time I met Henry. Darryl, who was close to Henry, was actively running the studio then and was in on everything, every script, chapter and verse. Darryl called to ask if he might send me the script of *Twelve O'Clock High*. I called back in a day or two and said, "You've got me if you want me."'

Greg was captivated by King's enthusiasm and relish for the project. 'I liked him from the beginning. We always got along in a kind of father and son relationship but in another way knowing Henry was like having an older brother. And in yet another way, our relationship was just one of two close friends.'

The project originated in 1947 when an unpublished novel found its way to Zanuck's desk. Flipping through it, Zanuck called it 'the best script I've ever read.' He was immediately struck by the real-life exploits of Air Force Brigadier General Frank Savage who, in 1942, directed the first US precision bombings behind German lines. He later suffered a mental breakdown; a condition generally alluded to only in whispers in post-war America. Screenwriter for the project and veteran flier Sy Bartlett saw the parallel in Zanuck and Savage: 'Zanuck ruled by rigid discipline, and, like Savage, Zanuck found he couldn't crawl into the goddamn cockpit.'

Next on Zanuck's order of business was securing the Air Force permission to use military planes and to get permission to locate

Second World War B-17 bombers. In return, the Air Force asked for and got changes to the script. The biggest objection was to the general's mental breakdown. 'We did not believe that a man with the strength of character as indicated and his moral fiber would burst out hysterically,' wrote an Air Force adviser. 'He would be more likely to breakdown with . . . just plain fatigue.' Zanuck, who recognized that the Air Force would provide a crucial aspect of the film's authentic portrayal of war, agreed to all changes.

As one of the few non-vets on the project, Greg was nervous. He told King: 'I never had any real military experience in my life.' The director countered: 'You'll be so surrounded by military people who'll be giving you advice that you'll find yourself thinking like a military man.'

Although his back injury made him a 4-F, Greg wanted to show he had the right stuff for the job. The town had plenty of actors with real combat experience and they would be scrutinizing his performance. Jimmy Stewart was one of those men. Nine months before Pearl Harbor, Stewart, at age 33, determined to become a combat pilot, and logged 300 hours of flying. He eventually led 20 bombing missions over Germany, hitting targets in Bremen, Frankfurt and Berlin. He won a succession of decorations, including the Distinguished Flying Cross twice, one of them for piloting the lead plane in a spectacular raid on key aircraft factories in Brunswick, Germany. He also received the Air Medal, a succession of oak-leaf clusters, six battle stars and the *Croix de Guerre* with palm.

As shooting got underway, Greg discovered his instincts were correct vis-à-vis Henry King. In the leathery-skinned director's blue eyes, there was always a sparkle. Like old-timers Raoul Walsh and William Wellman, King was thoroughly professional but there was a kind of playful challenge, always couched in an affectionate way, and never demanding, as if to say: 'Let's see what we can do. We'll play this game together. Let's give it the best we've got.'

Reflected Greg: 'I think we were cut from the same cloth, not merely as fellow actors, but more as Middle Americans. He was from Virginia. I was from California. But we seemed to share a lot of easy understanding without the need for further discussion. The values and the standards we held up for ourselves were in many ways similar, in spite of a 30-year age difference.

The more he talked about King, the more Greg sounded like an idealist young man who has found his all-time hero: 'I think that I learned by example, not so much by what he told me but by his being the kind of man he was and of the personal code he had. I also think of him as very American in character, old-fashioned in his ideals and extremely conscientious, kind and considerate with everybody on the set, but demanding and tough when things did not go right. He had steel in him. Those times were among the best of my working life. We both looked forward to the enjoyment of going to rushes together and watching a scene come out the way we wanted. I know that we both drove home feeling fine, satisfied that we had done a good day's work.'

While scores of actors and directors resented Zanuck's despotic ways, commanding his studio with a sawed-off polo mallet, Greg and King respected him enormously. 'He was amazing in his knowledge of maybe 30 to 40 different scripts,' said Greg. 'Almost line by line, he knew them and analyzed them and worked with writers and worked with directors.

'I remember going to the telephone with Henry King and we just couldn't make the scene work. We'd call up Zanuck in his office and say, "We're doing Scene 87 and this dialogue doesn't work for us." And he knew the dialogue we were talking about, and we would work it out on the phone and change the script.'

While Greg was in the midst of filming, Greta went into labor. On 17 June 1949 at 2.30 a.m., Dr Donald Tolleson delivered her third son who was named Carey Paul after Greg's co-star Harry Carey in *Duel in the Sun*. Five hours later, Greta had a call from Louella Parsons eager for the details. 'Of course, it was very inconsiderate of him to arrive at such an hour when his father is busy making a picture,' Greta responded as the dutiful wife of a movie star plugging his next film. 'He's on the set of *Twelve O'Clock High*.'

Twelve O'Clock High is considered a landmark film because it is one of the first post-war movies out of Hollywood to treat the war in emotionally complex terms. Framed by post-war prologue and epilogue as a flashback appreciation of wartime valor and teamwork, Greg did an outstanding job as Brigadier General Frank Savage, a callous, desk-bound leader who assumes command of a bomber squadron based in England after the previous commander is relieved of duty. At first, he has little rapport with the 918th bomber group, whose loyalty still belongs to their former commander. As they continue to fly dangerous missions over Germany, however, the group and Savage develop mutual respect and admiration, until the once alienated commander feels that his men are part of a family – where men's bravery transcends the rigors of rigid discipline and by-the-book leadership. The film's complex climax, in which the general waits patiently for his squadron to return to base – painfully aware that they may not return at all – is one of the most subtle yet emotionally intense scenes of any Second World War drama.

Savage cracks under the cumulative stress of putting his best face forward for men who 'don't have confidence in anything anymore.' Sitting paralyzed, with his hands clawed over his knees, then the arms of his chair, his cramped features project an utterly focused will, leading – in his mind – his pilots on a dangerous mission and bringing them safely home. Only the drum of returning planes unclenches his body, and brings him back to himself. The final scene, still disturbing today, must have stunned post-war audiences. As he stares dumbly into space, a comrade eulogizes: 'It's like a light bulb burned-out.' It was a risk for Greg. Here he was a screen giant suffering an on-screen nervous breakdown. However, the leap of faith paid off for audiences, the studio and Greg, who cinched a Best Actor Academy Award nomination.

Twelve O'Clock High is one of Greg's movies that is still talked about today. And he continues to be commended for his performance. In listing his favorite movies, producer Martin Scorsese wrote: 'I know all about Gregory Peck, don't read any further, Gregory Peck is Gregory Peck, when he's in a film you accept it for what it is, it's a given, like a theorem in geometry, okay, Gregory Peck. But here he's a man in war, dealing with his conscience and his fears. You figure, this guy's so tough he can take anything.

But then comes the moment when he has to get into the bomber, and the machismo breaks down. He can't get in the plane. And I love it.'

Stephen Farber and Marc Green praised the film in their book *Hollywood on the Couch* (1993). 'Although there is no psychiatrist in the cast of characters, *Twelve O'Clock High* is one of the most pro-psychiatry movies of the period, for it convincingly demonstrates the shattering effects of emotional trauma.'

Greg had an in-depth understanding of his character because he possessed the same duality of bravery and fear. 'I'm not nearly as confident as those hero characters are,' he admitted. 'Although I think in films like *Twelve O'Clock High* and *The Guns of Navarone* [1961], it seemed to me that I brought in a little ambivalence of character and vulnerability and self-doubt whenever there was an opening for it. But am I like these heroes in real life? No. Sometimes I'm courageous and sometimes less so.'

Ironically, at this point in his life Greg was sorely in need of psychological counseling. He was drinking excessively, popping sleeping pills and in denial about the difficulties in his marriage. But there's no record of him going into therapy and he was quite outspoken about his disdain for 'Freudian stuff' when it came to himself.

Twelve O'Clock High is used today by the military and corporations to teach leadership and teambuilding skills. It is a study of how to become a self-actualizing cohesive unit, to plan a mission, make choices and succeed. The US Air Force Academy uses *Twelve O'Clock High* in its pilot training program. As one cadet put it: 'This film demonstrates how military leadership has nothing to do with medals and parades, but is a constant battle to make a group of people do a thankless, inglorious job.'

One thing was certain: Greg put in a damn good performance and he was not deserving of a nasty swipe Bette Davis took at him, even if it was made in the privacy of her home. Her husband Gary Merrill, a laid-back, easygoing, make-do man, had played an Air Force squadron commander in *Twelve O'Clock High*. He preferred to enjoy the pleasures of life than kill himself working, a mindset that did not sit well with nervous, perfectionist, hard-charger Bette. He said to her one day: 'I wish I were Gregory Peck, so I'd only have to do one good movie a year and make some decent money.' To which Davis growled, 'If you're going to pick an actor to be, at least pick a good one.' The exchange sparked a fight. They separated a few weeks later.

It's interesting to note Greg's reactions to zigzagging across the country in Henry King's Beechcraft plane as they made their way from Los Angeles to Florida and back again. Watching King man the instruments, Greg felt shaky. And the weather didn't help. Big thunderheads were rolling by above as King – an expert flier – went 150 miles out of his way to duck the weather. Admitted Greg, 'I was a little jumpy about being up there in a single-engine craft. Henry seemed to me like an old man. Actually, he was a very hale 63 but to me that was old. I thought, "This man might have a heart attack up here at 12,000 feet." So I watched closely. And I watched the things on the radio, as we crossed over different towns. I was glued to those little levers and dials. I had on a pair of ear phones and I told myself if he suddenly became ill or had a heart attack, I might have a chance of getting myself down.'

If Greg was going to risk his life with anybody, he was happy to do it with King. Reflecting on the six movies he eventually made with the director, Greg said of *Twelve O'Clock High*, *The Gunfighter* (1950), *David and Bathsheba* (1951), *The Snows of Kilimanjaro* (1952), *The Bravados* (1958), and *Beloved Infidel* (1959): 'These pictures reflect on honor, integrity, being true to your word, living up to your commitments. They say don't lie; don't cheat; don't use anybody; be open-hearted and generous; do your duty; be a man – what some people would now think of as old-fashioned virtues. We never articulated these precepts; we never said: "Now we are going to reflect these values."'

'I could have gone on doing what I did in *Twelve O'Clock* – the martinet with the heart of gold; the hard driver, but the fellow who was doing it for good reasons, for an honest cause.'

The Gunfighter was Greg's next film. In it he gives a great performance. As the movie opens to a wishful air played softly on a mouth organ, the introduction scrolls on the screen:

'In the Southwest of the 1880s the difference between death and glory was often but the fraction of a second. This was the speed that made champions of Wyatt Earp, Billy the Kid, and Wild Bill Hickok. But the fastest man with a gun who ever lived, by many contemporary accounts, was a long, lean Texan named Ringo.'

The desperado rides into a no-name town in the middle of nowhere for a drink. At this point in his life, fast-gun Ringo is trying to overcome his bloody past. But he's challenged by an ambitious 'squirt' and shoots the kid down, whereupon he fades into the darkness again. Weary and despairing, he laments, 'I just want to be somewhere else!'

Greg's professional gunslinger could pass for any one of those lean, frowning, mustachioed Westerners who stare so flatly out of nineteenth-century tintypes. Waiting for his last chance at having a real home, he sweats it out in yet another bar, staring bleakly into nothing. He has risked his life for a reunion with his estranged wife and child only to be doomed by his fate. In a compelling swan song, he exonerates his youthful assassin so that the punk may live to follow his 'sire's' haunted path: 'Just wait,' he says to the boy, as the gunfighter is surprised in death.

The genesis of *The Gunfighter*, however, is rooted as much in an American masculine mystique of the Western gunfighter as in the tradition of the American bad man. Andre de Toth was a dashing Hollywood figure involved since the early 1930s in the direction and occasional writing of films. Among his close friends de Toth numbered three-times world heavyweight champion, Joe Louis, and actors Errol Flynn and Humphrey Bogart. De Toth noticed a curious thing: every time he accompanied Flynn to a nightclub inevitably someone would challenge Flynn, someone who wanted to demonstrate his prowess for his date. Bogart, he said, was especially vulnerable because 'Bogey couldn't fight his way out of a paper bag.' De Toth observed the same phenomenon when he went out to public places with Louis. Perhaps as part of the provocation a troublemaker would make a remark to the effect that 'You don't look so tough to me.' De Toth realized that after a while his friends quit going out to public places because of the risk of such competitive challenges. The more he reflected on this phenomenon, the more he became sure that here was the heart of a screenplay.

De Toth took the idea to a friend who was also a scriptwriter, William Bowers. They collaborated on *The Gunfighter* using ideas about the Old West derived from original sources. The hero would be a man upon whom the countless incarnations of Wild Bill Hickok, Wyatt Earp and other gunmen had been patterned. Like Joe Louis, he would be at the top of his line of work; and like Louis he would discover that the champ is constantly in the presence of challengers. They had an actor specifically in mind for the role, an actor who, like the hero, was now on the other side of the climacteric. His name was Gary Cooper.

The script reached Darryl Zanuck's desk. He went over the script with Nunnally Johnson who was to produce it: 'It could be made just as it is and it would be a hell of a good and rather unusual Western. I do feel, however, that this can emerge as a real classic in the field . . . as powerful as *Stagecoach* . . .'

Zanuck envisioned the film in sepia color with somber touches. But he didn't like the idea of going outside the studio to secure Cooper. Twentieth Century Fox had a perfectly good male star who also projected strength and integrity. Why not cast Gregory Peck instead? De Toth and Bowers worried he was too intellectual and contemplative.

At some point before the final version of the script (to which King also made his contribution) Greg was offered the leading role; he wanted especially to work with Henry King, whose direction in *Twelve O'Clock High* had stretched his abilities.

Later, Greg recalled: 'We particularly liked doing *The Gunfighter*. Early on, when we started preparing the picture and I had accepted the role, both of us decided that we wanted this fellow to look and dress in a motley collection of clothes like the people in the daguerreotypes of the early West. You see them with swallowtail coats and hard hats and ill-fitting homespun garments. They do not look like rodeo cowboys at all, and a very large number of the men wear beards and mustaches. So he and I decided that I should look like one of those fellows. We pored over all the books that we could find. Then located several models, long, lean, cut off, semi-educated, early Westerners – people who might have come from the east or even as far away as Scotland. They were out there to try to make a better life. I put on a handlebar mustache and a funny-looking, corduroy coat. They gave me a soup bowl haircut, a 15-Center – not all romantic looking. Then we started.'

For this picture King did not insist on extensive location work since the movie swells on the landscape of the mind. Nevertheless he would have preferred shooting in Texas. But finally Lone Pine, California, was chosen for the desert watering-hole scenes. Closer to LA, the stark mountainous area was used for countless Westerns.

At this point in production, Zanuck, for some reason or another, was not around, and his assistant, Spyros Skouras was in Europe. After *The Gunfighter* crew had gone a couple of weeks, Skouras came back. It was his custom to catch up on the rushes of current productions. He let out a howl when he saw Greg on the screen. He said, 'What the hell is that? Who gave you that haircut? Who put a mustache on Gregory Peck? He's a sex symbol. People don't like men with mustaches. And that funny-looking haircut and that crazy-looking suit? And a black hat?'

'He went into a rage about it, and the message came down to us on the set that Skouras would never forget it,' Greg recalled. 'For 20 years, every time I saw him it was: "You black Irishman. You! You ruined my picture." I am half Irish, and he would say: "Anyway, you don't even know who you are or what you are. You think the black Irish came from the sinking of the Spanish Armada. That's pure shit. It comes from the Greeks who were there 2,000 years ago. Where do you think you got the name Gregory anyway?"'

When Zanuck returned to the studio, King and Johnson ran the picture for him. Silence followed the showing. Zanuck groaned that he would give $50,000 (sometimes the figure in King's account is $40,000, sometimes $25,000) of his own money for Greg not to have that mustache. Zanuck was figuring the commercial consequences: 'This man has a young following. That mustache, I'm afraid is going to kill it.'

Although *The Gunfighter* was recognized as a film of unusual quality when it appeared, its reputation gains luster with the passing years. In the 1980s, Bob Dylan wrote a song about it titled 'Brownsville Girl,' which pleased Greg and formed the basis of a friendship between the two men. One writer of Western films, Walter

Kaufman, argued that *The Gunfighter* is the measure by which all Westerns would be judged. The film clearly instituted the trend in 'adult' Westerns. Just as Jesse James initiated a cycle of sympathetic outlaw protagonists, so *The Gunfighter* introduced so many weary gunfighters that the type has become a cliché. Another critic Allen Creek compared *High Noon* (1952) to King's picture; he liked especially King's ability to find 'truth in every situation,' and the sense of passing time without the looming clock faces so present in the latter film. Now the King picture is usually regarded as the better film.

With Greg as the outlaw loser Ringo, the story played out the cycle of the Greek tragedy. The action suggested Ringo's hopes for his wife and himself, while pointing the way to his death by bloodshed. This is the tragedy of a man with a reputation from his past. He now wishes to return to normal life with a wife and the son to whom he cannot reveal his paternity. But he reaches the point of no return and he can only go on shooting. Only death can relieve him of his search to be freed from his reputation.

Indicative of the movie's psychological probing is the fact that in this Western only three shots were fired. In the end, the cowardly young Hunt Bromley, intent on ruining Ringo's reputation, and the shuttle of the horse and rider leaving the community signals the deadly start of a new cycle. While the business of the story is grim, it is alleviated with some comedy. Ringo, for example, remarks that the good ladies of the town seeking to punish the outlaw seemed, ironically, as cold-hearted and malicious in their planning as the worst of gunslingers.

Once released, *The Gunfighter* received excellent reviews but did weak box-office. In fact, the shortfall appeared to validate Zanuck's estimate of public taste. For years, he and Skouras would accuse King and Greg and Johnson of letting 'their mustache' cost the studio a million dollars. As producer Johnson saw it, audiences, 'brought up with Jesse James were probably put off by the relatively realistic depiction of Ringo, especially since *The Gunfighter* was one of the first films to begin to dismantle the popular myths of the West.'

The year 1950 was the Westerns' watershed, marked by the release of *Broken Arrow, Devil's Doorway, Winchester '73, Wagon Master*, and *The Gunfighter*. Following kudos for his role in *The Gunfighter*,

Greg was immediately offered the lead in *High Noon*. George Chasin, his agent, urged him to take it. 'You've found the archetype,' he said. 'Stay with it and you'll be another John Wayne.' Greg turned it down and regretted it ever after. Gary Cooper won the Academy Award for it. Greg lusted for that golden statue. He said modestly, 'I don't think I would have been as good as Gary Cooper, but I still think it would have been a good film with me in it.'

At the time Greg felt it was too much like *The Gunfighter* and, what's more, he didn't want to be typecast as a cowboy. On the other hand, he knew that if you get in a groove you get better and better at it. Years later, he said: 'That's why those fellas were so magnificent playing the same part, because they'd played it 40 times. That's why John Wayne finally became a good actor in *True Grit* [1969]: he's got 150 of them behind him. Now he's developed a saltiness and an earthiness and a humor and a subtlety that comes from mining that same vein over and over again.'

Although he came to deeply regret his decision in the light of the splendid success of *High Noon*, he did receive compensation – of sorts. The Reno Chamber of Commerce appreciated his cowboy panache, and named him the top Western star for 1950, and presented him with the Silver Spurs award. A miffed John Wayne barked at Greg: 'Well, who the hell decided that you were the best cowboy of the year?'

Greg's next film, *Only the Valiant* (1951) holds a singular distinction in his career – and personal life. It's the film that leaves the bitterest taste in his mouth.

When Greg signed a contract with David O Selznick, there was the understanding that the actor would never have to appear in any film he opposed. But Selznick's financial condition had become so desperate, he couldn't ask for Greg's approval. Among those he made available for loan were Greg, Jennifer Jones, Shirley Temple, Joseph Cotton and Louis Jourdan.

So one day in 1950 Selznick's chief executive, Daniel O'Shea, told Greg to report to Warner Brothers for wardrobe tests. He would be starting a Western, *Only the Valiant*.

'Wait a minute,' Greg said. 'That's not the way my deal works. I have a nonexclusive contract.'

'Yes, but David has one commitment left under your contract,' O'Shea said, 'and he sold it to Jack Warner. He needs the money. He's committed to pay you $60,000, and Warner is paying $150,000. So David made a quick profit of $90,000.'

Feeling sorry for Selznick, Greg agreed to make the film for Warner Brothers. He was well aware of Warner's reputation for making quick, cheap movies and he realized *Only the Valiant* would be a potboiler. The pioneering Warner clan started out in a rented vacant store in New Castle, Pennsylvania, christening their theater the Bijou. With 99 chairs borrowed from a nearby funeral parlor (nickelodeons always kept to the magic figure of 99 chairs because no theater license was needed for under 100 seats), Sam ran the projector, while Harry and Albert attended to business. Jack, starting at age 12, sang illustrated song-slides during reel changes.

At Warner's, actors, directors and screenwriters worked at a pace more frantic than at the other major studios and usually at lower salaries. This often led to stormy clashes between management and employees. Wilson Mizner, a Hollywood wit who had been hired to write scripts at the studio, quipped: 'Working for Warner Brothers is like fucking a porcupine – it's one hundred pricks against one.' He took a particularly dim view of the head of the operation. 'Jack Warner has oilcloth pockets so he can steal soup.'

The picture was a torment for him. He hated being in it. And when a picture wasn't going well he would go into one of his black moods at home. He was madder than a boiled owl. After the success of *Twelve O'Clock High* and *The Gunfighter*, the star found himself having to settle for a second-rate Western. But the worst part was his luscious co-star Barbara Payton. Sexually irresistible, she carried with her the seeds of his destruction.

In 1946, a term created by the French critics, film noir, came into vogue. Literally translated 'black film,' it was coined in recognition of a darkened somber mood that had begun to emerge in many films produced in America. These movies were made primarily between the early 1940s and the late 1950s, and were distinguished by their shadowy appearance, and overall mood of hopelessness, pessimism, suspicion and fear. The females in these flicks were often evil and, at the same time, demonstrated spellbinding attributes. They were hard-hearted. *Femmes fatales.* 'Bad Blondes' was a term bandied about at the time. Barbara Payton was a 'Bad Blonde.'

In type Payton could be compared to Marilyn Monroe or Jayne Mansfield, but she never achieved the heights of her celebrated contemporaries. Of course, she never had their driving ambition. Plus, her unconventional lifestyle, public brawls and longtime bout with the bottle contributed to her eventual downfall. Her freewheeling personal pursuits and problems detracted from her ability to deliver a good performance. According to James Cagney who put her in a few movies including *Only the Valiant*, 'Barbara was an actress of impressive if limited skill.'

Romantically, Payton had a lot of balls in the air. For a while she was involved with Bob Hope who, like Greg, was married. Hope dropped her; fearful her loose lips could do serious damage to his reputation.

Veteran B-movie actor Mickey Knox also dated Payton. He remembered her as a compulsive and passionate lover who '. . . kept me in bed once for three days and nights, even feeding me [there]. She wouldn't let me get out of bed! I had to crawl out on my hands and knees.'

Payton gained much publicity in 1951 when actors Franchot Tone and Tom Neil engaged in a fierce brawl for the right to date her. Tone landed in the hospital with a fractured cheekbone, broken nose, and concussion. He eventually married Payton, but the union lasted just one month and she returned to Neil. She said of Neil: 'He was the only man I ever loved.'

Filmed on location in the New Mexico Desert, *Only the Valiant* deals with an Apache attack on a cavalry troop led by Captain Richard Lance (Peck). Although Payton's part as Greg's love interest was small, it gave her career a lift for a time before the booze and black eyes got to her.

Greg was part of her heyday. In her slushy memoir, she recalled: 'I was sitting on top of the world. My particular acting talents were worth $10,000 a week, and I was in constant demand. I know it sounds unbelievable, but it's true that Gregory Peck, Guy Madison,

Howard Hughes and other big names were dating me. Almost everything I did made headlines.'

Payton claimed to be having an affair with Greg during the filming of *Only the Valiant*. And while he never denied it (the liaison was described as an affair in a biography Greg authorized), he *never* mentioned her name. She was not so discreet, sharing details about their relationship that eventually ended up in *Confidential*, a scandal magazine of the 1950s. Published by a flip, sharp, racy Broadway agent named Bob Harrison, it rehashed almost every Hollywood scandal. Determined to capitalize on the public's yearning for gossip, Harrison ballyhooed *Confidential* and was eventually selling 3,700,000 copies on the newsstands – outselling even *Reader's Digest* and *TV Guide* with his screaming headline articles.

According to *Confidential* stories, Greg and Payton once held up shooting for an afternoon. They borrowed a single horse from the studio corral and Greg perched Payton in front of him. With one hand on the reins and another clutching Payton, he rode off into the hills. On other occasions, they ducked into each other's dressing rooms. When first assigned to the movie, Greg protested bitterly about his accommodations. His room had no windows and he complained it was stuffy. According to *Confidential*, he turned happily silent after trysting with Payton.

In egregious bad taste, Payton openly praised Greg's boudoir talents. She rated him as five-star material.

The magazine article didn't appear until sometime after the fact. In the meantime, there was talk about the two on the set and around town. Greg must have heard it and perhaps also Greta. In any case, his solution – though hard-hearted – is a testimony to his strong survival skills. According to Payton, he had her banned from the *Only the Valiant* set, except when she was scheduled to play in a scene. Yelped Barbara: 'I'm banned from my own movie.'

When *Only the Valiant* premiered on 11 April 1951, the *Los Angeles Times* observed: 'Barbara Payton had little to do but look glamorous, quite a trick in an early day New Mexico fort.'

This would be the last high-quality film for Payton. The misbegotten actress continued her downhill slide with public displays of drunkenness and, finally, into prostitution. In the years following the release of *Only the Valiant,* she moved into an old, shabby, rundown apartment building on the edge of Hollywood, amid unsavory characters. With all her furs and jewelry gone, she was sometimes spotted wondering Sunset Boulevard, waiting for a bus or hitchhiking.

In 1962, at age 35, she was found sleeping on a bench at the corner of Sunset Boulevard and Stanley Avenue. Her body, clad in a bathing suit and coat, was covered with bruises, her skin blotched and her front teeth missing. She told police she had been beaten by a youth gang. They charged her with being drunk and loitering. Frank Sinatra offered her a walk-on in *Four For Texas* (1963). Sadly she was never even given a screen credit if, indeed, she showed up for work.

A few years later, according to John O'Dowd, author of *The Barbara Payton Tragedy,* sanitation workers mistook her for a bag of trash scattered beneath a dumpster in a parking lot behind a Thrifty Drug Store on Sunset Boulevard and Fairfax Avenue in the heart of Hollywood. 'As they drew closer,' writes O'Dowd, 'they discovered instead the body of a woman lying on her side, wearing only a thin, cotton shift and a pair of slippers. With a smudge of dried blood caked thick around her nose and upper lip, the woman appeared, at first glance, to be dead. The woman's brassy blonde hair, with two inches of dark roots, was bunched in knots atop her head, like some tangled beehive gone awry. So battered was her appearance that it made it almost impossible to determine what she actually looked like underneath all the layers of blood and dirt. One of the men later said that the sight of her crumpled body lying on the pavement made it appear as if she had been "dumped out of the sky." When at last they noticed she was still breathing, the two workers rushed to get help.'

On 8 May 1967, her father E Lee Redfield discovered her ravaged body on the bathroom floor. She died of liver failure. Her physical appearance was so drastically changed that it was two days before the police realized who she was. One of them gasped: 'You mean, that was Barbara Payton the movie star? God, what happened to her?'

Whatever actually occurred between Payton and Greg, one thing was certain: he was not happy with himself or the world. After the heart spasm in La Jolla, he worried about his health. Like Frank Savage, in *Twelve O'Clock High*, he was holding his emotions tightly within himself while he tried to appear supremely in control. It was just a matter of time before his body would rebel.

In the meantime, his career sped forward like a fast-moving train. Fortunately for Greg, his dark Irish features qualified him for a lead in one of the pious sexy epics so popular in the early 1950s. His dense black hair in a split widow's peak had stray hairs that frequently fell over his brow. He also had a strongly carved nose, a finely molded mouth, the upper lip not as full as the more generous, and cleft, lower one; and hard-working jaw muscles. Studio executives such as Darryl Zanuck, ransacking through the Old Testament for hot stories, were on the lookout for faces like that. He got the lead in *David and Bathsheba* (1951).

The McCarthy years of fear and blacklisting coincided with the age of epic extravaganzas: *David and Bathsheba* (1951), *The Robe* (1953), *The Egyptian* (1954), *Land of the Pharaohs* (1955), *Alexander the Great* (1956) and *The Ten Commandments* (1956). Dramas based on the Bible and on ancient history responded to the conservatism of the time, and simultaneously allowed for lots of sex and gore.

Such films were inspired partly by Hollywood's exploration of large-screen technology as a weapon against the Lilliputian television screen. Beyond all such technical questions, though, beyond all commercial questions of the struggle against television (weekly moviegoing continued dropping from about 60 million to 40 million during the 1950s), these epics represented a kind of self-portrait of the Hollywood studios in their decline and fall.

In *David and Bathsheba*, Peck played opposite Susan Hayward. She was a tough, husky-voiced redhead known as the firebrand from Brooklyn. Hungry is one of those words that always seemed to come to mind for Susan Hayward: hungry for success, for money, for love and for work. 'I learned at a very early age that life is a battle,' Hayward often said. She knew exactly what she wanted (at this particular time, the title of the movie changed to *Sheva and David*). And she knew she had to fight for what she wanted. She stormed her way through the movies and its moguls. 'The only thing a woman should ever be afraid of in her life,' Hayward used to say, 'is never having lived.'

'I've never considered myself a beauty,' she also claimed. 'I can look at the mirror and know I'm not bad looking, but I'm no raving beauty by a long shot. I guess I never thought so much about glamour as ideas about becoming a good actress.'

If there was anybody who wasn't in the mood to crack the Bible and refresh their memory of the trials of 'Dave and Sheb', Greg was prepared to feed them a catchy synopsis of the plot: 'We have a great combination – religion and sex – in *David and Bathsheba*. David gets into as much Dutch as a fellow can get into. He has four or five wives before he spots the redhead [Susan Hayward]. His own son, Absalom, turns on him. The prophet (Raymond Massey plays that part!) warns him, but he goes so far out on the limb you think it will break. Then he goes straight to the Man upstairs and promises to work differently in the future. It proves that everything will be okay with the world if we can only get back to God.'

Greg needed a sense of humor to alleviate the tension building on the *David and Bathsheba* set. He put up a wall between himself and the other actors. One of the principals in the film said of Greg: 'I have never worked with any actor who held himself so totally aloof from the rest of the cast.' Susan Hayward was also miffed at him because she resented the close bonding between Greg and Henry King, figuring she was getting short shrift in terms of acting direction and camera angles.

Born in a Brooklyn tenement and growing up hell-bent on escaping squalor, she had evolved into an accomplished actress who found stardom playing alcoholics, a death-row inmate, and a ruthless rag-trade queen. She wasn't about to be dismissed as a pretty young thing in flowing robes. Once after filming a love scene with Greg, she asked her dresser for a cup of coffee and acted as if Greg wasn't even there.

To judge by the glowing reviews for Greg's performance as the standout in the film, her paranoia was justified. The *New York Times* claimed that without Greg as a convincing David, 'this combination of romance and religion would have been merely a two-hour dissertation no more exciting than a lantern-slide projection.

However, in Gregory Peck's delineation the producers have an authoritative performance. He is a man filled with anguish at the death of Jonathan and of Saul. He is a King willing to forego his regal right for his love and he is the frail vessel who movingly confesses his sins but one who also is strong enough to exclaim, "lift Thine hand from Thy people who suffer for my crimes."'

One morning Greg was undergoing make-up tests at the Fox studio. He suddenly felt his left arm go numb and an agonizing constriction in his chest. He found himself covered with sweat and said to the make-up man, 'I think I'm having a heart attack.' He was rushed to Cedars of Lebanon Hospital and given an electrocardiogram, which revealed he hadn't suffered a heart attack, but it was another indication that he was bottling things up and needed to slow down and unwind.

After the picture wrapped, Greg and Greta went to the Yucca Loma Ranch in Apple Valley, California, for a month's vacation. The children came for weekends.

Interviewed about this break in his routine, Greg said he didn't drink the whole time. His mentioning of abstaining seems to indicate that he was concerned about his drinking and its impact on his health. He didn't think of himself as particularly young anymore.

Around this time, a reporter asked him, 'How about Shakespeare? Ever had a hankering?'

'Now you've got me,' Greg said, grinning ruefully. 'You've pinned me to the mat. I had a hankering but I've overcome it. I've got it licked. I'm a thirty-fiver – halfway around the track. This is no time to begin coaching for a Shakespearean role.'

CHAPTER TWELVE

Gentleman Hero

'Here's to girls and gunpowder!'
Gregory Peck in *The World in His Arms*

When Greg signed on for *Captain Horatio Hornblower* (1951), he approached the project with high spirits because he liked C S Forester's story and he was gung-ho about doing a film that would finally give him a chance to travel abroad. As a bonus, he had the opportunity to work with a legend in filmmaking. 'There are directors for whom I would walk through fire,' said Greg 'and Raoul Walsh is one of them.' He considered Walsh 'a nineteenth-century kind of fellow, very funny, ribald, a curmudgeon.'

Roistering Raoul Walsh, known as 'the one-eyed bandit' was 66 years old when he directed *Captain Horatio Hornblower*. He had more than a hundred movies under his belt as actor, director, producer or a combination thereof. He tackled a variety of genres but was at his best with virile outdoor action dramas, which he often mellowed with moments of genuine tenderness. Producer Jack Warner contested this appraisal, maintaining: 'To Raoul Walsh burning down a whorehouse is a tender love scene.' Like King Vidor and Henry King, Raoul Walsh used his colorful early life as the wellspring for his imagination.

The son of a clothes designer, he ran away to sea as a boy and later broke horses in cattle drives in Mexico, Texas and Montana. He did some stage acting from 1910 and entered films in 1912 as an actor and assistant director to D W Griffith at Biograph. It was Griffith who gave him his first directorial assignment, in collaboration with Christy Cabanne, *The Life of General Villa* (1914), a seven-reel mixture of staged scenes and authentic footage of Pancho Villa's military campaign starring the Mexican bandit himself. Walsh's most notable appearance as an actor was in the role of John Wilkes Booth in Griffith's *The Birth of a Nation* (1915).

A straightforward storyteller, Walsh made many fine, unpretentious, smoothly paced films with the accent on entertainment and slick production values. Douglas Fairbanks Sr, Errol Flynn, James Cagney, Humphrey Bogart, Gary Cooper and Clark Gable were among the actors who typified the masculinity of his screen heroes. A dynamic, instinctive director, he was considered by many as one of the great primitive artists of the screen. Critic Richard Shickle contended: '. . . the fact that Raoul and his contemporaries had something other than movie making, had lived hand-to-mouth doing rather humble work, gave them an edge in their work. For one thing, it was impossible for a mogul to frighten them. Since they had survived and apparently even relished living on the margins of society, they could always turn away from the big do in the glamorous life of Hollywood and go back to the life they had known before.'

Adding to his mystique, Walsh sported an eye patch having lost an eye in an automobile accident in which a jack rabbit crashed through the front window. He liked to say: 'A buzzard plucked it out.'

Walsh was famous for his tall tales and practical jokes. One yarn – which he swore was true – concerned the borrowing of the corpse of his close pal John Barrymore. After the actor died, Walsh and two of his cronies bribed the undertaker into 'lending' Barrymore's body to them for an afternoon. Since Errol Flynn was a close friend of the departed actor, they took the corpse to his home and propped up the 'Great Profile's' body in Flynn's favorite chair behind the front door with a drink in hand ready to greet the swashbuckling star. Fortunately, Flynn got the joke. 'I forgave Walsh,' he said later. 'He brought this distorted touch of genius to his films.'

The part of Hornblower was tailor-made for Greg. He would once again play the role of the martinet who was really a softy beneath the grim exterior. Greg devoured Forester's books and appreciated the fact that Hornblower was not 100 per cent heroic and that 'he got seasick.' He was 'unhappy in love yet refreshingly humane, he turns his talents to the needs of his country.'

Greg's meticulous attention to detail can be seen in his approach to this film. He learned to 'shoot the sun' with the quadrant. He developed an intimate knowledge of gunnery. He learned the principles and the rules of navigation. And he could explain the intricacies of a square-rigged frigate or even a ship-of-the-line. What's more, he could splice a line with the saltiest of them. He also did a lot of general reading: naval histories, records of decisive sea battles and memoirs written by great naval figures. Homework paid off. As the lean and hard Captain Hornblower he paces the quarter-deck, shouts to his crew, and conducts himself as the epitome of Forester's fictional hero.

Walsh had the formidable challenge of bringing to the screen what many consider to be the greatest sea story of all time. 'The worst enemy a motion picture director can have,' said Walsh as the production got underway, 'is a preconceived notion.' He was referring to the preconceived notion held by hundreds of thousands of readers of Forester's *Hornblower* stories all over the world.

It was only proper that *Captain Horatio Hornblower* should be filmed in its natural British and Mediterranean setting; and Warner Brothers made use of two London studios, a couple of British seaports and much of the south of France, including coastal water there.

'Ever since I started acting, I've cherished the idea of playing this role,' Greg said, schoolboyishly excited about the swagger, romantics and excitement of the part. 'We shot in four months,' Greg said. 'We worked a six-day week all through the picture.' With Greta and the boys in tow, he journeyed along the French Riviera and also rented a house in London for part of the shoot. He recalled: 'We had an Irish staff. It was all very fine, except the cooking; but they were such nice hearty girls I didn't have the heart to ask them to leave.' A nurse came along for five-month-old Carey and Jonathan and Stephen attended nursery school where they got a kick out of seeing Scots lads in kilts. One aspect of their London stay, which received a lot of publicity, was a visit to the set by Princesses Elizabeth and Margaret. They came specifically to see Peck – Princess Margaret admitted he was her favorite actor – and were disappointed when they learned it was his day off. Adding to

Greg's mystique, his co-star Virginia Mayo proclaimed him 'the best kisser in the business.'

For Greg, the European sojourn opened new worlds to him – and widened the distance between himself and Greta. It brought out a restless longing in him and he wasn't sure where it was going to lead. The French Riviera completely captivated Greg, so much so that years later, he bought a house in Cap Ferrat. His entire being responded to the tranquility of the olive trees, exotic flowers and superb light. And the people loved him. Everywhere he went Greg was given a warm reception. At Cagnes sur Mer, a small medieval village not far from Nice, where Walsh was shooting a number of scenes for the film, the young country girls lined up to give him flowers.

Walsh recalled a funny incident during the shooting: 'I had this big frigate down in a place called Villa France in the Mediterranean, south of France. And I had a sailing scene with Peck standing up, giving the helmsman orders to bring it up to this big wharf. Now, right close by this wharf is a series of cheap apartments. Most of them have a balcony. They are very cheap places; in fact, they are all inhabited by prostitutes. So when we got ready to take this scene – all of a sudden, up on one of these balconies, a naked woman appeared. Stark naked. Right in the center of the camera. So I had to stop the scene.

'I told my French assistant to call out to her, that if she wanted to watch the scene, would she please put something on? She disappeared. Then we turned the boat around and came back, and as we started to approach the dock again, out she came, stark naked, with a big picture hat on.'

Filming outside of America affected Greg's tax position and there was concern as to 'whether or not Peck would be entitled to any tax exemption under the tax treaty [between the United States and Britain].' It was not clear that Greg was working for an individual or company currently resided in the United States. This sort of tax bargaining would eventually appear to work in his favor and lead to his shooting several films overseas.

Arriving home in LA, Greg was once again put under the microscope and pressured to present the image of the happy husband and ideal father as promoted by the film studios. He had been named Father of the Year back in 1948 and so it was not surprising that *Good Housekeeping* magazine paid the Pecks a visit on the couple's return so they could chronicle the star's blissful family life.

Greg explained the family routine to the reporter: 'Early in the evening is my play hour with the boys; they have an early dinner and then to bed. I am not a "romper," but we have some good times together just the same . . . The boys do not have dinner with us except on special occasions. That is the one time of the day when Greta and I have a chance to talk.'

Greg went on to explain that Jonathan was attending public school. As a couple, they favored 'good-sized classes where there isn't much individual attention and where he has a chance to shift for himself. Greta has been a member of the PTA and I make it a point to drop in and visit his schoolroom occasionally, when I arrive a little early to pick him up.'

Then Greg told the reporter about an interest of Jonathan's that didn't appear to be alarming at the time. However, in the light of Jonathan's tragic death in 1975 by self-inflicted gunshot, it is prophetic. 'He has dozens of technical questions about guns, which fascinate him,' explained Greg. 'They fascinate most boys and it seems to be a natural interest. Rather than fight it, I'm going to teach him how to use one. He's been promised a BB gun when he's eight and a .22 when he's ten, and I'll take him out into the woods and teach him how to shoot. That's better than letting him go along fascinated by guns, but knowing nothing about handling them. That's just plain foolhardy – dangerous.'

It was hard to get away from the studio pressure on actors and actresses to conform to the image that they were just regular folks by day who transformed into gods and divas by night. Often reality had to be adjusted to fit the image. Sid Avery, the iconic Hollywood photographer of the 1950s and 1960s remembers arriving to photograph Marlon Brando for a spread on the actor's supposedly normal 'everyday life.' He wanted to take a picture of Brando in the kitchen, but it was filthy. 'It was up to your chest in old bags and paper cartons and a lot of other things,' said Avery. 'I don't think he'd ever cleaned it, and I hinted, if you'd just clean up your act a little bit, then we could take pictures.' The result: a homey shot of one of Hollywood's biggest stars taking out the trash.

Yet, when stars went out on the town, the studios insisted they shine like supernovas and encouraged them to huddle together in order to generate more glitter: no hobnobbing with underlings. Shelly Winters remembered: 'There were definite rules on how stars were supposed to behave when they were out in public. You are to be photographed only with someone as important or more important than yourself.'

Given specific instructions by Universal on the proper conduct of a star, Winters went to a cocktail party that preceded the Golden Globe awards. She recalled she was 'looking gorgeous and chatting with gorgeous Gregory Peck. We were discussing something banal, and a character actor I knew stopped by, said hello and joined us and improved the conversation.' Just then, one of the foreign photographers wanted to take a picture. Winters was dismayed by what followed: 'Gregory Peck edged me away from the unimportant character actor so that we two stars could pose by ourselves – it would be safer for our careers. No doubt Peck had been given the same pep talk by the Selznick publicity office and was trying to obey his orders. I was offended. If being a star meant I couldn't associate with character actors, who weren't stars, I wanted no part of this kind of studio system.'

True, Greg did what he could to accommodate both the studios and the press. And the gods rewarded him. In January 1951 he received the Henrietta, an award from the Foreign Press Association, proclaiming him the world film favorite, based on a world-wide poll that garnered more than a million votes.

In theory, Greg should have been able to ease up on his killer work hours. 'I had so many contracts, managers and agents that I felt more like a corporation than an actor,' said Greg of the years he had put behind him. 'That's when I determined to ride out my commitments and work towards becoming an individual again.'

The script for *The World in His Arms* (1952) entertained Greg so thoroughly that he accepted the offer to star in it less than an hour after he finished reading it. (An added inducement was his guaranteed $100,000 and part of the profits.) Adapted from a novel by adventure writer Rex Beach, it was an action-packed yarn to be directed by Raoul Walsh, who was just right for the fast-moving tempo of the story. 'A picture needs action, action and more action,' said Walsh at the time. 'That was the theme of the earliest picture and it's the theme of the successful ones today. Keep things happening on the screen.'

In this adventure story, Greg tries to buy Alaska from the Russians but settles instead for Ann Blyth, one of the lesser-known Romanovs. The so-called historical background (seal fisheries and Russian commercial imperialism) was an excuse for swashbuckling melodrama, which involved battles royal, wild sea chases, and prodigious amounts of drinking and boasting.

Walsh's directorial style included lots of drinking and action as well. He liked to act out his scenes behind the camera while his actors were performing in front of it. In fact, he was known to lose as much as 15 pounds during the production on a picture with his blow-for-blow offstage antics. Greg was a hearty admirer of his impromptu vaudeville act, referring to Walsh as a 'one-man stock company.' When Greg blew his lines in the middle of a sequence, he excused himself by saying he was only waiting for Walsh to catch up with him. On lunch breaks Walsh fueled his spirits with spirits and Greg usually joined him for a couple of stiff belts over steak.

'Dutch courage' came in handy. Walsh, a veteran actor, stipulated that a fight scene in a motion picture had to measure up to the standards set by him when he was appearing in such scenes himself. 'In those days we had to really put on a show,' reminisced Walsh. 'I hadn't been in the business ten years before I had broken both arms – one of them twice – had my nose broken three different times, and had been knocked absolutely unconscious more times than a punch-drunk fighter.'

Even with such a stellar role model, Greg was no Errol Flynn. He just couldn't throw caution to the winds when brandishing a sword or pummeling someone with his fists. *Theater Arts* magazine wrote him off as a 'prim' swashbuckler.

Thank God for Ava Gardner! Just when there was a possibility

Greg's life could disintegrate into humdrum routine she showed up, this time cast opposite him in the screen adaptation of a superb Ernest Hemingway short story, *The Snows of Kilimajaro* (1952). By this time, Gardner had been married to Frank Sinatra for eight weeks and dramas in her personal life were playing out a mile a minute. She was sorely in need of Father Peck's pastoral counseling.

Since *The Snows of Kilimanjaro* was a slim story, screenwriter Casey Robinson took it upon himself to pick his way through Hemingway's body of work and lift here and there to fill out his script. Naturally, 'Papa' didn't take well to this idea. He fumed: 'I sold Fox a single story, not my complete works. This movie has something from nearly every story I ever wrote.' He took to calling it *The Snows of Zanuck*.

While Hemingway didn't play a part in the shaping of the movie, he did ask Zanuck to cast Ava Gardner as Cynthia Green. Papa had admired her performance in *The Killers*, a 1946 film based on his short story and, in fact, referred to her as the greatest actress in films.

In the movie, Greg plays Harry Street, a writer with whom Greg shared similarities in personality – a burning temper and melancholy moods. Harry languishes on his deathbed thanks to a gangrened leg. A writer of too easy popular success, he reviews his life with much bitterness. He lies on the slope of Africa's famous mountain and thinks back on his life while awaiting medical attention. 'Africa' is this case is a back screen projection; fortunately, the majority of the film is told through flashbacks set in France, Spain, and parts of the 'Dark Continent.' Harry's relationships with various women (played by Susan Hayward, Ava Gardner, and Hildegard Knef) are at the center of his recollections, but the overall thesis is a very Hemingway-esque summary of the responsibility of a writer to get to the truth. His Harry is a thoroughly honest and courageous, but confused and somewhat embittered twentieth-century man. The film paints a wide canvas of his involvement in the Spanish Civil War, in game hunting and after that, in the frivolous fun and games of international high society.

If *The Snows of Kilimanjaro* was made today, the crew would go straight to Africa. As it was, they played in front of a big set against the painting of Mount Kilimanjaro which went two-thirds the way around the sound stage, creating massive problems for the sound technicians. Then they put in trees, brush, tents – all sorts of things – to make it look like Africa. The trees and foliage had to move, there were wires and wind machines everywhere. When hunting wild game, Greg found himself shooting against a blank screen.

Casey Robinson's job was to put words in Greg's mouth that came tripping off the tongue. 'I was worried that his propensity to think words through, in this case, would make them seem false,' remembered Robinson. 'I was in great doubt about my screenplay, which used a stream of consciousness method with many flashbacks, new to the screen. There was no time pattern. I guess we both were a bit wrong, for it turned out to be one of Peck's best films, and it amassed a box-office record, up to that time, for Twentieth Century Fox.'

While making the movie, Greg's name was linked with German actress Hildegard Knef. Even Robinson claimed Greg 'was experimenting with all kinds of dames on the set.' In the case of Knef, however, she was by no means an easy 'dame' with which to experiment. 'Through the profession of acting I was catapulted to Hollywood,' Knef reminisced, 'where I thought the war was over and everybody loved everybody. I found out nobody loves anybody, and the resentment against the Germans was so tremendous it made me absolutely speechless. I was put on ice and dragged out every time they needed a glamorous spy for a Darryl Zanuck movie. I went from a dictatorship to a dictatorship operetta.'

Gardner came to the production but with strings attached. Sinatra's career had hit a low ebb, and he wanted her with him. When the shooting went over the allotted ten days of her contract, Sinatra and Gardner revolted in the midst of a battle scene, which involved more than 400 extras. Robinson blamed Sinatra: 'I hated the little bastard because he was making my girl unhappy.' Gardner confessed to Robinson that she did not understand some of the language and the thought processes of her character, but she succeeded with it quite nicely and launched her career as an international star. Hemingway told her: 'The only two good things in it were you and the hyena.'

Stick it in your ear, Papa! The critics loved Greg. For him, *The Snows of Kilimanjaro* represented a peak in his career. It marked his return to playing a sturdily American character, where most critics felt his true strength resided. While he still had rough going ahead of him in his personal life, professionally the best was yet to come.

CHAPTER THIRTEEN

When in Rome – and Paris

'Half a century ago a coal miner who found himself in a fashionable restaurant would not have the faintest idea of how to behave; nowadays he has only to ask himself, "How would Gregory Peck do it?"'

Frederick Lewis Allen, *The Big Change*

Her name was Veronique Passani, and she was stunning. Greg would never forget the first time he met her in the spring of 1952. He was on his way to Rome to film *Roman Holiday* (1953), a light comedy about a runaway princess and a suave newspaperman with ulterior motives. She was a fledgling reporter on assignment for *France Soir*. And this assignment was a feather in her cap.

Greg was at the height of his fame. Many people considered him to be the handsomest man on the planet. The French press tagged him 'No. 1 Great Screen Lover.' He deserved the title, they said, not for his romantic fire, but for the finesse he displayed in any love scene. The French love finesse. So there was much curiosity about the star.

'We had lunch on the Left Bank in Paris in a bistro,' he remembered. 'She was 19, and I was 36 years old. She was a journalist, and I was immediately attracted to her.'

Veronique was a petite Parisian with great almond eyes, raven hair and an intriguing smile. She was also coy, careful not to unnerve Greg with a barrage of questions. Perhaps she had heard he reacted to the journalistic interrogation process like a patient strapped to a dentist's chair, flinching, squirming and grimacing. So she waited patiently and looked at him worshipfully as he found the right words to express himself.

Her technique worked. He spoke knowledgeably and thought-fully in that deep, almost hypnotic voice. 'We just talked,' he remembered. 'There was sort of a wonderful gaze and a deep intelligence and great poise about her, though she was only 20.'

When he recollected this meeting, Greg referred to it as 'the luckiest day of my life.' He didn't mention Greta was with him. Yet, according to Greta, Veronique interviewed both of them. Of course, it might not have been *that* interview she was referring to. It could have taken place in Rome. Veronique popped up there and interviewed Greg for *France Soir* while he was on location. And Greta said she had seen the French woman five or six times. In any case, the stage was set for a long hot summer.

Riding the express train from Paris to Rome with Greta and the boys, Greg was filled with high spirits. Everything was falling into place. Ever since the European filming of *Captain Horatio Hornblower*, he had been itching to live in Europe for a while. Now his dream was being realized partly through the auspices of the Internal Revenue! They had recently put through a ruling that if you lived abroad for 18 months you didn't have to pay US income taxes. So Greg was joining the exodus of movie stars who started to take up residence in Paris, London and Rome. His plan was to stay there with his family for at least a year and a half.

Roman Holiday also offered him the opportunity to star in a film comedy, a welcome change from the heavier stuff he'd been doing. And, what's more, the reverse Cinderella plot had the earmark of a winner.

As the story begins, Princess Anne (Audrey Hepburn), who is the daughter of a king of an unnamed European country, is touring the capital cities of Europe. Her life is one long round of appearances on behalf of her country's government. To make matters worse, the lovely young princess is constantly being ordered about by her guardians, and even the maids, who all want her to act decorously and to be exposed only to things that are suitable for a princess.

Anne, on the other hand, aches to experience life. So she simply breaks loose one evening on a visit to Rome and flees her country's embassy. Unfortunately, her maid had popped a heavy tranquilizer in her nightly glass of warm milk, and the drowsy Anne falls unconscious out on a public bench. Tough guy news reporter Joe

Bradley (Peck), who is an American assigned to Rome and is perpetually broke, takes pity on her. What can he do but take her to his apartment to sleep it off? The next day he discovers who she is, but hoping to get a big story that will boost his career, he teams up with a photographer (Eddie Albert) and they give the princess a truly hilarious Roman holiday, while gleefully snapping pictures for their 'exclusive.'

A catchy story indeed, but little did Greg know it would become one of the most charming, whimsical and beautiful comedies ever brought to the screen. And the reason for that, of course, had much to do with the splendid directing of William Wyler and the film's exquisite female lead, a Belgian ingénue named Audrey Hepburn.

Hepburn was born in Brussels as Edda Kathleen van Heemstra Hepburn-Ruston, the daughter of a Belgian countess and a British banker. Trained as a dancer, she played the cigarette girl in the opening scene of Charles Crichton's *Lavender Hill Mob* and, while acting in Jean Boyer's *Nous Irons a Monte-Carlo* in Paris, had been chosen by Colette herself to play the title role in the future musicalization of *Gigi*. Soon, she caught the eye of Hollywood.

One of the people who noticed her was William Wyler. He'd picked up the *Roman Holiday* project from Frank Capra and he knew that in order to pull it off he needed an actress with continental poise. After looking around in London and interviewing several girls, Wyler decided to test Hepburn. She had a delightful affectation in voice and delivery that was controlled just enough to have charm and serve as a trademark, as well as the looks and poise to make her role of a princess of a not-too-mythical-country come over strongly. Although the studio was pressuring him to use Elizabeth Taylor, he decided on Hepburn.

However, Wyler did have some initial reservations. After viewing her screen test, he told Hepburn, 'I thought you were a bit fat.' She admitted it was absolutely true at the time of testing. 'I ate everything in sight, having been undernourished during the war. You know, whole boxes of chocolates. I was ten pounds more than I ever weighed in my life. It's funny to think I might not have gotten the part because I was too fat, because from then on everybody thought I was too thin.' Separately, Hepburn also heard that Wyler 'stuck his neck out' for her because she was 'not only an unknown, but a thoroughly inexperienced unknown.'

Wyler was able to get Audrey Hepburn because the signing of Gregory Peck satisfied Paramount's demands for a star with marquee value. 'According to Hollywood mathematics, now that I had a male star, I didn't need a stellar leading lady. I wanted a girl without an American accent to play the princess, someone you could *believe* was brought up as a princess.'

Greg, too, gave her career a big push. 'In those days stars had approval of script and co-actors,' said Hepburn. 'Greg could have said at the time, "She's just a little dancer, and perhaps we'd better get someone more established."'

Alighting from the train in Rome, Greg helped Greta settle the children with their nurse in a hotel, then the couple took a moonlight stroll through the Eternal City. The next morning they moved into the beautiful villa – complete with waterfall – they rented in Albino, 25 miles outside the capital.

Before leaving the United States, the Pecks packed large stores of food for the children, which turned out to be completely unnecessary. Jonathan, eight, and Stephen, six, went pasta crazy. Even little Carey, age three, learned to love Italian dishes. Greta hired a tutor, a Mr Ricknor, and the children took to him right away. They were even managing to pick up a little Italian. Greg beamed with pride when his two older boys taught some Italian youths how to play baseball.

Reporting to the Cinecittà Studios, Rome's biggest film complex, Greg joined other members of the cast who gathered around William Wyler for a quick meeting before launching into the film. 'Now, boys and girls,' said the director, 'there's just one prima donna on this picture and I'm that one. And I want that understood from the beginning!'

Nobody questioned Wyler's authority to pull rank. He may have been irascible, tempestuous and highly demanding, but he was also a superb craftsman and one of the most inventive stylists of the American screen. Some of the best-loved movies of the 1930s and 1940s were Wyler films. He had racked up eight Academy Award nominations for Best Director prior to *Roman Holiday*, winning his

Oscars for *Mrs Miniver* (1942) and *The Best Years of Our Lives* (1946). Known for his sensitive direction of great actors, he worked with some of the best, including John Barrymore, Bette Davis, Humphrey Bogart and Myrna Loy.

His ascent to the peaks of Hollywood began in a gingerly fashion. His daughter, film producer Kathryn Wyler, remembered: 'His very early start came when he rigged up a smoking machine for an editor who was editing nitrate film which was very combustible, and the guy was dying for a smoke. So, my father, as a young twerp at the studio, rigged up a long piece of metal pipe. He could have a cigarette out the window and be inside and smoke. And that was my father's entrée into the editing room.'

Greg knew going into the project that the story was really about the princess. In fact, Cary Grant had turned down the role for just that reason. He was willing to accept this limitation because he wanted to play comedy. Nothing prepared him, however, for the allure of his co-star. The princess role was perfect for her. She was stunningly beautiful, a gamine with a long neck and thick eyebrows that drew attention to huge limpid eyes. Everybody on the set fell in love with her; and it quickly became obvious that the public was going to be enchanted.

With a mischievous glint in his eyes, he said to Wyler: 'Willie, this new girl is stealing the movie right under our noses. Don't bother about camera angles. Just shoot the picture fast!'

Greg, of course, knew that his name on the marquee carried the film's value, but it didn't seem fair to Hepburn. He explained: 'I called my agent after two weeks, and I said, "George, you've got to change the billing." The billing was to be "Gregory Peck in *Roman Holiday.*" He said, "Why? What's the matter with you?" I said, "Nothing's the matter with me, but I'm smart enough to know this girl's going to win the Oscar in her first picture, and I'm going to look like a damn fool if her name is not up there on top with mine."'

For the rest of her career, Hepburn expressed gratitude to Greg for such a magnanimous gesture. And, considering the vanity of movie stars, it was a definite show of gallantry even if she was going to win an Academy Award.

Screenwriter Garson Kanin once tried to encourage Spencer

Tracy to show similar generosity toward Katharine Hepburn since the two were paired so often on screen and were lovers in private. 'It was always Tracy and Hepburn. I chided him once about his insistence on first billing. "Why not?" he asked. "Well, after all," I argued, "she's the lady. You're the man. Ladies first?" He said, "This is a movie, chowderhead, not a lifeboat."'

Chris Chase, a struggling actress during the 1950s, took Audrey Hepburn's good fortune personally. Writing about her own picaresque adventures in *How to Be a Movie Star, or A Terrible Beauty is Born,* she describes sitting in a darkened movie theater watching Audrey Hepburn playing opposite Greg in *Roman Holiday*: '. . . I realized there were first breaks and first breaks. There was a girl being given her baptism by silver screen, and it wasn't in any alley with a NO TOILET sign. The director had set her, like a jewel, into the middle of beautiful Rome, with beautiful clothes and beautiful Gregory Peck, and it made me sick.'

In the script of *Roman Holiday,* Hepburn's Princess Anne pretends to be a student and tells Greg's Joe Bradley she would like to do what her heart dictates for at least one Roman holiday. Joe goes along with her and they make the scenic rounds of Rome with Eddie Albert, as 'fotog', tailing along with his cameras. (Bradley extracted a promise of a $5,000 bonus from his editor for an exclusive account of the princess's real personality.) It is a gay, fancy-free day for Princess Anne and Joe Bradley. They have pleasant adventures, dance on a barge in the Tiber, tangle with secret service agents and become affectionate.

Exhilarated by shooting outdoors, Wyler used the ancient buildings and streets of Rome as a colorful and beautiful backdrop for his production and direction, and the Eternal City is an unusually effective part of the entertainment. He shows the workaday Rome; of sidewalk cafés, of the Pantheon, of the Forum, of such various landmarks as the Castel San Angelo and the rococo, mirrored grandeur of the Colonna, Brancaccio and Barberini Palazzi.

Wyler deftly used ordinary Italians, not professional actors, to play themselves in the picture with a fluency not often found in films. There is a cab driver, for example, who refuses to be responsible for the seemingly intoxicated girl, thus forcing Joe to

Greg holds the collar of his best friend Bud. A mutt with Airedale in the mix, Bud could outdistance Greg's father's car going 30 miles an hour.

Left: A pharmacist in San Diego, Gregory Peck Sr. stands next to his pride and joy. Hoping his college age son would become a doctor, he tried to steer him away from acting. He warned: 'You'll be broke at 35 and you'll end up borrowing from me.'

Left: A fleeting presence in his youth, Greg's mother, Bernice Peck Maysuch, relishes the role of grandmother. As Greg tries to calm his sons, Bernice (nicknamed Bunny) holds Jonathan and Stephen.

Below: Greg attends a soiree with second wife Veronique and their daughter Cecilia, accompanied by actor Adrian Passer. He regarded Veronique – a clever, cultivated French woman – as the great love of his life.

Above: Greg shares a light-hearted moment with first wife Greta and sons Jonathan and Stephen. She supported Greg in his journey from unknown actor to one of Hollywood's hottest stars.

Below left: Veterans Day 2000. Steve Peck, 54, joins Greg, 84, and Greta, 89, at a reception honoring servicemen. Although divorced, Greta remained loyal to Greg.

Below right: Jonathan Peck committed suicide in 1975 at age 31. The tragedy almost destroyed Greg.

Opposite: London, 1960. Hearty laughs on the set of *The Guns of Navarone* (1961). Greg and Stanley Baker trade quips with David Niven, who is dressed in formal attire for a day at the races.

Above: Wrapping up *Roman Holiday*, Greg embarked on a whirlwind romance with June Dally-Watkins. He invited the Australian model to follow him from Rome to Paris. She refused.

Right: Greg took a fatherly interest in Kansas student Jeff Lang, who created a website dedicated to the star. He cited Lang as 'the reason I'm famous on the Internet.'

On the set of *Spellbound* (1945), Ingrid Bergman and Greg take direction from Alfred Hitchcock. The sexual heat generated between the two actors raised eyebrows on the set.

Below: Playing lascivious Lewt McCanles (a role he loved) in *Duel in the Sun* (1947), Greg is united in death with sultry Pearl Chavez, portrayed by Jennifer Jones. Dubbed lust-in-the-dust, this high camp Western incurred the wrath of film censors.

As swashbuckling hero *Horatio Hornblower*, Greg braves the high seas with radiant beauty Virginia Mayo. He was ideally suited to play the courageous captain, who exudes leadership but is plagued by self-doubt.

Portraying Hemingway's hard-living protagonist Harry in *The Snows of Kilimanjaro*, Greg meets his match in Cynthia, played by tempestuous Ava Gardner. The two stars developed a deep friendship. Greg appreciated Gardner's unflinching candor and ribald sense of humor. He often called her his favorite leading lady.

Maverick director John Huston adjusts Greg's unruly hair during filming of *Moby Dick* (1956). Though intrigued by Huston's wild imagination and reckless approach to life, Greg eventually called it quits to their friendship. Nonetheless, Huston claimed: 'Greg is one of the nicest, straightest guys I ever knew, and there's a size to him.'

What's a Western without a fistfight? Here, Greg slugs Chuck Connors in *The Big Country* (1958). Off-screen, Greg feuded bitterly with brilliant director William Wyler with whom he co-produced the film.

Sophia Loren and Greg go belly down in *Arabesque* (1966), a cunning spy caper directed by Stanley Donen. Reviewers criticized it as a Hitchcock knock-off.

Above: During a break in filming location shooting for *The Guns of Navarone* on the island of Rhodes in Greece, Greg faces down master chess player Anthony Quinn as Anthony Quale studies their moves. *Navarone* proved to be one of the most popular World War Two movies ever made. It garnered seven Academy Awards.

Above: As southern lawyer Atticus Finch, who defends a black man accused of rape in *To Kill a Mockingbird*, Greg plays the quintessential American hero. He identified completely with the part.

Omar Sharif played a priest and Greg an anti-Fascist hero in the Spanish Civil War film *Behold a Pale Horse* (1964). Directed by Fred Zinnemann, the film faltered at the box office. Surmized Greg: 'It lacked passion and that's a big lack.'

In *The Omen* (1976), a horror film with a Satanic twist, Greg plays the Devil's foster dad. Co-star Lee Remick was an elegant Yankee beauty, who started out playing saucy flirts.

Harrison Ford and his girlfriend Calista Flockhart join leading movie industry figures and the general public for a memorial service honoring Greg at Our Lady of Angels Cathedral in Los Angeles. Among the approximately 3,000 mourners were Harry Belafonte, Anjelica Huston, Brock Peters and Michael Jackson.

In *Roman Holiday* (1952), Greg plays a dashing journalist in love with a princess. Smitten with his co-star Audrey Hepburn, Greg admitted: 'I liked her a lot. In fact I loved Audrey. It was easy to love her.'

put her up for the night in his own room. There is the barber, played by Paolo Carlini, who cuts her hair reluctantly and then invites her to dance with him by the river. Rome's citizens loved the spectacle and joined in the spirit of the film. Greg recalled acting in front of 'a gallery of about 5,000 Italians, every one a critic and actor.'

A scene just about everybody remembers from the movie is the scooter ride. Greg careens through the streets, alleys and market places with Hepburn shrieking with delight and bear-hugging him for dear life.

This was Americans' first exposure to the jaunty Italian Vespa. The movie launched a trend. For several decades it was the cool means of transportation for American college students, academics and artists. The Italians loved that Americans adopted their motor scooter. For people living in Italy the Vespa is a piece of their history. 'It symbolizes the reconstruction of Italy after the war,' said Roberto Leardi, head of the Vespa Club of Italy. 'I can still remember the days when a family of four would pile on to a Vespa. The father driving, the mother behind and the children on both ends.'

Greg threw himself into the spirit of the street theater. 'I've lost 16 pounds, worked every day, from dawn to long after dark, grabbed a sandwich on the run, and have been so exhausted I couldn't sleep, but every second has been worth it. In Hollywood you get ingrown. Here, working in the natural settings with live audiences, has been wonderful. The other day Audrey and I did a cozy little love scene with 4,000 Romans crowded around us.'

The Italians couldn't get enough of the friendly Yank they called 'Gregori Peek.' Everywhere he went mobs of people followed him. The *American Weekly* newspaper said he was the most popular American ever to visit and work in Italy. A member of the US Embassy admitted that Greg's behavior toward the Italian people had probably done more to make friends for Uncle Sam than the entire diplomatic corps. 'He became one of them overnight,' he said.

Greg thrived on the adulation. 'The Italians sure do love me,' he said with a wide smile. 'Let me tell you about the first time I really got caught in a mob after a baseball game between an Italian and Spanish team. I threw out the first ball and sat in the box but after the game the crowd got out of hand and 25 police helped me get into a room with a heavy door.'

It was tough finding time to see his family. When they filmed at the Coliseum, he worked 24 hours straight. And it was difficult making the commute to and from Albino. Once his car broke down and he was an hour late to the set. Wyler forgave him but Greg was so mortified he never forgot it. When he did have an afternoon off, he and Greta, with Jonathan and Stephen, wandered about the city snapping pictures, always followed closely by mobs of people, young and old. The newspapers freely speculated about a romance between Audrey Hepburn and Gregory Peck. And that can not have enhanced domestic relations.

In the middle of July 1952, Greta flew with the boys to London to join her 74-year-old mother, Emily Piipari, who was arriving there after having taken her first plane ride. Mrs Piipari was a homebody who seldom ventured from her 127-acre farm in the Finger Lakes region of New York State. She loved crocheting and knitting. In fact, she crocheted 20 pairs of curtains for the windows of her farmhouse. But that wasn't her only forte; she also spoke four languages – Finnish, Swedish, Russian and English – fluently, and had studied German. Although she was eager to venture out and practice her language skills, she was anxious about the trip. To ease her apprehensions, Greg had sent Mrs Piipari a number of cards and letters explaining in detail everything she would need to know in order to have a good time. While in London, mother and daughter saw *Call Me Madam* and *The Deep Blue Sea* at the Duchess Theater.

From there they journeyed to Helsinki for the XV Olympic Games and a visit with relatives. Mother and daughter hadn't been back to Helsinki since Greta was a child. What a fascinating time to check into the old hometown. The Soviets were returning to the Olympic fold after a 40-year absence. Ironically, they chose to make their comeback in Finland, a country they had invaded twice during the Second World War. The competition of East versus West dominated the atmosphere. Bob Hope single-handedly intensified the Cold War when he said on a telethon to raise money for the US team: 'I guess old Joe Stalin thinks he is going to show up our soft, capitalistic Americans. We've got to cut him down to size.'

At Greg's request, Paramount studios arranged for Greta and her mother to be greeted with bouquets of red roses and furnished with an automobile. Emily Piipari attended four of the Olympic events and Greta watched them all. If she was worried about Greg's wandering eye, she didn't show it. With her characteristic effervescence, she strengthened the bonds with her large Finnish family. For their part, they were thrilled she'd married a movie star.

Back in Rome, Greg was doing his best to turn in a fine performance for William Wyler. A perfectionist and a taskmaster, Wyler had acquired the nickname '90-take Wyler' for the many takes he filmed of every shot until he was satisfied that he had achieved a desired effect or nuance. Many performers resented his tyranny on the set but being a perfectionist himself, Greg didn't mind.

There wasn't the smallest detail that escaped Wyler's attention. He molded the performance of his actors as a sculptor molds his clay, until after innumerable takes he got what he wanted. Someone asked Greg: 'How can you stand working with a director who insists on 37 takes for a two-line scene? Doesn't it drive you right round the bend?' To which Greg simply countered: 'I want to reach for my ultimate best. Once it's on film, it's there forever.'

Buoyed by the on-screen romance and the after-hours adulation from the 23-year-old Hepburn, Greg did all he could to help her turn in a polished performance despite her inexperience. There was nothing of the hardened professional about Hepburn and it wasn't just a matter of her youth. Greg could see that in her character she didn't have any backstabbing, grasping, petty or gossipy aspects. And that was *very* rare in an actress. He recalled warmly: 'It was my good luck, during that wonderful summer in Rome, to be the first of her screen fellows, to hold out my hand, and help her keep her balance as she did her spins and pirouettes. Those months [were] probably the happiest experience I ever had making movies.'

Another time he reflected: 'Everyone on the set of *Roman Holiday* was in love with Audrey. We did that one picture together, and I think it was the happiest experience I ever had on a movie set. There were a lot of tender feelings that we projected on to the screen.' The two stars frequently dined together.

Although their names lit up the tabloids, a good guess is nothing happened beyond heavy flirting and perhaps a few stolen kisses. Hepburn told writer Michael Munn: 'If there was anything going on, it didn't last long because most of our time was taken up with work. It's true that I had an enormous crush on him. But I was engaged at the time [to Jimmy Hanson, son of a wealthy Huddersfield businessman] and I even had my wedding gown hanging in the wardrobe of my Roman hotel room. And Greg was married to Greta. I knew that he wasn't happy, that his marriage was not good even though they had three lovely children. Maybe he did feel something for me, maybe there was a little chemistry between us that made our scenes work. I was in Rome, being treated like a princess, and it was not difficult for me to believe I was the princess in the film, and it was not difficult for me to believe I was in love with Gregory Peck.'

In the meantime, Veronique Passani had managed to get herself the assignment from *France Soir* to write a story on *Roman Holiday*. It's not clear how much time she spent with Greg that summer in Rome. Observers said she became infatuated with Greg and stayed in Rome to be near him. And around this time, Greg started backing off from the press. An editorial in a Rome newspaper took him to task for being a 'temperamental representative from Hollywood, who refuses to cooperate with, or even to see, Italian reporters.' How could this be? Greg was once voted 'most cooperative actor' by the Hollywood Women's Press Club.

Greta flew back to Rome after the Olympics. Then she packed up and took Jonathan, Stephen and Carey to Paris, the city she and Greg had decided on as their European base, to get the two eldest enrolled in school. Emily Piipari, who had stayed on in Finland to visit with relatives, flew to Paris to join her. Happy to exercise her grandmother skills, she spent a month there and often took the children to school or accompanied them home.

Even with her mother's help, it wasn't easy for Greta to be a woman, without a husband, raising three children in a strange city. The Paris that greeted her in the autumn of 1952 was threadbare and full of arduous challenges. La Ville Lumière still had not recovered from the war. Neglected for years, public and private buildings needed repainting and other repairs. Antique buses plied the city streets. Otherwise the resourceful Parisians got around by bicycles, tricycles, horse carts, rickety trucks and dilapidated cars, propelled by kerosene or charcoal engines.

Back in Italy, Greg embarked on his own personal Roman Holiday. His companion in this adventure was June Dally-Watkins, an Australian beauty of 25, who was touring the world in a one-woman fashion show. A country girl from an isolated small town in New South Wales, Dally-Watkins had been born illegitimate and, like Greg, grew up outside the setting of the nuclear family. But she was lucky, just like him. God kissed her face – and he didn't do a bad job with the rest of her. Endowed with classic features, a tall graceful frame and a zest for life, she went on to become Australia's top model in the period following the Second World War.

In her memoir, *The Secrets Behind My Smile,* Dally-Watkins recalls her touring solo fashion show and the rigors of climbing into and out of 20 ensembles in record time. It was 'as ambitious and as comical as a one-person band. As both compère and mannequin, I spoke to the audience about the next outfit I was to model, disappeared backstage to frantically change clothes, then reappeared trying not to look frazzled as I walked amongst the seated audience.'

In Rome, Dally-Watkins checked into a boutique hotel at the top of the Spanish Steps, directly opposite the exclusive Hotel Hassler where Greg was staying. As an Australian model, she was something of a novelty and invited everywhere. At the wind-up dinner for *Roman Holiday,* Dally-Watkins found herself seated next to Greg. Sparks flew in both directions.

Greg offered to show her the town. So for one week Dally-Watkins played hooky from her fashion duties and let herself be swept off her feet. No, they didn't gallivant on a Vespa. Instead, Greg escorted her in a sleek black Mercedes. And the week passed like a dream. Hand in hand they wandered through St Peter's Square, tossed coins in the Trevi Fountain and idled for hours in sidewalk cafés. Just like Joe Bradley and Princess Anne in *Roman Holiday,* they strolled through the silent ruins of Rome's once mighty Forum. Greg held her in his long arms and kissed her over and over again. Here's where Princess Anne would have whispered: 'If I were to die at this moment, I would die knowing I had always loved you.'

Dally-Watkins didn't have a scriptwriter. Still, romantically speaking, it was a sublime moment. Greg urged her to join him in Paris.

She really wanted to go. He certainly seemed sincere. What's more, he was coming across like a man who wanted a serious relationship. He told her he was unhappily married and gave her the impression he was separated. Yet he didn't appear traumatized by his domestic troubles. In fact, he was relaxed and ebullient.

'My insecurity was very deep,' explained Dally-Watkins about why she turned down his offer, 'and I felt if I followed Greg to Paris I may be hurt. I could not believe a person like Greg would want me.'

Being a virgin, she was apprehensive about taking the relationship to the next stage. 'I would not have known how to make love anyway,' she writes in her memoirs. 'There were no sealed sections in women's magazines giving explicit instructions on the intricacies of sex and it was never discussed with girlfriends or my mother. All the while, Mother's warnings surfaced from the back of my mind: "Don't throw yourself at a man, he'll take advantage of you. Don't trust men. He will respect you more if you don't sleep with him."'

So Dally-Watkins returned to Australia. She continued her modeling career, developed a highly successful deportment and business school, married and raised a family. Like Audrey Hepburn, who became an ambassador for UNICEF, she volunteers and represents Crossroad International, a relief organization. Is she sorry she didn't follow Greg to Paris? Oh, yes. 'If I wanted to look at it romantically, I would say, Yes, I have big regrets! But it wasn't meant to be. That's the way real life goes; it can't always be like a fairytale and I feel privileged to have known him for the time I did.'

Now that the filming was completed, Greta and her mother returned to Rome to join Greg. The three enjoyed the sun in Santa Margherita on the Italian Riviera before returning to Paris by automobile. As they wended their way back to Paris, Greg took them on innumerable sightseeing tours including the Casino at Monte Carlo.

If Emily Piipari was aware of the friction between Greta and Greg, she kept quiet about it. On the contrary, she was highly effusive in her praise of her famous son-in-law as a husband, father and celebrity. She said, 'He's so friendly with everybody.'

Having pounded the streets of Rome for four months, Greg was looking forward to a period of extended relaxation before starting another movie. He told a reporter he wanted to 'study French, play golf, go to the horse races and stay up all night.'

At Greg's suggestion, Greta had selected a French Norman house out of a realtor's catalog. The place was located in St Germain, a highly sought-after suburb of Paris. 'It had central heating and two fireplaces but he called it a miserable cold barn,' Greta remembered bitterly. 'He stayed away from home.'

Particularly hurtful to Greta was the night they were invited to the home of Dr and Mrs Jack Voskamp. 'We went there an hour or so, and he decided to leave. He got his coat and hat and was going down the stairs. I followed him and asked if he wanted me to go along, and he said it really didn't make any difference. I went back and I stayed the night. I saw him the next afternoon.'

Despite the practical limitations of post-war Paris, the American expatriate community was thriving. Though despondent at the state of his marriage, Greg was constantly out on the town with other members of the film and theater world.

Irwin Shaw, a master of the short story who had written *Sons and Soldiers*, which briefly stared Gregory Peck on Broadway, was now a fixture in the City of Light. He was part of a colorful band of expatriates, some of whom invited Greg to their parties. The expats included George Plimpton and Peter Matthiessen who were launching *The Paris Review*; actors and directors such as Gene Kelly, Kirk Douglas, William Wyler, John Huston who arrived to make films as word got out about the tax loophole. The list goes on and on: James Jones, Janet Flanner, Mary McCarthy, Allen Ginsberg, Man Ray, Alexander Calder, and even Julia Child, who taught cooking in Paris. It was a splendid time to be an American in Paris – particularly if you were tall, dark, handsome and famous.

One night, columnist Art Buchwald encountered Peck on the street and took him home to meet his wife – a very surprised Ann

Buchwald. Buchwald recalled: 'The city attracted every type of American after the war . . . Besides con men and Americans on the make, there were poets holed up on the Left Bank, writers hoping to finish a great novel, painters who planned to set the world on fire, and CIA agents who were infiltrating every organization they possibly could.'

This community of rakehell opportunists and verbally adroit sophisticates wasn't Greta's scene. She wasn't focused on the latest music, art, literature and restaurants. Her domain was her home and her children. Yet for Veronique – though barely out of her teens – it was her natural milieu.

The daughter of a White Russian mother, whose family had lost their money in the Revolution, and a French aristocrat father, who worked as an architect in Paris, Veronique was *une jeune fille bien élevée*. At 18, she graduated from Marymount, a private school for girls located in Neuilly, with a working command of English. This gave her an edge in her chosen profession.

Veronique's mother occasionally submitted articles and photographs to magazines which most likely gave the young girl the desire to storm the gates of tradition and work on a newspaper. Soon she was skipping all over Paris, interviewing such luminaries as producer Sam Goldwyn, Senator Estes Kefauver, Melina Mercouri and Jean-Paul Sartre. A resourceful journalist, she managed to get pictures of the interior of General Eisenhower's home near Paris when it was off-limits to French papers. She got her scoop by hiding in a furniture van.

But once she interviewed Greg, her priorities changed. She confided to a friend, 'I'm going to marry him.'

Very surprised, the friend blurted: 'You must be crazy. Gregory Peck is in Paris with his wife and three sons.'

Veronique, then 20, smiled and reportedly said: 'You will see.'

A tabloid article said Greg and Greta got into an argument at a housewarming party they were giving at their house; the cause was a woman and it was most likely Veronique.

But the Pecks were together for the holiday season of 1952. They spent Christmas to New Year's week at the Hotel du Palais, a luxury hotel in St Moritz, Switzerland. The deposed King Farouk of Egypt and Queen Narriman were there as well as Fritz Mandl, the Austrian arms dealer, and columnist Art Buchwald.

At dinner each evening family groups would be relegated to a low walled-off section near the kitchen. 'Families sat there,' recalled Hollywood screenwriter Col. Barney Oldfield, who was vacationing with his wife Vada the same week as the Pecks, 'and the kids made whooping noises and improvised slingshots with their spoons. One family tended to arrive late, and tried to be unnoticed. That's quite difficult when the father was the great screen star, Gregory Peck. Art Buchwald, the then *New York Herald Tribune* columnist, was there and came by our table. He asked us to have an after dinner Coca-Cola with him. We said we would.

'What he didn't mention was that Greta and Gregory Peck would be with us, too. Greta tried hard, but tears came now and then. Vada sensed something was wrong. And she was a good and sympathetic listener. Let us guys gab about movies – favorite this and thats. Greta chose to sit with Vada and tell her about her three sons, how proud of them she was. When the group broke up, Greta took Vada's hand in hers and said she looked forward to their seeing each other again. "I mean that," she said it with tears in her eyes.

'En route to our room, I said, "You seem to have made a new friend." When we were inside the room, Vada put her hands on her hips like an Irish washerwoman: "*You* don't know the half of it. He's going to divorce her. This is their last Christmas together as a family."'

In Hollywood, Barney and Vada Oldfield always attended the American Film Institute's Life Achievement Awards, but in 1989 – the year Greg was to receive the award – Vada said she would prefer not to go. Ultimately she did attend. When Greg gave his acceptance speech and eulogized Veronique and 'their children,' Vada nudged Barney and suggested they leave. As they drove home, she said: 'That was my vote for Greta. I know who his kids' mother was. And who got him where he was tonight.'

On 13 January 1953 Greg drove Greta and his sons to Le Havre where they boarded the *Ile-de-France* and he watched them set sail for home. He wasn't exactly sure when he'd see them again. Later, he recalled feeling 'very Dostoyevskian, practically suicidal.' Driving back to Paris, he stopped at a café and downed a row of double cognacs. By the time he reached his room at the Hotel Lancaster, he was pie-eyed. It was the onset of a deep and protracted depression, complicated by drinking binges.

Roman Holiday garnered ten Academy Award nominations – amazing for a comedy – with statuettes awarded to Audrey Hepburn for Best Actress, Edith Head for costumes, and Ian McLellan Hunter for the film's story.

Eventually the world would learn Hunter wasn't the real author of *Roman Holiday*. It was actually written by Dalton Trumbo, one of the infamous Hollywood Ten and, as a blacklisted writer, banned from work. 'Dalton was flat broke,' explained his wife Cleo. 'He had just emerged from ten months in jail for refusing to testify before the House UnAmerican Activities Committee. His only solution was to write.' So he penned *Roman Holiday* and asked his friend Hunter to front for him. But he never received credit for the movie until 1993. By then he was deceased, so the Academy of Motion Picture Arts and Sciences presented the award to Cleo Trumbo.

The movie made Audrey Hepburn an instant star. A week after the movie opened at Radio City Music Hall on 27 August 1953, *Time* put her on its cover. 'Amid the rhinestone glitter of *Roman Holiday*'s make believe, Paramount's new star sparkles and glows with the fire of a finely cut diamond. Impertinence, hauteur, sudden repentance, happiness, rebellion and fatigue supplant each other with lightning speed on her mobile face.'

Hepburn's classic, chic style presented a wonderful contrast to other contemporary actresses who were more likely to be blonde, buxom, and sexy. Billy Wilder, who was slated to direct her in *Sabrina* (1954) marveled: 'She's like a salmon swimming upstream. She can do it with very small bozooms. Titism has taken over this country. This girl single-handed may make bozooms a thing of the past. The director will not have to invent shots where the girl leans way forward for a glass of Scotch and soda.'

Although the lively, cynical wit of Joe Bradley would have fit Cary Grant like a silk glove, Greg was actually perfect for the role. Greg, the model of all-American manhood, provided a fortuitous balance for Hepburn. His long, lean, Yankee look, the taciturnity and the mileage of years gave Hepburn something solid to play against.

Roman Holiday is still a popular movie. Why? Because for generations, films like this one have taught viewers the meaning of love. We learn how to court, romance, seduce and be seduced from watching how the stars do it. When Gregory Peck abandons his stuffy reserve and hops on a Vespa with Audrey Hepburn, our hearts leap and we write ourselves into the scene. 'In every movie I have ever watched, starting with *Roman Holiday*, I was in love with Audrey Hepburn,' confessed clothes designer Ralph Lauren. 'I played every part. I was Gregory Peck a long time ago!'

CHAPTER FOURTEEN

Wrestling with Demons

'Peck's name on our marquee is the best box-office insurance
we can have. Thousands of women in this neighborhood, I
guess and every neighborhood, feel that here is one guy who
would sooner chop off his right arm than cheat on his wife.'

Los Angeles Theater Owner

'I was like a bear in a log,' Greg said. 'I just felt awful about the
boys.' He remembered the dark time of January 1953 – the sudden
break with his family that put them on one side of the Atlantic and
himself on the other – as one of seclusion and retreat. He claimed
not to have left the Hotel Lancaster for two weeks except to walk
the streets of Paris at night. But unhappiness has a way of blurring
memory.

In reality, professional obligations forced Greg into the spotlight.
Two days after his family sailed from Le Havre, *The Snows of
Kilimanjaro* opened at the Park Theater in Stockholm. Such a wild
commotion! Greg's arrival sparked a near riot. An estimated crowd of
3,000 people – a good many of them screaming teenagers – jammed
the streets trying to glimpse the world-famous movie star.

A dozen mounted police and at least 20 foot patrolmen held the
crowd at bay. Fans tried to tackle Greg as he made for the back door
of the theater. Inside, Swedish actress Signe Hasso introduced him
to the premiere's audience of 400. Amazed at the melée outside, she
said: 'I've never seen scenes like these, even in the United States.'

In Copenhagen and Oslo, the reaction was much the same. But
in Helsinki, the welcome was more personal. Greta was a Kukkonen
(shortened in America to Konen) and this large family traced their
genealogy back for hundreds of years. The descendents kept in
touch with each other. In fact, many of her relatives welcomed Greg
and threw a party for him in which they made him a present of five

Scandinavian knives. When a reporter asked what his concept of the ideal woman was, he replied, 'My perfect Finnish wife.'

Back in Paris, the 'log' or hotel where he 'holed up' wasn't exactly Spartan. Just off the Champs Elysées on the Rue de Berri, the Hotel Lancaster was nicely situated in the heart of Paris – and conveniently located close to Veronique's mother's apartment on the Avenue Franklin D Roosevelt. It was run like a luxurious private home, filled with a fascinating collection of furniture, antique clocks, paintings, chandeliers, lamps, tapestries, velvets, silks and damasks, crystal and porcelain. Its courtyard, once the stables of a private house, was one of the prettiest in Paris.

Vigilant about its low profile, the hotel prided itself on being one of France's best-kept secrets. The clientele of the Lancaster was international and highly select, its rooms serving as the Parisian home of Joseph Kennedy, Greta Garbo, Clark Gable, Alec Guinness, Marlene Dietrich, Katharine Hepburn, Spencer Tracy and John Huston.

Any lonesome American could just wander across the street to the *Herald Tribune* building. From 11.30 p.m. to midnight, Americans congregated in front of the building to get their paper fresh off the press. They felt better just by reading an English-speaking paper to make sure everything – their stocks, the homeland – was all right.

It's not clear at what point he reconnected with Veronique after seeing her in Rome the previous summer during the filming of *Roman Holiday*. William Wyler claimed the romance started in Rome during the filming of the movie. Because Greg was married, they concocted elaborate ruses to keep it out of the public eye. Some accounts put it in the fall of 1952. Greg claimed it was early 1953. He called her at the office of *France Soir* only to find out she had joined the staff of *Paris Presse*. When he invited her to Longchamps to the races, she hesitated. She had an appointment to interview Dr Albert Schweitzer at the apartment of Jean-Paul Sartre. When Schweitzer didn't show up, she opted to go to the races with Greg. He quipped, 'You made the right choice, kiddo.' Years later, when she was asked what would have happened if she had kept the appointment, she laughed and said, 'I might have been a missionary's wife in the Congo.'

Calling on Veronique, Greg was welcomed into the Passani family. Veronique's mother was divorced from her father. During the war, Madame Passani had been briefly married to an American with whom she had a son named Cornelius. When this second marriage ended, Monsieur Passani adopted Cornelius and gave him his last name. Although he didn't remarry his ex-wife, Monsieur Passani dropped by the apartment each morning for coffee. In such an unconventional setup, a married suitor wasn't out of place.

Veronique quickly became Greg's life raft, his anchor, his savior. Here was someone to cling to at a time when he felt as if he was drowning. 'She had huge, glowing eyes and a face brimming with vitality and intelligence and humor,' he remembered. Verging on 21, she gave him hope and avid admiration. And she was a good reason not to lose himself in the heavy drinking bouts that had become his method of blotting out his troubles with Greta. Squiring Veronique around in his Porsche, he ventured around Paris and its environs looking for out-of-the-way restaurants and quiet cafés. The lovers devised imaginative stratagems to outwit the paparazzi in hot pursuit of a good story. It didn't always work. Their pictures appeared in the papers.

In Los Angeles, Greta had her hands full. She was the stabilizing influence for the boys – Jonathan, nine, Stephen, six, and Carey, three – who missed their father terribly and were confused and traumatized by the separation. To make things even harder for Greta, the press wouldn't leave her alone. They wanted to know why she had packed up in such haste when she was supposed to stay on the Continent with Greg for 18 months. Hoping to save her marriage, Greta replied to inquiries with credible excuses. Also, she cut Greg slack. Being older and in some ways wiser, she knew Greg was in too much emotional turmoil to know what he wanted.

Responding to Marsha Saunders, a particularly persistent reporter, she said: 'The children and I came back to California, because it's just too difficult to try to raise them abroad under Greg's schedule. He's in Italy for a few months, France for a few months, England for a few months. He likes to have his family with him, and we just can't keep moving all the time.

'It sounds very romantic, but how would it be dragging three small boys to India for a couple of months (a location considered for a future movie *The Purple Plain*), enrolling them in school, getting everything set up and then just when you've got your household organized, start packing and return to France?' She went on to say: 'Greg wanted us to remain with him.'

Saunders kept up the interrogation. How about reports of Greg being seen around Paris with a very young reporter? Greta didn't rise to the bait: 'When he is away, he's entitled to a little companionship.'

Pressed even further, Greta turned starchy: 'Greg and I are not separated. There will be no divorce. We are on the best terms, and if you don't believe it, you can talk to him at the Hotel Lancaster in Paris.'

At the Lancaster, Greg blew his top when the reporter asked him if he contemplated dropping Greta in favor of some younger woman. 'How in heaven's name do these things get started?' he exploded. 'I'm not separated. I'm not getting a divorce, and I'm very happily married . . . Greta and I had a great time and I wanted her to stay, wanted her to stay very much, but she is a wonderful mother – she's always thinking of the boys – and she figured they would be better off in California.'

In the spring of 1953, Greg rented a house in London near Buckingham Palace and invited Veronique to join him. He then began making deals with the British film industry, the first major American name with box-office clout to do so. His first was for a comedy called *The Man with a Million* (1954) for which he was paid $350,000. The English title, *The Million Pound Note*, follows the title of the Mark Twain story on which the movie is based. Greg plays a shabby young man who dines in a restaurant and then casually hands over a million-pound banknote, while murmuring, 'I'm awfully sorry, but I don't have anything smaller.' The character, stranded in London with an authentic million-pound note, finds he cannot cash it, he can only flash it. Although ingratiating, it failed completely in the United States though it did better abroad. According to *Variety*, the picture was 'too soft and mushy to reach a contemporary crowd.'

Very much in love, Veronique dropped her journalistic career and focused her talents on helping Greg by acting as his secretary, traveling companion and hostess. In her new life, her training as a reporter stood her in good stead. She knew the journalism game and she now used the tricks of the trade to make sure Greg presented himself in the best possible light.

The Man with a Million was shot in Hyde Park, in Belgrave Square and in Savile Row, all central London locations, which inevitably attracted crowds. Greg's handling of the importunate fans was an object lesson in patience and concentration. He must have chuckled, though, when a spectator caroled: 'How silly of them to use that man. He is nothing but an imitation Gregory Peck.'

Around this time, Greg engaged the public relations services of Johnny Kimberley, 4th Earl of Kimberley. The Earl was a jovial extrovert whose interests included shark fishing, UFOs and winter sports. Known as 'a glorious failure,' he was a godson of Winston Churchill and a cousin of the humorist P G Wodehouse. His checkered career also included serving in the Guards Armoured Division as an officer in the Second World War; competing as a member of Britain's national bobsleigh team; holding his own as a championship tiddlywinks player; breeding prize pigs; and being an amateur steeplechase jockey. Kimberley was a free-spending, hard-driving member of London's beau monde, taking weekends at Deauville, losing at all-night chemmy sessions and bedding as many women as he could. By the time Greg met him in the 1950s the clients on his successful public relations business included Robert Mitchum and 'that bald bugger' as he referred to Yul Brynner.

During that same spring, William Wyler needed Greg to overdub some dialogue and called him back to Rome from London. The actor and director had become fast friends; their relationship would turn into a business partnership as well. What's more, Wyler's wife Talli developed a rapport with Veronique.

In Rome, the paparazzi dogged their every move. 'Veronique and I were a hot item for the tabloids,' Greg said. 'Willie and Talli were on our side. They loved her.' To get away from the press, Wyler suggested the four of them slip away to Lake Como, near the Swiss border. After several days, believing they had made a safe escape, they took a motorboat to Coccina, a tiny island with Roman ruins, in the middle of the lake.

'It was unbelievably picturesque,' Greg recounted. 'We were all having a great time at lunch. Suddenly Talli froze. Something caught her eye. We all turned around and a camera went *click!* from behind a tree. Willie and I jumped to our feet. We were the only customers in the restaurant. We thought we were the only people on the island. Willie and I started chasing this guy up the slope. I didn't want to be photographed with Veronique for obvious reasons. It was an absolute comedy. Willie took a flying tackle and grabbed him from behind.'

The photographer proved too fleet of foot and escaped with his film. (William Wyler told the same story. However, he claimed it happened the previous summer during the filming of *Roman Holiday*.)

Greg next signed on to star in a cloak-and-dagger yarn called *Night People* (1954). Set in Berlin, it concerns the efforts of the US Army Intelligence Corps to get a young American soldier, who has been kidnapped, out of the Russian sector. Greg was cast as a US Intelligence Officer who knows how to deal with the Russians. They are 'a methodical bunch of lice' and 'head-hunting cannibals.' To be sure, the level of the film's anti-Communism wasn't too sophisticated.

The film's screenwriter Nunnally Johnson insisted later that he didn't set out to write a propaganda piece, he was aiming for a fast-paced thriller. In fact, he described the picture to *Time* magazine as 'Dick Tracy in Berlin.'

Johnson had made his mark in Hollywood as an iconoclastic writer whose screen credits included *The Grapes of Wrath* (1940), *Tobacco Road* (1941*)*, *The Three Faces of Eve* (1957), and *The Gunfighter*. An urbane former journalist from Georgia, few people could match his off-the-cuff wit. Foreign correspondent Alistair Cooke remembered: 'Like many another Southerner, he maintained a surface courtesy and tact behind which glowed an owl-like skepticism about human motives, whether in Columbus, Georgia, or Beverly Hills, California . . . He had the luck of his inheritance and his gifts: a wry, uninhibited humor from his father, and a prose style of great clarity he developed on his own . . . [He adopted] a pose not very different from that with which two other small-town boys, Mark Twain and James Thurber, were able to cope with rich and complicated people and also to earn their applause.' Cooke explained that Johnson adopted, as a second nature, the air of a bewildered mouse in a world of tigers and jaguars. Greg liked him and was in awe of his drollery.

Eager for a new challenge, Nunnally Johnson approached the film's producer Darryl Zanuck and told him he wanted to direct *Night People*. Zanuck agreed as long as Greg went for the idea. Zanuck said, 'Peck's a big star, and he's got a right to an okay on the director, and he certainly has the right to say he doesn't want a man who's never directed before.' So Johnson took off for London to confer with Greg.

Since Johnson had written the script for *The Gunfighter*, Greg knew him; he respected his talents and appreciated his humor. Greg said, 'Well, you wouldn't be the first writer that turned director. It's all right with me.'

While in London, Johnson ran into Henry Hathaway, who had directed *The Desert Fox* (1951) for which Johnson wrote the screenplay. Hathaway warned him he wouldn't be any good as a director and when Johnson asked why, he replied: 'Because you're not a bastard. Look at the big directors, all of them bastards, John Ford, George Stevens, Fritz Lang, Willie Wyler.'

Before filming started, Greg leased an apartment in Paris to use as a base. Then he flew to Berlin for *Night People* and Veronique joined him. Once shooting got underway, Greg began to wonder, 'Have I committed myself to a guy who may not know what the hell he's doing the next minute?' But, as the shooting continued, Greg went out of his way to help Johnson make the transition to director.

However, a rumor started that the two men were feuding. In early September 1953, a front-page article appeared in the *Hollywood Reporter* saying the two men were having difficulties; Greg was being temperamental and holding up production. Johnson said: 'Peck's a genuinely nice man. He's stubborn. He's very opinionated, and sometimes I thought he was rather slow witted, but he really isn't. He just has to be convinced of the necessity of doing something before he'll do it. It can become pretty exasperating because it takes up time, but he helped me on *Night People* in so many ways. He would make suggestions, but never try to impose his ideas.'

Johnson – a man who reached in the air and caught ideas on the fly – couldn't get over Greg's compulsive approach to acting. He noticed Greg kept a typed, bound script of the film with him at all times. It was filled with a strange conglomeration of hooks, curlicues, scribbled footnotes, and peculiar flourishes. Each little dot, dash, or doodle meant something.

Greg realized Johnson didn't have any sort of noticeable, dazzling directorial brilliance, but he did have professional competence and Greg went out of his way to help him in his new line of work. Knowing he had gone the extra mile to get along with Johnson, Greg was furious about the articles, bristling at the suggestion he wasn't a total professional about his work. Johnson, on the other hand, took the negative publicity in stride. Rather than being intimidated by the power of the press – particularly the gossip columnists – Johnson reveled in jousting with them.

Once he was asked by the editors of the *Saturday Evening Post* to rewrite an article about Louella Parsons because the original writer skewered the daylights out of 'Lolly' and her proctologist husband 'Old Velvet Finger.' Johnson's rewrite was none too charitable and was supposed to be anonymous, but he admitted, 'It was the worst-kept secret in town.'

The day it hit the stands, Parsons appeared in Darryl Zanuck's office, weeping and furious. 'I expect you to fire him!' she told Zanuck, who was his boss.

'I can't do that, he has a contract,' said Zanuck.

Zanuck sent for Johnson. 'Why did you get me mixed up in this?' he asked. 'Louella has a lot of power.'

'What power?' Johnson asked him. 'She hates me more than anyone in town – and she can't get me fired, can she?'

Harry Brand, who was the head of Fox's publicity department, was in the meeting. 'But, Nunnally,' he said, 'after all Louella's *done* for you . . .'

'What has she done for me?' he demanded.

'Well,' said Brand, 'when you were picked up for drunken driving, she didn't print the item in her column, did she?'

'She didn't have to,' Johnson retorted, 'seeing as how her city editor had put it in headlines all over the front page!'

A few days later Parsons counterpunched. Johnson had just married Dorris Bowden, and he picked up the paper to read: 'I saw Dorris Johnson the other day. Poor Dorris. Before her marriage, she looked so lovely . . .'

'That,' Johnson admitted with admiration, 'was *really* shooting around a corner.'

Greg cared too much about his public image to ignore the criticism. He was already vulnerable to negative publicity on two fronts: living with Veronique and taking advantage of a tax loophole by residing abroad. Many Americans struggling to pay their taxes and stay square with Uncle Sam frowned on movie star breaks. Also, the unions in Hollywood objected vociferously to 'runaway productions,' i.e. movies made abroad. They singled out Peck for his role in taking money out of Hollywood.

Together in a foreign country, the bond between Greg and Veronique grew stronger. She was tolerant of his moods and weaknesses and she shared his sense of adventure about experiencing exotic places. In Berlin, she was a comforting presence in a city still scarred by war and seething with political unrest.

Working in Berlin in 1953 had its nerve-wracking moments. They filmed one scene near the Brandenburg Gate, which was heavily guarded on the Russian side. The scene involved a girl in a telephone booth, and as with all such sequences, the unit had its own portable telephone booth, which could be set up to get the best camera angle. As they tried out the booth in various locations, the top of the Brandenburg Gate began to fill up with Russian soldiers with binoculars, trying to figure out what sort of American trap this moveable phone booth was.

After the film wrapped, Greg gave a thumbs-up to the new technology employed: 'The CinemaScope method of picture making gives the actor somewhat more range in his work. It is the closest thing that I have encountered to the stage, and yet we were able to avail ourselves movie-wise of all the natural advantages offered by the new locations in Germany.'

As summer rolled into fall, Greta finally admitted publicly that she and Greg were separated. Her comments carried none of the fury of a woman scorned. 'He's a wonderful father and he has always been very good to all of us,' she bravely told reporters. 'If he wants a divorce, I am going to let him have it.' Then, with self-abnegation, she added: 'I feel, however, that any announcement must come from Greg. He is the important one in my family.'

When the going got tough, Greta played fair. At the same time, she was a realist about money. She hired Jerry Geisler to handle the separation for her. 'Get me Geisler!' was a Hollywood joke line. 'If you were in trouble, you knew whom to call,' said Lana Turner. No one in Los Angeles could match Geisler's skills before a jury. Not only did he handle many high-profile divorces, he also successfully defended Charlie Chaplin and Errol Flynn on rape charges. For his part, Greg hired Laurence Beilenson, who represented Ronald Reagan in his divorce from Jane Wyman.

As Christmas drew near, Greg arranged for Jonathan to join him in St Moritz for the holidays. There, he signed the boy up for ski lessons and also gave him the opportunity to get to know Veronique who had joined them. In this way father and son returned to the same resort they had visited the year before when the family was intact.

Greg's next picture, *The Purple Plain* (1955) took him to Ceylon (present-day Sri Lanka). In this Second World War thriller, he plays a neurotic pilot, flying with his navigator and tentmate, who has to crash-land his plane in enemy territory. They make their way to safety, carrying the navigator, who is seriously injured. After several brutal days of trudging through the jungle, the tentmate shoots himself, but the navigator is eventually saved by the compulsive pilot.

Greg agreed to make the film, with two provisos. First, it had to be shot in Southeast Asia. Secondly, the role of Emma (the female lead) had to be played by an Asian woman. Over 200 females showed up to audition for the role; many just wanted to get a chance to see Greg up close. Director Robert Parrish selected Win

Min Than for the part. Blessed with exotic, exquisite beauty, she had an unfortunate way of shaking her head back and forth; consequently, the production team had to devise a brace to remind her to keep her head still. She also possessed a wildly jealous husband who insisted she eat garlic before smooching with Greg. Another difficulty was location. Because of its proximity to the Chinese border, no company would insure Greg; Rank considered canceling the film but Robert Parrish prevailed.

During the shoot Greg gave Parrish a terrible fright. On the first day of shooting in the jungle, the crew finished two hours before sundown, had a delicious native-cooked meal and were warned not to go outside after dark 'because of the kraits.' Parrish thought the kraits might be some hostile, head-hunting savages, but they turned out to be extremely venomous nocturnal snakes. They were about the size of a pencil and usually lay in wait on low-hanging branches of trees.

Parrish shared a tent with Greg and knew that – with Veronique in Ceylon and Greta in Los Angeles – the star was preoccupied with personal problems. The director recalled most nights Greg would crawl on to his mosquito-netted cot, turn on his flashlight and read. Some nights he would lie there on his back staring at the ceiling of the tent. Parrish would usually flop on his cot, say, 'See you tomorrow,' and sink into a dreamless sleep. From time to time, he would wake up at some odd hour and look over at Greg. He was always reading or staring.

'One morning,' wrote Parrish in his memoirs *Hollywood Doesn't Live Here Anymore*, 'at about 2, an ungodly scream woke me up. I saw Greg jump out of his cot, knock the center tent pole down, and disappear through the flaps of the front entrance, his mosquito net flowing behind him. I fought my way out of my mosquito net and the collapsed canvas and chased after him. He was screaming like a wounded $250,000-per-picture banshee and heading, barefooted, for the jungle, the kraits, and the end of a $2-million British-American co-production. I ran faster and yelled, "Greg!" a couple of times, but that seemed to speed him up even more. He tripped on the mosquito netting, got up, and plunged on.

'At the edge of the compound I caught up with him and tackled him. I tackled Gregory Peck, one of the most famous movie stars in the world.

'"Are you all right?" I asked. He stared at me, dead-eyed, then put both hands over his face and gasped for breath.

'"Are you all right, Greg?" I asked again.

'After what seemed like a very long time, he took his hands away from his face and said quietly, "I'm fine."

'"Well," I said, "would you like to come back and help me rebuild our tent so we can get some sleep before we start shooting four hours from now?"

'He nodded his handsome head and said, "I'd like that very much."

'I helped him to his bare feet and led him back to our tent. We put the tent pole up and crawled on to our cots. Greg said, "Some kind of nightmare, I guess," and went right to sleep. I lay there, wide awake, thinking. When our breakfast arrived at 5, I went over and shook Greg awake.

'"How do you feel?" I said.

'"Fine," said Greg. "Why?"

'"Do you remember what went on here last night?" I asked.

'"More or less," he said, and smiled his shy, expensive smile.

'"Do you mind if we use it for the opening scene in the picture?" I said.

'"Be my guest," said our gracious star, still smiling.

'Two nights later we shot the scene. They got it all in one take.' Parrish concluded: 'I guess that's because Greg and I had rehearsed it so well.'

Perhaps what troubled Greg most was his voluntary absence from his children's lives. He knew he didn't need to make movies half way around the world. He was missing his kids' birthday parties, their appearances in school plays, and even Father's Day. Years later, when he looked back and thought about how many celebrations and special moments he excluded himself from because he was striving in his career, he had deep regrets.

There were, however, lighter moments. While driving into the mountains during his time in Ceylon Greg spotted a sign into a tiny village. It read: 'Gregory Peck. Fine gentleman's tailoring.'

'I couldn't resist,' Greg said. 'I went and there was a little man sitting cross-legged with a needle and thread, sewing a jacket. His jaw dropped when he realized I was really Gregory Peck. I said, "Why? Why do you want to do this?" He said, "To attract the public."' Greg relished the absurdity of the situation.

Alas! The paparazzi surfaced in Ceylon. They hounded Greg about Veronique. 'She's just a girl I met in Paris,' Greg said non-commitally. 'Nothing serious, I see her once in a while – just like an old friend.' But what was she doing in Ceylon? 'I think she came out here to buy some tea for her mother.'

When Greg and Veronique stepped off the plane at Orly airport in Paris from Ceylon in 1954, they were exhausted from the flight. Walking toward the immigration office to have their passports checked, Veronique removed her dark glasses. A photographer dashed out, clicked his shutter and disappeared just as quickly.

Veronique had developed tricks for outwitting the press. She disguised her appearance and traveled under various names. But after a couple years of tracking her in London, Paris, the French Riviera and Ceylon, the press was able to recognize her. One photographer said, 'No girl can go around with Gregory Peck and hide behind sunglasses forever!'

Veronique did her best to keep the reporters at bay: 'Gregory Peck is a good friend and I am a *journaliste* and this is my own private business and I will answer no questions about it.' In the meantime, a friend of hers said, 'Veronique is a shrewd girl and she expects that Greg will divorce his wife eventually and marry her.'

There's such a thing as too much Irish charm. Greg wasn't aware of this when John Huston sidled up to him at a London cocktail party with a tempting offer. The director was a lean, rangy man, 6 feet 2 inches, with pitch-black hair that he wore slicked down with water, although some of the front strands fell raffishly over his forehead. His eyes looked watchful and belied the hardiness of his manner. He was trying to get his production of *Moby Dick* (1956) up and running and he needed a star of Greg's stature to get financing. Greg's slice of the pie was generous: $250,000 for the picture and a percentage of the film's takings.

Originally published in 1851, *Moby Dick* is Herman Melville's adventure classic of the feud between a whaling skipper and the great white whale that caused the loss of his leg. Consumed by an insane rage, Captain Ahab has but one purpose in life – revenge on Moby Dick. As the skipper of a whaling boat, *The Pequod*, Ahab uses his command to sail the high seas in an unrelenting search for his prey.

John Huston, son of one of the great film actors of his generation (Walter) and the father of one of the great actresses of her generation (Anjelica), had been captivated since boyhood by Ahab's obsession. 'In pursuit of one whale he is committing a sin,' said Huston. 'This was really the heart of the matter. Ahab saw Moby Dick as the embodiment of evil, and he sees God. This is, of course, in Melville: "When will the judge himself be tried before the bar?" He is assaulting the Almighty, it is his naked fist against the deity.'

With such classics as *The Maltese Falcon* (1941), *Key Largo* (1948), *The Treasure of the Sierra Madre* (1948), *The Asphalt Jungle* (1950), and *The African Queen* (1951), under his belt, Huston was case-hardened about the treachery involved in turning a good story into a finished movie. One of the most admired, rebellious, and shadowy figures in the world of motion pictures, he once said: 'It's a jungle. A close knit, tight, frantically inbred, and frantically competitive jungle. And the rules of the jungle are predatory and fascinating and tough.'

Huston had a theatrical way of punctuating his speech with melo-dramatic intensity and the smooth patois of a snake-oil salesman. Lauren Bacall characterized him as 'daring, unpredictable, maddening, mystifying and probably the most charming man on earth.' He talked Greg into playing Ahab in his movie version of Melville's classic novel. When he first conceived the project, he planned to use his father Walter Huston, but the veteran actor had died.

The maverick director once told *New Yorker* writer Lillian Ross: 'I've been around actors all my life, and I like them, and yet I never had an actor as a friend. Except Dad. And Dad never saw himself as an actor. But the best actor I ever worked with was Dad.'

With his star in place, Huston put an enormous amount of time into research for the film. Locations were scouted, and the director settled on Youghal, a port town on the South Irish Coast, as the film's New Bedford. The film would be shot on the Irish Sea, in the Canary Islands, and in the studio in London.

Huston chose science fiction writer Ray Bradbury, author of *The Martian Chronicles,* to co-write the screenplay. A child of 'pop' culture, Bradbury credited his success as a creative artist to his early exposure to the horror movie, the carnival, the circus and the comic. When Huston called him about writing the screenplay for *Moby Dick*, he confessed he had tried it once but couldn't get through it. Huston pressed on: 'Read as much as you can and tell me tomorrow if we can kill the white whale.'

Second time's the charm. According to Bradbury: 'Melville and I had the same midwives: the Bible, Shakespeare. Melville had poor eyesight. He couldn't read Shakespeare because the print was too small. Then he found a large-type edition, threw out his whaling equipment and wrote *Moby Dick* in a few months.'

Max Wilk, a collector of Hollywood anecdotes, recalled that at the halfway point in the writing of the script, John Huston came in one afternoon looking grave. He handed writer Ray Bradbury a telegram, which read: CANNOT PROCEED WITH FILM UNLESS SEXY FEMALE ROLE ADDED. It was signed: JACK WARNER.

'Has this man gone insane?' Bradbury shouted. 'This is terrible! We can't stick a woman on board! My God, he can't be serious!'

Huston shook his head. 'That's Hollywood, Ray. Warners is paying the bill, and if they want love interest, we'll just have to get it in somehow. Maybe Ahab could have an affair with Gina Lollobrigida as a disguised stowaway.'

Furious, Bradbury crumpled up the telegram and threw it to the floor. Then he looked over at Huston. 'John was doubled up on the couch, laughing like a big monkey,' he says. 'That's when I knew he'd sent the thing. I was so relieved I couldn't get sore.'

As for Greg, he dove into the project with gusto. 'I'm as excited about it as if I'd never made a picture before,' he admitted. 'Ahab is the best part I've ever had. Ray Bradbury and John Huston wrote the script, and it's the finest – poetic, big, and suspenseful. It will be shot as an allegory and not an adventure yarn, and all the qualities of the book have been retained in the script.'

He let his hair grow and sprouted whiskers. 'I'm getting grizzled by the minute.' And he eagerly looked forward to navigating on a wooden leg. 'What a stickler for realism this man is!' Greg said in admiration of Huston when they were still in the honeymoon phase of their relationship. 'We were all set on a "chelsea peg" that's the old seafaring artificial leg. It looks like a cup into which the knee fits with a wooden peg from there to the ground. But that didn't satisfy John. He said that Captain Ahab lost his leg in the South Pacific and that the ship's carpenter made one out of whalebone. So he wanted a leg to look like it'd been made under those conditions.'

In July 1954, Greg flew home to Los Angeles for a two-week visit. Greta and the boys greeted him at the airport with enthusiastic hugs. He was thrilled to see Jonathan, Stephen and Carey who looked to him as if they'd each grown a foot. He said later he wanted to see Greta one more time to see if there was any spark, any kindling of feeling to save the marriage. There wasn't. After a week he took the boys camping.

Off in the woods and around the campfire, he drew on his Moby Dick stories, regaling the boys with scary tales of the sea. Stephen Peck recollected in the American Film Institute's *Gregory Peck Tribute Book*: 'He wore a full beard and a conspicuous slash of gray in his hair, and often Captain Ahab would emerge without warning. One eyebrow would raise, and he would fix my brothers and me with an intense, slightly crazed look.

'"Well now men, and who are we after?"

'"Moby Dick," cried the three little sailors.

'"And what do ye say about this Moby Dick?"

'"A dead whale or a stove boat!" we shouted.

'"Aye lads, that's it!"

'He had drawn us into his make-believe world for a moment. I could hear the sound of the creaking ship and see the giant white whale as Dad described it for us, for he described it not as a movie, but as real life.'

It was a time to treasure. Something good to reflect about in the weeks that followed when newspapers ran headlines about his split with Greta.

Greg returned to Europe with his impersonation of lunatic Ahab hunting down his quarry. Angelica Huston, the director's young daughter, took to him straight away. 'I remember seeing him at four-years-old in Fishguard, Wales, with a peg leg and a big top hat. And that was the beginning of my love affair with Gregory Peck.'

'This was probably the most difficult picture I've ever done,' John Huston recalled in his memoirs. 'The imponderables were so great. A lot of mistakes were made, shortcuts were taken that we paid for. Some of them that had been made I wasn't even aware of. The weather turned out to be the biggest antagonist in getting the film shot. It was a record-setting stormy season on the seas where they filmed. Lifeboats were capsized. I don't mean our boats, but the coastal lifeboats that went out to vessels in distress. Ships were blown on the rocks. We lost masts three times. Once there was no question in my mind we were heading for the bottom and were just saved by a miracle of seamanship.'

Huston counted it as a miracle they didn't lose any lives. 'We did lose whales, however,' he wrote. 'The reason we'd lose whales was that there would come that moment of choice: should we save the people in the boats or should we save the whales we made. Being humans ourselves, our sympathy went towards these men rather than these plastic fabrications. Then we would have to build another whale. These whales were some 90 feet long, constructions of steel, covered in latex – big, expensive articles. It would some-times take three weeks, and we would have to shoot something else while we were waiting for another whale to be made.'

Off the coast of Ireland, Greg had an encounter with a rogue wave that almost proved fatal. Location shooting in 12-foot seas off the coast of Western Ireland, he floated off into the fog clinging to the huge rubber model of Moby Dick. He feared for his life. Still, he kept piercing the whale with his harpoon and cursing him. 'It got very choppy,' he recollected, 'and I felt if I slipped into the water, I'd be a goner. I didn't know which way to swim. Should I swim towards Ireland or Wales, the South Pole or the North Pole? I was completely disoriented so I began to shout "Ahoy there!" and "Help!" Eventually the camera boat found me and I was glad to slide off the rubber whale.' Safely rescued, he denied the newspapers the headline 'Actor Lost on Rubber Whale.'

Although Youghal was selected as the town that most closely resembled New Bedford, Massachusetts, in 1841, the construction crews had to place special wooden shells over the front of the stores to make it look more authentic. The transformation was so dramatic the locals had a hard time finding a way around. The only thing remaining was Paddy Linihan's pub, the Moby Dick saloon. One drawback was the harbor wasn't dug out deeply enough, so that instead of having several hours a day shooting they shot only at high tide. All these things affected the picture and its budget.

Meanwhile, back at Warner Brothers, the company that was bankrolling the production, the executives were apoplectic about the wildly escalating production costs. They wondered if they might have a flop on their hands. At lunch one day, H M Warner began to confide in George Axelrod (a screenwriter who hit the jackpot with his feverishly witty 1955 satire *The Seven Year Itch*): 'I've just spoken to Huston,' he said. 'John is a very headstrong, difficult man. I tried to explain to him, we had World War I, World War II, and the Korean War – everywhere in America, in practically every home, there's some family with a veteran who was wounded – so I asked John, why does Gregory Peck have to have one leg?'

Herald Tribune columnist Art Buchwald went to Youghal to report on the production. He dropped by a pub where the cast hung out, mainly because the brother of one of the local production assistants owned it. The bar was jammed with horse fanciers. All they talked about was horses, until Huston and Greg walked in. Then the patrons broke into song with 'Did Your Mother Come From Ireland' or 'My Wild Irish Rose.' Huston and Greg were suckers for that sort of malarkey.

The day before shooting began, Buchwald noticed a man with a wooden leg standing at the bar. His name was Paddy Ryan, and he was being treated as a hero by the townspeople. Word had gotten out that Gregory Peck would need a stand-in for the Captain Ahab long shots, and Paddy was the only one in the county with a wooden leg.

'Does he have the job?' Buchwald asked.

'No. He's going over the casting in a few minutes,' came the reply.

It sounded like a good story, so Buchwald accompanied Paddy over to the casting office. He said cockily, 'I hear you need someone with a wooden leg.'

The casting director leaned over the table and said, 'Wrong leg.'

Though giving it his best shot, Greg couldn't get over the feeling Ahab was just an old crackpot. However, he didn't cross him off as an ordinary nut. In analyzing him, Greg concluded: 'Ahab was a one-man rebellion against fate – a slightly insane, crude champion of humanity. He wanted to find out a little more about the mystery of life, the mystery we live in. To him, his personal existence meant nothing.'

Down the years, Greg was asked how he would play Ahab differently. 'Better, I think. I should've been more ferocious in pursuit of the whale, more cruel to the crew, and I think I'd have a better grasp now of what Melville was talking about. He was trying to find an answer to the eternal mysteries. Ahab focused all his energies on pitting himself against the whale, but he was trying to penetrate the mystery of why we are here at all, why there is anything. I wasn't mad enough, not crazy enough, not obsessive enough. I should've done more.' Greg took a long breath: 'At the time, I didn't have more in me.'

Huston was neither a high-strung auteur like Orson Welles nor a despot like Erich von Stroheim. He was, rather, a man who believed in facilitating the gifts of others. He believed in giving his actors as much room to find their own performances as possible, which is why he managed to get such marvelous performances out of less gifted actors. What's more, he believed in adhering to the elements that made great novels in the first place.

Huston was one of the last of the Renaissance men. A voracious and wide-ranging reader, writer, and painter, he was a true raconteur as well as conversant on such subjects as neo-realism and Sartrian existentialism. He explained: 'I tried to direct as little as possible.'

The final sea sequences of *Moby Dick* were scheduled to be shot in the Canary Islands. Greg, accompanied by Veronique, joined the crew of a hundred with fingers crossed that no catastrophe would sabotage the project any further. Huston was in a state of high anxiety. He had to supervise the building of another great white because of the two lost in the Irish Sea. The picture had already cost half as much again as it was budgeted for. If they lost this whale, it could mean the end of the picture.

Greg approached his last critical scene with much apprehension. The shot was to be of Ahab lashed to the back of Moby Dick with harpoon lines. It was dangerous but a stunt man could not fill in because of the close-ups.

John Huston recalled: 'The model – which was a section of the head and body of the white whale – was actually a big hole for Greg to put his leg through, and then he had to be quite securely fastened as the model was slowly revolved in the sea at the end of a long pier. All this time the wind machines were roaring and there were torrents of water as Greg was submerged time and again so that the "harpoon lines" would appear to be wrapping around his body, lashing him forever to his mortal enemy. The model was 20 feet in diameter, so Greg was underwater for a good long time each rotation. The danger, of course, was that the contraption might get stuck while he was underwater.' Fortunately, everything went as planned. It was a perfect take. Huston said, 'That's it!'

Greg shook his head. 'Let's do it again, John, and make sure.' Huston was certain they had it, but Greg insisted.

'We can never come back for it, John. Let's do it again.' So they did it again and the second time also everything went perfectly.

In December 1954 Greta filed for divorce in Los Angeles. Smartly dressed in a conservative dark suit and white hat, she remained composed before the Superior Court as photographers trained their cameras on her. Still, the images published for the world to see revealed the face of a woman who had suffered profound anguish. There was no doubt she'd been through the wringer. She had lost the love of her life.

In her complaint, Greta said Greg was guilty of mysterious absences from home, refusing to explain where he'd been. She stated he was a source of 'anguish, embarrassment and humiliation.' Their parting, nearly two years before, was the result of Greg's 'cruel and inhuman manner.' The statement went on to say: 'He has pursued a course of conduct toward his wife of such character as to constitute extreme cruelty . . . he has caused her to endure grievous mental suffering, extreme nervousness, and she can no longer live with him as his wife.'

The next day Greg issued categorical denials of the charges of cruelty launched against him. Still, he did not contest the divorce. Subsequently, Greta informed the court that she and Greg had agreed on a settlement in which she was to get custody of Jonathan, ten; Stephen, eight; and Carey, five as well as providing for division of community property and for support for herself as well as the boys. The court approved the agreement and ordered Greg to comply with its terms.

Greta was awarded one of the largest settlements in Hollywood history. She received half of the couple's community property including the house Greg loved on San Remo Drive in the Pacific Palisades and substantial interests in three motion pictures, *The World in His Arms*, *Roman Holiday*, and *Moby Dick*. She was awarded 20 per cent of the first $100,000 Peck earned annually for the next ten years, 12.5 per cent of the second $100,000, 10 per cent of the third $100,000, 7.5 per cent of the fourth $100,000 and 5 per cent of his earnings until she remarried (she remained single). In addition, she won $250 a month for each of their three children.

With the money issue resolved, Greta let bygones be bygones. When reporters asked her opinion of Veronique Passani, she said simply: 'I saw her half a dozen times, but I really don't know her very well. I hope they'll be happy.' Then she volunteered that she was allowing Greg to stay in the family home at 1700 San Remo Drive with their sons while she traveled east to visit relatives. Greta explained she wanted to make it 'as easy as I can' on Greg because 'I want to protect my sons from any scandal.'

Greg called it an 'amiable divorce.' Although in a moment of candor, he told Michael Freedland: 'You get a divorce because you can no longer stand each other.'

The Parisian newspapers ran front-page stories claiming Greg was engaged to Veronique Passani. One reporter telephoned Veronique's mother at the apartment on Boulevard Franklin D Roosevelt.

'Madame Passani, is it true that your daughter is engaged to Gregory Peck, the American film star?'

'I don't know,'

'But the newspapers are filled with stories to that effect.'

'I've seen them.'

'Are they true?'

'All I can say, is that my daughter has known Mr Peck for say, three years. They have much affection for each other, but beyond that I cannot say.'

Greg returned to the United States in 1955. The previous year he was voted the best box office draw by 7,000 exhibitors in the country and more than 11,000 all over the world. This extraordinary vote of confidence in his career did not assuage Greg's insecurities. He was prepared to fight hard to stay on top and repair any blemishes to his reputation.

Since the divorce wouldn't be final for 11 more months, Greg played cagey with the press. 'Veronique is a good friend and an intelligent, charming woman,' and 'I know I am exceedingly happy in her companionship,' he would tell reporters.

Veronique flew to the United States on 10 March 1955. At the airport in New York, Greg kept himself hidden in a luncheonette while his emissary rushed forward to greet her. She checked through customs, then entered a chauffeur-driven Cadillac with the stand-in and drove off. On the outskirts of the airport field Greg made his first appearance. He hopped in the car and it roared off.

In New York, Greg mixed business with pleasure, taking Veronique to several shows and attending meetings in connection with *The Purple Plain*. When they arrived in Los Angeles he arranged for her to stay at the Bel Air Hotel. For himself, he leased a house in the Pacific Palisades. It was modest, but big enough to accommodate Jonathan, Stephen and Carey. In fact, the boys could bike from their house on San Remo Drive. Greg introduced her to his close friends but they rarely went out socially.

One of Greg's first orders of business was to present Veronique to 'Auntie Lolly.' He knew Veronique had to pass muster with Louella Parsons if she was going to win over the film colony. The gossip columnist reported to her faithful readers: 'She is entirely unlike what I expected. She is a very pleasant girl, without any affectation and she is not a great beauty. Her eyes are violet in color, and her best feature.

'For a girl who's lived in Paris most of her life, I expected a fashion plate. But she wore a very simple dark dress and a mushroom-shaped pink hat. We talked about the newspaper business.

'It is her intelligence and a certain indefinable charm that has held Greg rather than her glamour. You never could call her a glamour girl in any sense of the word.'

Pressed by Parsons about his intentions, Greg said, 'I have no plans to marry Miss Passani.'

Greg played cagey right up to the last minute. When his divorce became final on 30 December 1955, he married Veronique 19 hours later. For the wedding, officiated by a Justice of the Peace, Greg chose the ranch of his friend Channing Peak in Lompac, California. Only Greg's parents, their spouses, the Peaks' children and a few friends attended. There was little time for a honeymoon because Greg had started filming *The Man in the Gray Flannel Suit* (1956). It was a modest celebration for what would become one of Hollywood's rare, enduring love stories.

CHAPTER FIFTEEN

Perils of Producing

'He doesn't get familiar with strangers. But once you get to know him, he's a charming bohemian character who always loses at poker.'

John Huston on Gregory Peck

Moby Dick landed in theaters in 1956. Impressed with the many outstanding aspects of the production, critics gave it high praise. 'One of the great motion pictures of our time,' rejoiced the *New York Times*. 'A brilliant film,' exclaimed *Time* magazine. William K Zinsser of the *New York Herald Tribune* went so far as to proclaim '*Moby Dick* may be the finest film this country has achieved.' Despite being a box-office success, it failed to win a single Oscar nomination at the 1956 Academy Awards.

The stark beauty of the movie impressed viewers no end. This consummate artistry was achieved through the creative use of color and sound. John Huston and cinematographer Oswald Morris came up with a new process by making one Technicolor negative, another one in black and white, then printing them together. It suggested old whaling engravings. Reviewers also congratulated Huston for having the guts to tackle such an unfilmable behemoth. And several of the actors were singled out for their performances: Richard Basehart as Ishmael, Leo Genn as Starbuck and Orson Welles as Father Mapple. It was a triumph for all concerned – *except Gregory Peck!*

Ahab was a choice role for an actor lusting after an Oscar. In the eyes of many critics, Greg fell woefully short. *Time* magazine wrote: 'The most difficult role, Ahab, is unfortunately handed to the actor probably least able to cope with it: Gregory Peck. Visually, he has an unlucky resemblance to a peg-legged Abe Lincoln, and he is not always convincing as a man at war with Heaven and arrogant enough to "strike the sun if it insulted me." But his failure is only a measure of the high success of the rest of the cast: Peck merely lacks art, not courage or intensity of purpose.'

Some years after the fact, *New Yorker*'s Pauline Kael wrote: 'Though Huston might conceivably have made a great Ahab himself, Gregory Peck could not: that nice man did not belong in the whirling center of Melville's vision.' The *Saturday Review* lamented, 'Peck's make-up for his role is expert, but the force needed for conviction is seldom present.' More biting was the implication by his peers that his range of talent was limited. *Moby Dick*'s screenwriter Ray Bradbury said, 'Greg Peck is never going to be a paranoid killer or a maniac devourer of whales.' And a director who saw the film agreed: 'It's a wonderful picture. But the role of Captain Ahab gave Greg one of the choicest dramatic opportunities of his life and he flubbed it.'

Put on the defensive, Greg cast aspersions on Ray Bradbury's script: 'I felt it was overly reverential with those great dollops of Melville's prose, and it basically lacked the forward drive and motives of a film.'

What stuck in Greg's craw was that when he first agreed to do the film, he did not realize Huston wanted him for Ahab and not for Starbuck, a role he knew and understood, having played it at Berkeley. He finally agreed to portray the lunatic sea captain even though he had trouble imagining himself in the part. Why? Because Huston cast his spell and Greg succumbed. Years later he learned Huston really wanted Orson Welles (after his first choice, Walter Huston, died). But Warner Brothers insisted he sign up a movie idol like Greg before they would finance the deal.

Of course, Huston didn't come out and tell Greg that. He made him think he wanted him for his own sweet self. Later, when he knew the score, Greg lamented: '*Moby Dick* was the end of my innocence.' Orson Welles, who was cast as Father Mapple in the *Moby Dick* production, wasn't so easily taken in. He called Huston 'A Mephistopheles, an outrageously seductive, unfrocked cardinal, an amiable Count Dracula who drank only the best vintages of burgundy and never bared his teeth except to smile.'

For Huston, the deception of Greg was just business. Nothing personal. He didn't become the legendary director of all those classic films by playing Mr Nice Guy. Morally, he was in the same camp with David O Selznick who once said: 'If you are primarily concerned with something called personal artistic integrity, you don't belong in the business of making movies.'

Greg kept quiet about his resentment toward John Huston, and the two men continued to hang out together and enjoy mutual pursuits, such as racehorses – they shared ownership of a couple of thoroughbreds – and primitive art collecting. Professionally they made plans to work together on Melville's *Typee* and *The Bridge in the Jungle*, but the projects never got off the ground.

Still, the fact that Huston wanted him for the lead in *Moby Dick* only to finance the film, continued to rankle. After several years of being boon companions, Greg cut him out of his life without explanation. It's not clear what happened. In trying to fathom the rejection, Huston remembered an occasion where he gave Veronique a friendly kiss, but she pulled away in a 'queer, clumsy piece of behavior . . . and from then on Greg avoided me.'

Given Huston's propensity to consume alcohol and the way it plays tricks on memory, there's a good chance Huston made a crude pass at her but didn't remember it clearly once he sobered up. Greg's avoidance of him bothered the director past the point of forgiveness. When, some years later, Greg saw Huston on a studio lot and acted friendly, Huston turned away. 'It was too late to start over.'

Greg avoided speaking ill of Huston, but he conveniently forgot they had once been close buddies. He told Patricia Harty of *Irish American* magazine: 'Certainly, he was a colorful character, a fine raconteur, but I didn't get to know him on an intimate, friendly basis. I only knew him as a film director.'

After receiving such searing criticism for *Moby Dick*, Greg felt a new urgency to find roles in which he could grow. Though regarded as an accomplished actor in the technical sense, 'good' and 'adequate' were two adjectives people frequently employed when describing his ability. No critic had ever lauded a performance by Greg as truly great. His name was never mentioned in the same breath with Laurence Oliver, Marlon Brando or Rod Steiger.

Though commanding $300,000 a picture, he was filled with self-doubt. Yet, damn it! He wanted an Oscar (he'd been nominated four times). To a self-torturer like Greg, the solution was to drive himself harder. Pick better scripts. 'Of the movies I've done, there isn't much I really like,' Greg admitted. '*The Gunfighter, Roman Holiday, Twelve O'Clock High* I feel were my best.'

The Man in the Gray Flannel Suit wouldn't catapult Greg into Oscar territory, but he had high hopes for it anyway. Based on Sloan Wilson's best-selling novel of the 1950s about a Madison Avenue executive trying to solve his marital problems and cope with his guilt over a wartime affair, the story fit the nation's zeitgeist.

Historian David Halberstam called Sloan Wilson's book one of the most influential of the decade. It was a largely autobiographical account of Wilson's own struggle upon returning from the Second World War to find fulfillment in a pencil-pushing job at Time-Life Inc. Set in 1953, the novel shed an unflattering light on corporate and suburban life in the 'Fabulous Fifties.' For Wilson, the gray flannel suit represented a material culture that rewarded conformists who put career above family. He wore those suits like a prison uniform, as does the book's frustrated protagonist, 33-year-old Tom Rath (as in anger).

One reason the book struck a nerve was that it dramatized the lust for affluence and status rampant in American society. Neither the Korean conflict nor McCarthyism could distract Americans from their rush to claim a place in the rapidly expanding middle class. The standard rerun of the period features sincere men in gray flannel suits and contented women in kitchen aprons smiling at the disinfectant Mr Clean. Split-levels sprouted in potato fields, Cadillacs grew fins, and families snuggled up to television sets, where they learned to love Lucy and eat prepared dinners packaged in tinfoil trays.

The film brought Greg back to the Fox lot with Darryl Zanuck as producer, Nunnally Johnson as both screenwriter and director and Jennifer Jones, his hot tamale from *Duel in the Sun,* as co-star. Greg had high expectations for the film. He optimistically told Johnson: 'I hope it turns out to be *The Best Years of Our Lives* [1946] ten years later with the same man who came home.' He was referring to a popular film directed by his friend William Wyler about the difficulties war veterans experienced adjusting to civilian life.

Gray Flannel's lead character, Tom Rath, represented a pleasant bit of typecasting. 'Gregory Peck happens to be by nature the actor in the gray flannel suit,' wrote journalist Lloyd Schorr. 'He's stolid, conservative, hardworking.'

In the film, Rath has to come to grips with the repercussions of his overseas affair while he is trying to adjust to civilian life. He takes a job as a Madison Avenue public relations man but finds himself caught in the dilemma of succeeding in his high-pressure job or maintaining his integrity.

His wife (Jennifer Jones) is pushing him to take another offer and become the assistant to Ralph Hopkins (Fredric March), president of a major TV network. It would raise his salary, prestige, and workload. But he feels that his family, and the time he spends with them, is more important than the new opportunity. The story has lots of melodrama, guilt, and a revelation about a son he fathered in Italy.

Such irony. Here we have Darryl Zanuck, Nunnally Johnson, Jennifer Jones – and Greg – making a movie about opting for hearth and home over the excitement of career. All had put their careers first and each paid a bitter price.

The Man in the Gray Flannel Suit was Zanuck's 'golden swan song.' Bored with the Hollywood grind, worried about middle age and his virility, and besotted with his mistress Bella Darvi, Zanuck had decided to decamp for Paris.

In many respects, Zanuck's life paralleled that of Ralph Hopkins, the tycoon in the story, who must face a wife who barely knows him. Worse, Hopkins' daughter sees him as a failure as a parent and hates his super-corporation values. She defies him by running around town with disreputable men. Zanuck's marriage of 32 years was breaking in pieces and he had a severely strained relationship with his daughter Susan because of his workaholic attitude and salacity. He admitted to his biographer: 'My mood was to escape, to get away from the scene, the social scene, the studio scene, and everything connected with it.'

Outfitted in a three-button, single-breasted suit he would wear in the film, Greg prepared for his role as 'the gunfighter of Madison Avenue' by visiting advertising agencies, walking along Madison

Avenue and taking trips on the New York City commuter train. Camouflaged by his gray flannel suit, he quietly observed the behavior of the men sitting in the commuter cars reading their copies of the *Times*. Few people recognized him.

Such is the life of an actor. In Sweden, three years before, teenagers shrieked with delight at the sight of 'the handsomest man in the world.' Now, he blended seamlessly into the faceless army of organization men.

Having acted under Nunnally Johnson while making *Night People* in Berlin, Greg knew him to be competent but lacking in the extra depth of insight to qualify as top notch. Johnson enjoyed the idea of being a director and he certainly appreciated a percentage of the profits, but the job itself didn't light his fire.

Greg figured: 'It may be that if he heard his own words played back in a lively way he thought, "That's as good as they can do it." It may be that if he'd gone on a little more, he could have gotten more of a personal contribution from the actors, to shed a little more light on his lines.' Others said: 'He only directed to protect his lines.' Though Johnson wrote, produced and directed eight pictures, he was, first and last, always a writer, a compulsive, dedicated storyteller. Nothing else – professionally or personally – interested him as much, and producing and directing were afterthoughts.

Both Greg and Johnson found Jennifer Jones's on-set behavior disturbing. When Greg had played opposite her in *Duel in the Sun*, there was an ambiguous, intense, edgy quality to her acting that made her compelling. Since then she had married David O Selznick (in 1949), and her ex-husband, Robert Walker, had died (in 1952). Now, her personal life was getting in the way of her professionalism. Selznick still kept a very tight rein on her career. Although he had no part in the production of *The Man in the Gray Flannel Suit*, he tried to dictate to Johnson the manner in which Jones was to be dressed, made up, and filmed. Johnson passed the missives on to Zanuck who responded: 'Listen, you fucker, keep your fingers out of my film.'

Jones's neurosis set her up to give a disturbed performance. Johnson recalled, 'Her eyes were rather out of focus, I couldn't tell whether she was hearing me or not.' One scene was close to catastrophic. Shooting on the lawn of a house rented for the purpose on Long Island, Jones was supposed to run out of the house after a fight with Greg, who then catches her and kisses her as they fall on the ground.

'She came out like an impala,' Johnson explained. 'God, she's a big, leggy girl, you know, and Greg has a limp anyway, so she forgot all about that spot [actor's marker on the ground] and was leading him by about eight lengths when she passed it. I said, "Cut." I said, "You must have forgotten, Honey, we've got to get you in the camera." She said, "Well, I thought I was supposed to be real."'

The next take seemed to be going perfectly, except that Jones started to lose it. 'She just opened up my face,' said Greg. 'There were big claw marks there.'

Johnson recalled: 'By this time, eight doctors and nine make-up men were surrounding him. He said, "I don't call that acting. I call it personal. Can't you get her to do the scene right?" I said, "I don't know. You worked with her in *Duel in the Sun.* I thought you'd know how to cope with this particular thing."'

They had to do it again, for a close shot, and 'This time,' Johnson remembered, 'she butted him. You never saw a madder actor. He said, "Have we got to do it again?" I said, "Well, if we do it again, you wear your cup, because I don't know what's going to happen." I talked to her . . . what do you say to a woman who is fighting savagely when you're supposed to be make-believe? She listened to me, looking past me, and then walked back to her dressing room. She didn't answer . . . One time she did a kind of emotional scene, and much to everybody's astonishment she suddenly made a gesture and knocked everything off the dressing table. It looked right, so it stayed in.'

The Man in the Gray Flannel Suit was worth the aggravation, for the picture proved a financial success. The promotion of the film was tied in with the garment industry. *Look* magazine carried fashion spreads showing a wife waiting at the train station for the return of her husband, both garbed in the very practical gray flannel slacks and suit with the tag line: 'Gray flannel is in the limelight from Hollywood to the Eastern suburbs.' Comedian Bob Peck even parodied the film with a popular song titled 'The Moth in the Gray Flannel Suit.'

'Togetherness' was a catchword of the 1950s celebrating the kind of domesticity portrayed in *The Man in the Gray Flannel Suit*. Women's magazines such as *McCall's* and *Ladies Home Journal* overused it to the point of nausea. *Chez* Peck, togetherness was taking place on a much more lavish level.

Veronique had furnished the couple's sprawling ranch house in Brentwood – then a sleepy if luxurious suburb – with an eye to comfort. Everywhere there were casual corners where Greg could relax for reading or conversation. Occasionally he chose a sunny corner of the garden as a place to study scripts for possible production, or retired to his pleasantly cluttered study. The room was filled with mementos from his films, including a saddle from a long-forgotten Western, small Greek marble horses and life-sized wooden *santos* from Spain 'because you can work better if you are surrounded with beautiful things.'

Veronique wore simple yet expensive clothes, drove Greg to work in the morning, cooked him fine French meals and treated him as the master of the house. She had to adjust to having stepchildren around and vice versa. She was only a decade older than the boys; the period of adjustment took time.

Greg's youngest son Carey remembered: 'My parents had a custody agreement they stuck in a drawer somewhere and forgot about.' The boys moved freely between the two houses. In fact, they could hop on their bikes and cut across a polo field to their father's house in Brentwood.

Soon Veronique learned she was pregnant. When she reached the second trimester, she dialed Louella Parsons. 'You think any other woman in Hollywood was able to keep the secret of the stork's coming visit four months?' she crowed. 'How did it happen you didn't find out!' Although said in a playful manner, the message was clear. The Peck household was now under new – and very smart – management.

In the meantime, Greg was looking for laughs. After slogging through *Moby Dick* and *The Man in the Gray Flannel Suit*, he was itching to do a lively light part, but was he up to the challenge?

There's a telling line by Edmund Gwenn, who played Santa Claus in *Miracle on 34th Street* (1947), that's also been ascribed to Edmund Kean, Edwin Booth, David Garrick, William Holden, Groucho Marx, Marcel Marceau, Noel Coward and Oscar Wilde. In any case, according to Peter Hay in *Movie Anecdotes*, as Gwenn lay dying, Jack Lemmon visited him and asked about dying. The heaven-bound actor replied, 'Oh, it's hard, very hard indeed. But not as hard as doing comedy.' For Greg, the hard part was getting a shot at performing in a comedic role. After *Roman Holiday*, he expected to be deluged with offers. It didn't happen. So, when an amusing, sophisticated screenplay blew his way, he leapt at it.

Designing Woman (1957) is a charming tale about a sports reporter (Peck) who marries a dress designer (Lauren Bacall) in haste and they soon suspect they have nothing in common. Marilla and Mike Hagen are both from New York, but they meet in southern California, and their brief romantic courtship is not intruded upon by the disparate realities of their respective worlds at home. Once they arrive back in New York as man and wife, however, she is dismayed by his prosaic apartment and he is intimidated by the elegance and spaciousness of hers. Bowing to practicality, Mike moves in with Marilla. The two are then introduced to each other's friends and milieus. Much of the humor derives from the convergence of four separate worlds: fashion, news reporting, the theater, and the underworld. Marilla is sickened by the sight of blood at a prize fight, and Mike is contemptuous of the ceremonious gentility of a fashion show. Complicating matters further, both Mike and Marilla must resolve their previous romantic involvements. The story was suggested by famed costume designer Helen Rose who ultimately created 132 outfits for Lauren Bacall to wear in the movie.

Dore Schary, MGM's production chief, originally wanted James Stewart and Grace Kelly for the film's leads. Kelly stalled, first having to complete two other films, *High Society* (1956) and *The Swan* (1956). Then she accepted Prince Rainier's proposal of marriage and got caught up planning the wedding. The delays caused Stewart to back out. So Greg was offered the male lead. When director Joshua Logan also retreated, Schary asked Vincente

Minnelli to direct the movie. Then he turned to George Wells to develop the screenplay; the script would win an Oscar.

Although Minnelli had experience directing comedy with *Father of the Bride* (1950) and had just completed filming the Broadway drama *Tea and Sympathy* (1956), he was best known for his splendid musicals: *Meet Me in St Louis* (1944), *An American in Paris* (1951), *Bandwagon* (1953) and *Brigadoon* (1954).

Greg let Minnelli know how much he looked forward to getting started on *Designing Woman*. 'Greg, the king of the underplayers, was raring to go, like a banker at an American Legion Convention,' recalled Minnelli. Greg was also gung-ho about Lauren Bacall playing opposite him. Having known her from her days as a 17-year-old usherette and photographers' model, he had watched her rise from obscurity like a rocket from a silo. He said: 'No one else has her looks, her style, the way of moving and wearing clothes, the sharp mind.'

Lauren Bacall, independent, self-aware, represented the best of the new kind of mysterious woman. Allegedly she was discovered by director Howard Hawks' wife, Slim, who spotted Bacall's picture in a fashion magazine. Coached by Hawks himself, who every day for a year had her work out in an empty lot, shouting until she was hoarse in order to lower the register of her voice, Betty, as she was called, magnetically modernized the screen with her odd mixture of gossamer and lemon. Tall, rangy, she was, according to Marjorie Rosen, author of *Popcorn Venus: Women, Movies and the American Dream*, the only screen female since Marlene Dietrich who had the resources, or chutzpah, to look as if she might be mentally undressing every male with her gaze.

But the charismatic pairing of Bacall with Humphrey Bogart in such winners as *To Have and Have Not* (1944) and *The Big Sleep* (1946) early in her career stunted her growth. Without Bogart she floundered. Alone, she was acid, just a little too brittle and serpentine. This worked against sustained stardom, especially if the vehicles were unsuitable, and in the early 1950s her luminosity would seem diminished – or misused – in *How to Marry a Millionaire* (1953), *Woman's World* (1954), and even the highly successful and romantic *Written on the Wind* (1956). But the script of *Designing Woman* offered her material witty and stylish enough to engage her attractively. So she jumped at the chance to appear in the film.

There was another personal reason she campaigned to play Marilla Hagen. Humphrey Bogart had been diagnosed with esophageal cancer. Although she proved stalwart throughout her husband's illness ('That's the way you tell the women from the broads in this town,' he said admiringly), she desperately needed a release from the sickroom atmosphere of her home. Yet nobody would consider her for a role. 'My career had come to a dead stop,' she confessed. 'No one offered me anything – I was caring for Bogie.'

When she heard about the part in *Designing Woman*, she called Dore Schary, told him she could play it, wanted to, and when she cut her salary in half, he finally said yes. 'I swallowed pride and everything else that got in the way to get that part. For some reason, a test was not mentioned, but Gregory Peck, the leading man, had the right to approve his leading lady, which he did, thank heaven.'

The news that Bogart had cancer of the esophagus deeply saddened Greg as it did many people in Hollywood. He didn't know Bogart well, but he admired his ability to become king of Hollywood in the 1950s and still hold on to his essential character.

'Bogie was a curious mixture,' wrote Bacall. 'He wasn't cynical. He didn't expect too much, he never realized he would leave the kind of mark he has left. He never tried to impress anyone. I've never known anybody who was so completely his own man. He could not be led in any direction unless it was the direction he chose to go.'

Before Bogart's illness, Greg used to run into the couple at Romanoff's, the chichi restaurant run by a fake nobleman that served as a hangout for the film elite. There, Bogart always occupied the second booth on the left off the entryway. When Bacall joined him, she could be depended upon to arrive in a smashing outfit. Led by the maître d' or by Mike Romanoff himself, Bogie and Betty would step royally through the archway and down three steps into the main dining room. With a roomful of eyes riveted upon them, they sat down but rarely dined alone. On a given day, they might be joined by any of the following: Nunnally Johnson, Holmby Hills neighbors Judy Garland and her husband Sid Luft, Bogart's agent,

Irving (Swifty) Lazar, writer Nathaniel Benchley, composer Jimmy van Heusen or Frank Sinatra.

Greg was a great appreciator of Bogart's antics. 'He was feisty,' recalled Greg. 'He'd tackle somebody on religion or on politics or on their opinions about most anything, and he'd get somebody else to contradict them, and he'd sit back and laugh.'

Following his cancer diagnosis, Bogart was on the operating table for eight hours, undergoing surgery that one doctor called 'the worst a human being can undergo.' His stomach was raised 12 inches. Two inches of his esophagus were removed, and one rib was discarded. The public was told that the operation had been a success, but Bogart lost 34 pounds. Radiation treatment at the Los Angeles Tumor Institute followed, but the prognosis wasn't good. Despite his condition, Bogart encouraged Bacall as she went off to the set of *Designing Woman* each day.

Greg never worked with a director quite like Vincente Minnelli. He was unusual in that he could visualize the finished product long before it was even put on paper. This is a rarity. What's more, the sets had to conform to his preconceived idea, his whole photographic conception and his cutting and editing of them long before he started a picture. The man knew what he was after. He knew what he wanted to see on the screen. This meant serious demands: more money, more time, more effort. Some people resented it. Some people went along with it. But never did he ever let up with his one feeling of this was going to be the kind of picture he wanted it to be. And generally his films turned out beautiful. *Designing Woman* was a prime example. With a generous budget of nearly $2 million, Minnelli gave the film the polish of his musicals, starting with the opening scenes set at the exclusive Beverly Hills Hotel.

Greg was heartened to see Bogart join Bacall for the first day's shoot at the pool of the Beverly Hills Hotel. Accompanied by his children, Steve and Leslie, Bogart stayed off to the side and quietly observed the action. And for the sailboat sequences in the movie, he felt well enough to take out his own yacht *Santana*. During their lunch break, Bacall and Greg boarded his boat, but there was no getting around the fact that Bogart's days were numbered.

Bacall continued to regard *Designing Woman* as a godsend. 'Greg and I played characters very much in love, working in different worlds, fighting a lot. In one scene I was leaving him after a fight, running on a cobblestone street in spike-heeled shoes – and of course proceeded to fall and sprain my ankle. It was a romantic movie and I seemed to be constantly running toward Greg or away from him, so I had emotional and physical release to compensate for keeping everything inside at home.' And it didn't hurt that she regarded her co-star as gorgeous. 'He was probably the most beautiful creature I'd ever seen,' said Bacall. 'And when he looks at you, he sees you, he connects with you completely.'

The high point of *Designing Woman* is the pasta scene. Greg takes Dolores Gray (Lori Shannon) to a top restaurant to tell her that he is going to marry Bacall. Their conversation is calm and civilized and she seemingly accepts his long-winded explanation without emotion. Quietly she reaches over and tips a large plate of ravioli into his lap. He makes no reaction and continues as if nothing has happened, and they bid each other goodbye. Greg loved the scene, especially when George Burns complimented him. Greg boasted: 'George told me that he thought my "take-it" was one of the best he had ever seen, and to be told that I could make him laugh was as good as getting an Oscar.'

On the home front, Greg and Veronique looked forward to the birth of their first child. A month before Veronique's due date, her mother, Alexandra Passani and half-brother, Cornelius, who was ten years old, arrived from Paris. Greg arranged for Cornelius to be enrolled in Beverly Hills public school and he taught his mother-in-law to drive.

When Greg signed the contract for *Designing Woman* with MGM, he insisted upon a clause allowing him 24 hours off when the baby was born. When he got the call, he paced the corridor at Santa Monica Hospital. On 24 October 1956 Veronique gave birth to a 7-pound 14-ounce boy. Mindful that Louella Parsons' memory for slight would have done justice to an elephant, Greg phoned her with the news before she heard it from anybody else. He told her about his new son, Anthony, adding he was returning to work even though he had been up all night. A big fashion number was scheduled and he didn't want to disappoint the company. Greg was 40 when Anthony was born and Veronique was 24.

After *Designing Woman* wrapped, Greg continued keeping in touch with the Bogarts. In November, Bogie was readmitted to the Good Samaritan Hospital for treatment of nerve pressure caused by the growth of scar tissue on his throat. He was sent home after the operation, but never recovered.

Visiting Bogart in his last days was a heart-rending experience. Still, Bacall insisted to friends that as soon as they crossed the threshold of the Bogart home, they were invited to pick up his spirits. Since the guests were there to cheer Bogart, he, in turn, wanted to live up to their expectations. As his illness progressed, he grew too weak to walk downstairs and refused to be carried, but he was determined that he would visit with his friends in the Butternut Room rather than upstairs in his sickbed. 'He would lie on his couch upstairs at five o'clock,' John Huston wrote, 'to be shaved and groomed and dressed in gray flannels and scarlet smoking jacket. When he was no longer able to walk, his emaciated body would be lifted into a wheelchair and taken to a dumb-waiter, the roof of which had been removed to give him headroom. His nurses would help him in, and sitting on a little stool, he would be lowered down to the kitchen where another transfer would be made and, again by wheelchair, he'd be transported through the house into the library and his chair, and there he would be, sherry glass in one hand and cigarette in the other, at five-thirty when the guests started to arrive.'

Greg was deeply pained by Bogart's condition and found it difficult to engage in the gossip and verbal repartee the situation required. 'You weren't allowed to talk about his illness. We told jokes. I had a long one prepared, and as I was trying to edit this story in my head, Bogie cut across it and said, "Great God Almighty, if you don't get to the punch line soon, I won't be around to hear it!"

'I remember getting home that night, walking into the garden and my eyes just filling with tears.' Bogart died in January 1957.

Some reviewers saw *Designing Woman* as too derivative of the screwball comedies of the 1930s and, most particularly they felt it harkened back to the 1942 Tracy–Hepburn classic, *Woman of the Year*. Viewed without that reference point, it's a fine film. Thirty-five years later, Greg and Bacall were happily reunited in a made-for-television movie *The Portrait*. The film itself would have a television spin-off in the 1990s sitcom *Designing Women*.

'Greg, it's a helluva thrill to make a movie,' director William Wyler had said to Greg one day in Rome when they were filming *Roman Holiday*. 'We start with just an idea, get it on paper, put it before a camera, and then people pay money to look at a blank wall and see what we've put there.'

Greg did a lot of thinking about that conversation. He admitted: 'Just walking in front of the cameras gets a bit thin after ten years.' If he went into producing, he would not only exercise more control over his career, he would also make more money. Economically, the mid-1950s were unkind to him. A change in tax laws retroactively opened up his European earnings – 80 per cent of his income that was supposedly tax-free. That bill of nearly a million dollars was added to the $100,000 a year alimony for Greta, and the $750 a month child support for his sons. He said at the time: 'One day, I was a millionaire. Then the phone rang and I was told the tax law had been changed. I don't think anyone ever said "goodbye" to $900,000 as suddenly as that before.' After that sobering experience, producing looked like a practical venue to expand his income. It was a great way to save on taxes, which is what an actor does when he incorporates himself as the producing company and shares the profits instead of working for a salary.

Greg formed an independent production company, Anthony-World, named after his infant son Anthony, with William Wyler to make a movie called *Thieves Market*. When that deal fell through, they bought a project called *The Big Country*. It came to them through Greg's agent George Chasin who had been sent the property for Marlon Brando – a 50-page treatment of a book with the same name.

Working together, Greg and Wyler conceived the movie on a vast scale: strong men and beautiful women of the Old West against gorgeous scenery and magnificent music. Their film would capture the sweep and grandeur of the Great Plains at a time when men's passions were as volatile and untamed as the great frontier itself. Greg referred to it as a 'Grand Hotel' of Westerns.

Greg wasn't the only actor determined to get a bigger slice of the movie pie. In the post-war era, independent production had increased from 40 films in 1945 to 265 by 1957. United Artists alone had 50 independent filmmakers on its roster, among them John Wayne, Frank Sinatra, Bob Hope and Kirk Douglas. Now they had Greg for *The Big Country* (1958). Furthermore, 'independent' was no longer synonymous with low-budget.

The more he talked with Wyler, the more optimistic Greg became about the new direction his career. 'As an actor I didn't have any real authority,' Greg explained. And he also reasoned his producing experience with the La Jolla Playhouse provided him with solid preparation for his new role. Close to 60 plays, 10 every summer – that's a track record. But putting on plays in a high school auditorium – even with professional actors – is not the same as taking on the enormous responsibility of a multimillion-dollar movie.

Before the actual physical process of shooting a movie could begin, the script had to be in shape, the cast and crew chosen, and the locations decided upon. The physical process of making movies is fiendishly elaborate. Dealing with the egos is a job in itself. For instance, when Charlton Heston was approached to be in *The Big Country*, he initially refused because Greg had the lead. Then Heston's agent talked him round. 'Kid,' he said, 'you don't know what the fuck you're talking about. You have an offer to work with Greg for maybe the best director in film, and you're worrying the *part* isn't good enough for you, you *have* to do this picture!'

Playing in David O Selznick movies, Greg had a chance to see the greatest producer of Hollywood's golden era at work. Selznick believed that a producer, in order to be able to produce properly, must be able, if necessary, to sit down and write the scene, and if he is criticizing a director, he must be able not merely to say 'I don't like it' but to tell him how he would direct it himself. He must be able to go into a cutting room, and if he doesn't like the cutting of a sequence, which is more often true than not, he must be able to re-cut the sequence. 'The difference between myself and other producers,' he said, 'is I am interested in the thousands and thousands of details that go to into the making of a film. It is the sum total of all these things that either makes a picture or destroys it.' In sum, the way Selznick saw it, the producer's function was to be responsible for *everything*. Such an all-encompassing role appealed to Greg's obsessive-compulsive instincts but he didn't have Selznick's experience and Selznick had never had to act in front of a camera while producing a movie at the same time.

For the moment, it was blue skies all the way. Who better to make a film with than William Wyler? Actors working for him have been nominated for Academy Awards more than 30 times, and won a dozen Oscars, plus countless lesser awards. Looking back over his filmography, it seemed unbelievable that one man could be connected to so many of the cinema's greatest films, but Wyler was. Not to mention the great number of stars who did their first films with him: Laurence Olivier, Henry Fonda, Barbara Hutton and, of course, Audrey Hepburn. Wyler was also able to guide cinematographers and writers, to make movies we can never forget.

Another plus for Greg was he responded well to Wyler's directing style. Greg didn't like a lot of the detailed analytic chatter he got from some directors; it tended to confuse him. 'But Wyler waits for extra values, extra insights,' Greg enthused, 'and he knows when you capture something special, a new shred of illumination – Wyler is this kind of director, he isn't terribly articulate, doesn't talk a lot, but he knows it could be better and he'll say so over and over again.'

The groundwork for their partnership was laid not only professionally, but personally. Dinners, vacations – it was the Pecks and the Wylers. Peas in a pod. Banking on the bond of friendship and avidly wanting to make a film with him, Greg discounted the fact that Wyler was – in the words of his biographer, Jan Herman – one of the major Hollywood 'son-of-a-bitches.' Like Huston, his movies were the most important thing in the world to him. If a friendship was sacrificed in the process, so be it.

'I don't care what goes on on the set,' claimed Wyler. 'I don't care if we all hate each other. I only care what the finished product looks like when the audience goes to the theater.'

The story of *The Big Country* was bone-hard and uncluttered, and the cast Greg and Wyler assembled was first rate. The tale is essentially one of two feuding families, their cattle, their need for water that belongs to a school mistress (Jean Simmons), and their settlers' conviction that as big as the country is, there is no room for both of them. The Terrills, led by the Major (Charles Bickford), stand for culture and live in luxury, but they are as brutal in their own way as are the Hannasseys, who live in squalor under the patriarchal domination of Rufus (Burl Ives).

What made *The Big Country* a Western with a difference was its hero, James McKay (Peck), a man who refused to act according to accepted standards of behavior, the Western code of ethics. McKay is a gentleman sailor from Baltimore coming West to wed Patricia Terrill (Carroll Baker), whom he met and wooed while she was attending a New England finishing school. He faces opposition from his competitor in love (Charlton Heston), his adversary in business (Ives), and his skeptical father-in-law (Bickford).

But the myriad problems connected with the film started with the script. Jessamyn West, who had worked with Wyler on *Friendly Persuasion* (1956), tried her hand; she was followed by Leon Uris, Robert Wyler, and Robert Wilder, with input from Greg as well. James Webb and Sy Bartlett finished the script, but with dire consequences. The writing amounted to 170 pages, most of which were shot. Millions of dollars were lost in cutting the film down to size (more or less), as the budget grew from the projected $1,100,000 to more than $4,200,000 million.

To shoot *The Big Country*, Wyler chose Franz Planer. Together, they chose Technirama and Technicolor. Wyler thought the new giant screen was eminently suited for the Western because the whole idea was to have space. With the wide screen, he soon discovered, it was awkward in intimate scenes because it tended to let the audience's eyes wander from principal characters toward incidental bits.

With cast and crew assembled in Stockton, California, Greg hired his three eldest sons as extras. They were on school holiday. The mischievous kids can't be missed in the opening scenes depicting Greg's arrival in a dusty, sun-scorched frontier town. As Greg, in his Eastern clothes and bowler hat, alights from the stagecoach that has brought him from faraway Baltimore, he is greeted with derisive looks and grins from the boys dressed as ragamuffins. The youngsters were affectionately known as Peck's bad boys for between-scenes pranks.

'Because you're acting, this is the one and only occasion when you'll be allowed to laugh at your father,' Greg, with a smile, warned his offspring as Wyler called 'Camera!' and the episode began.

Later, he said reflectively: 'I want to do a good job with the boys. I hope to teach them the right values, to work and develop their minds. I don't want them loaded with too much spending money. They'd miss all the good things that form character in kids.'

As a side income for his sons, and a possible vocation, Greg had gone into the cattle business on a large scale, leasing grazing land in Santa Barbara, San Luis Obispo and Modesto. 'I had dreams of owning a ranch,' said Greg. 'I would take part in roundups, the roping and the branding. It was part of my life at the time.' He hoped the boys would want to learn all they could about animal husbandry and some day take charge of the cattle business.

As shooting got underway, Greg experienced one rude shock after another about the realities of making movies. 'Producing is a hell of a thing,' he admitted. 'When you're just acting, production details never come to your attention. You only know you have a call for 7.30 a.m. for scenes 423 through 427. But when you're a producer, you're always aware of money going down the drain. One key figure sticks in my mind. On locations, it costs us $35,000 a day. That's about $4,300 an hour!'

Despite the escalating costs, Greg arranged for 4,000 head of cattle, at $10 apiece, to be used for the shot in which he comes out of the house on the first morning at the Terrill Ranch and surveys the landscape. It took Greg the producer several days to arrange for the vast herd to be gathered from various ranches for the single day. But he arrived on the set to find only 40 cattle; Wyler had cut the number to save money.

'It'll be enough,' Wyler assured him.

'But this was my decision,' roared Greg.

'Godammit,' yelled Wyler, '$40,000 for just one shot!'

Because of the remote locations and constant script revisions, tensions mounted on the set. Wyler expected a lot from everyone.

His towering reputation, and his track record, gave him the license to be as difficult as he wanted – and damn anybody who questioned his approach.

The vibes on the shoot began to reflect the mood of the picture. Jean Simmons said the atmosphere felt 'very dodgy – the sort of prevailing tension that invites paranoia, causes you to wonder, "What have I done?" . . . I guess Willy was in a position to know what it took to achieve great performances, but he also seemed bent on making things difficult . . . and there was all that constant rewriting. We'd have our version, then receive yet another rewrite the following morning. It made the acting damned near impossible.'

The major crisis started when Greg was looking at the dailies of an important early scene in a buckboard with Carroll Baker. He felt he could do a better job on his close-up. So he asked Wyler to do a retake, not uncommon for an actor of Greg's stature and reputation, even were he not a co-producer. Wyler responded, reasonably enough: 'Let me do a rough assembly of the whole scene first. If you're still unhappy with the shot, we'll do it over.'

But Wyler kept putting him off. With the production about to pack up and move from Stockton into the Mojave Desert, Greg urged: 'Take a part of the day and do the retake!' Wyler barked: 'I'm not going to do another retake. We don't need it.' Spurned by the director, Greg voted with his feet. He marched to his trailer, packed up his things and headed home to Los Angeles. His working relationship with Wyler as a co-producer was well and truly shattered.

Wyler decided that he could finish the film at the studio where all the interiors were to be shot, but Greg, still fuming, refused to return for the final week of filming. George Chasin and Veronique finally persuaded him to change his mind. Wyler insisted Greg make a public apology in front of cast and crew for his tantrum, but Greg would not, and Wyler had to drop his demands or risk not getting the film finished. Greg reported for work at the studio and for the final week.

The feud wasn't over. Wyler supervised the editing and delivered a film to United Artists that ran to four hours. Greg complained, 'he'd overshot by an hour's length, which had to be cut. We went way over our budget and in the end spent $4.1 million.'

Wyler tried to stop Greg's name going on as co-producer and lawyers were called in to fight it out. Veronique and Talli Wyler tried to get them to sort out their problem amicably but both men stubbornly refused. Greg felt it was a question of ethics, of keeping your promises and he wouldn't give an inch. As for Wyler, he announced: 'I wouldn't direct Peck again for a million dollars and you can quote me on that.'

Storming off the set is career suicide in Hollywood. No sooner does the word get around, than the arrogant fool who committed such a transgression is sentenced to sit by a silent phone. Greg had to act fast, or risk perdition. But what could he do to convince a town he was not inordinately thin-skinned, throwing a hissy-fit because he didn't get his way? Then it came to him. Play against type. People think you're a prickly loner? Toss a splashy party. Get everybody talking about what a fun fellow you are.

So he flew Ted Straeter's orchestra from New York to Los Angeles. He gave directions for the parking lot of Romanoff's restaurant to be transformed into a miniature Versailles and ordered thousands of roses and enough caviar and champagne to have stocked Maxim's for months. He paid one of the biggest restaurant checks in local history – but it was worth it! Cary Grant and Clark Gable told him it was the best party ever given in Hollywood.

Despite its virtues, *The Big Country* – two and three quarter hours in length – received a lukewarm reception from the critics and, though profitable at least on paper, failed to become the hugely successful blockbuster United Artists anticipated. Wyler and Greg would have done well to heed Alfred Hitchcock's advice: 'The duration of a film should not exceed the capacity of the human bladder.'

Greg lost more than Wyler did from their feud. If he had stayed close to Wyler, there's a chance the director would have found another romantic comedy like *Roman Holiday* in which Greg would have had the opportunity to stretch his comedic potential or have grown in another way under Wyler's superior direction. As it turned out, Greg never formed an ongoing relationship with one director in the manner of Cary Grant (Alfred Hitchcock and Howard Hawks), James Stewart (Alfred Hitchcock and Frank

Capra), and Henry Fonda (John Ford). His career seemed to suffer because of it.

The Bravados (1958) came next. In this saga of outrage and revenge, Greg plays rancher Jim Douglas, a man whose wife and child have been murdered. He is very different from James McKay, the protagonist in *The Big Country*. With six-shooter at the ready, Douglas sets out to execute their killers. In retrospect, Peck said, 'I did not care for the picture because my character is unbelievably grim and straight-faced . . .' Though he initially turned down the role, he ultimately said 'yes' because the script was re-worked by veteran Western writer Philip Yordan. Also, his good friend Henry King signed on as director.

Veronique packed up baby Anthony and joined Greg on location in Mexico. It certainly would have been understandable if she had chosen to stay home since she was pregnant again. But for her, Greg would always be top priority. She understood movies were an obsession with Greg. When working on a film, he became totally immersed in it. Everything else seemed trivial by comparison. She knew he needed a woman who could live with his obsession and not be jealous of it. And she was also aware sex was rampant on locations. So she created a cocoon within the hustle and bustle of the movie set. Her strategy proved sound. Happy to have his family near him, Greg didn't mingle with the cast. (The other actors in *The Bravados* were in awe of him, though they considered him austere, aloof and disinterested in them.) In fact, he even paid scant attention to Joan Collins, his leading lady.

Collins had not exchanged many words with Greg until they came to a scene where they rode side by side, hard and fast and expertly for days. She recalled in her biography *Past Imperfect*: 'He was a wonderful-looking man, tall and rangy, with a classically handsome profile and a strongly carved nose,' she wrote in her biography. 'His aloofness, I found out when we rode for so long, was a form of shyness. He was basically not at ease around new people. I found he had a wonderful sense of humor, and knowing my fear of riding, he was considerate toward me.

'But on the last day he teased me unmercifully by riding so fast that I was sore for a week. "Come on, Collins" he yelled as we cantered faster and faster beside a deep canyon that I knew with a sickening lurch meant plunging to certain death if Adonis [her horse] placed a hoof wrong. "They say you English women can ride," Greg said mock-scornfully, digging his spurs in and making his mount fly even faster. "Let's see you show 'em *all*, Collins – show 'em you're a real horsewoman, will you?" He galloped even faster. The wind almost took off my Stetson and I jammed it down like Greg's until it covered my eyes. It was enormously exhilarating. I felt in command of that three hundred pounds of sinew and muscle beneath me; I wasn't afraid at all, in fact it was a wonderful, free and joyous feeling I had of space, power and purity.'

The camera car was hard put to keep up with them. They hadn't expected Greg to gallop so fast, and even less expected that Collins would be right alongside him, urging her horse to ever greater speed. Even when Henry King yelled 'Cut,' they continued galloping faster and faster into the distance. They were laughing now as they heard the assistant director plaintively calling them back to their positions. They reined in the horses. Collins amazed herself with her newfound expertise.

'Thank you, Greg,' she yelled over her shoulder as she galloped away, out-racing him!

'For what?' he called.

'For curing me of my fear of horses – you really did it. I'm not scared anymore.'

'Don't mention it, ma'am.' He smiled gallantly.

Reminiscing about making *The Bravados* with Collins, Greg told Michael Freedland in the 1970s: 'She was a sensational young girl . . . a kind of knockout. I see Joan today and, if anything, she is prettier now than she was then.'

Another Peck baby arrived at Santa Monica Hospital on 1 May 1958, and Greg dutifully contacted 'Auntie Lolly'. Parsons led off her column: 'In a matter of minutes after Miss Cecilia Peck made her appearance in this world, her happy father, Greg, was on the telephone to tell me his good news. He said, "This is the fifth time I've called you with news of a birth, but this is the first time I could say it's a girl." He added, "She's a real gift from heaven."'

For his next production, Greg set out to show the human face of war. As co-producer and star of *Pork Chop Hill* (1959), he took great pride in making a picture depicting the futility of combat. Even though it failed to make a killing at the box-office, Greg still called it 'One of my favorite pictures. We made a realistic war film, without sentimentality, without mom's apple pie, without letters from out in the old hometown. I like it because of the extreme, tragic irony.'

Based on the true account of Brigadier General S L A Marshall, the gritty film is a harshly realistic depiction of the bloody capture of a hill with no military value during the final days of the Korean War. While peace negotiations are being conducted in Panmunjon, not 70 miles from the Chinese-held ridge, the company of Lieutenant Joe Clemons (Peck) must take the hill to prove to the Chinese diplomats that the US is 'serious.'

The ambivalence of the soldiers, many of whom feel the hopelessness of fighting for ground that is simply a diplomatic token, is contrasted with the gung-ho attitude of those who believe that they must do their patriotic duty. If not outright anti-war, *Pork Chop Hill* showed soldiers questioning their involvement.

After breaking the bank with *The Big Country*, Greg scouted about for unknowns in lieu of name stars and put together a superb cast. Among the troops are Forstman (Harry Guardino), Fedderson (George Peppard), Lieutenant Russell (Rip Torn), Marshall (Martin Landau) and Velie (Robert Blake).

Greg chose Lewis Milestone, an excellent craftsman with a fluid camera style, as his director. In 1930, Milestone helmed the landmark *All Quiet on the Western Front* – probably the greatest of pacifist, anti-war films. He also directed other combat films: *Edge of Darkness* (1943), *The Purple Heart* (1944) and *A Walk in the Sun* (1946). Like William Wyler, he knew his own mind and by the time *Pork Chop Hill* was ready for release, Milestone was fed up with Gregory Peck.

In S L A Marshall's book, also called *Pork Chop Hill*, the brigadier general describes Joe Clemons as a young West Point graduate with no fighting experience. As a greenhorn officer, he made some fundamental military errors. Greg, now 42 years old and a guardian of his image, played Clemons as the stereotypical hero.

Greg said he took Milestone's edited version of the film and 'sharpened it up and speeded it up,' while Milestone claimed the 20 minutes of footage that did not feature Greg was cut out, allegedly at the suggestion of Veronique. (She was becoming a familiar figure in the editing rooms of her husband's films, standing in the back, not talking, but taking everything in.) So a picture with a noble purpose became the source of lasting friction between Greg and his second co-producer. *'Pork Chop Hill* became a picture I am not proud of,' regretted Lewis Milestone, 'because it looked as if it were cut with a dull axe. All that remained was Gregory Peck and a gun.'

Greg liked money. No doubt about it. But it isn't what drove him to continue producing movies. More than anything, he wanted 'to make or appear in a great film – the kind that shows every year or so at New York's Museum of Modern Art or is hailed as a great film world around.'

In the meantime, he was off to Australia to make *On the Beach* (1959) with Fred Astaire, Anthony Perkins and Ava Gardner. Oh, that Ava! How happy he was to be getting together with his bosom pal from *The Great Sinner* and *The Snows of Kilimanjaro*. With 'the Barefoot Contessa' around, life was *never* dull.

CHAPTER SIXTEEN

Role of a Lifetime

'*On the Beach* is a movie about the end of the world. I cannot think of anywhere better to film it than Melbourne.'

Attributed to Ava Gardner

In the quiet city of Melbourne in 1959, Greg and Veronique rented the elegant Victorian mansion of Sir Norman Brookes, a former tennis star. With them were Anthony, three, Cecilia, 18 months, and Carey, ten.

One of the well-wishers on hand to greet Greg was June Dally-Watkins, the model he escorted around Rome in 1952. This time they connected as old friends.

'Are you happy?' she asked him.

'Yes,' he answered. Then he added that he not only liked being married to Veronique, but he was thrilled to finally be the father of a little girl.

Carey Peck found to his surprise that he was behind grades of Australian children the same age.

'What do I do, Pop?' He asked Greg.

'Surpass them,' said Greg. Just as he was tough on himself, he also held the bar very high for his children.

Although the house was staffed with servants, Veronique brought along her French chef and between the sumptuous food and splendid drinks the estate soon became a mirthful refuge for the cast of *On the Beach*. It gave the besieged actors a chance to let their hair down unobserved by their besotted Melbourne fans.

Very few Hollywood faces had thus far been seen in Melbourne, a city of eager moviegoers. In the 1950s, the locals were still suffering from 'cultural cringe.' So it is no wonder that Greg, Fred Astaire, Ava Gardner and Anthony Perkins were fêted, cheered and mobbed wherever they went.

On the Beach was to be a movie based on best-selling novelist Nevil Shute's bleak, moving tale about the consequences of full-scale nuclear war. Only the inhabitants of Australia and the men of the US submarine *Sawfish* are left after the Big One goes off in the Northern Hemisphere. Who started it? Fred Astaire's character, a cynical scientist gives his take on the tragedy: 'Some poor bloke probably looked at a radar screen and thought he saw something . . . he knew that if he hesitated one thousandth of a second his own country would be wiped off the map and so he pushed the button. And the world went . . . crazy.'

As *On the Beach* opens, the radiation cloud is slowly moving toward Australia, where the only pro-active role left for people to play is to minimize the suffering of radiation sickness, and take their own lives using the government-issued suicide pills. A glum story.

Ava Gardner's arrival brightened things considerably. This was particularly true for Greg. Seven years had passed since they made a picture together. Now he could resume his role as rescuer and confidant. Though her spectacular beauty – with its luminous skin and languid eyes – was gone, her face was still arresting. She was looking bruised and world weary, which ironically suited her character in *On the Beach*. What could be more fitting than to have Gardner play Moira Davidson, a Melbourne party girl finding love too late?

By now, Gardner was divorced from Frank Sinatra but the drama rolled on. Their epic fights spanned the globe – he followed her to movie locations in Spain, Australia and England – and usually ended up with one of them leaving on a plane. Gardner tossed out words like primitive, passionate, bitter and acrimonious when describing their romantic jealousy. Journalist Pete Hamill believes if they had stayed together it would have got very violent and somebody would have died. Yet their love endured.

Since the locals didn't meet many women who 'live for the moment,' Gardner's arrival was put under intense press scrutiny. Her resolve to lay off drinking and her conscientiousness about her tennis lessons with professional player Tony Trevor were evidently dashed by the boredom of Melbourne. She was eagerly awaiting a visit from Sinatra. And the press kept badgering her because she was such great copy. She tossed off tidbits like: 'Deep down I'm pretty superficial'; and 'Everybody kisses everybody else in this crummy business all the time. It's the kissiest business in the world. You have to keep kissing people when you're penned up and working together the way we are. If people making a movie didn't keep kissing, they'd be at each other's throats.'

Her much-quoted remark about Melbourne being the end of the world was actually invented by Sydney journalist Neil Jillet. When Jillet was working in the Melbourne office of the *Sydney Morning Herald* in 1959 he was told to do an interview with the actress. She was unavailable, so he wrote a few paragraphs about her inaccessibility and about the number of cigarettes and bottles of whisky going into her South Yarra flat (Gardner was frequently drunk by noon). To spice up his copy, he dropped in the infamous line about Melbourne.

Jillet expected a sub-editor to spot the joke and cut it out, but it was printed that way in the *Sydney Morning Herald*. He now wryly comments: 'It's not easy to live with the fact that, after 48 years as a journalist, I have only once written anything worth repeating – and someone else got the credit.'

Another cast member Greg looked forward to working with was Fred Astaire. Smooth, suave, debonair, dapper and intelligent, Astaire was in high spirits at the prospect of taking a break from his song-and-dance movies and trying his hand at a straight dramatic role. About to turn 60 and not looking a day younger, the project also made him nervous. On the long flight from California to Australia, he found himself sitting next to Donna Anderson, the 19-year-old discovery of the director, Stanley Kramer. She admitted she was terrified on her first trip out of the United States. She added, 'My great-grandmother told me not to worry, that Mr Astaire would take care of me.'

Astaire grimaced. 'Your *great*-grandmother! Couldn't you at least have said grandmother?'

It is hard to imagine anyone but Stanley Kramer having either the power or the inclination to tackle Nevil Shute's novel. A self-possessed and candid man, with a wiry body and angular features, he had a reputation for producing movies with social relevance:

Home of the Brave (1949 – racism), *The Men* (1950 – post-war veterans), *The Caine Mutiny* (1954 – battle fatigue) and *Inherit the Wind* (1960 – educational freedom).

Kramer was never regarded as a distinguished stylist, preferring to blend his progressive themes with conventional storytelling techniques. His critics labeled him self-righteous and self-congratulatory. They disparaged his films as manipulative and sentimental, peopled by cardboard characters representing social types and beliefs.

'I'm not interested in message films,' Kramer insisted, '– of which I have been accused – because I don't have messages. I do have provocations, thoughts, doubts, challenges, and questions to offer.'

At this stage of his career, it was Kramer's practice to load his films with big-name stars, thus ensuring that his productions were deemed sufficiently 'important' to go into general release, despite their sometimes controversial subject matter. With *On the Beach*, the film reflected a shifting away from the then popular attitude that a nuclear bomb is a friendly deterrent to the position that it is a clear and present danger.

As the film got rolling, Greg found himself studying Astaire as the two men went through scenes. He knew Kramer had worried about removing all indications of Astaire the dancer and even considered weighing the great dancer's legs to eliminate his inimitable walk. But that didn't prove necessary. Astaire developed his own characterization, and even abandoned his toupée.

Praising Astaire, Greg said: 'He wanted every move set – the lighting of a cigarette, the body language, every gesture and movement.' He was in total agreement with Astaire's willingness to rehearse endlessly in order to get that effortless quality. As Astaire said, 'A scene must look as if it's being done for the first time.'

In their free time, the two men developed a strong friendship. 'Fred and I sometimes sneaked off to the dog races. The track was a semi-shabby place where the low life of Melbourne congregated, and Fred enjoyed the raffishness. Fred wore a trench coat and pork pie hat, and he darted about unnoticed. I wore dark glasses, and a trench coat, but eventually I was spotted. While I signed autographs, Fred disappeared. I was amazed what a fast mover he was. After the races, he and I met at the gate and went home.'

Greg looked forward to playing opposite Gardner. He had witnessed from the inside how Gardner had been kicked around by the best in the business. Such prominent figures as Humphrey Bogart, John Ford, Louis B Mayer and George C Scott had each in their own way let her know they considered her a minimally talented actress.

This crippled her self-esteem and certainly played a role in her heavy drinking. As her friend and protector, Greg wanted to do all he could to make sure she turned in a solid performance in *On the Beach*. He took her aside and coached her in her role.

Greg prized the fact that Gardner could be fun in tough situations. 'There was a spell where the temperature was over one hundred degrees,' recalled Greg about location shooting on the movie. 'Ava and I, our characters having become lovers, were trying to play a lighthearted romantic scene on a beach. But the air was so thick with flies they almost blackened the skies. There would be thousands of flies crawling on Ava's forehead and in her hair, and the effects men would rush in with a smoke gun and blow smoke in our faces. That would get rid of the flies for a minute or two and allow us to say a few more lines before they settled in again.

'I have worked with a few actresses, who will remain nameless, who would just not work under those conditions. But Ava was never, never the kind of actress who would complain about her working conditions. She took it like a trouper and we just kept plugging away despite everything until we got the scene.'

Greg was better for Gardner than any of her lovers. Over and over again he proved to her he was a true friend who was always in her corner. Years later, when she died, he brought her housekeeper Carmen Vargas back to Los Angles to live and work in his home. And he even adopted her Welsh Corgi, Morgan, who was not an easy dog. Yet Gardner could never have fallen for a man like Greg. As she put it: 'Nice guys are the kiss of death.'

To mount his production, Kramer leased the 72-acre Royal Showgrounds, the site of Melbourne's yearly agricultural fair. For interior shots, he put up a sound stage in the cavernous Agricultural Hall. But rustling up a US submarine presented a challenge. The State Department refused his request. Kramer recalled an officer said 'I was taking myself too seriously and the film too seriously. There might be four or five million casualties, but it wouldn't be the end of the world.' Not to worry. The British came through with a 'Guppy,' rigged up to pass for a nuclear-powered sub.

During the course of filming the movie, there was a lot of bad blood between the book's author, Nevil Shute, and Stanley Kramer. Shute was an English-born Australian, a well-mannered country gentleman and an accomplished storyteller. In his novel, the central character, Dwight Towers, is loyal to his dead wife right to the end. For this reason, Shute was livid at the way Kramer distorted the two main characters – Greg's Towers and Gardner's Moira Davidson to give the inference that the two of them 'hit the sack' in a mountain hotel bedroom scene. The whole point of *On the Beach* was that they rose above themselves and the relationship did not become sexual.

Greg fought with Kramer to retain the integrity of the author's story. Kramer felt that it was totally unreasonable for a man in Towers' situation to remain loyal to his convictions. Moreover, he believed that the audience needed the relief of some romance and sex. As critic, Stanley Kaufman wryly noted: 'Kramer, like the rest of us, doesn't want the world to be blown up. But he doesn't want to lose money saying so.'

The Hollywood spin didn't quite work. The relationship that develops between Dwight and Moira is close to clichéd; we've seen it in too many other films for it to have the intended impact. Worse, Kramer chose to focus upon the couple in preference to the film's other characters. Consequently, the slow building of atmosphere that the film requires never occurs. The continuous cuts to Dwight and Moira take away from developing an appropriate sense of tragedy and impending doom.

Nevil Shute's daughter, Shirley Norway, claimed Kramer's film was 'by far the worst interpretation of any of his books that had been turned into film.' She even contended: '. . . we've always believed in our family, that *On the Beach* killed him.' As to Shute's relationship with the principals involved, she added: 'Stanley Kramer's film crew and actors, with the exception of Fred Astaire, were persistently and uniformly ill mannered to Dad, and I don't think he went anywhere near them.'

Did she really mean *all* the actors, including the male lead? 'Gregory Peck, we could never talk to Gregory Peck. We always had to talk to his people and it was, you know, would Thursday be convenient? No, I don't think so; Mr Peck is busy on Thursday. And what about Friday? Well, we'll let you know. And so Friday morning – is Mr Peck coming to lunch? Oh, no, no, no, he's not doing anything like that. Anyhow, this sort of thing went on, until finally one day they called us and said, Mr Peck can come to lunch with you today, and my mother said, I'm sorry, it's not convenient.'

Despite this shortcoming, Kramer devised an inspired closing sequence, which has no counterpart in the novel itself. The Queen Victoria Hospital, symbol of healing, becomes a dispensary for suicide pills, and the classical façade of the Public Library, con-ventional symbol of culture, becomes the backdrop for Melbourne's Savonarola to call the city to repentance, under the banner 'There is still time . . . brother.'

Kramer secured the unique arrangement of having *On the Beach* simultaneously released in 18 world capitals in December 1959. The Pecks used it as an excuse to visit Russia. The picture became one of the most celebrated anti-bomb films, and attracted much attention in Moscow because it was the first full-length American feature to have a premiere in the Soviet Union.

'We flew to Moscow in a blizzard on December 17,' recounted Greg, 'and the policemen at the airport were on horseback dressed as though they were going to the North Pole – fur hats and fur collars. I don't know what the temperature was, but it was certainly maybe twenty or thirty below zero. It was a strange experience, the sky was very dark, the blizzard was blowing and it was freezing cold.' Kramer and Greg were surprised when the Russians told them they would have given the film a happy ending. 'We would not allow the world to blow itself to smithereens.'

The *New York Daily News* review of the movie on 18 December 1959 is a measure of the sentiment in some quarters at the time: 'This is a would-be shocker which plays right up the alley of a) The Kremlin and b) the Western defeatists and/or traitors who yelp for the scrapping of the H-bomb . . . See this picture if you must (it seems bound to be much talked about), but keep in mind that the thinking it represents points the way toward eventual Communist enslavement of the entire human race.'

Now we come to one of Greg's 'turkeys.' In *Beloved Infidel* (1959), he found himself absurdly miscast as the frail, alcoholic writer, F Scott Fitzgerald. Although Greg was proud of his raucous drinking scenes in the movie, it was always one he preferred to forget. 'Every film is a risk, artistically and financially,' Greg said philosophically, 'and none of us is bomb-proof.'

His co-star, Deborah Kerr, proved equally unsuited to her role as Fitzgerald's on-the-make mistress, Sheilah Graham. The refined and elegant English actress gave the impression of being, in the words of Laurence Olivier, 'unreasonably chaste.'

As with many projects that are better skipped, Greg agreed to co-star in *Beloved Infidel* as a matter of expediency. He admitted: 'Deborah Kerr and I both did it to kill off final commitments we had made to Fox.' (Kerr was a top name in the late 1950s, demonstrated by her 1959 Golden Glove as the world's most popular female star.)

The movie was based on a memoir Sheilah Graham wrote in collaboration with Gerald Frank. It was revealing enough about the quarrels and reconciliations of the couple, about Fitzgerald's disastrous binges and equally disastrous behavior, but it was tainted by purple prose. Eager to have the book make money, Gerald Frank added a sense of violins trembling near the surface of every sentence. He portrayed Fitzgerald as a wounded genius and Graham as his self-sacrificing nurse.

Fitzgerald's years before his death in December 1940 contained enough drama for a compelling film – with his relationship to Sheilah Graham fitting in as a small sub-plot to the big issues. That's how Greg saw it and there is much to support his point of view. By the time Graham met Fitzgerald, the dazzling young man of the Jazz Age was now in his early forties, down on his uppers and working as a screenwriter for the big Hollywood studios.

Many of Greg's friends and acquaintances had known Fitzgerald personally during the last period of the writer's life. Screenwriter Nunnally Johnson observed his valiant efforts to conquer an alien medium. Recalled Johnson: 'He had simply wandered away from the field where he was a master and was slugging around in an area for which he had no training or instinct.'

Anita Loos, who created some of the most memorable screenplays of our time including *Gentlemen Prefer Blondes* (1953), considered Fitzgerald a sad sack: 'Poor Scott had quit drinking and, from being a nuisance when tight, had taken on that apologetic humility which is often characteristic of reformed drunks. I would hear a tap on my door in the Thalberg Building and know it was Scott because nobody else ever bothered to knock before entering my office. I'd ask Scott to join whoever happened to be there; he'd enter a couple of steps, then stop. "You people don't really want to see me!" he'd say with an embarrassing meekness. We were sorry for Scott because he seemed so alone. He never mentioned a girlfriend who popped up after his death.'

It was only after Fitzgerald died on 21 December 1940 that the world learned he had actually been using his Hollywood experience to write *The Last Tycoon,* an extraordinary 'insider's book' about the film industry. For despite all its inherent contradictions and curious puzzles, *The Last Tycoon* is a heroic – though unfinished – book; a fascinating work that established beyond any question that Fitzgerald had indeed regained his ability to write as well as he ever had in the past. In a letter penned to his daughter Scottie in 1939, he told her: 'I am not a great man, but sometimes I think the impersonal and objective quality of my talent and the sacrifices of it, in pieces, to preserve its essential value has some sort of epic grandeur.'

Greg dismissed the Graham–Frank *Beloved Infidel* book as a potboiler. 'What Sheilah Graham wrote was a Cinderella story: a cockney girl who clawed her way to the heights, which means becoming a syndicated Hollywood gossip columnist.'

Graham, who had been hired as a consultant on the film, strongly objected to the casting of Greg and Kerr as the leading figures in her personal drama. She later wrote: 'Greg was too tall and self-contained for Scott, Deborah Kerr too thin and ladylike for me. (I had second thoughts about the latter after reading Stewart Granger's autobiography in which he implied that he and Deborah had an affair in a taxi in London.) Marilyn Monroe or Jean Simmons would've been better in my part, and for Scott, Richard Basehart, the poetic fool in *La Strada*.'

Except for the fact that they both were of Scots-Irish origin, Greg and Fitzgerald couldn't have been more dissimilar. Fitzgerald was 5 feet 7 inches with fading blond hair and a delicate almost feminine mouth. His biographer, Andrew Turnbull, described him as faun-like and a friend of the Fitzgeralds recalled his appearance as 'too pretty for a man.' By the time he met Graham, Fitzgerald had lost the glow of his scintillating youth. His strong physique had become soft and flabby and there were deep circles under his bloodshot eyes. The first two fingers on both hands were stained to the palm with nicotine. His hair was thinning and his medicine chest was a forest of dandruff cures. There seemed to be no colors in him. Greg, on the other hand, looked strikingly fit for a man of 43. And most of the time he projected the confidence of success.

Knowing he'd be laughed at for trying to resemble Fitzgerald, Greg sought to resolve the problem by getting the script changed. He urged director Henry King and the film's screenwriter, Sy Bartlett to transform the story into the last episode in the life of an American writer of great stature. Stick to the theme of the besieged writer, reasoned Greg, but give him the *gravitas* of a John Steinbeck, William Faulkner or Ernest Hemingway.

Through each stage of the movie's production, Greg bombarded King and Bartlett with letters urging and pleading for changes. One letter was 18 pages long. The studio then turned the script over to Robert Allen Arthur, but he too failed to satisfy the producers or Greg.

Greg recalled: 'They were pulling and tugging at the script from start to finish, and I don't think those two schools of thought were ever resolved. Sometimes you get into such situations when we'd be writing the script from day to day as we went along. There were even two little groups of writers, I think, at one time: one group tugging toward the Cinderella story and the other tugging it toward something meaningful. I think it landed somewhere in between, and didn't do either story justice. Although I don't think there was any justice to be done to Sheilah Graham's story.'

Too many cooks stirring the script made it exceedingly difficult not only for Greg but also for Kerr. 'The film wasn't all bad, but it became disjointed, between Sheilah's original story, the film script and Greg's own writers, and I was unable to characterize, because half the poor woman's personality was cut out. It was difficult for me to pick up the threads halfway through her life and, for my own self, be genuine. I wasn't able to show where she came from, and what she was, and why she became the way she was later on.'

Doomed movies call for desperate measures. Greg believed, '. . . you do your best acting in your worst pictures because this is where you must provide the coherence that is lacking in the script.' In this case, Greg decided to showcase his 'best acting' with the help of some 'Dutch courage.'

'I had a big drunk scene,' Greg explained. 'I pushed her and slapped her around. She ran for a gun and I wrestled it away from her. Finally, the gun went off and brought me to my senses. Well, I had rehearsed that at home about 200 times. We rehearsed it on the set, and while they were setting it up, I had a couple good shots of vodka to set me on edge – because I wanted to go all out. I wanted there to be a certain wildness and an uncontrolled frustration and fury in this man.'

As Sheilah Graham tells it, she found a gun in Fitzgerald's dresser drawer and he tackled her to the floor to get it back. Graham threw it across the room and screamed, 'Take it! Shoot yourself, you son of a bitch! See if I care. I didn't pull myself out of the gutter to waste my life on a drunk like you!'

As Greg remembered it, the scene was 'funny, outrageous and very true to life.' Maybe a little unorthodox but 'still we got a helluva scene out of it.'

The director, Henry King, wasn't amused. In fact, he was shocked. He contended, Greg 'scared Deborah Kerr half to death. You would think he was a drunken demon.' And one has to wonder about the *in vino veritas* factor. Greg had a strong temper and he liked to drink. Plus, he was big and strong. Did his wife, children or friends ever see him behave in a frightening manner after imbibing?

After viewing the rough cut of the movie on 20 November 1959, Greg fired off yet another three-page, single-spaced letter regarding the script flaws. He pleaded for a postponement of the film until the script could be reworked altogether, but to no avail.

It probably wouldn't have made much difference. Above all, movies are a visual medium. A performer with Greg's engaging good looks would have to possess extraordinary gifts as an actor to be believable as a dilapidated writer who was about to die. As it is, the viewers of *Beloved Infidel* see a gorgeous guy and they wonder: if this man needs money and he works for the studios, why doesn't he get an acting gig, pay off his debts, and pump out books on the side?

Nobody was happy with the movie – at least, almost nobody. 'I was heartbroken that *Beloved Infidel* did not do what it should have done,' said Kerr, 'but, on the other hand, I understood Gregory Peck's point of view, and I was happy to work with him.' Sheilah Graham was scathing in her criticism of the film, claiming 'even Bing Crosby' would have made a more credible F Scott Fitzgerald. She waited anxiously for the reaction of Fitzgerald's daughter, Scottie, assuming the young woman would also hate it. But Scottie never saw *Beloved Infidel* in the theaters. At a later date, she caught it on television, adored it, and phoned Graham to say: 'I thought Gregory Peck was so like Daddy!'

Not long after *Beloved Infidel*, Greg accepted a tempting offer. It was to play opposite Marilyn Monroe in a movie titled *The Billionaire*. The film's original producer Jerry Wald was looking for an actor 'with the audience image of a shit-kicker – a Gary Cooper, Jimmy Stewart, or Gregory Peck – so that his inability to perform would be all the more funnier.'

Finally, another shot at comedy. Who could tickle his funny bone better than Marilyn Monroe? He needed to be paired with a force of nature like Monroe who, with her mock innocent charm, could crash right through his granite defenses and startle a spontaneous performance out of him. Her comedic talent was remarkable. Joshua Logan pronounced her 'as near genius as any actress I have ever known.'

As soon as he approved the script, he gave his agent, George Chasin, the go-ahead to make the deal. Then he reported to the studio for singing lessons and even learned to 'croak a few songs.' He also tried his feet at dancing.

Alas, at this point in time Monroe was accelerating her downward spiral. She had lost a baby, increased her dependence on sleeping pills, and almost died from an overdose. She could not find happiness with her husband, Arthur Miller, or have his child, two things that might have reconfirmed her self-worth.

Monroe's tremendous success in comedy roles such as Sugar Cane in *Some Like it Hot* (1959) only inflamed her wild anxiety. This translated into work habits that were diametrically opposite to those of punctual Greg. Here was a man who did everything in his power to make sure a picture came in on schedule. There was no time lost on temperament, clowning, blown lines or hangovers. Monroe, on the other hand, liked to boast: 'I've been on a calendar but never on time.'

She would keep a set in a perpetual incendiary state with her lateness, lack of preparation and inability to remember lines. This did not make her a favorite with her co-workers. During the filming of *The Prince and the Showgirl* (1957), Laurence Olivier fumed: 'Why must you be so fucking late?'

Marilyn looked at him in wonder, replying sweetly: 'Oh, they have that word in your country, too?'

Greg's friend Nunnally Johnson wrote *How To Marry a Millionaire* (1953) starring Monroe and may have shared with Greg some of his experiences with the darling blonde: 'Marilyn was blowing take after take, either fluffing or forgetting a line completely,' remembered Johnson. 'Every man and woman on the set was loathing her. I said: "Don't worry, darling, that last one looked very good." She looked at me, puzzled, and said: "Worry about what?" I swore then that I'd never attribute human feelings to her again.'

Tony Curtis, who played opposite her in *Some Like it Hot*, came away with similar sentiments. He claimed embracing Marilyn Monroe was 'like kissing Hitler.' When Billy Wilder, the film's sardonic director, was asked if he would ever work with her again, he said: 'In the United States, I'd hate it. In Paris, it might not be so bad. While we were waiting, we could all take painting lessons on the side.'

Marilyn Monroe was happy to have Greg as a co-star and everything was perking along beautifully until Greg noticed that the script of *The Billionaire* was undergoing mysterious changes. 'My part began to diminish,' he recollected. 'Marilyn's part started getting bigger and bigger, and the whole thing stopped being funny.'

The script had obvious problems, Monroe agreed to do the film in order to fulfill the Fox commitment, and Miller agreed to revive the screenplay. Miller recalled: 'During the shooting of *Let's Make Love* [the eventual title of *The Billionaire*] and *Some Like it Hot* I had all but given up any hope of writing; I had decided to devote myself to giving her the kind of emotional support that would convince her she was no longer alone in the world – the heart of the problem, I assumed. I went so far as to do some rewriting on *Let's Make Love* to try to save her from a complete catastrophe, work I despised on a script not worth the paper it was typed on.'

Although Hal Kanter (another writer drafted in to work on the script) did not acknowledge that any important script revisions were being made, he did admit 'we are deepening the character a little for Marilyn and . . . writing in some special parts for others . . .'

Greg confronted George Cukor, the film's director, who seemed to be avoiding him. 'What the hell is going on here?' he fumed. 'This isn't the script I agreed to do!'

'Well, Arthur Miller is rewriting it,' Cukor said.

How ironic. One of Greg's aspirations was to work for Miller and it was turning out to be in a second-rate vehicle.

At this point, Cukor got uppity and reminded Greg: 'He's one of the greatest writers in America.'

'Yes,' Greg agreed, 'but he's *not* funny. And my part is getting smaller all the time.'

When Greg met with Miller, the playwright said: 'You don't think the script is funny?'

'It's about as funny as pushing grandma downstairs.'

'Well, *Marilyn* loves it.'

'Well, I'm hardly surprised!'

The script ended up completely rewritten and Greg backed out of the deal. French movie star and cabaret singer Yves Montand assumed Greg's part and it was released under the title *Let's Make Love* (1960).

Montand went into the project knowing full well it was a dud. But, unencumbered by Greg's set of ethics, he gingerly set about making the most of a small opportunity. To wit: he charmed Marilyn Monroe into bed. When the picture wrapped, he started packing for Paris. Suddenly, he heard someone knocking at the door of his Beverly Hills Hotel bungalow. Hedda Hopper breezed in uninvited just as the phone rang and the hotel operator told him he had yet another call from Miss Monroe. As Montand was telling the switchboard operator to refuse all calls from Monroe, Hopper fixed him a drink. 'I stirred up one hell of a martini to get him talking.'

'You deliberately made love to this girl,' provoked Hedda. 'You knew she wasn't sophisticated. Was that right?'

'Had Marilyn been sophisticated, none of this ever would have happened,' Montand replied. 'I did everything I could for her when I realized that mine was a very small part. The only thing that could stand out in my performance were my love scenes. So, naturally, I did everything I could to make them good.'

Montand returned to his wife Simone Signoret. And Monroe made *The Misfits* (1961), with the script written especially for her by Arthur Miller. She co-starred with Clark Gable who died shortly after its completion. By the time the film went into production Monroe's mental health was in steep decline. Her frequent illnesses and depression contributed to the film going far over budget. As the tensions grew, she upped her dosage of sleeping pills and started mixing them with liquor. On 21 January 1961, a week before the opening of *The Misfits*, she divorced Arthur Miller. On 5 August 1962, her housekeeper discovered her body nude and lifeless on her bed.

Greg emerged from the experience with little sympathy for Monroe's problems. Speaking of Hollywood's capacity to destroy people, he said: 'Monroe may have been a bit of an extreme example, but she was given the best stories to suit her talents, she was stroked and cared for and treasured and treated like a little princess, treated as a valuable, talented person. What it was that led her to drink and take pills, I don't know. I don't think anyone can put it all together, but it's too easy to say that Hollywood wrung her out and exhausted her, strained her nerves and destroyed her. I think she'd have gone to pieces even sooner without the adulation and the care she received at the hands of her directors and producers and the big studios.'

Greg's next project had the hallmarks of a top box-office attraction. *The Guns of Navarone* (1961) was based on a book by Alistair MacLean, a storyteller whose novels played out like motion pictures. Costing an unprecedented $6 million, *Navarone* started a vogue for all-star international action adventure pictures that continued for about 20 years. It featured Gregory Peck, 44, David Niven, 50, Anthony Quinn, 45, and Anthony Quayle, 47. One critic described the film as 'an elderly gang goes to war.'

The Guns of Navarone marked a comeback for writer and producer Carl Foreman. His screenwriting credits included *The Bridge on the River Kwai* (1957) and *High Noon* (1952). But Foreman had refused to cooperate with the House Un-American Activities Committee, causing him to be blacklisted. So, for a long stretch during the 1950s, he had been forced to write under an assumed name.

The script of *The Guns of Navarone* was a bright feather in Foreman's cap. It has a strong story and a credible attempt at realism. And it has depth. He lifted the story from being just an ordinary adventure/thriller into something that was far more sophisticated. 'He really brought up all these moral and ethical issues,' said Greg. 'It was really very well written. A lot of people thought it was this great, rousing war film, but it was really very anti-war.'

The plot focused on a single, seemingly impossible mission – the taking of an enemy arsenal. To accomplish this feat, the regular fighting unit was banished, replaced by a specially selected team of men, each with his own particular craft to enlist for the mission, and each a fairly well-defined character. As a movie format, it was basically sound, for it could showcase a pantheon of male stars.

The six members of the British team are Greg, the captain who takes over command when Anthony Quayle, the major, breaks his legs; David Niven, the explosives expert; Anthony Quinn, veteran resistance fighter; Stanley Baker, telegraphist; and a young Greek –

American James Darren, who is 'schooled in juvenile crime.' The two partisans are portrayed by Irene Papas and the perhaps too pretty Gia Scala.

Even the planner of the mission, the head of British military intelligence for the Middle East (James Robertson Justice), doesn't see much hope for its success. He laments to his aide: 'It's a waste of six very good men, although I don't suppose that matters much, considering how many have been wasted already. Still, who knows? Maybe they can get there, and maybe they can hold off. Almost anything is possible in a war. Smack in the middle of absolute insanity, people seem to find the most incredible resources – ingenuity, self-sacrifice, nobility, courage . . . '

'Getting there' is getting on to the Greek island of Navarone, occupied in 1943 by the Nazis. 'Pulling it off' is blowing up two giant cannons, mounted in a seemingly impregnable fortress cave, with which the Germans have been blasting British warships and the channel between Navarone and a nearby island. However, the mission is doomed unless two enormous German guns are destroyed, allowing Allied troops to arrive by boat.

To pull it off, however, requires walking a tricky tightrope. 'We played half a dozen commandos somehow able to perform miracles,' explained Greg, 'outwitting a whole German regiment, getting right into the middle of them, stealing their uniforms and masquerading as Nazis. Well, to do that you'd have to do with the Nazis what Mack Sennett did with the Keystone Cops. There were 550 chances for them to kill all of us.'

All location filming was done in Greece, on the island of Rhodes and some of it in Athens. Undoubtedly receiving word about the epic, the no-expense spared scale on which *The Guns of Navarone* was to be cinematized, the Greeks embraced cast and crew with open arms. Greg arrived on 7 March 1960. He recalled: 'They even removed the scaffolding from the Parthenon for us. It has been under repair since 1832, kind of a long job.' The King of Greece and his family even paid a visit to the set.

On Rhodes, the company settled in for several months of shooting. With remote locations, donkeys were used to transport equipment and personnel. The base of operations was the Hotel

Miramar. The film was supposed to wrap in July of 1960, so Greg rented a place in Cap Ferrat for the summer. As it happened, the shoot went over schedule and he could only fit in a few weekends. Greg's first exposure to this earthly paradise had been when he was filming *Captain Horatio Hornblower*. Reminiscent of an F Scott Fitzgerald novel, it is one of the loveliest places on the Mediterranean coast.

A surprise setback occurred when the film's director, Alexander Mackendrick, was fired. Carl Foreman quickly hired British director, J Lee Thompson. With only ten days before he was to start shooting, he approached the cast, according to Greg, 'frightened to death.' Greg added, he was a 'highly strung individual' who required the medication of stiff drinks to keep himself calm.

Still, Thompson was very excited to be given a chance to direct his first American picture. He said: 'And they immediately liked my way of directing, which was to rehearse the whole scene that we were about to shoot, and explain each setup that we were about to do, before we actually shot anything. Sometimes the rehearsals would take two or three or four hours, and we'd go a whole morning without having got a shot. But then in the afternoon, we'd get 10 or 11 shots done and complete the scene, because everyone knew exactly where they were going and knew exactly what setup was going to follow the previous one. And it became a delight for the actors – they really liked this technique and they were supportive to the hilt. Many of the actors had theater backgrounds. That kind of rehearsal method is very common in that world and it must have very much put them at their ease.'

As shooting got underway, the actors jostled for position. They were afraid one might get the advantage over the other. Greg felt threatened by Anthony Quinn – and the feeling was reciprocal. (Admitted Quinn: 'We all wished we looked like Gregory Peck and sounded like him.') Knowing that the wily Mexican-American was a natural born scene-stealer, Greg didn't want him running away with the movie.

Quinn was a roughneck who played by the rules of the street. The earthy peasant with the tanned, craggy face was born poor in Chihuahua, Mexico. He got himself into movies in the most humble of ways, as an extra, having already worked at colorful macho jobs that added to his mystique: hod carrier, construction worker, boxer, taxi driver and so forth. But he was gaining ground fast and audiences loved him.

'To see him was not particularly to love him or to fear him or to hate him; it was to feel him,' observed journalist Stephen Hunter. 'Quinn's specialty was the almost wordless projection of temperate masculine force, a father's gravitas, a brother's loyalty, a boxer's stamina, a gladiator's courage, a saboteur's guile and will to violence.' No wonder Greg considered him competition.

Fortunately for all concerned, Quinn got the cast playing chess, which bonded the group and kept them out of Thompson's hair. It also helped relieve boredom. One can only drink so many glasses of ouzo and smash so many plates.

Playing the 'lean-limbed, laconic mountain climber,' as the *New York Times* described his role, Greg was to emerge as the film's leader, partly because of the plot, partly because he was the most prominent star in the cast, and partly because he kept sending notes of script changes to Carl Foreman that improved his part.

Greg's personal favorite among the cast was David Niven. He called him 'the most wonderful male companion I've ever had.' The durable star possessed an abundance of urbane wit and dapper charm, plus he was an elegant gossip. Although he had proven himself on several occasions an accomplished dramatic actor, he lacked confidence in his ability. Rather than grabbing the spotlight, he preferred instead to portray himself as an untalented but happy-go-lucky adventurer who took a chance on Hollywood and by a fluke became a star. What Greg admired – and perhaps envied – about Niven was that he parlayed his picaresque escapades into two of the best-selling autobiographies of all time: *The Moon's a Balloon* and *Bring on the Empty Horses*. *Balloon* alone sold more than five million copies worldwide.

Most of the film was shot at Shepperton Studios in London. There, the guns themselves were constructed. At the time, it was one of the biggest sets ever built for a film in England and all did not go smoothly. 'We had a storm one day,' explained Thompson, 'and the whole set collapsed. A torrential rain beat down upon it, and the cave portions of the set started to crumple. It was all just plaster. And it took three weeks to rebuild.' Fortunately, they had plenty of other scenes to shoot in the meantime.

The boat that transported the fighters was built and placed on rockers in a huge water tank. Explained Thompson: 'This water would hit the artists with such force that some of them would get knocked right out of the boat. Then there was the danger of slipping underneath the boat, which was rocking. Of course, the water could not be warmed very much. It was a very tough sequence, but the actors were absolutely magnificent. They never complained and went back into the tank for shot after shot. And I think that is still one of the best storm sequences on film.'

With his leavening touch of humor, Niven recounted the experience from the actors' point of view: 'A lot of the scenes were shot waist deep in freezing water, from nine in the morning until six in the evening. To ward off chills and cold, there was an abundance of brandy and rum in flasks, handed out between shots. Greg's capacity for drinking and working was astounding. By noon, all the rest of us would be roaring, or close to it. But not Greg. He matched us drink for drink but none of us saw him so much as stagger or muff a line. Really quite disgusting to see a man able to handle liquor like that. What was even more annoying was his humorous, superior attitude toward us.'

Despite the setbacks, *The Guns of Navarone* was a smash hit. It was nominated for Best Picture, Best Director, Best Screenplay from another source, Best Sound, Best Scoring for dramatic picture, Best Editing, and Best Special Effects at the Oscars. Polls of critics by *Film Daily* and the Hollywood Foreign Press Association both tabbed it as the best film of 1961.

Greg received $2 million from his share of *The Guns of Navarone*. It was his biggest hit until he starred in *The Omen* in the 1970s. In 1960, he purchased a splendid vacation home for his family in Cap Ferrat on the Cote d'Azur, far from the hothouse of Hollywood.

Situated approximately ten kilometers from Nice to the west and Monaco to the east, verdant Cap Ferrat is reachable by the Basse Corniche, the low road that hugs the sea. Its tranquility and warm climate have long made it a favorite holiday destination for

European aristocracy and international millionaires who have built large estates on the water, including one which formerly belonged to the King of Belgium, Leopold II.

The Pecks' house was planned by Veronique's architect father. It opened up a new chapter in Greg's personal life. Here Greg could protect himself and his family from the relentless curiosity of the public; he could relax for protracted periods of time. 'We golf, swim, lie in the sun, have a few friends in – it's all very casual and idyllic. I spend a lot of time gardening, because that's one of my favorite hobbies. Veronique cooks while I garden. We are a great combination. She makes great fish casseroles, marvelous salads and my favorite of favorites, Boston cream pie.'

They could wander along the port or drop in for casual dining at the restaurants along the wharf with their shady terraces. Through David Niven, the Pecks became friends with Princess Grace and Prince Rainier who frequently invited Tony and Cecilia Peck to come over and swim at the palace.

One day, Tony socked Prince Albert on the nose. Fretting about it, Greg called Grace. 'Don't be silly!' she insisted. 'It was the best thing that ever happened to him! It was the first bloody nose he's ever had, and the first time anyone has ever punched him!' Over time, the boys became friends and studied at Amherst together. There, Tony introduced Prince Albert around campus as 'Big Al.'

Despite his royal blood, the effects of rubbing elbows with movie stars had an effect on Prince Albert. He recounts that when he was a teenager, he became aware that men like Greg were luminaries. 'It really amazed me who I was meeting and that I could interact with them. I used to think, hey, I may be the only 14-year-old in the world who could pick up the phone and ring Frank Sinatra or Gregory Peck or Cary Grant and actually get them on the phone.'

Fresh from the triumph of *Navarone*, Greg launched into making a movie with his own company, Melville Productions. His choice, *Cape Fear* (1962), looked intriguing because it had the straight construction of a horror movie. 'I thought this was quite good, quite tight,' said Greg. 'As for what made it so frightening, that was Bob Mitchum. He was so excellent. He was reptilian and subtle and very threatening. That piece of casting was essentially my idea. I thought of Mitchum because I remembered *The Night of the Hunter* (1955). I knew what Bob was capable of doing in a good part.'

An ex-con named Max Cady (Robert Mitchum) arrives in a Southern town in search of the man he holds responsible for his imprisonment, the lawyer Sam Bowden (Peck). The bluntly effective thriller shows the effect a devious psychopath can have on a middle-class family – husband, wife (Polly Bergen) and teenage daughter (Lori Martin). Their pet dog is poisoned, the daughter is tracked and narrowly escapes assault, and the wife is continually threatened over the phone by the vicious avenger.

Cape Fear reunited Greg with several familiar talents. Sy Bartlett and James Webb had written and produced screenplays for earlier Melville Productions: *The Big Country* and *Pork Chop Hill*, and J Lee Thompson had just directed *The Guns of Navarone*. The script for *Cape Fear* was adapted from a John D MacDonald pulp novel called *The Executioners*.

Max Cady's character was the juicy part in the movie. However, it took some enticing on Greg's part to get Mitchum to agree to play the part. The two men were neighbors when Greg and Greta first arrived in Hollywood and lived in a little gray house up in the canyons off Mulholland Drive. In the years that followed, Greg carefully acquired the polish and cosmopolitan tastes necessary to hold his own in international circles while Mitchum went in the other direction and merrily exploited his hipster edge.

On the first day on location, Mitchum sang: 'How dear to my heart are the scenes of my childhood, when fond recollections presents them to view.' This puzzled J Lee Thompson until Mitchum reminisced further about 'scenes from his childhood.'

His part Native American father was killed in a train accident when he was just two, and after 12 years of living with his mother and then his aunt, Mitchum ran away from home and wandered the roads. He made ends meet by stealing from bums he came across, and while strolling through Georgia, he was picked up for vagrancy and forced to be part of a chain gang.

Obviously not wanting to spend his days splitting rocks with hammers, Mitchum escaped after two weeks and headed out West, an instant real-life fugitive. There he continued his roughneck ways by becoming a professional boxer and fought in 27 fights. An unexpected bonus of his boxing career was the acquisition of his most pronounced physical feature – sleepy eyes – which, coupled with chronic insomnia, produced the world-weary look that set female hearts pounding. But beneath the half-closed lids and bored exterior was an enormous reservoir of angry energy that made him fascinating to watch.

By the time Greg became drinking buddies with him, Mitchum was already a popular actor with a large teenage following, and his credentials as a sexually irresistible cynic were well established. In the late 1940s he was busted for marijuana use and spent 60 days in prison. ('Just like Palm Springs,' he said, 'but without the riff-raff.') This only seemed to strengthen his appeal.

Mitchum's approach to acting could not have been more different from Greg's. While Greg labored prodigiously to master every aspect of his craft, Mitchum had a cynical disregard for acting. He didn't care much about his 'image,' which led him to appear in films that ran the gamut from classic to barely watchable. He just couldn't take movies or himself too seriously. And in the process he created some of the more honestly amazing characters to light the screen. Critic Pauline Kael described him as 'almost a lawless actor. He does it all out of himself. He doesn't use the tricks and stratagems of clever, trained actors.'

Perhaps he sensed that Greg had moved on and considered Mitchum too unpolished for his new life. For whatever reason, Mitchum had a chip on his shoulder vis-à-vis Greg during the shooting of *Cape Fear*. He told the press: 'I show up at nine and punch out at six. That's all I do.' And he added: 'The picture belongs to the other guys and I don't care too much.'

The movie was undeniably disturbing. In fact, the original trailers promised moviegoers they were going to 'feel fear!' The film derived much of its frisson from Cady's antisocial attack on the goody-goody culture of the 1950s. Here was Greg in his best pillar-of-rectitude manner with a wholesome wife and a sweet daughter. Then Cady appears in town. He is furtive and unscrupulous and has what Terence Rafferty described as 'the unnerving quick-strike elusiveness of a guerrilla fighter – the now-you-see-it-now-you-don't quality that can give human malevolence the aura of the demonic.' Upon seeing *Cape Fear*, novelist Barry Gifford called Mitchum 'the angel of death with pain, put on earth to give men pause.'

After filming, Mitchum claimed he had acted Greg off the screen. 'I had given him the role and had paid him a terrific amount of money,' said Greg. 'It was obvious he had the better role. I thought he would understand that, but he apparently thought he acted me off the screen. I didn't think highly of him for that.'

Several critics didn't think highly of Greg for producing the movie. *New Yorker* reviewer, Brendan Gill saw it as 'a repellent attempt to make a great deal of money out of a clumsy plunge into sexual pathology,' and asked, 'what on earth is Gregory Peck doing in such a movie?'

'If *Cape Fear* doesn't turn out to be box-office I'm through as a producer,' Greg said, voicing his frustration. 'I'll be a freelance actor again.' And indeed, *Cape Fear* bombed at the box-office. Grossing somewhere between $1.6 and $1.9 million against a cost of $2.6 million, the picture brought an end to Melville Productions.

Thirty years later, Greg was rewarded substantially. In 1991 Martin Scorsese remade the film for Universal with Nick Nolte as Sam Bowden and Robert De Niro as Max Cady. It was a big financial success. From distribution of television and home video rentals, the owner of the story rights, Gregory Peck, was doing very nicely on his initial investment.

At this point in time, Greg could have rested on his laurels. Lunching with writer Lyn Tornabene at the Colony Restaurant in New York, he confessed: 'I'm a semi recluse. I'm only in Hollywood when I have to be: lately, about six months out of the year.' When he said in Hollywood, he didn't work there. He said he wouldn't. 'I would have three homes: an apartment in Paris, a house in England or Ireland, and ranch in Southern California. Maybe four places . . . I'd like a plantation in Mississippi. I anticipated the picture, *Cape Fear*, in Georgia, and though I have the same objections to some Southern attitudes you probably have, I grew fond of the people and the landscape.'

Sitting in his office one day, he paused to reflect with Joe Hyams, a reporter for the *Los Angeles Times*. Greg complained it was next to impossible to get out from under the paraphernalia of being a movie star. When Hyams pressed him to explain 'the paraphernalia' of Hollywood stardom, Greg replied: 'Look at it this way . . . If you're established in a $3,000,000 a picture or up level and you suddenly decided to do a film for next to nothing, what you're doing is putting an established commodity on the block cheap. That commodity is likely to come out shopworn and shoddy when the picture is finished.'

At the beginning of 1961, producers Alan Pakula and Robert Mulligan sent Greg a copy of *To Kill a Mockingbird*. Written by first-time novelist Harper Lee, the story centered on racial prejudice in a small Southern town of the 1930s. 'It had been on the best-seller list for months,' said Pakula, 'but Hollywood had not nibbled at it yet. There was a kind of rule of thumb that pictures about kids were successful if they were made by Disney.' Pakula and his partner, Mulligan, envisioned Greg in the lead role of Atticus Finch, a widowed lawyer trying to raise two school-age children during the Great Depression.

After dinner, Greg picked up the book and started reading it and he didn't put it down until he had gone all the way through to the last page. By then he knew he had found what he had always been looking for: '. . . in twenty years of making movies, I never had a part that came close to being the real me until Atticus Finch.'

The gentleness of Atticus Finch's philosophy pervades the novel. He is the sort of man who symbolizes humanity at its best. He loves and nurtures his children, Scout and Jem. He treats all those around him with respect and consideration. He renounces violence but stands up for what he believes in.

Greg identified completely with the character. Here he was, the father of five children, trying to be exactly the kind of father in the novel – a sophisticated Atticus Finch – stern but fair, compassionate and concerned, always the traditional father figure.

To Kill a Mockingbird relates the story of tomboy Scout, growing up in an Alabama town, 'where there's no hurry, there's nowhere to go.' But, as in a child's world, marvelous, unexpected things happen just the same. Like Scout, we watch her quiet, widowed father, Atticus Finch, attack dangers that can destroy everybody's peace: a mad dog on the loose; and racial prejudice that pours over into another kind of madness. The tranquil world is set astir by the winds of change and shattered by terrors both real and imagined. The real terror stems from Atticus's defense of the Negro who has been unjustly charged with the rape of a white girl, and from the stigma and violence this brings upon the family.

Reading the book reminded Greg of his boyhood in the sleepy town of La Jolla where he ran barefoot, climbed trees, and, like Scout, would curl up in a tire and roll down the streets. Yet the innocence was balanced by an equally forceful memory recalled by Greg in a letter to Klanwatch: '. . . the burning cross in front of a house rented by a black family . . . it was in the early 1920s, when I was about five years old, but I remember it well.'

The novel gets its title from a warning Finch makes to Jem and Scout on the use of guns. 'I'd rather you shoot at tin cans in the backyard,' he says to his children, 'but I know you'll go after birds. Shoot all the Blue Jays you want, if you can hit 'em, but remember it's a sin to kill a mockingbird. Mockingbirds don't do one thing but make music for us to enjoy. They don't eat up people's gardens, don't nest in corncribs, and they don't do one thing but sing their hearts out for us.'

The novel also deals with changes in the lives of the children and a growing awareness in them, and also with prejudices, mainly racial, of the older people around them. It's a story about loss of innocence, people's first contact with evil, the tragic quality of life and how people learn to deal with it. It represents the fantasy childhood we all wanted. Here are these two children who have their first experience with evil, and they are taken through that experience by this fantasy father, the father all of us have dreamt of having.

'I finished at about midnight,' Greg said of reading the novel given him by Pakula and Mulligan, 'and wanted to call them immediately, but I managed to wait until morning to tell them that I would give almost anything to play Atticus.'

Alan Pakula came to the movies from the world of 1950s live television, and *To Kill a Mockingbird* has something of the feel of the urgent, naturalistic black-and-white dramas of that period. He began his film career as a producer, teaming with director Robert Mulligan to create the 1957 film *Fear Strikes Out*, about the breakdowns and subsequent recovery of the baseball legend, Jimmy Piersail. The two went on to make six more films. Mulligan had considered becoming a priest before joining the Navy and later entering the entertainment world through television.

A deal was set up in which *To Kill a Mockingbird* was to be distributed by Universal and produced by two independent film companies, Pakula–Mulligan and Brentwood Productions, with Brentwood co-owned by Greg.

Pakula was heartened to discover the real Gregory Peck was the same as the reel actor. 'It's very tough to go through the Hollywood mill – the excesses, the vulnerabilities, hysteria of huge star success – and not come out of it corrupted or scarred. You're almost encouraged to remain an infantile narcissist by the way people treat you. That didn't happen to Greg.'

In January 1961, Greg and Veronique made a trip to Monroeville (population 7,000) in southwest Alabama to see the place upon which the novel was based and to meet the author, Nelle Harper Lee. They stayed at the LaSalle Hotel and ate at the Wee Diner.

With Lee as his guide, Greg moseyed around downtown and spent time in the old courthouse (which was replicated exactly for the film).

'All the women dressed up and painted up and put on earrings and came to town to see him,' said George Thomas Jones, a retired Monroeville businessman. 'But he was real low key and down to earth, no fanfare at all. He just wanted to get the feel of the town.'

Monroeville shaped Harper Lee and her writing. After dropping out of law school, she moved to New York and worked as an Eastern airline reservations clerk. Determined to tell her story, she quit her job and moved into a cold-water apartment and subsisted on tuna fish sandwiches. When *Mockingbird* hit, she divided her time between New York and Monroeville.

'You see, I never expected any sort of success with *Mockingbird*,' she said. 'I didn't expect the book to sell in the first place. I was hoping for a quick and merciful death at the hands of reviewers, but at the same time I sort of hoped that maybe someone would like it enough to give it encouragement. Public encouragement.'

Giving Greg the once-over, Harper Lee wasn't sure he was right for the part. He appeared too young and handsome. Greg won her over just by sitting and chatting with her. It was a *coup de foudre* between the two of them – although strictly platonic.

'You have to consider who we Southerners are,' Lee said in explaining what makes her tick. 'We run hard to Celtic blood in influence. We are mostly Irish, Scottish, English, Welsh. We grew up in a society that was primarily agricultural. It was not industrial, although it is becoming so, for better or for worse. I think we are a region of natural storytellers, just from tribal instinct.'

The author introduced Greg to her father, A C Lee, the model for Atticus Finch. A tall man, who dressed like Atticus, A C Lee's legal defense of an African-American in 1923 formed the basis of the novel. 'He was a fine old gentleman of 82,' recalled Greg, 'truly sophisticated, although he had never traveled farther than a few miles from that small Southern town. I studied him intently and when he became aware of it, he said, "You're taking a very close look at me, aren't you?"' What struck Greg was the resemblance in character between Mr Lee and his own father.

The next challenge for Pakula and Mulligan was to have the novel turned into a screenplay with all its values intact. Horton Foote was drafted for the job. In the 1950s Foote wrote for the prestigious *Playhouse 90* and the *Philco-Goodyear Playhouse* among other shows – serious television work from the early years of that medium. Much to the joy and relief of all concerned, his screenplay was faithful to the letter and spirit of Lee's novel. 'There was a marvelous rapport between Horton Foote and Harper Lee,' said Greg. 'They were in complete accord as to how the story should be told on the screen.'

After scouting various locations, Mulligan settled on the backlot of Universal and, on 15 acres, created an authentic-looking Macomb. The buildings in the vintage early Depression town did double duty off-camera serving as dressing rooms for the actors, plus a schoolroom for the children in the cast.

Brock Peters, who made his film debut as Sergeant Brown in *Carmen Jones* (1954) with Dorothy Dandridge, Harry Belafonte and Diahann Carroll, was chosen to play accused rapist Tom Robinson.

Peters recounted how, shortly before he was to start filming, he was awakened early on a Sunday morning by a phone call from Greg welcoming him to the production. 'I was surprised and stunned,' said Peters. 'This was an idol of mine, both as an actor and a person. I'd only just been cast to play Tom Robinson and suddenly found myself ear-to-ear, voice-to-voice with Gregory Peck – and I dropped the phone.'

Harper Lee visited the *Mockingbird* set in February 1962. Greg was in the midst of doing wardrobe tests for the film. He needed to stand in front of the camera to see if his costume looked right. The test was taking place on a little street where the set had been erected. Lee's first glimpse of him was when he came out of the dressing room in his Atticus suit. There was no attempt to disguise his incipient double chin. His hair was half-groomed and his handsomeness was partly concealed by glasses. 'It was the most amazing transformation I had ever seen,' recalled Lee. 'A middle-aged man came out. He looked bigger; he looked thicker through the middle. He didn't have an ounce of make-up, just a 1933-type suit with collar, and a vest and a watch on a chain. The minute I saw him I knew everything was bound to be all right because he *was* Atticus.'

For the whole of the first day on the set, Robert Mulligan recalled watching Greg pacing the porch of the Finch home, entering its doors then reemerging as the completely realized Atticus Finch. 'You could feel him putting on the clothes in the skin.'

In the film's first take, the children run to meet their father, and Greg remembered Harper Lee standing nearby; there was a glistening on her cheek. Anticipating a comment about the power of his performance, Greg was dismayed and delighted by her comment.

'Oh, Gregory,' she exclaimed. 'You've got a little potbelly just like my daddy.'

'That's great acting,' he quipped.

The music-box-type sounds in *Mockingbird* – bells, harps, single-note flutes – suggested a child's world. For composer Elmer Bernstein it wasn't easily arrived at: '. . . it took me weeks and weeks,' he confessed. 'After the longest period of time, it came to me that what was going on here were a series of real-world adult problems seen through the eyes of children.'

Of the many distinguished aspects of *Mockingbird*, one of the most remarkable is the acting of its children. Mary Badham, who plays the role of Scout Finch, has a comradeship with a neighborhood chum, played by John Megna (based on Harper Lee's childhood friend Truman Capote), that is as believable as a backyard fence. She and Philip Alford, who plays her older brother Jem, were amateurs from Birmingham, Alabama, chosen from some 2,000 applicants in seven Southern States.

Encouraging these youngsters to play games and make-believe and initially keeping the camera at a distance, Mulligan gradually reduced their self-consciousness while retaining their authentic characterization. After running through a disturbing scene, Mary Badham cuddled up to Greg for comfort. Off camera, he was her foster father in Hollywood, and on weekends she came up to play with his own children in Brentwood.

Greg moved through the film with astonishing ease. 'I just put everything I had into it – all my feelings and everything I've learned in 46 years of living, about family life and fathers and children. And my feelings about racial justice and equality and opportunity.'

He had finally found his quintessential role. 'It was relatively easy to do because I had emotional involvement, and when you have that . . . Well, I read not long ago an interview with Henry Fonda, and he talked about *Mr. Roberts*, and he said that every night it was such a joy to play, and that they were on a kind of emotional wave that carried them through, and the thing took off every single night with a different audience.'

One can't ignore the role discipline and training played in Greg's performance. The voice, the body, timing and movement were the result of techniques developed over the years. According to Greg: '. . . every single facial expression, every movement of the body, even to the crooking of my little finger, was a total effort to bring Atticus Finch to life. Every move and every voice inflection were the result of hours of trial and error, of use and discarding.'

The courtroom scene is the high point of the movie. Ordered by their father to stay home on the day of the trial, Finch's children go secretly to the courtroom, determined not to 'miss the most excitin'' thing that ever happened in this town.'

'The thing that I remember most,' recalled Greg, 'was when I was questioning the accused man, Brock Peters, on the witness stand. It was a very dramatic scene, and all of a sudden Brock started crying. I was so moved that I myself starting choking up. I had to stop myself. We couldn't have both the defendant and the lawyer blubbering all over the courtroom.'

As the trial develops, lawyer Finch reveals that the accuser, a lonely, backcountry girl, actually made a sexual pass at the accused. Discovered on the spot, she was beaten by her father, who then cynically pinned the 'unspeakable crime' on Tom Robinson.

The truth doesn't matter to the jury: the accused is pronounced guilty. But not before some of the most eloquent words ever uttered in film for the basic rights of Negroes are said by Finch in defense of 'this quiet, respectable Negro who has had to put his word against two white people.'

One of the most affecting moments is that in which, following the verdict, the Negroes sitting in the balcony rise to their feet in respect for Atticus, who is leaving the courtroom. The Finch children are up there with them, having been smuggled in. Old Reverend Sykes whispers to Scout: 'Stand up. Your father's passin'.'

On 3 May 1962, the film wrapped eight days behind schedule. The editing process went relatively smoothly. 'I remember seeing a rough cut,' said Greg. 'I usually have lots of suggestions and I like to write suggestions. I can badger a director or producer, and have many times, with suggestions for rewrites and certain suggestions for editing. So I trot in there with my yellow legal pad and I watched about 15 minutes and I just waved the pad in the air. I didn't want to make any notes. Bob and Alan laughed.'

Greg yearned for the respect of his peers – and he sure got it. 'After the preview of *Mockingbird* the other night, a number of actors whom I admire and respect – Shirley Booth, Karl Malden and Paul Newman, among others – told me they thought I had done a good job.'

Sissy Spacek was raised in a small East Texas town. As a child she saw *To Kill a Mockingbird* which floored her because it evoked so many feelings and images from her small town. 'I thought it was a children's movie when I first saw it,' she said. 'And I was overwhelmed with the familiarity of the world that they lived in. Not until later, when I saw it as an adult, did I understand the deeper dimensions of it. It's so rare to have a film hold up over so many years, and to have seen it from two such different perspectives, yet to have it work for you on both levels so deeply.'

Harper Lee's father died while the movie was being filmed. A year later, Greg lost his own father. Greg said: 'I'm sorry the two of them couldn't have lived to see the picture. I think they would have been pleased.' Lee gave Greg her father's gold watch. It became his good luck talisman.

Asked if he thought any human being could be as noble and idealistic as Atticus, Greg said, 'I've met two in my lifetime – my own father and Harper Lee's.'

Although many wonderful things happened to Harper Lee after writing *To Kill a Mockingbird*, it appears it brought her bad luck in terms of her progress as a writer. She had such high hopes for herself when she was young. But a great success with one's first book can be stifling. Back in 1964, she said: 'I want to do the best I can with the talent God gave me. I hope to goodness that every novel I do gets better and better . . . In other words all I want to be is the Jane Austen of south Alabama . . .' Lee hasn't published any books since *Mockingbird*.

Released in time for the 1962 Academy Awards, the film elicited rapturous reviews and Oscar nominations in eight categories. Greg dashed off a note: 'Dear Harper, Congratulations on your eight nominations for the Academy Awards.' He also took the precaution of wearing her father's pocket watch on the night of the Oscars.

When he went to the Santa Monica Auditorium that night, he fully expected to lose. After all, he'd been through 19 years, 34 pictures and 5 Oscar nominations. He was so certain Jack Lemmon would win for *The Days of Wine and Roses* that he wasn't even nervous. In fact, his approach to the event was totally out of character. Normally a firm believer that the best impromptu speeches are written well in advance, he had prepared nothing.

'I had sat in the audience before and I had lost,' said Greg. 'I had already accepted the fact that I would lose again. Then, when Sophia Loren read my name, it was as if I'd been struck on the head or suddenly drugged. A peculiar feeling about reality came over me. I'd never quite had a physical sensation like it before. It was numbing.' On his way up to the stage, he touched Jack Lemmon gently on the shoulder. Once in the spotlight, he had no speech to give. His 'thank you' was brief, emotional, and sincere.

Success is so sweet. Greg didn't temper his unalloyed delight in getting the Oscar. When asked how it felt to win, he blurted: 'I was damned pleased to get it. My heart was ready to jump out of my chest. I managed to keep my emotions under control. But I really was damned pleased to get it. It meant the approval of my fellow actors and technicians and artists. I was in my forties and the middle of my career. I thought, well, I've got a long way to go. It was kind of a punctuation in my life, which is definitely worth having.'

Greg particularly enjoyed gadding about with his new identity. 'I think Atticus Finch was a popular man,' he jested. 'I'm a very busy fellow on the freeways, waving back to well-wishers, all the while speeding along at 50 miles per hour. At red lights, other motorists grin at me, and I grin right back!'

CHAPTER SEVENTEEN

Antiheroes

'Kennedy after all has lots of glamour – Gregory Peck with an atom bomb in his holster.'

William F Buckley Jr

Kennedy was dead. That cruel November day in Dallas changed the fabric of American life forever. Greg – who knew and admired JFK, and had just received an invitation to the White House – took his two youngest children, Tony and Cecilia, to morning mass to pray for the President. Later, he honored Kennedy by narrating a United States Information Agency (USIA) film, *Years of Lightning; Days of Drums*. With his soul-stirring voice – called 'one of the world's great musical instruments' by violinist Isaac Stern – Greg told of the major programs put forward by Kennedy: the Peace Corps, Alliance for Progress, Civil Rights and the Space Program.

'The times they are a-changin'' went the song. The 1960s had arrived; exciting, revolutionary and turbulent. New forms, new energies, new values were bursting into national consciousness. The martini hour was ending, replaced by pot and LSD. Spreading his psychedelic gospel, Timothy Leary exhorted the youth of America to 'turn on, tune in, and drop out.' Moneyed people dressed in hobo chic and poor people turned raucous and highly vocal about their discontents. Men tossed out three-piece gray flannel suits and grew straggly beards. Women stopped wearing bras and started swearing like Marine sergeants. It was a tough time to be a gentleman actor. One sign of the times; the new Hollywood stars had strange names like Rip, Rory, Tab and Rock.

Greg wasn't sure how his career was going to fit into the altered landscape. The young warned, don't trust anybody over 30. He was pushing 50. Producers were casting about for an antihero, not a stalwart leader with a strong arm and a heart of gold. In place of

John Wayne, Burt Lancaster and Gregory Peck, they were discovering Jack Nicholson, Dustin Hoffman and Richard Dreyfuss. A new wave of directors commanded the public's attention: Sydney Pollack, Mike Nichols, Arthur Penn and Stuart Rosenberg. Their films centered on characters of ambiguous values, while the males Greg played belonged to a simpler age when the difference between right and wrong was more clear-cut. Critic Judith Crist put it very well: 'They had faces then, the men who took over the still-silver screen during and after World War II, providing proper role models for the boys and romance for the girls and in some cases, satisfying performances and rewarding, even enduring, portraits and perceptions for grown-ups.'

Greg was indeed the epitome of honor as the reporter who exposes anti-Semitism in *Gentleman's Agreement*, the lawyer who fights racism in *To Kill a Mockingbird,* the heroic Captain Horatio Hornblower, the Air Force general pulling together a demoralized bomber group in *Twelve O'Clock High*, and the captain of an atomic submarine facing a dying world in *On the Beach*. What's more, he prided himself on his 'man who delivers' reputation. He claimed: 'You don't want an anti-hero to perform brain surgery.'

What were actors of Greg's generation to make of the scripts being written in the 1960s? Movie stars who had made their names under the antediluvian Hays Office rules, which dictated that even married couples had to be filmed in separate beds, were astounded by the new freedom. Quipped Bob Hope: 'They are doing things on the screen now that I wouldn't do in bed. If I could.'

Only a handful of stars from the 1930s and 1940s endured. Greg was one of them – but his future was uncertain. From his point of view, it seemed as if nothing recedes faster than success. After winning an Oscar, Greg had every reason to expect an avalanche of great scripts and movie offers. This didn't happen. It didn't help that some of the new upstart critics took condescending pokes at him.

The 1960s and early 1970s were heady moments for reviewers. Invested with more cultural authority than in previous decades, reviewers fully exercised their power in deciding the success or failure of a film. Two favorites with young people were Andrew Sarris of the *Village Voice* and Pauline Kael of *The New Yorker*.

Commenting on his rival, Sarris compared Kael's bullying but often on-target movie reviews to papal pronouncements of infallibility.

Provocation was the name of the game. Sarris recalled when he started writing for the *Village Voice* in 1960, 'I got so much angry mail that the editors were very impressed with me. At that time people who could arouse controversy were very valuable.' When *Mockingbird* came out, Sarris refused to join the collective hosannas. Instead, he wrote: '*To Kill a Mockingbird* relates the Cult of Childhood to the Negro Problem with disastrous results. Before the intellectual confusion of the project is considered, it should be noted that this is not much of a movie even by purely formal standards.'

Taking pleasure in skewering establishment actors, Kael aided and abetted the impression in the public mind that Greg was a self-righteous, wooden and over-the-hill actor. Her basic philosophy was that movies were like sex – some good, some bad – and that what mattered was what turned her on. Underwhelmed by *To Kill a Mockingbird*, she carped: 'When Gregory Peck got the Academy Award for best actor for his performance as an upstanding widower practicing in a small Alabama town in the early 30s, there was a fair amount of derision throughout the country: Peck was better than usual, but in that same virtuously dull way. (There was the suspicion that Peck was being rewarded because the Lincolnesque lawyer shot a rabid dog and defended an innocent black man accused of raping a white woman.)'

Stella Bruzzi, a more recent authority on films and currently writing *Bringing up Daddy: Fatherhood and Masculinity in Postwar Hollywood*, asserts Greg took himself out of the running for a number of roles because he played in three movies as the head of a family. According to Bruzzi, becoming a father is a masculine renunciation. Despite fatherhood functioning as proof of his virility, the man now forsakes his right not only to beauty and vanity but sex as well.

'There are diverse reasons for Hollywood's reluctance to permit a man to be both erotic and a father,' Bruzzi explains, 'Freud's theories of seduction being but one. The sexual father transgresses psychological and symbolic boundaries and the appearance of

Gregory Peck and other notable Hollywood fathers in gray suits, woolen cardigans, drab trousers and glasses testifies to their castration.' The author contends Greg went from being one of the most heavily promoted of Hollywood's pin-ups in the 1940s and 1950s, to someone trapped in his repressing, desexing wardrobe. 'Not only are the daddy's clothes notably un-alluring, but you never see his flesh. The father's body has been subsumed into his social, paternal role – and it certainly isn't used for fun and games.'

Off screen, Greg reveled in the role of father. He regarded his children as the most rewarding part of his life. In raising his three boys by his first marriage, he had a supportive partner in Greta. Back when they were together, he had said to her: 'I think we'd be better friends if we weren't married.' And that turned out to be the case. Greta valued Greg: 'He gave me three wonderful sons.' Plus, he had been her magic carpet to Hollywood glamour.

On the wall next to the steps leading to the second floor of her home, Greta hung photos of herself and Greg in the 1940s attending celebrity events. She took the boys to see Greg's movies and she'd travel with them to San Francisco to visit Greg's mother and stepfather, Bunny and Joe Maysuch.

Greta visited Greg at his house in Brentwood and she welcomed him at her home. But after Tony and Cecilia were born, Veronique cooled to the open-door policy. Greta told Tommy Hinkkanen, a Finn now living in Los Angeles: 'She didn't really like having me around. She didn't want me seeing him.' So Greta and Greg limited their contacts to events related to their children's activities.

Years later, an Armenian reporter submitted a list of questions to Greg's publicist for review. The journalist included a query about Greta's whereabouts and the publicist scratched it out and cautioned the reporter that under no circumstances would Greg discuss Greta. Why? Out of respect for Veronique, the reporter was told. First wives don't fit neatly into fairytales. Nor, sometimes, do the children from the first union. Carey Peck's second wife, Lita Albuquerque, told Bonnie Clearwater: '. . . he's not completely accepted by his stepmother.'

One area where Greg and Greta didn't agree was the boys' schooling. He balked when she insisted on sending Jonathan,

Stephen and Carey to the conservative Harvard School (no relation to the University; presently called Harvard-Westlake). It was an academically competitive old-line preparatory school where the boys wore military uniforms. Greta even bought a house at 908 N. Beverly Drive in Beverly Hills because it was closer to Harvard School.

She reasoned since the boys had such a peripatetic father, they needed roots and connection to community and friends. (By Greg's own estimate, he was only in Los Angeles half the year.)

For his part, Greg didn't want his children exposed to Hollywood values. 'They have everything there is and they're surrounded by affluence,' Greg said of the local youth. 'They lose their ambition. And they lose their desire to study, to accept a set of rules to live by, and they just become useless appendages of their parents.'

In 1962, Greg became one of the vast numbers of Hollywood stars to be given a part in the extravagant epic about the taming of the frontier called *How the West Was Won* (1963). The film was presented in segments, linked by the narration of Spencer Tracy. It was directed by John Ford, Henry Hathaway and George Marshall. Along with Greg, the cast included John Wayne, James Stewart, Debbie Reynolds, Raymond Massey as Lincoln, and Henry Fonda, in a walrus mustache, as a buffalo hunter. Throughout the production, the operative word was 'big.' According to the *How the West Was Won* publicity book, the star-studded cast was supported by 12,617 extras, among them 350 Native Americans from five different tribes.

If the circumstances had been more auspicious, Greg would have rejoiced in his role as a charming rogue. He usually welcomed a chance to play against his type. But *How the West Was Won* was shot in Cinerama – a ridiculous huge-screen process contrived as a vain attempt to defeat television – and Greg hated it. He lamented: 'I found it impossible to act realistically in front of the giant machine with three lenses.'

Greg's real problem, however, was Henry Hathaway. The director for his segment of the movie viewed him with contempt. Hathaway was an ornery character who had been in the business of making Westerns a long time, and had gained the reputation of being a skilled craftsman who handled his material straightforwardly with few complications and pretensions. Several years later, when Hathaway was required to direct Greg in a Western called *Shoot Out* (1971), he snorted Greg was 'the worst son of a bitch in the world for this picture. He is a cold, indifferent actor. He had no love in him.' Another time he railed at Greg's impenetrable reserve: 'The bastard wouldn't let me in.'

Greg found Hathaway 'a charming fellow at dinner,' but hell on wheels on the set. 'He just yelled and screamed and foamed at the mouth and chewed cigars all day long,' recalled Greg. 'The terrible tempered Mr Hathaway.' While Hathaway's indictment of Greg was harsh, there was no doubt Greg had undergone subtle changes since picking up his Oscar. For one thing, he voiced his opinions more freely. There was an element of braggadocio in his comments. When it was suggested to him that movie acting is a lightweight enterprise compared to the demands of live theater, he scowled: 'I've seen them all, Olivier and Burton and Gielgud and the rest. Most of them are simply vocalizing. It's fancy speaking and declaiming. To me, it is a highly developed parlor trick, learned in schools of recitation, just as schoolboys learned to recite. Eventually, as with Burton, if practiced long enough, it becomes a kind of acting.

'But I believe it goes no deeper than the vocal cords. It is like opera. Playacting. These actors fail to differentiate between life and acting. The old sock-and-buskin school is what it is. But performances have little or nothing to do with reality. When I see them emoting on a stage, I feel their minds are wondering, perhaps worrying whether the laundry has been returned on time.'

Though some critics saw *How the West Was Won* as a saga of dim-witted bunglers who couldn't do anything right, the public loved it. The film was one of the most popular to hit the screens in 1963 and eventually earned over $50 million.

When he wasn't making a movie, Greg continued to enjoy relaxing at his villa in Cap Ferrat, and hanging out with the 'horsey' set in England. ('We have many friends in the English racing crowd,' he explained. 'They don't know about movies and could care less. I like that.') Greg also enjoyed gathering with his family at their sumptuous apartment on Avenue Foch in Paris near the Arc de Triumphe. Sophia Loren was a neighbor.

Designed by Baron Haussmann during the nineteenth century so that rich people could easily reach the new and fashionable Bois de Boulogne, Avenue Foch is one of the most prestigious residential addresses in the world.

In the summer of 1963, John Bell – a friend of Greg's eldest son, Jonathan, from New Zealand – showed up at the Pecks' Avenue Foch apartment. He was supposed to meet Jonathan there. The two friends had planned to travel to Germany where they each had girlfriends named Karin. (Jonathan's girl, Karin Ruhle Von Lilienstern, had worked as a maid for Greta in Beverly Hills.) But when Bell arrived, he learned Jonathan was still in the south of France visiting 'a princess somebody or other.'

Although Greg and Veronique had never set eyes on Bell, they welcomed him like a member of their family. 'I obeyed their rules and what not,' he recalled, and made himself useful playing with Anthony, seven, and Cecilia, five.

Over lunch at a café, Greg asked Bell about his plans following the trip to Germany. Bell recalled: 'My ambition was to travel through Europe all the way back to New Zealand by bike except in those places where I was required to travel over water. But with all the turmoil in the Middle East, countries like Israel and Palestine presented a problem.'

'You should talk to the New Zealand ambassador,' said Greg.

Bell thought, 'Yeah. Here I am, 17 years old. What chance have I got of meeting the New Zealand ambassador?'

Returning from lunch, Greg rang up the New Zealand Embassy and arranged for Bell to meet with the ambassador that afternoon. Veronique accompanied Bell to the meeting. The ambassador graciously explained to Bell his plan was dangerous.

'Being a stupid, naive teenager,' Bell recalled, 'I said something to the effect: "Well, what's the use of having an embassy here if you can't help citizens like me?"'

That evening, Veronique told Greg what happened. 'He dressed me down like he would any of his sons,' said Bell. 'He said, "I set this up for you and my wife tells me you were rude to the New

Zealand ambassador. You shouldn't do that sort of thing." He corrected me in a very gentlemanly yet fatherly manner. He put me in my place. I was embarrassed as hell. I apologized profusely.'

Then Greg asked Bell if he had an alternate plan to biking to New Zealand. To which Bell replied: 'I think I'd like to hang around Paris and work.'

Greg called a studio in Paris and made inquiries about a job for Bell. He was told it was very difficult for foreigners to find employment because a French working card was required.

Bell never forgot Greg's kindness. 'He tried to help me even after I abused the New Zealand ambassador,' marveled Bell, comparing Greg's behavior to Atticus Finch. Like the fictional character, Greg was firm, authoritative and forgiving.

In *To Kill a Mockingbird*, Atticus says: 'You never really understand a person until you consider things from his point of view . . . Till you climb inside his skin and walk around in it.'

It's unclear how much Greg knew about what was going on inside the mind and heart of his oldest son. To all appearances, Jonathan looked like a promising, polite young man not given to reckless behavior. Beneath his reticent manner, however, he was growing increasingly troubled by his role as offspring to a world-famous father. His struggle to become a person in his own right would ultimately prove tragic. But back when he was a teenager and Greg was becoming even more prominent as a leader and a symbol, chances are he didn't comprehend the depth of Jonathan's inner turmoil.

John Bell didn't pick up on his friend's angst for some time. The two boys met when Jonathan – a high school middle-distance runner – traveled to Auckland, New Zealand, in the summer of 1962 to train with Arthur Lydiard, a fabled name in the sport. Lydiard was the country's top marathon runner in the 1950s who went on to become an internationally respected track coach for middle-distance runners. Lydiard-trained athletes such as Peter Snell and Murray Halberg had competed successfully at the Olympics.

At 17 years old, Jonathan was 6 feet 1 inch, weighed 165 pounds, was good-looking and soft-spoken, yet awkward and shy with braces on his teeth. He was also the spitting image of his dad

– the black hair and brown eyes, the strong classic features, the baritone voice, prominent ears and the long lean frame with the distinctive walk.

Like Greg, he kept his feelings wrapped tightly inside himself. But his father could escape his inner torments by playacting in a movie role. Jonathan wasn't so lucky. 'Dad and I both think one actor in the family's enough,' he said, following some unsuccessful theatrical attempts at Harvard school where he was a C+ student. 'I'm not star material.'

When Jonathan landed in New Zealand, his arrival was trumpeted in the newspapers. In the early 1960s the country was still isolated from the rest of the world. 'Jonathan would have made the papers even if he hadn't been Gregory Peck's son,' explained Bell. 'It was very exciting to have an American in our midst. People wanted to meet him just so they could listen to his accent.'

It soon became obvious that Jonathan was a good kid. Kind and unspoiled, his joy was running, not drinking or drugs as one might expect from a Hollywood visitor. And he never traded on his father's name. 'Jonathan wanted to make it on his own,' recalled Bell, who became one of Jonathan's closest buddies. 'That's the distinct impression I got after the first few days I met him. And I maintained that impression throughout our friendship. He never gloated or bloated about his famous father.'

When it came time for Jonathan to return to America, the coaches and athletes threw a farewell party for him. They toasted him, giving speeches, telling jokes, reliving the good times he brought to the summer running camp.

Jonathan was so overjoyed to receive accolades for an identity he had clearly established in this group on their terms – dedicated runners and good sportsmen – he ran outside with Bell following him. Said Bell: 'He had himself a good bawl. He bawled his eyes out.'

The next summer, after Bell's stay at the Pecks' apartment, the two boys traveled to Germany to visit their Karins. Then Bell returned to New Zealand and Jonathan started Occidental, a liberal arts college located in the Eagle Rock section of Los Angeles (later to appear in the television series *Beverly Hills 90210*). Jonathan chose the school because they had a strong track team, and he was determined to continue his excellent track record from high school and thus achieve an identity independent of his father.

He could not escape being the great man's son. Not only was his father a stellar character both professionally and personally, he also felt a deep need to project the image of perfection to the public. This can be very tough on a young person trying to find himself. Here was Jonathan, who inherited Greg's facial features, his height, voice, gestures and athletic build. But these physical endowments, which had provided Greg with a passport to fame and fortune, were visited upon Jonathan like a curse. People couldn't look at him without thinking of his father.

To compound the problem, Jonathan only knew his father as a success. Lost in the mist of time was the gawky Greg who stumbled through high school riddled with mediocre grades, no girlfriend, minor athletic achievements and no accomplishments as an actor. Nor did most strangers know Greg as anything but Hollywood royalty. So it was not unusual for people to look Jonathan over and think: 'Does he have the old man's brains and charisma?'

Throughout Jonathan's school days and into his working life, Greg's fame brought him attention he didn't want and deprived him of the attention he did want. 'Poor Jonathan,' remembered his friend Nancy Stesin. 'He was always the son of Gregory Peck. When people introduced him they didn't even say his first name.'

Greg knew it wouldn't be easy. 'I foresaw that possibility. Which is why I didn't name any of my kids Gregory Peck Jr. I was very careful not to do that.' (Jonathan was christened Jonathan Gregory Peck.)

At Occidental, a friend on the track team recalled a telling incident. One day Jonathan won a race. Greg was in the crowd cheering for him and Jonathan could look up and see him in the stands. It was a moment to savor. Afterwards, in the locker room, Jonathan burst into tears. They were tears of joy, remembered his friend. His father was applauding him – instead of the other way round.

Perhaps it was this race day that an interviewer heard about when he visited the Peck household about that time. In his account of an exchange between father and son, we see how these happy family moments are played out for an observer, so they became as much a tribute to Greg as a model parent as they are to his son's accomplishment.

Wrote the reporter: 'The day before my visit, Peck's son Jonathan, a freshman at Occidental College – he wants to be a diplomat – had just won the half-mile race against the UCLA frosh, and Peck had spent the afternoon watching that race, and also the final leg of the mile relay, both of which the boy won for his team. When Jon Peck came into the house, he was in his black-and-orange sweat suit, standing tall and straight like his dad in his youth. It was a warmly moving scene, to an outsider, to see Peck shake his son's hand and clap him on the shoulder gruffly, in congratulation.

'"Well done, Jon," said father Peck. "Congratulations. I'm proud of you." It could have come from one of his pictures. And Peck, playing Peck, was never better.'

At Occidental, Jonathan corresponded with John Bell in New Zealand. Said Bell: 'He'd write things like "Life's a bitch." It sort of went out of the top of my head. We were teenagers. And life's always a bitch then. But it cropped up often in his letters. I began to realize he wasn't happy.'

In a letter dated 7 March 1964, Jonathan wrote: 'Believe me there's nothing I'd rather do than come down this summer (your winter) to help you and your dad cut down those trees in Orewa [a beach community near Auckland]. Nothing like a little work to make a man feel like a man.'

Then Jonathan complained school was driving him nuts. He added, 'We learn about great men and how they did this and that but we never get a chance to do anything great or big ourselves. Everything is served up on a silver platter – it's enough to make anybody go crazy.'

Ever on the alert for interesting new projects, Greg heard from a friend of his named Sy Lamont, who was a professional reader. Lamont suggested Greg's production company, Brentwood Productions, make a movie out of a current best-selling novel *Captain Newman, M.D.* Enthusiastic about the idea, Greg hired husband-and-wife team Henry and Phoebe Ephron to develop the screenplay, pacing it with the kind of humor they wrote for *Desk Set* (1957) and *Take Her She's Mine* (1963).

Newman is an interesting drama of an Air Force psychiatrist whose duty is to his patients first, the military brass second. The resulting film links comedy and combat in a way that was not unusual in traditional war films, but the hospital setting, the emphasis on war-induced diseases, and the barracks humor anticipated the more contemporary style of *Catch-22* and *MASH*.

Captain Newman, M.D. (1963) was an instant hit. The movie depicted the struggle of a humane doctor to repair the shattered psyches of three battle-weary soldiers. Greg, fresh from his Academy Award-winning performance as Atticus Finch, was the cinematic paragon of decency and virtue. He was the ideal actor to embody Hollywood's exaltation of the psychiatrist as a caring, courageous sage.

Greg assembled a cast that included Angie Dickinson and Tony Curtis as well as pop singer Bobby Darin. Dickinson and Curtis were members of Frank Sinatra's celebrated Rat Pack, the mainstays of which were Dean Martin, Sammy Davis Jr and Joey Bishop. More sporadic participants included Shirley MacLaine, Juliet Prowse and Tony Curtis's wife, Janet Leigh. Also known as 'The Clan,' the group became the focus of inordinate public attention in the late 1950s and early 1960s. Rat Pack 'broad,' Angie Dickinson was hot copy for gossip columnists because she had reputedly been a mistress of President Kennedy.

After some forgettable roles in mostly B-movies, she managed to jettison her contract with Warner Brothers in favor of a similar pact with Universal Studios. The carrot was an opportunity to co-star with Greg. She next starred as the deceitful 'Sheila Farr' in the 1964 remake of *The Killers*, co-starring John Cassavetes, and in his last screen role (and his first as a heavy), the future President, Ronald Reagan.

Dickinson was thrilled to be cast opposite Greg. 'Universal said I had to sign a long-term contract if I wanted to play Fran. I thought, 'What could be worth that chunk of my life? Then I thought Gregory Peck. And I said, "Oh hell – what's seven years anyway?"'

For his part, Greg was intrigued by Tony Curtis's comic antics and conjuring tricks. Christened Bernard Schwartz, Curtis was the son of an immigrant tailor and grew up in poverty in a tough section of the Bronx. By age 11, he was a member of a notorious street gang. He began his acting career with a stock company that toured the Catskill Mountain 'Borscht Circuit', then appeared briefly on Broadway. Though Hollywood built Curtis up as a star based on his pretty-boy looks, he proved to have more range. In 1957, he surprised critics with his nervously energetic performance in *The Sweet Smell of Success* as the unprincipled press agent Sidney Falco. Another successful performance in the Roaring Twenties comedy *Some Like it Hot* (1959) led to many light roles in films of the 1960s including *Captain Newman, M.D.*

After the film wrapped, Greg phoned Curtis and suggested that they team up as a comedy duo in future movies. Curtis was polite but later confessed in his memoirs he found the idea of playing a comedy with the stalwart Greg, well, laughable: '. . . he wasn't exactly a comedian,' Curtis wrote, 'and people came down hard on him about being stiff and kind of wooden in that film. Gregory either didn't know or didn't give a shit what they thought.'

The tepid reviews by critics did not enhance Greg's chances of being seen by the public as a vibrant star for the Aquarian Age. In its critique on 23 October 1963, *Variety* said: 'Peck's portrayal of the title figure is characteristically restrained and intelligent. Perhaps his best scene . . . is the one in which he quietly but expressively reacts to Darin's high-powered histrionics.' Although some critics perceived the film as being not focused enough, it earned $3,325,000 at the box-office.

Greg next co-produced and starred in *Behold a Pale Horse* (1964) a movie about an anti-Fascist hero in the Spanish Civil War in the late 1930s. The cast included Anthony Quinn and Omar Sharif and was directed by Fred Zinnemann. Greg's interest in the Spanish Civil War dated from his Berkeley days when he was caught up in the fervor of the war and even considered signing up with the Abraham Lincoln Brigade. When the movie did poorly, Greg admitted: 'Yes, that didn't come off – I think, because we didn't commit ourselves. We followed the current fashion of posing a question instead of taking a moral stand.'

Zinnemann added: '*Behold a Pale Horse* was a big flop everywhere in the world except Lebanon. It was a smash hit there because Omar

Sharif was born there. My mistake on that picture was assuming that people remembered and still cared about the Spanish Civil War. Apparently they don't because nobody cared about the picture.'

Fortunately for Greg's career, he managed to garner some upbeat reviews. Said the *New York Daily News*: 'Greg and Quinn, and other members of the cast, play their roles with complete conviction. Peck's characterization . . . tops his prize-winning performance in . . . *Mockingbird* . . .' *Variety* concluded: 'Peck is a worn-out, untidy, broken man who once again surges with force and energy in a characterization that ranks among the better in his long and respected career.'

Greg next chose *Mirage* (1965), a diverting thriller. In it, he played a man who believes he has amnesia and starts to retrace his past, and subsequently becomes involved in a murder plot. Walter Matthau (he claimed his name was originally Walter Matuschanskayasky but it could have been one of his tall tales), played a detective hired to unravel the mystery. The film employed the trappings of *The Twilight Zone* and the villainy of *Mission Impossible*. Greatly in its favor is the stylish direction of Edward Dmytryk and his use of New York City as a setting.

Perplexing and never quite believable, Greg sometimes drew a blank when asked about *Mirage*: He admits: 'I forget what the hell it was about.' Critic Leonard Maltin had much the same reaction, calling it 'An utterly confusing yarn.'

Despite *Mirage*'s ho-hum reception, Greg prided himself on sticking to his policy of hiring only top-notch people rather than choosing lesser talents whom he could easily outshine. He was acutely aware his value as a contender depended upon his ability to 'bounce off' his performance against the best. He often cited the tremendous lift given the careers of the actors who played in *From Here to Eternity* (1953): Burt Lancaster, Deborah Kerr, Montgomery Clift, Frank Sinatra, Donna Reed and Ernest Borgnine.

With regard to *Mirage*, Greg said: 'I think my main contribution to the film was that I hired Walter and virtually launched him on his screen career.' Indeed, Matthau's rapid rise was helped in no small way by the beautiful part of the detective he had in *Mirage*. However, Greg exaggerated his role in Matthau's ascent.

Matthau, whose gravelly voice and lugubrious bloodhound face is now famous the world over, was an actor whose career could have gone way up or down. He was a chronic smoker, an eccentric eater and a gambler; he claimed to have lost over $5 million through gambling by the time he reached middle age, and once, in the course of one or two weeks, had lost $83,000 just betting on spring training baseball games. His wife Carole Matthau took it all in her stride – except when he paid attention to other women. Once overhearing him ask an upwardly nubile young female what her age might be, Carol cut in: 'Why don't you chop off her legs and count the rings?'

Matthau seemed destined to become one of those character actors like William Demarest and Sydney Greenstreet who are in constant demand, helping to populate Hollywood's special world, yet never taking center stage. But when Billy Wilder finally recognized his great talent for comedy, he turned in an unbroken string of truly memorable performances in *The Fortune Cookie* (1966), *A Guide for the Married Man* (1967) and *The Odd Couple* (1968).

In *Mirage* he played a crafty New York private eye who gets bumped off by the military-industrial establishment for assisting Greg. Someone on the set of *Mirage* congratulated Matthau on a particularly well-played scene, assuring the struggling actor: 'You should have a great career in films. You can be a top character actor.'

'Character actor, Hell!' snorted Matthau. 'I'm going to be a top leading man.' And lo and behold, he surprised everyone but himself by becoming the first character actor to successfully make the transition to playing the romantic lead.

For his part, Greg found producing no bed of roses. Having been brought along by a gaggle of flamboyant, extravagant moguls who seemed to value good stories more than the bottom line, he was finding himself bogged down in accounting duties and chronic worry about potential failure. Two pet projects of Greg's which had to be jettisoned for practical reasons were *The Martian Chronicles*, again with Robert Mulligan and Alan Pakula, which could have been the *Star Wars* of 1966 and *The Bells of Hell Go Ting-a-Ling-a-Ling*, a drama about First World War aircraft crews. *Ting-a-Ling* got as far as a whole film production staff starting to work on location in

Switzerland. Costumes were designed, made and fitted. Aircraft of 1917 vintage were adapted and, in some cases, manufactured specifically for the film. Greg and the rest of the company assembled in Switzerland ready for the takeoff – but it never came. After 25 days of solid rain and three weeks of mist, which obscured everything that needed to be photographed, the picture was abandoned.

Such setbacks triggered Greg's dark Irish moods. During one funk, he quaffed Jack Daniels and revealed his feelings to Charles Hamblett with uncharacteristic candor. Hamblett was writing a book called *The Cage*. It was a series of interviews about how Hollywood – the weirdest small town in America – had a way of closing in on movie people and making them feel trapped.

On the day of their meeting, a coastal haze made the Pacific kingdom of Movieland look like a fading dream. Arriving at Greg's Summit Ridge ranch house in Brentwood, Hamblett was surprised to find an unshaven, sleep-deprived man deep in reflection. As they sat in the garden near the pool looking out at the vertiginous view of sun and sea, Greg knocked back his drink and admitted: 'There are times when I could cheerfully walk out on the whole God damn setup. I don't have to make pictures anymore. When I first came out here to work from the New York stage, I was carved up in all directions, a dumb actor tied to a slew of contractual clauses. Today I'm my own man, free, off the hook. This is a collective business, I know. But now it's up to me to decide the stories we use and the kind of picture in which I'm prepared to get involved. I'm no longer the dumb and trusting ham being shuttled from picture to picture at someone else's whim. I'm a company boss who has to make big decisions right or wrong, responsible only to myself in the long run.'

Greg shifted his great legs in the canvas chair and continued grousing, sounding to Hamblett like a drugstore cowboy: 'For years, we actors have been fighting for our so-called artistic freedom. We wanted to get rid of the moguls and their accountants. We damned the studio Shylocks for their materialism and lack of taste. Now, most of us are on our own. So what happens? This morning I had to call my office and scrap a production on which people had been working for months . . . I decided it would be best to chuck it rather than risk making a bad picture. All night I've been pacing up and down the house trying to make the right decision. I tell you there are times when I wish Hollywood actors had retained the status of bums and gypsies and left the planning to others. Right now, I'm tempted to say "the hell with all of it." '

Greg's tirade gained stentorian force: 'The picture has changed, my friend. The old omnipotent caliphs are dying fast. Television plus the weight of years has weakened the survivors. It will need energy and a fresh executive approach to redirect the creative drive, re-channel the talent. The monopolies of the studios have been broken. The anti-trust laws have severed their distribution outlets. The shackling of actors to loaded long-term contracts is virtually a thing of the past. In effect, I have complete control over what I do. A year or two back this was considered some kind of victory of art over tyranny. Now I'm not so sure.'

The more he talked, the more Greg sounded like the guileless young man he was when he first hit town: 'I'm a free soul, you remember. Before I became an actor, I wanted to be a writer. Freedom of mind and action is important to me. Right now I'd like to take off for Mexico and fish for a while and swim and read books without wondering whether they would make a good picture. Now I'll have to follow another production through from the drawing board to the cutting room. And then go out on the road and sell it with personal appearances. It can be stimulating. A challenge, as they say at Chasens. But there are times when actors like myself find themselves wishing we could resurrect Thalberg and pass the ball to him or people like him. The town's wide open for any operator with the ability to finance, package and sell motion pictures.'

Finally, looking over at Hamblett, he sighed: 'You're lucky. As a writer, you can go anywhere you like. You carry your studio in your mind's eye . . . you don't have to worry about lights and cameras just so long as you have a couple of ballpoints. You guys are fast, mobile. If we're the heavy artillery, you're the guerrillas. The guys who can hang out in the hills and harass the enemy with minimum equipment.'

Clearly, Greg needed something to lift his spirits. Fortunately, he was presented with a delectable mood-enhancer in the shape of

Sophia Loren. The belle of Naples had signed on to do a picture with him.

Born 31 years before, illegitimate, in a ward for unwed mothers, Loren had gone on to become a rich and talented actress. Commenting on her extraordinary emotional equilibrium, columnist Rex Reed noted: 'For a woman who has spent most of her life in the headlines, been threatened with excommunication by the Roman Catholic Church, jail sentences by the Italian government, rape by German soldiers, robbery at gunpoint by thugs, scandal and sometimes even death, she remains sane, natural, and unpretentious.' Still, she was no pushover – as Greg would soon discover.

Producer-director Stanley Donen, whose *Charade* (1963) with Cary Grant and Audrey Hepburn had recently been a box-office smash, wanted to team Sophia Loren with Greg and do a similar romantic thriller titled *Arabesque* (1966). Donen intended to start production in England at the end of April 1965, which suited Loren and Greg. The two stars had discussed the possibility of working together two years before at the Oscars ceremonies.

Cary Grant had been Stanley Donen's financial partner in several of their movies together, and he was originally supposed to star in *Arabesque*. But after taking flak from the critics for his love scenes with the considerably younger Audrey Hepburn in *Charade*, Grant decided that he had grown too old to continue playing romantic leads. He recommended that his close friend Gregory Peck, his junior by 12 years, replace him. (Peck grumbled good-naturedly: 'Every script I get has Cary Grant's paw prints on it.') No doubt Grant also nominated Loren for leading lady. They had become romantically entangled while filming *The Pride and The Passion* (1957) in Spain. If Loren hadn't been committed to marry Carlo Ponti and Grant not been already married to Betsy Drake, the relationship might have gone somewhere. In any case, he was still very fond of her, often phoning her long distance just to chat.

Loren would have preferred Cary Grant. Friends of hers claimed Greg had been taking himself too seriously as an actor since winning the Oscar for *To Kill a Mockingbird*. But Loren found him amiable and easy to work with, although his technique lacked the comedic sparkle of Cary Grant.

Arabesque was a contrived, not altogether successful chase melodrama set amid lavish international settings. Instead of the Paris of *Charade*, *Arabesque* used London, Oxford, Ascot, and the English countryside for backgrounds. As he did for *Charade*, Henry Mancini composed the title song and music score. The title *Arabesque* suggested undulating suspense but also played on the word 'Arab,' a major element in the story. At Greg's suggestion, Donen chose it over *Cipher*, the title of the Gordon Cotler novel on which the script was loosely based.

Donen later said: 'It wasn't a good script and I didn't want to make it, but Gregory Peck and Sophia Loren, whom I loved, wanted to be in it and the studio implored me to make it, because, they said, "It's ridiculous not to make a film with Peck and Sophia." '

Though Greg was no young stud, he proved to be an attractive on-screen love interest for Loren. (He kept in shape by bicycling, swimming, and exercising on a slant board.) At a time in life when many stars see their best features succumb to gravity, Greg was fulfilling a prophecy made in the 1940s. 'For the camera purpose, his lean, bony face is the sort that is practically indestructible. For the next 20 years, he is not likely to look older, enough to damage him as a leading man.'

Loren had the benefit of an eye-catching wardrobe. Due to the success of *Charade*, in which Audrey Hepburn made fashion news in Givenchy creations, Donen was able to persuade Universal to spend $100,000 on a wardrobe for Loren at Christian Dior. So before setting down in London for the shooting, Loren stopped in Paris for fittings with Christian Dior's Mark Bohan, who designed all her outfits for the movie, plus 25 pairs of footwear that went with them.

Loren played the mistress of a murderous Arab tycoon who is plotting to take over the world oil supply, while Greg was cast as an American exchange professor at Oxford University who is trying to decipher a secret message written in hieroglyphics. *Arabesque* repeated a plot device in *Charade*, where the audience never knew for certain whether the hero was the murderer or not until the climax. In contrast, however, this film had what some saw as an excess of clever plot twists. As the director admitted, 'I kept my sequences all right, but I ruined the movie.'

One of the lead actors' first scenes together required the fugitive professor to run and hide in the shower stall occupied by the nude Loren. Since they hardly knew each other, Greg tried to put her at ease. 'Don't be embarrassed,' he told her. 'It's all in the game. Strictly professional.'

Loren looked at Greg with those giant almond eyes. 'What makes you think I would be embarrassed?' she asked as she slipped out of her robe and into the shower. 'Absolutely nothing at all,' Greg replied, as soon as he caught his breath.

Asked about how he felt about the shower scene later, Greg said only that the view was 'Spectacular!' Allan Ladd, who played opposite Loren in *Boy On a Dolphin* (1957) had a more alarmed reaction to coming into such close proximity with the Italian beauty's famous *poitrine*: 'It was like being bombarded with watermelons.' For her part, Loren liked to say: 'Everything you see I owe to spaghetti.' Lest anybody get the wrong idea, she would insist in her broken English: 'I am not a sexy pot!'

Relations between the principals weren't always so lighthearted. Later in the film, Loren and Greg were being chased through a cornfield by villains driving a deadly thrashing machine. Since suffering permanent injury during the riding accident incurred just before filming *Yellow Sky*, Greg struggled with all his might trying to keep up with Loren. Ignoring Greg's pain, Loren kept getting ahead of him. Finally, he pleaded with her, 'Sophia, would you please slow down? Remember, I'm supposed to be rescuing you.'

Loren just laughed: 'Greg, you can do better than that. Just try harder.' In her drive to look young and vigorous in the film, she even went to Stanley Donen and insisted 'make him run faster.' But Greg was in such pain, Loren finally had to cooperate or there would have been no scene.

Greg wanted to grow in new directions. It seemed like everybody he knew was engaged in restless travel and radical politics, in drugs and spiritual quests, or seeking new forms of love and work. Cary Grant was experimenting with LSD and even admitted to dropping acid more than a hundred times; Frank Sinatra recharged himself by taking a *very* young Mia Farrow for his bride (hearing the news, Ava Gardner howled: 'I always knew Frank would end up in bed with a boy'); and numerous other stars were partying with Bunnies at the Playboy mansion in the Holmby Hills section of Los Angeles. Greg didn't have any great yen to snort cocaine, take off for India with the Maharoonie, or fill his bed with upwardly nubile starlets. Although he was friendly with the Rat Pack, he was not about to sully his White Knight image with heavy boozing and gambling in Vegas. So, while it seemed that half of Hollywood was 'letting it all hang out' and looking for exciting new ways to raise hell, Greg went from good – to gooder.

Taking a three-year break from making movies, he devoted the lion's share of his time to the American Cancer Society, the National Endowment for the Arts, and the Academy of Motion Picture Arts and Sciences. He also agreed to act as general chairman of the Motion Picture Relief Fund's 15-year endowment and building relief campaign. 'I want to be useful,' he said. 'I don't want to concentrate just on my own career.'

Aside from his heartfelt desire to make the world a better place, Greg had another spur. In a spirit of provocation, Gore Vidal once said to him: 'C'mon now, don't you think acting is really a feminine job?' Incensed, Greg shot back: 'You mean feminine like Tracy and Cooper and Bogart?'

Actually, Vidal hit a sore spot. Acting has always been considered sissified – as Doc Peck told the young Greg in no uncertain terms. It was not a respectable job for an Alpha male. 'Scratch an actor and you find an actress,' claimed Dorothy Parker – who did a lot of scratching. And while Greg evoked the name of his idol Spencer Tracy, that star never thought much of the profession. 'Why do actors think they're so God damn important?' he bellowed. 'They're not. Acting is not an important job in the scheme of things. Plumbing is.' Warren Beatty put it another way: 'Movies are fun, but they're not a cure for cancer.'

So Greg wanted to step up his humanitarian efforts and make some solid contributions to his country. He had never defended America in war, and acting was just playing at heroism. A movie might show him parachuting behind the lines in Nazi Germany, but the person in the parachute wasn't even Greg, but a double. Besides, even at his most ambitious, he had never been a taker. As we have seen, a broad streak of idealism was evident since schooldays. Over the years, Greg had devoted, often quietly and without much public notice, a great deal with his time and energy away from the cameras and sound stages and locations to a wide range of charitable and humanitarian activities.

In 1966, he embarked on a personal crusade. Recalling the excruciating last days of his intrepid grandmother, Catherine Ashe, who succumbed to ovarian cancer, as well as those of friends and a more recent experience with his father's widow, Dorothy Peck, who had pleaded with him 'You've got to get them to let me die. I'm so sick,' Greg accepted the office of National Chairman of the American Cancer Society. With Veronique, he crisscrossed America on a breathless circuit of 24 cities, and raised $5 million.

Greg's inadvertent role in aiding the spread of lung cancer went unspoken. Like many of his confreres, he had bolstered his income by posing for cigarette ads – in his case Chesterfields. The ads were backed up by 'product positioning,' the ubiquitous flaunting of cigarettes by the characters he portrayed in films such as *Gentleman's Agreement* and *Twelve O'Clock High*. In retrospect, Greg undoubtedly felt great anguish for advertising cigarettes once the link between them and cancer was disclosed in the Surgeon's General's report in 1964. Unfortunately, the damage is still being done. With the frequent airings of his movies on television and with video rentals, he is helping to sell tobacco products to a new generation of viewers.

On a sunny day in September 1965, Greg stood only a few feet away from President Lyndon B Johnson in the White House Rose Garden. Johnson had invited him to witness the signing of the Arts and Humanities Act, which made the United States Government, for the first time in history, an official patron of the arts. Novelist John Steinbeck, violinist Isaac Stern, composer Leonard Bernstein, choreographer Agnes De Mille and Greg were among the founding members of the Arts Council. Other appointees included actress Elizabeth Ashley, sculptor David Smith, and film director George Stevens.

'It was a very special day for all of us,' Isaac Stern later wrote. 'Many of my colleagues were world-renowned artists, others well-known leaders in the arts. Each one had known exciting and moving occasions in their disciplines. But this day was unique, for we were joined together in an extraordinary mission. Our task was to help develop excellence in the arts and to make that excellence more widely available and accessible to all our people.'

Greg also conferred regularly with the newly formed staff of the Endowment for the Arts using his extensive contacts throughout the United States to rally support for the arts. With Veronique at his side, he shuttled back and forth to Washington, becoming a familiar figure in the White House. Lyndon B Johnson vividly recalled Greg's first appearance in the West Wing offices. His assistants and secretaries, who had remained calmly at their desks during visits of kings, chiefs of state and other dignitaries, practically trampled each other to look at Greg.

Down the street at the Endowment for the Arts, Greg was a favorite with just about everybody. The rank and file troops knew he and Isaac Stern were the standouts on the Council when it came to hard work. An attractive secretary with corn silk blonde hair, wide cheekbones and white Scandinavian complexion became quite smitten with him. She willingly put in long hours typing his correspondence. For her efforts, Greg responded with the utmost gallantry, greeting her with smiles and hugs and sometimes presenting her with bouquets of bright red roses. Watching the kind way he treated the secretary, celebrated architect William Periera, who was also a Council member and knew Greg from the actor's early days in Los Angeles, shook his head: 'You know, she looks just like his first wife. Greg will never get over his guilt for leaving Greta.'

Greg served six years on the National Arts Council. One of his first campaigns was to help strengthen the regional theater movement in the United States. With Veronique, he visited theaters in 26 cities. As a result of this scouting expedition, he wrote a report recommending that federal money should be allocated to 16 regional theaters. Among them were the Long Wharf Theater in New Haven, Connecticut, the A.C.T., then in Pittsburgh (it is now permanently located in San Francisco), the Arena Stage in Washington and the Boston Theater Company. 'It was small potatoes,' said Greg, '$10,000 to $15,000 for a theater, but it helped them elevate their standards.'

The standards sorely needed elevating. Andre Gregory, who had served as artistic director of the Theater of the Living Arts, in Philadelphia and the Inner City Repertory Company in Los Angeles, said at the time: 'I'm scared that the regional theater, by the time it is mature, will have bored the shit out of millions of people all over the country.'

Council members wrestled with the question of how the new funding agency for the arts should deal with film, a task that required some creativity and analyzing what the nation's needs were when it came to nurturing film as an art form. The Endowment's role was more obvious in music, where funds could be channeled to symphony orchestras, and in dance, where ballet companies were in need of support. But the highly commercial nature of filmmaking in the United States made the question of governmental assistance more complex. No area of the arts was closer to Greg's heart than the establishment of the American Film Institute.

Sitting with George Stevens Jr in the garden of his Georgetown home in Washington, Greg impressed Stevens with his precision in the use of the English language in drafting the mission statement for the American Film Institute and in the depth of his commitment and concern for rescuing and preserving classic films, so many of which were either lost or in some state of decay. Reflected Stevens: 'Idealism was never a hot ticket in Hollywood, and Gregory Peck's willingness to raise his voice and lend his stature to an institution devoted to the cultural worth of film and television gave much-needed strength to the fledging organization.'

Without question, Greg was riding high. His name posted on the masthead of a charity guaranteed a large turnout. People said he was so perfect he was scary. Even the most celebrated producers, directors, screenwriters and agents held him in awe. Responding to a phone message from Greg, an industry insider confessed: 'I couldn't call him back right away because my mouth was so dry I couldn't swallow to talk.'

At home on Cliffwood Drive in Brentwood, Greg sought tranquility in his sprawling brick ranch house and his garden. There were Transvaal daisies just outside the white-walled living room; plus walls of bougainvillea and deep rows of roses. Greg himself planted a vegetable garden where he grew beefsteak tomatoes, Japanese eggplant, cucumbers and zucchini. He rejoiced: 'Working in the garden is to me pure pleasure.'

Across town at Occidental college, Jonathan pretty much kept to himself. Fortunately, his good friend John Bell moved from New Zealand to Los Angeles and they spent time together. 'Jonathan wasn't much of a drinker,' said Bell. 'We'd have a couple of beers and that was about it. Once in a while he'd bunk on my couch just to get away from school and have someone to talk to.'

Both Jonathan and Bell owned guns and enjoyed target practice. Once they ventured into the desert near Palm Springs and practiced shooting tin cans. 'He liked guns,' said Bell. 'In fact, he was *dedicated* to his gun. He used to make his own bullets.'

When Bell turned 21, he decided to marry an American girl named Judy. Jonathan stood tall as his best man while Stephen and Carey Peck served as ushers. Greta went all out to give the couple a festive reception. But, once he was married, Bell found that with a wife and a job, he had embarked on a lifestyle quite different from that of Jonathan at college.

Jonathan called his friend one night and urged him to come to his apartment at Occidental, so Bell went, taking Judy along. They found Jonathan setting up a movie projector to watch *The Guns of Navarone*. 'I thought it was odd that he wanted to watch one of his father's movies,' said Bell. 'I'd seen it three or four times myself.' He wondered how many times Jonathan had viewed it. But Bell and his wife stayed the evening and watched the movie. They didn't want to leave Jonathan. His loneliness was palpable.

CHAPTER EIGHTEEN

Power Players

'. . . there's only going to be one actor to be President, and the right one – as I keep telling him, he would never listen to me – is Gregory Peck. Bad actor, but he'd be a helluva President, you know.'

Orson Welles

Greg was so adept at raising cash for his arts and humanitarian projects, that some didn't notice his secret weapon: Veronique. As his young wife moved into her 30s, she proved to be a formidable ally. Chic, funny, imaginative, and no-nonsense, she was a man's woman, one way or another. And her impact was not to be underestimated. Totally focused on Greg, she was a force to reckon with in the brittle, bitchy world of Los Angeles society.

Veronique had been practically mute during her first years in Hollywood, but she now occasionally talked to the press. She sounded genuine, rehearsed and reverential. 'Actors have so much talent to give; and they can't give it in their youth – they must work for their own futures,' Veronique told the *Los Angeles Times*. 'Gregory really wants to give back something of what America gave to him. He feels he was lucky, and he just wants to pass some of that luck on.'

While Veronique gave the outward appearance of deferring to Greg, she was proving highly adept at managing his affairs. Without any apologies to feminists, she asserted, 'I just participate in everything Greg does. I like it this way; I am not a career woman.' Wherever he went, she went. No matter if it was a 28-city barnstorm to stump for cancer research money, or a small dinner to raise money for the Motion Picture and Television Relief Fund. Whatever the endeavor, Veronique was at Greg's elbow, listening to him, reassuring him and generally giving him unconditional love – the life-blood of actors.

Rather than being called a housewife, Veronique preferred *maitresse de maison* in the French style. In any language, she was a high-powered professional partner. She kept track of the niggling details of their complex lives and sometimes played the heavy. 'They run in rhythm,' observed Harper Lee, who had become close friends of the Pecks during the filming of *To Kill a Mockingbird*. 'He doesn't begin to understand her feminine wiles, but he sure does appreciate them.'

Keeping a low profile, Veronique grew and arranged profusions of flowers; stage-managed exquisite luncheons and dinners; sat quietly while her husband gave fundraising speeches as well as advising him on motion picture scripts and the roles that would showcase him to best advantage. Composer Elmer Bernstein, a friend of the Pecks, considered her 'formidable.' He observed: 'I don't think she suffers fools gladly.' For himself, Greg said: 'Veronique is my subliminal sub rosa associate producer. She has a lot of very good ideas and I welcome her suggestions and advice. I like the way she dresses, too.'

She traveled well. Over the years the Pecks could be seen at Kennedy picnics on Cape Cod, Princess Grace's swimming parties in Monaco, and at little French bistros with Jacques Chirac. Stationed at Greg's side, Veronique enjoyed watching his effect on females: 'When women swoon over Gregory,' she claimed, 'it makes me very proud. I even give him pointers to perfect his technique.'

While Greta had resisted uprooting the children and living out of suitcases, Veronique packed at a few moments' notice; then turned a sterile hotel room into a home from home. For longer trips, she could move lock, stock and barrel, to England, France, Switzerland, Australia, or their other home in Cap Ferrat. She was keenly aware that a man as attractive as Greg should not be left alone for long. No matter how crazy his schedule, she traveled with him and tried to make him as comfortable as possible. In that way she became indispensable to him.

'We go wherever Greg goes,' explained Veronique. 'He wants his family around him.' The constant travel separated her from her two young children, Anthony and Cecilia. It took her away from the house she loved. But her life was built, by design, around the involvements of her much-sought-after husband.

Of course there was sniping and gossiping in the tight little world of Hollywood, but that went with the territory. Hedda Hopper scoffed at what she called Veronique's ambition to be 'a real big-star hostess.' And she shared with her readers what she heard about how the famous couple got together. 'Veronique pretended to be a writer so she could get a private interview with Gregory when he visited Paris with his first wife, Greta, and openly told a companion, Brenda Helser of *Diplomat* magazine: "I'm going to be the next Mrs Peck."'

It wasn't easy for Veronique to find her place in the tough sorority of entertainers' wives. In *The Club Rules*, a book about how to make it in Filmland, social critic Paul Rosenfield confides: 'I discovered the truly monstrous women in Hollywood are the stars' wives. Don't tangle with them. They never forget anything ever. And then they ghostwrite their husbands' autobiographies, and get even with everyone their husbands slept with, or got rejected by. They are the Greek chorus that speaks the truth – because they are protected by layers of club agents, attorneys, managers, business managers, maids, masseurs, manicurists, dress designers, and so on.'

Veronique was better looking and possessed more *savoir-faire* than most of the actors' mates. In this Gucci jungle, her worldliness may have made her the target of jealousy but it was also a great asset. She was intellectually concerned with public affairs and appreciated the arts. Plus, she was shrewder than most. She attended the other wives' tented fêtes, luncheons and charity balls and they, in turn, supported the causes she espoused. Quid pro quo is vital for turnout. 'All social life now is charity,' commented actress Anjelica Huston. 'I get 15 or 20 letters a day for everything from Yugoslavian dog illnesses to marathon diseases.'

Veronique's big moment came when she wooed space age Paris couturier André Courrèges to Los Angeles for a benefit to help the fledgling Inner City Repertory Theater, a downtown group which played, free, to 4,500 bussed-in teenagers every week. With a handful of her powerful friends, she pulled off the coup of the year by persuading Courrèges to fly right over the heads of New Yorkers with two assistants and six great trunks from his new collection to give his first showing in America. Barbra Streisand, Ethel and Robert Kennedy, Jack Lemmon, Steve Allen, Lucille Ball, Gene Kelly, Kirk Douglas, Charlton Heston, Fred Astaire, Milton Berle, Marlo Thomas, David Niven, and Shirley MacLaine – all of them, plus about 400 others, paid $250 per couple to do honor to Courrèges. For her efforts, Veronique was named Los Angeles Woman of the Year of 1966.

Now that his oldest son Jonathan had come of age, Greg was eager for him to make a successful transition to manhood. 'Every youngster,' Greg said, 'somewhere in his late teens, should take time out and test himself, climb a mountain, or take off for Outer Mongolia, or run in front of the bulls in Pamplona, or do something out of the ordinary. He should stand on his own two feet and test his stamina and his courage.'

The Peace Corps represented the kind of adventure that excited Greg's imagination. In his inaugural address for 20 January 1961, Kennedy, the founder of the Peace Corps, challenged a new generation of Americans 'to fight tyranny, poverty, disease, and war . . . To those people in the huts and villages across the globe struggling to break the bonds of mass misery, we pledge our best efforts to help them help themselves.'

In 1966, Jonathan Peck, having graduated from Occidental College, became one of the 15,000 volunteers who heeded the Kennedy call.

On 5 July 1966, Jonathan reported to Syracuse University for Peace Corps training to spend two years in Tanzania, one of the world's poorest countries. Blair Bolles, another volunteer, remembered walking into the area where the recruits signed in. A message scrawled on a blackboard caught his eye. 'Jonathan Peck. Call your father.' Then Bolles joined the group on the lawn outside.

'We were sitting outside waiting for some official greeting,' said Bolles. 'There was this guy sitting next to me. Very handsome. He looked just like Gregory Peck. It was spooky. Really spooky.'

Bolles mustered the courage to say: 'I wasn't going to ask you this, but I *have* to ask you. Are you related to Gregory Peck?'

'Yes,' Jonathan answered without elaborating.

Bolles replied, 'I can't tell whether you're shittin' me or not.'

They both laughed. Then Jonathan added, as though embarrassed by his relationship to a celebrity, 'Well, I can't help that.'

Jonathan liked chess. So did Bolles. 'I'm a total wood pusher. A putzer,' explained Bolles. 'Jonathan had a real knack for chess. He carried around a portable set with pegs on the bottom.' So the two young men played during their breaks in training.

With 85 per cent of Tanzanians living on the land, the Peace Corps volunteers were training to be agricultural workers and teachers. 'We were all so idealistic,' said Bolles, 'and enthusiastic. They told us to go to the shed and get hoes. Jonathan and I sprinted to get out tools. With his runner's training, he was really moving. Trying to keep up with him, I said, "This is probably the only time in our lives we'll race to pick up a hoe."'

In Tanzania, Jonathan was assigned to Kisiju, a little fishing village about 30 miles from Dar es Salaam, the vibrant and bustling commercial capital of Tanzania. Explained Peace Corps volunteer Carter Black, 'It wasn't far from Dar in terms of miles but it was really remote. Bush country. The boonies. You hardly ever saw a white person there.'

In his village, Jonathan taught English, science and agriculture. 'I had to get used to an entirely new way of life. I lived in a house made of mud, with no electricity or running water. It was quite an adjustment, but I'm happy I did it.'

Filled with pride, Greg boasted Jonathan learned Swahili in 90 days. He was happy his son had ventured so far and was seeing the world's great natural wonders such as Kilimanjaro. He quipped: 'The nearest I ever got to it was Beverly Hills [referring to the Fox sound stage where *The Snows of Kilimanjaro* was filmed].' Greg didn't visit Jonathan during his African sojourn.

Paul Sack was the Country Director in Tanzania for the Peace Corps. It was his job to check in with the volunteers in the villages and give them guidance and support. He found Jonathan to be an upstanding young man, though quiet. 'He was well spoken. Of course, he sounded just like his father. He was well composed. Wonderful manners. Everybody liked him.' Sack remembered Jonathan told him his father's age was 52.

'My God,' said Sack, who was 39, thinking of photographs of Peck. 'I wish I looked that good now.'

'Well, he works at it full time,' Jonathan replied. 'Very hard. A number of hours a day.'

Carter Black remembered Jonathan never complained about the bare bones lifestyle of rural Africa. Some volunteers didn't work out, he explained. They stepped on the toes of local officials and had to be sent home for diplomatic reasons. Still, Black picked up on an emotional delicacy in Jonathan, who did not talk about his feelings. 'You just sort of sensed there was a lot going on back there.'

On weekends, Jonathan ventured up to Dar es Salaam where he would hang out at the Kilimanjaro Hotel or the Bottleneck Bar at the New Africa Hotel, both popular meeting places with expatriates.

'The female volunteers thought he was terrific,' said Paul Sack. Blair Bolles watched with admiration as Jonathan persuaded a girl to come back to his primitive village with him. 'I remember being impressed because he lived in as remote a place as any of us.' He surmised: 'It was an advantage to look like a famous movie star.'

Similarly, Carter Black was sitting on the veranda of the New Africa one day with Jonathan and two American girls who had traveled up from South Africa. After Jonathan left, Black told the girls who Jonathan was. 'They just flipped out.'

Years later Jonathan confided to Nancy Stesin that during his Peace Corps stint in Africa he had an affair with a missionary's wife. She was an avid fan of his father. And when she climaxed during lovemaking with Jonathan, she cried out 'Gregory!'

After the first year, the Peace Corps volunteers in Tanzania were given a break. Most of them traveled around the country together. Greta visited Jonathan, who arranged to meet her at the airport in Dar es Salaam.

'He asked me to iron a shirt for him,' said Peace Corps volunteer Susan Casey, recalling it was a safari style. 'He wanted to be properly dressed for her.'

Jonathan spent the break traveling in India with Greta. The other Peace Corps volunteers in his group saw it as an indication that his lifestyle was on a different plane from theirs. Said Carter Black: 'It had an element of important people being whisked off in airplanes.'

But as the second year progressed, Susan Casey recalled Jonathan was under pressure from his father to do something significant with his life. There was talk Greg was using his pull with Lyndon B Johnson to get Jonathan into Annapolis. This is unlikely because Annapolis appointments are given to seniors in high school. In any case, following the Peace Corps Jonathan enrolled in the University of Virginia to study law. He dropped out after the first semester.

In the meantime, Greg's prestige continued its upward trajectory. Here he was, looking like Lincoln and sounding like God. So it's no wonder some of his Democratic colleagues started to view him as presidential timber. Wouldn't it be nice if a *real* movie hero – one with brains – took over the White House?

The buzz had started during the California campaign of 1964 when California State's Democratic incumbent Pat Brown was running against Republican Ronald Reagan. It was Brown who – unasked – threw Greg's name into the political ring. Recalled Greg: 'We had a whistle-stop tour, speaking from the observation platform of the train around California. And, on election night, when he lost to Ronnie Reagan, Governor Brown said, ruefully, I guess, "Hell, if they're going to run actors against us, maybe we should have run Greg Peck."'

Democratic leaders rejoiced at the idea. Pit Peck against Reagan. If Atticus Finch can take California, then the next stop's the Oval Office. Greg's colleagues inundated the press with positive comments about the star. Roger Stevens, chairman of the National Endowment for the Arts and former treasurer of the Democratic Party, said: 'They'll be lucky if they can get him.' Added a White House aide: 'He's first rate as far as giving of himself. He's a real doer, a favorite of the President, and our best circuit rider for culture.'

Some skeptics contended a background in government and law was better preparation for the highest office in the land than a career in films. Others saw no conflict. Jack Valenti, Chairman of the Motion Picture Association, said recently that some individuals believe actors and politicos spring from the same batch of DNA. To him, it made perfect sense: 'They are both addicted to power, anxious to please, always onstage, inhabiting an unpredictable, sometimes glamorous world, hooked on applause, lured by publicity, and usually reading from scripts written by someone else.'

Greg promptly retrieved his hat from the political ring. He told the press in no uncertain terms: 'I have had enough of the limelight to last a lifetime. I am not tempted by the idea of political power.' He wasn't playing coy. For a man as ferociously private as Greg, who recoiled from strangers invading his personal space and touching him, a man who insisted on controlling how he was perceived by the public, life in the White House fishbowl would have been pure hell.

At the same time, he was immensely drawn to power. While working on *The President's Country* (1966), a documentary about Lyndon B Johnson, Greg had an opportunity to get close to the chief executive. The film focused on LBJ's stomping ground, southwest Texas, showing the President's attachment to this land and particularly to his ranch; he was born down the road on a farm that had originally been settled by his grandfather. (Produced at a cost of $87,612, *The President's Country* was not shown in the United States. Copies of the film were sent to the USSR and to 97 other embassies.)

The Pecks were invited for weekends at the Johnsons' Texas ranch and must have seen some eye-popping sights while hob-nobbing in the Texas Hill Country down by the 'Purd'nallis' River. Stories were making the rounds in Washington of LBJ's terrifying hell-for-leather drives in his Lincoln Continental over his ranch as a back seat full of white-knuckled foreign dignitaries sat frozen while the President tossed out beer cans and shouted his observations about the great American way of life. (Said his assistant Roger Wilkins, 'Lyndon Johnson filled the air with his tongue.') Or of Johnson telling a visiting official from India, 'Hell, man, we don't worship cows in this country, we eat 'em.'

Veronique and Lady Bird Johnson were natural allies – since they both had the same agenda. Mrs Johnson sought to protect the President from members of the press who might not view LBJ in the same affectionate light in which she saw him. He was cut off from anyone who might find him lacking in the standard niceties.

Greg and Johnson seemed like an odd match, but they appreciated each other. To the backwoods president, Greg represented elegance and dignity. LBJ desperately needed to be associated with both. The respectful awe given John Kennedy was not to be accorded LBJ. He seemed unable to catch the country's imagination; there was little affection for his homespun personality. More than most presidents, he was the source of constant conjecture, appraisal, and gossip. Except as a political master, LBJ was a hard man to idolize. Perhaps he appeared too much the average person. Americans like in presidents the glamour and refinement that they may not have in themselves.

On Greg's part, he got a backstage view of the Presidency and a chance to glimpse the troubled mind of the leader of the free world. LBJ was a Shakespearean character, vulgar, cynical, consumed by raw ambition. A good houseguest, Greg never commented on the fact that Johnson was devoid of cultural or literary curiosity and had no interest in filling in these gaps in his education. Philip Gevelin writes in *Lyndon B. Johnson and the World* that the President 'cannot remember having read six books all the way through since college.' Johnson was eternally restless, seldom able to sit through a movie, but instead turning constantly to talk to others in the audience. He liked to sit around the living room in the evening with some cronies, drinking Scotch and rehashing his legislative triumphs. If displeased, he was given to bullyragging, temper outbursts and cruel sarcasm. Since Greg hung out with Sinatra, such histrionics were old hat.

Besides, the two men had many interests in common. Although Johnson's Great Society vision was being obscured by the frightening headlines about the war in Vietnam, Greg and LBJ were both ardent Democrats. They shared high hopes for the President's sweeping civil rights, social security, education, and housing programs. It would have been interesting to have watched the two of them huddled in conversation: Greg, with his characteristic ironing-board stiffness and LBJ crowding in close to him. Russell Baker, then White House correspondent for the *New York Times*, recalled it was hard to keep a physical distance from press-the-flesh Johnson. 'One of his favorite postures for conversation was leaning down over you and pressing his nose down toward yours until your spine was bent so far back that you couldn't think of anything but your aching vertebrae.'

As the 1960s progressed, the country continued on its long, strange trip. The terror and madness of Charles Manson, the regret and bitterness of Vietnam sent out signals that the country was teetering on the edge of chaos. Johnson became the focus of tremendous hostility. From the Oval Office, the President only had to look out his window to see anti-war demonstrators with their fists raised in protest shouting: 'Hey, hey, LBJ, how many kids did you kill today?'

Amid rising personal unpopularity, and in the face of the lingering war and racial strife at home, LBJ removed himself from political life with words that stunned the nation and the world: 'I shall not seek and I will not accept the nomination of my party as your president.'

On Johnson's last day in office, he awarded 20 Americans – including Greg – the Medal of Freedom, the highest civil honor the chief executive can bestow. Medal of Freedom recipients must have made exceptionally meritorious contributions to the security of the national interest of the United States, through world peace, cultural or other significant public or private endeavors. 'He is a humanitarian to whom Americans are deeply indebted,' the citation read.

Lyndon B Johnson lived for four years and two days after he left the White House. The Pecks returned to the Johnsons' Texas ranch after the President left office. Greg was startled to see Johnson's deterioration; he'd become a broken man. 'I saw a Shakespearean tragedy enacted before my eyes with a man I knew so well,' said Greg.

During this period of acclaim in the civic arena, Greg hadn't paid a great deal of attention to his film career. After *Arabesque*, he was not seen on the screen again until 1969 and unfortunately the four films released that year did little to further his popularity: *The Stalking Moon*, *MacKenna's Gold*, *The Chairman* and *Marooned*.

The Stalking Moon is the best of the three. It is a slow-paced, dark and moody Western, well directed by Robert Mulligan, who had worked so well with Greg on *To Kill a Mockingbird*. With the resurgence of old films through video, this film may garner new respect as time goes by. In critiquing it for *Films in Review*, Page Cook commented: 'The role of the retiring Army scout is ideal for Gregory Peck, whose ability to project moral strength plus compassion is one of the most inspiring things today's screen affords.' But the *New York Times* was more cutting: 'Peck is so grave and earnest it seems he must be thinking about his duties on the board of The American Film Institute, rather than on survival.'

In *MacKenna's Gold*, an overblown and overproduced Western, starring Greg and Omar Sharif, Greg is cast as the marshal who knows where a fabulous fortune in gold is hidden, and Sharif is the villain who wants to get his hands on it. Critics leapt to attack the film, and Western film expert, Brian Garfield, labeled it, 'The most expensive star-studded two-hour B-movie ever made, a gargantuan dud of absolutely stunning dreadfulness.'

The Chairman was a little far-fetched. Picture if you will Greg behind the Chinese bamboo curtain on a spy mission, with an explosive device sewn into his head ready to be detonated. *Look* was flat out exasperated with the star: 'I don't know what's been getting into Gregory Peck, but I do know what Gregory Peck's been getting into: *MacKenna's Gold* and *The Chairman*, a pair of drowsy pictures . . . Will he please read the scripts before getting into more movies like these?'

Next came *Marooned* (1969), an adventure story about astronauts stuck in space. NASA lent ample assistance to the *Marooned* production, including location shooting at Houston and Cape Kennedy and a commendation to the producers for the accuracy of the film.

Variety's preview cited the 'hokum' of the film's ending as fakery that could 'cool word of mouth enthusiasm.' Another critic called the timely arrival of the Russian space craft, 'deux-ex-space machina.' Pauline Kael faulted the casting: 'Who in his right mind would cast the three leads with Gregory Peck, Richard Crenna, and David Janssen, when anybody can see they're all the same man.' British writer David Shipman made Greg sound much too dignified to *ever* be considered for a racy part. He said of Greg: 'He seems to represent some sort of ethos, the sort of man you'd like as your bank manager or your kid's tutor . . .' The box-office was kinder. *Marooned* was ranked 33rd in earnings for 1970, with $4,100,000 qualifying it at the time as one of Greg's all-time hits. On Thanksgiving Day 1992, HBO's late-night 'Mystery Science Theater 3000' provided a comic commentary on *Marooned*, with jibes like, 'Hey look they're wearing jock straps on their heads' and 'Yeah and they double as flotation devices.'

Particularly biting was a jab from industry insider Stanley Chase of the *Hollywood Reporter*. Audiences had reached a saturation point according to Chase, fed up with seeing big names like Gregory Peck in all too repetitive formula roles. 'There are stars, I believe, who will keep people away from the theater,' maintained Chase. He claimed that in 1969 there were 'increasing instances where big names not only failed to perform their ordained magic at the box-office, but where their presence in a film actually discourages people from buying tickets.'

Greg's next two pictures added to the downward drift of his career: *I Walk the Line* (1970), in which he played a middle-aged sheriff hot for the body of a moonshiner's lusty daughter, and *Shootout* (1971), a remake of the 1934 film *The Lone Cowboy* and an imitation of *True Grit* (1969). Reviewing *I Walk the Line*, *Playboy* magazine made the interesting comment: 'Even though members of the Gregory Peck Fan Club may cavil at their hero's new image as a horny old lawman with a penchant for young stuff, Peck hasn't had so appealing and warm-blooded a role in years.'

There was no question in the minds of many. Hollywood's number-one-concerned-citizen needed to lighten up. 'Pompous!' sniped Marlon Brando in commenting on his acting colleague. Hubris was the classic defect of doomed characters in Aeschylean drama and Greg always had to be aware of it.

Tuesday Weld, his nubile co-star in *I Walk the Line* recounted playing a love scene with Greg in which she was in bed wearing a see-through garment. Greg was too inhibited to see through. He sat on the mattress with her, but was careful to keep on his 'businessman shoes'.

Years later, Rita Gam, Greg's romantic co-star in *Shootout*, had drinks with him and kidded: 'You remember when we were making *Shootout* and had to be in bed together all morning? We both leaped out of bed at the same time at the coffee break, and when my dresser handed me my bathrobe, you snorted, "A little diplomacy, please." I always wanted to know if that was because you had seniority.'

With a deep chortle, Greg asked her, 'Was I being pompous?'

Her reaction. No, just dear. In fact, despite his starchy side, she considered him one yummy hunk of masculinity. Gam came away from their meeting asking herself: 'Why aren't there more men like Gregory Peck?'

About this time, Greg was wondering why there weren't more women around like Audrey Hepburn and Ingrid Bergman. The feminist movement was catching fire by the late 1960s and some of the adherents scared the daylights out of him. In principle, Greg agreed with the feminist agenda. He favored the right to abortion, equal pay and the option to live with a man without benefit of marriage. He just felt a real woman should primp before she wrote her manifestos and burned her bras. What ever happened to leg shaving, perfume dabbing and gardenias in the hair? And to tell the truth, Greg wasn't much of a liberal when it came to dirty work. Pressed by *Coronet* magazine, he confessed: 'I haven't washed a dish since I was in college and I'm not planning on it, and I've never changed a diaper. I think it's a bad part for a man.'

There was nothing he dreaded more than matching wits with a hardcore feminist. 'Usually it's at a cocktail party with a mixed bag of people, and usually it's crowded and noisy and people don't know each other well,' explained Greg. 'There's usually a liberated female intellectual with horn-rimmed glasses. They usually have wrought-iron bracelets, and some sort of home-craft jewelry. They have a tendency to wear gunny sacks. They wear their hair very slick and parted in the middle. They usually graduated from one of the Eastern girls' colleges, and I've found myself pinned in the corner by these liberated females and I tell you this terrifies me. But they want to get right to the point – no fooling around, no frills, no preliminaries, no small talk. They realize it's a fleeting encounter and, by God, they're going to get it out of you, what it is that makes you tick. Well, I never have told them, and I'm not about to. I don't know whether they're man-haters or whether man is the enemy with them, but it just isn't a very friendly way to get to know somebody.'

Greg was given an opportunity to unbend. Jack Benny invited him to perform on his new variety show. There he was singing 'Steamboat Whistles Blowing' as one-third of a potential top-40 group called Two Bushels and a Peck and doing the old soft-shoe. A reporter for TV watched the dress rehearsal. He said: 'I have never seen a performer so nervous. He seemed absolutely terrified of the studio audience, and finally relaxed only when he heard the audience laughing.'

On the home front, Jonathan was casting about trying to find a career that suited him. Stephen, next in line, was less of a perfectionist than Jonathan, more conciliatory, and more emotionally stable. A graduate of Northwestern University, Stephen had been a US Army artillery officer in Vietnam. 'He was in combat the whole time,' Greg said. 'I was sleepless until he came back. I see no dichotomy in love for my son and the fact that I admire him for serving his country in Vietnam, and my philosophical objection to our whole policy there.' Carey, popular and more relaxed than his father, studied government at Georgetown University. Following in Jonathan's footsteps, Carey also joined the Peace Corps, going to Senegal and working on sewerage disposal projects. 'He's becoming,' Greg joked, 'one of the great latrine specialists of our time.'

To protect the two younger teenage children, Tony and Cecilia, from the shallow values of the Los Angeles movie set, Greg and Veronique enrolled them in Aiglon, a first-class British boarding school set high in Swiss Alps, 4,000 feet above the Rhone Valley. The lure for many globe-trotting families is the 'portable diploma' or International Baccalaureate (IB) which is well regarded by universities in most countries.

Greg explained that he and Veronique waited until the children were 14 because 'we wanted to enjoy their childhood.' 'We shipped them off, with their consent, I must say,' said Greg, 'to get them out of Beverly Hills.' He added: 'I think we did the right thing. Aiglon has an English headmaster. It is a bit like Gordonstoun, though not quite so severe. They do have cold showers in the morning and plenty of outdoor sports. They also study very hard and learn French and German – international bunch of kids.'

'They're fine kids,' Greg said of his brood, 'but they don't talk to me much about life.' He might have given a clue why they avoided confiding in him when he said: 'Money doesn't mean anything to them.' Or, at another time, 'My kids didn't have it as tough as I did when I was young.'

Of course they didn't. The impact of the Depression is readily identifiable in those of Greg's generation. They turn off unused lights, save pennies and nickels in a jar and avoid throwing food away. 'I have a personal coming-of-age test,' said Greg. 'When my boys reach the age of 18, I give them each $50. It's up to them to go as far away as they can for as long as possible to see if they can stand on their own feet. When I was 18, I got from California to New York City on $50. But so far, the long-distance record for my sons is California to Mexico. Maybe $50 doesn't go as far as it used to.'

For one thing, the Peck children had perhaps heavier baggage than their old man. Stephen Humphrey Bogart, once wrote: 'The heaviest thing I have ever had to carry is my father's fame.'

Veteran actor Sam Jaffe noted: 'I've lived with celebrities and with stars, great people, great directors, and I can tell you that the children always have to suffer. You just cannot live up to the reputation of a parent who becomes successful. To have to follow in those footsteps is a very big handicap.'

As the 1960s came to an end, Jonathan joined the speechwriting staff of John V Tunney of California who was making a run for the US Senate. A 36-year-old politician, Tunney cavorted with the Kennedys and was very much in their style. His father, prizefighter Gene Tunney, was a legend in the sport. And Tunney, like Jonathan, suffered by comparison. 'The lightweight son of a heavyweight champ,' he was called. Still, his family fame and his Kennedy connections made his campaign a hot draw for young people. Two women who would have a deep impact on Jonathan's life also joined the staff. Their names were Nancy Stesin and Connie Farrow.

'You'll never guess who that guy is,' Jamie Auchincloss, half-brother of Jackie Kennedy said to Nancy Stesin. Auchincloss was motioning to Jonathan who was sitting at a desk typing. 'That's Gregory Peck's son.' Auchincloss saw a kindred soul in Jonathan because they both struggled under the weight of a famous name. 'You have to watch what you do,' said Auchincloss. 'For example, you're careful not to have a couple of drinks and drive fast because if you're picked up for speeding, your name gets in the papers and it reflects on the family.'

Nancy looked over at Jonathan and was immediately smitten. 'He was gorgeous,' she said. 'I was just drooling.' After they got to know each other, she fell hard for his dark sexy looks, deep voice and athletic body. Soon they were intimate. Because of his extraordinary resemblance to his father, she found the experience unsettling. She admitted: 'It was hard to distinguish between loving Jonathan and not thinking about who his father was.'

Jonathan lived in a guest room in a wing of Greg's house in Brentwood. Although he had a separate entrance to his quarters, it struck Nancy as odd that a man in his mid-20s wouldn't want to strike out on his own. At the same time, she enjoyed her visits to the Peck household and observing the relationship of Greg and Veronique. 'They did their dance,' said Nancy, in describing a couple very caught up with each other. 'Greg could be cold to Jonathan and his other children. His loyalty was to Veronique. She ruled the roost.'

Nancy called any mistakes Greg might have made with Jonathan 'benign neglect'; he was too focused on his busy life to stand back for a while and let his son take center stage. But the closer she became to Jonathan, the more she realized how difficult his life was. 'He was a C+ or B person in an A+ world,' said Nancy. 'Not that he wasn't intelligent. He just didn't have the goal direction of the hard chargers.' For example, some years before, Veronique's half-brother, Cornelius, had moved in with the Pecks along with Veronique's mother. Cornelius went to Beverly Hills high school, then to Harvard. Now he was studying to become an orthopedic surgeon. Nancy sensed that although Jonathan liked Cornelius, he felt he was the kind of high-achieving son his father wanted. Although Greg had floundered in science classes while at Berkeley, he always liked the idea of being a doctor. 'He couldn't take it,' Nancy said of the unspoken comparison. 'I don't think Greg meant any harm to Jonathan, but a lot of harm was done.'

Although Nancy loved Jonathan and wanted to marry him, she gradually realized he was emotionally immature for someone in his mid-twenties and 'didn't know boundaries as far as women were concerned.' At work one day, he told her he had a crush on the campaign manager's wife. 'Don't be ridiculous,' Nancy told him. 'She's not available.' Then she found out Jonathan was sleeping with Connie Farrow, an intensely bright Berkeley graduate who also worked on the campaign. But what really caused an upheaval in their relationship was when Jonathan knocked on the door of Nancy's apartment one Friday night. When she didn't answer right away, he walked across the courtyard and rang the bell of a young woman who was a friend of hers. After a brief conversation, he said: 'Would you like to have dinner with me? Then, maybe, we could spend the weekend together.'

'You know I'm Nancy's friend,' the girl said outraged, slamming the door.

After Nancy's anger subsided, she decided she would simply have to be a loving friend to Jonathan rather than look upon him as a potential husband. In contemplating the incident with her neighbor in the courtyard, she said: 'As mad as I was with him, I still understood. He was very, very lonely. It was heartbreaking. He was so alone.' Now that their relationship was on another level, Jonathan told Nancy about a woman he dated whom he used to bring back to the Peck house when nobody was there. The woman insisted on making love in Greg's bed.

Nancy's role as 'loving friend' came quickly into play when Tunney campaign worker Connie Farrow committed suicide. A deeply disturbed Jonathan came to Nancy for solace. But there was little she could do. He told her: 'Connie called me the night she killed herself but she couldn't reach me.'

As the months went by, Jonathan persisted in his state of emotional upheaval. 'His reaction to her death was one of absolute devastation,' said Nancy. 'I don't think he ever got over it.' Nancy voiced her concerns to Madame Passani, Veronique's mother. Madame Passani was a straight shooter who smoked Gauloise cigarettes and took a genuine interest in Jonathan. Looking for a solution, the two women visited Nancy's psychiatrist. His questions only pointed up the severity of the situation. Nancy concluded Jonathan was 'an accident waiting to happen.'

Shortly thereafter, Jonathan settled on a career direction. 'Politics was exciting,' he said of the Tunney campaign, 'but what I found more to my liking was working with the press.' He added enthusiastically, 'I made up my mind to get a job as a news man.' So he moved to New York and worked for United Press International in New York for 18 months.

During this time, Greg decided to produce, rather than act in, a modest movie about nine anti-war resisters who staged one of the era's most dramatic protests, dousing a bonfire of draft records with homemade napalm at a Selective Service Center in Catonsville, Maryland, burning 387 files of potential draftees. The play *The Catonsville Nine* was written by ex-Jesuit Daniel Berrigan who with his brother Philip, also a former priest, helped inspire a generation of anti-war dissenters.

As a writer as well as a protester, Daniel Berrigan saw the dramatic possibilities inherent in the situation: 'The air of the court was charged with grandeur, with damnation, with bathos,' he wrote of the trial. 'Spite, blindness, danger, gentleness, the interplay of wit and dim wit, an overriding sense that here, in one place almost against our will, by choices that bore us headlong, the tragic ingredients of the war were being pressed into a single concentrate. Was it named hemlock?'

In Greg's eyes the Berrigan brothers, the nuns and teachers involved in the 1968 destruction of draft files in Catonsville, MD, were patriots and firebrands cut from the same cloth as early American colonists. 'The sanctity of human lives, both Vietnamese and American, is more sacred to them than the laws they broke,' he said.

Greg's production of *The Trial of the Catonsville Nine* (1972) was replete with human ironies and odd coincidences. The play was originally produced for the New York stage by Leland Hayward, Greg's first agent. Assisting on the film was Greg's son, Stephen, a 25-year-old combat veteran by this time, then studying at the

University of Southern California. Greg noted: 'He came back safely, thank God. But he said it was the most dehumanizing experience of his life and we didn't belong over there.'

Greg wanted a quality movie. He had no intention of making popular entertainment, and he set a low budget of $300,000, half of his own money, the rest donated by friends. Preserving the drama format, the movie was shot in just eight days at the old David O Selznick studio. Sneak previews in college settings such as Berkeley and Santa Barbara, California, provided encouragement, but in Covina, California, 200 people walked out, some muttering obscenities.

Greg recalled he was almost literally carrying cans of film around town, looking for distribution. 'I thought to take it to Robert Evans and Frank Yablans, because they had two enormous hits, *The Godfather* and *Love Story*. They agreed to see it. Bob Evans was ecstatic. He said: "This is shameful, this is a blunder of historic proportions. Everyone must see this picture," and Yablans said, "Not with my *Godfather* money."' Finally Don Rugoff's Cinema V distributed the film for a few screenings in only five cities, after which it folded.

Greg noted wryly: 'As Sam Goldwyn said, if people don't come to the box-office, you can't stop them.'

Greg never regretted making it: 'You see, I've come to love the process of putting a film together, because as a producer I meddle and take part and contribute and have more to do with the whole operation than obviously I could have as only an actor.'

The film had mixed reviews. Said *New York* magazine: '*The Trial of the Catonsville Nine* works on many levels, as a courtroom drama, as a contemporary document, as a statement of conscience, and as a challenge to your own courage.' *TV Guide* said: 'The play itself doesn't hold up well on screen, with the actors seeming to do more preaching than acting.'

Soon after making the film, Greg learned that his public opposition to the war had earned him a place on Nixon's infamous 'enemies list,' along with Jane Fonda, Paul Newman and other Liberals. A previous grudge could also have helped put Greg on the list. The President might have remembered Greg's vocal support of

Helen Gahagan Douglas, wife of actor Melvyn Douglas and a tireless New Deal Democrat, who ran unsuccessfully against Nixon in 1950 for the US Senate. In one of the nastiest campaigns on record, Nixon characterized Douglas as 'soft on Communism.' In fact, he accused her of being a conduit through which decisions made by Josef Stalin in the Kremlin flowed to the US Congress. In any case, the distinction of making the 'enemies list' caused wary backers of Greg's projects in Hollywood to renege on a handshake agreement to make three films.

In Europe the film was well received, and many cities praised the free atmosphere in America which allowed the film to be made without censorship.

Daniel Berrigan, who was in the audience at Cannes when it showed there, received a standing ovation. 'I'd screened the film for Dan Berrigan the week he got out of jail,' reflected Peck. 'It was an experience to show a man a film that he's written, that's about himself, that is going to make him and his views known perhaps to the whole world. I wanted him to like it and he did, thank God!'

At this point, Jonathan had returned to Los Angeles and found a job at KNX radio, a CBS affiliate. 'I'm 28, single, have a small apartment and I'm delighted to be working at KNX,' he told reporter Hal Evans. 'Someday I hope to do on-the-air work as a field reporter and anchorman.'

Nancy Stesin ran into Jonathan one night at a Baskin Robbins in West Hollywood. He invited her for a hamburger and told her about his apartment. 'He was so proud of it,' Nancy said. 'And boasted it had a waterbed.' They returned to his place and made love. The spark between them was still there.

Once they started seeing each other again, however, Nancy realized Jonathan's problems had deepened. He didn't drink excessively or do drugs; nonetheless, he was a lost soul. 'It wasn't hubris. It was a lack of ego,' she said. 'He had no self-confidence.' Plus, he was still tormented by the suicide of Connie Farrow.

Almost three years separate *Shootout* and Greg's subsequent feature *Billy Two Hats* (1973), also a Western but considerably more interesting, although not destined to do much better business. It was made entirely in Israel, where the rugged landscapes easily pass for the Wild West, and it presents Greg in his first real non-glamorous character acting – as a bewhiskered old bandit of Scottish birth and brogue.

Panned by the critics, *Billy Two Hats* quickly disappeared from view. Greg worried. 'I made four or five turkeys in a row before I realized that all I was accomplishing was going downhill with pictures like *Shootout* and *Billy Two Hats, Marooned* and *MacKenna's Gold.*' Now 58, he tried to stay upbeat, hoping that his career hadn't permanently tanked: 'People remember us for our best work, thankfully,' mused Greg. 'No one comes up and says, "I hated you in *I Walk the Line.*"'

For his next entry as a producer, Greg chose to make a film of Robin Lee Graham's adventures sailing a 23-foot sloop around the world. The Californian was a teenager when he undertook the voyage and later put it into book form. The celluloid result, *The Dove* (1974) is a beautiful travelogue, thanks largely to the superb Swedish cinematographer Sen Nykvist – but it is short of excitement. Although it didn't do well on its American release, it broke house records in South Africa and Japan and some other parts of the world.

Nancy Stesin was working at the Israeli consulate. Since *Billy Two Hats* was the first American Western made in Israel, Greg was in and out of the consulate for meetings related to the film. Greg and Nancy talked on several occasions. She showed him a screenplay treatment she'd written about herself, Jonathan and Connie Farrow. The story revolved around three young idealists working on a political campaign and one of them commits suicide. The character based on Jonathan was a very unhappy person. Greg became intensely interested and asked to read it. 'I knew it was amateurish,' said Nancy. 'And I realized Greg didn't have a professional interest in the project. But I could see he was worried about Jonathan and his reason for reading it was to try and figure out what was bothering him.'

Increasingly troubled, Jonathan moved back in with Greg and Veronique in Brentwood. At 30, he didn't have a spouse, a child, a house or a realistic career plan – and it bothered him. His goal was to be a television news anchorman but he was getting started late in the game. He lacked the sterling journalistic credentials as well as the hard-charger mindset required to land a top spot in television. Large numbers of journalists constantly angled for these prestigious and big salaried jobs. His brother Stephen concluded: 'Jonathan's greatest problem was that he set goals which were too high. Part of the reason he set such high goals was that he was the son of a famous man.'

At this point, Jonathan started seeing Micki Rosten (now Katz). Like Nancy, she was impressed by his extraordinary good looks. Micki also appreciated his exquisite clothes and manners. 'My mother loved him,' she said, adding he projected the air of someone 'to the manor born.' But he also seemed sad and he gave her the impression that his father couldn't communicate with him very well and treated him like a lackey. Upon reflection today, Rosten realizes that Jonathan was depressed at the time. It wasn't that he wasn't loved. 'He had a disease,' she said by way of explanation. When Jonathan started seeing a recently divorced woman with two small children, Micki ended their relationship.

Jonathan landed a job at KCOY, a television station in Santa Maria, a small town about 100 miles north of the coastal city of Santa Barbara. He was a rookie on-air news reporter. His 'beat' was the entire city of Santa Barbara. In Santa Maria, he rented a $150-a-month apartment. He was frequently strapped for cash. Sometimes Greg helped him out. In fact, Greg offered to pay for psychiatric sessions. Jonathan went a few times and let it drop.

KCOY was a small station that made big demands on its reporters. 'I just heard this,' a local news manager at a station like KCOY would say. 'Are you on your way?' If it's a fire, 'Did you get any big flames?' Jonathan was required to turn in three stories a day. 'No story? Well write it as best you can.' The pressure was incredible. He had first to line up the stories – build up contacts with police, the town's clergymen, the hospital and the University of California and at the same time keep his finger on the pulse of the Santa Barbara social and artistic set. Bloody crimes, fires and accidents, teary-eyed victims, cute kids and animals, street protests, whatever, he was expected to be on the spot ahead of the competition. Then he had to set up his camera and tripod and report and film. Come hell or high water, he had to be sure the three stories were on the Santa Maria bus at 1 p.m. every day. It's not a bad job if you have tremendous energy and thrive on pressure.

Incapacitated by depression and anxiety, Jonathan was sinking fast. On top of that, his father didn't fully understand his situation. A stringer is a low man on the totem pole. He has to justify his existence every day.

'Can't you tell them you need some help,' asked Greg, 'that they must find you a legman? That they should get someone to write for you, scrounge for you, or just work the camera?'

'No,' said Jonathan. 'They won't. This is small station on a budget.'

By the summer of 1975, Greg was long overdue for an extended period of leisure. As was the custom of Greg and Veronique, the couple flew to Cap Ferrat for the summer. Here Greg embraced the good life at its most sublime: Mediterranean food, bouquets of flowers, the sun on his back, swimming, taking strolls and listening to music

Greg also kept up his heavy schedule of compulsive fast reading, delving into Dostoyevsky and Trollope and devouring reams of newspapers. Veronique believed Greg could keep so many interests going because he 'has intense concentration. He can focus totally on one thing, then shut it off and go to something else.' The difficulty with children – even grown ones – is that they need a parent's attention when they need it, not necessarily when the parent has time.

Then came the nightmare phone call. Jonathan had shot himself in the head with a .44 rifle. The news ripped Greg's heart in two. His 31-year-old son was gone. There was no note.

CHAPTER NINETEEN

Picking up the Pieces

'It's just the worst thing that can happen to anyone. It's on your mind every day. You never get over a thing like that. Something will remind you that he ought to be here, and he isn't, that he impulsively took the wrong way out.'

Gregory Peck on Jonathan's death

Greg and Greta buried Jonathan in a private ceremony at Forest Lawn Memorial Park in the Hollywood Hills. After 21 years apart, they were now united in profound grief. Veronique and the four surviving children shared their anguish.

Although there was no indication of foul play, Greta never believed Jonathan committed suicide. 'She thought it was an accident,' said John Bell. Years later, she confided to Tommy Hinkkanen that she suspected he had been murdered. After all, Jonathan bought groceries the day he died, she reasoned. Why would he do that if he were planning to leave this world? And the absence of a note. Didn't that say something?

Greg accepted the county coroner's report. Death occurred at 3.30 in the afternoon. It was the result of a massive skull fracture. A .44 caliber revolver lay close to the body. When Jonathan failed to submit his news stories to KCOY-TV, a co-worker came by his apartment and discovered the bloody scene.

Every suicide is a mystery. Jonathan left many people wondering why such a decent, kind, handsome, and *fortunate* young man would kill himself.

Somebody likened his departure to the Richard Cory poem by Edward Arlington Robinson.

Whenever Richard Cory went downtown,
We people of the pavement looked at him:

He was a gentleman from sole to crown,
Clean favored, and imperially slim.

And he was always quietly arrayed,
And he was always human when he talked;
But still he fluttered pulses when he said,
'Good morning' and glittered when he walked.

The poem goes on to say: 'we thought he was everything to make us wish we were in his place.' And then: 'Richard Cory, one calm summer night, / Went home and put a bullet through his head.'

In cases of death by accident, illness, old age, alcoholism, and homicide, the family knows what killed the deceased. They have something specific on which to focus their feelings of guilt or anger. With suicide, however, loved ones often become preoccupied with wondering how the suicide could have happened. In large part, Greg blamed himself. All those years of striving, the separations from the children while he was in Europe, now yielded bitter fruit. Echoing the situation of many movie star parents, he admitted: 'When you're working you have to get out at five in the morning. When you come home at the end of the day you are too tired to talk to your children. You can't give them the time they need and all you really have to give them is time. If not you lose them.'

When it was suggested that there was poor rapport between Greg and his son, Veronique spoke out. 'Jonathan and his father were very close. If anyone tells you they had a bad relationship it's not true.' Then she added: 'The autopsy showed that Jonathan had a serious heart condition [premature arteriosclerosis]. We think that maybe the oxygen flow to his brain was cut down and – in an irrational moment – he shot himself not really realizing the importance of what he was doing.'

Premature arteriosclerosis is rare in a man of 31, particularly in one such as Jonathan who was in excellent physical condition. 'I've never been sick a day in my life,' he told Nancy Stesin in the period before he died. But one thing was certain: Jonathan had been in a precarious mental state.

Years after the suicide of Connie Farrow, he continued to brood about her. Suicide experts caution about a ripple or copycat effect. For this reason, newspaper editors often underreport such deaths, not giving the method and not including a photograph of the deceased for fear of over-dramatizing the act. More recently, Jonathan had been rejected by a newly separated woman who refused to move in with him. So he was depressed. Although most depressed people are not suicidal, most suicidal people are depressed. Depression can twist thinking. A person in a state of mind like Jonathan's should not have had easy access to a gun. Most US suicides result from gunshots.

Thirty is a critical age. It can be especially cruel for a man living in the shadow of a famous father. Psychiatrist Dr L James Gold said that when the children of famous parents realize their goals are unobtainable, they experience a sense of loss that confirms their feelings of hopelessness. 'The result is severe depression and it can be suicidal.' Dr Gold pointed out that many of these kids see their celebrity parents as 'awesome supermen or superwomen,' and not as ordinary human beings.

Angst is so widespread among the descendents of superstars that it is referred to as the Paradise Syndrome. A significant number of Hollywood offspring take their own lives. The son of producer Ray Stark jumped out a window as did the daughter of Jennifer Jones and David O Selznick. Marlon Brando's son murdered his half-sister, Cheyenne's, lover. She compounded the Brando misery by hanging herself. Louis Jourdan's son committed suicide by drowning. Carol Burnett's daughter, Charles Boyer's son, Carroll O'Connor's son – all took their own lives. In 1978, Paul Newman's son, Scott, overdosed on pills and alcohol. Reflecting on the tragedy, Newman said: 'There are about 180,000 liabilities in having me as a father. The biggest one is that there is always an element of competition between children and their parents.'

As Jonathan knew only too well, the children of famous parents are treated differently by their peers. Mary Francis Crosby, the daughter of crooner Bing Crosby, explained the pressure to Joey Berlin when he interviewed her for his book *Toxic Fame:* 'Being a celebrity's kid either goes one of two ways. You either become a mess or you become very strong. The questions aren't any different. 'Who am I? What am I? Where do I want to go with my life?

'All of those things everybody has to deal with. The only difference is, if you're a celebrity's child you have to deal with those questions earlier. If you don't establish a very strong sense of your own identity, people will project on you what they want, as so-and-so's son or daughter.'

Jonathan's friends reeled from the news. They asked themselves, why didn't anybody pick up on the signs of this impending catastrophe? John Bell was shocked and devastated. He sought out a doctor friend of the Pecks. 'Why did he do this?' he pleaded. The doctor alluded to the huge chasm between Jonathan's achievements and Greg's. 'He just couldn't do it like his old man.'

The first thought that came to Paul Sack's mind, having known Jonathan in Tanzania was: 'Why did he choose a profession like television broadcasting which somewhat put him in competition with his father?' Susan Casey, another friend from Peace Corps days, became angry with Greg when she heard the news. She recalled the pressure Greg put on Jonathan to move forward in a respectable career.

Following Jonathan's death on 27 June 1975, Nancy Stesin wrote a condolence letter to Greg. On 6 August she received a reply with a handwritten postscript from Greg: 'I'm sorry. I know this must have been very painful for you too. Love, G.' The words 'have been' struck Nancy as odd. Jonathan's death was so recent. She showed the note to her psychiatrist who told her Greg had already pigeonholed the tragedy in his mind, placing it in the past. But, of course, he hadn't. Nor had Nancy. For her, Jonathan's memory is still alive today. Occasionally, she'll rent *Gentleman's Agreement* because Greg's physical appearance in that film reminds her so much of Jonathan. Laments Nancy: 'I've never gotten over Jonathan.'

In the months that followed, Greg sank into a horrible depression. America venerated him as Atticus Finch, the splendid role model for fatherhood. And somehow he had failed his son. He brooded obsessively about things he could have done differently. He anguished: 'Whatever the causes were, whatever the mistakes his mother and I have made, whatever influences he was subject to that made it apparently impossible for him to withstand that particular set of pressures at that particular time I don't know. But my regret that I will live with for the rest of my life was that I was in France instead of here. I felt certain that had I been in Los Angeles he would have called me, because he often dropped in to talk things over with me. If only he could have picked up the phone and said, "Things are just bearing down so much on me." I would have said, "Quit your job. We'll go off to Tahiti."'

Veronique was afraid that it might break him completely. The bereaved are often at risk of suicide themselves. 'She was his rock,' said talk show host Larry King. It was she more than anybody who brought him a feeling of hope. Veronique told Michael Freedland it was 'a great expression of his love for her, for Tony and Cecilia' that Greg came through it.

Although he continued to be miserable about Jonathan, gradually Greg's life again became full of friends and projects and aspirations. Part of his mending process was to become an outspoken advocate for gun control legislation.

Religion also played a role. Greg was not a traditional orthodox Catholic. This powerful conservative branch of Roman Catholicism holds to papal authority and historic church doctrine. Rather, Greg was a modern, liberal Catholic who took a pro-choice stance on abortion and supported gay rights. But, in addition to the heartbreak involved, the issue of suicide must have troubled him on a spiritual level. After all, Jonathan was a creation of God. It was not solely his life to do with as he saw fit. To kill oneself is to deny God.

Greg's religion was one of broad sympathies and high moral passion. He looked to the Bible for guidance in the immense mystery of death and creation. 'Faith is a force,' he said, 'a powerful force. To me, it's been like an anchor to windward – something that's seen me through troubled times and some personal tragedies and also through the good times and success and the happy times.'

Although his beliefs and those of the Catholic hierarchy were not in sync, Greg, nonetheless, found strength in the structure and rituals of the church. Having once considered becoming a priest, he liked and respected the clergy. He counted his introduction to Pope John Paul II as a high point in his life. Without reservations, Greg swore: 'He impresses me more than any other man I've ever met and I've met a lot.'

The Pope came to Washington during Jimmy Carter's presidency in the 1970s, and the Pecks were among 500 prominent Americans invited to the White House to meet him. 'My wife and I happened to be seated on one of the aisles,' Greg said, 'and the Pope came right down and he saw me and smiled. The smile was genuine, not a politician smile, the *practiced* smile. He shook hands with me and went on.

'And then Carter said, "Hello, Gregory, what are you doing here?" and I said, "Well, Mr President, you invited me." He said, "Just a minute" – and damned if he didn't run after the Pope, grabbing him by the arm and pulled him back. He said, "Your Excellency, this is one of our best-known, most-loved American film actors." And he looked at me, ah! – there was a glimmer as if somehow he must have seen me in a movie. His eyes widened and he took me in his arms. And he sort of grabbed me by the elbow and said, "God bless you, Gregory. God bless you in your mission." And he went on.'

Greg's next spiritual encounter was decidedly more bizarre. His agent, George Chasin, presented him with the script of *The Omen* (1976) and inquired: 'Would you be interested in playing the Devil's foster dad?' This was a tale of Satan's return to earth.

You betcha. Greg had a poor run of movies behind him. He'd also become exasperated with producing movies that lost money, so he perused the script and gave a quick thumbs up. 'I remember reading it and thinking, this is going to be a commercial success, but I didn't know it would be that kind of blockbuster. I really thought it would be a good paperback thriller. The success is almost obscene.'

The time was right for satanic cinema. *The Exorcist* (1973) had changed the face of horror. Plus, the very late 1960s birthed *Rosemary's Baby* (1968), a creepy classic about a woman who is stalked by a satanic cult. So a movie about raising the Antichrist looked like a good bet.

In *The Omen*, Robert and Kathy Thorn (Peck and Lee Remick) give birth to a child. Is it the spawn of Satan? No. It's actually stillborn. But Robert decides to swap an orphaned boy for his own lost son without letting anyone know. Switching kids is risky at best. Robert discovers he's made one hell of a mistake. Little Damien doesn't seem like a devil, but something's amiss. Maybe it's the eyes, little soulless gray coals. Maybe it's the steel-melting stare. Perhaps it's the fact that his nanny hangs herself in his honor. Things grow more intriguing as Rottweilers show up around the boy, as well as an evil replacement nanny. Then, Robert comes to realize his son is *really* different.

The documentary *666: The Omen* provides an intriguing glimpse into the casting of the child to play the pivotal role of Damien, the Antichrist. Director Richard Donner instructed Harvey Stephens: 'When I say "Action," I want you to fight me as hard as you can, and quit when I yell, "Cut."' Donner yelled, 'Action,' and Stephens launched into a barrage, kicking him in the testicles and failing to stop even after Donner yelled, 'Cut!' At that moment Donner knew he'd found his Antichrist. 'He was a good kid,' Donner confides 'but I would not want him to be my own.'

Though Damien was no little darling, it must have been excruciatingly difficult for Greg to run through scenes in which he held and caressed a small boy when so little time had elapsed since Jonathan's death. He admitted he thought of Jonathan 'every day, every hour.'

On the first day of shooting, Greg sent Lee Remick two dozen roses with the note: 'At last we get to work together on such a jolly little subject.' The movie was shot primarily in England with other units filming in Jerusalem.

Like Greg, Remick was more interested in the craft of acting than in the attention generated by stardom. An elegant Yankee beauty who started out playing saucy flirts, she was soon billed as 'America's answer to Brigitte Bardot.' Her ascent as an actress was swift and distinguished. At age 22 she sizzled as the drum majorette in *A Face in the Crowd* (1957); then she attained stardom in *Anatomy of a Murder* (1959), and, maturing as an actress, was nominated as Best Actress three years later for her role in *Days of Wine and Roses* (1962).

The Omen caused an outcry from churches and theologians. With some justification, the latter group attacked the movie's suppositions, especially since they were based on a non-existent source, a doggerel from a fictitious 'book of revelations,' which sounded enough like the Bible's Book of Revelations to unsuspecting patrons.

> When the Jews return to Zion
> And a comet rips the sky
> And the Holy Roman Empire rises
> Then you and I must die.
> From the eternal sea he rises
> Creating armies on either shore,
> Turning man against his brother
> 'Til man exists no more.

Despite some reviewers dismissing the story as sheer hokum, *The Omen* was a huge, huge hit. In its first weekend, the film grossed $4,500,000. By January 1977, *The Omen* had earned $27,851,000. That placed it third behind *One Flew Over the Cuckoos's Nest* ($56,500,000) and *All the President's Men* ($29 million). By 1989, the film returned over $65 million. Reportedly, the star also got 10 per cent of the gross (*Daily Variety*, 13 March 1989). 'I owe a great deal to films like *The Omen*,' laughed Greg. 'I'm terribly pleased about all the money I made from it.'

The film restored Greg's popularity. People were congratulating him on the street. It also re-awakened studio interest, and he was offered $250,000 (the same as Charlton Heston at that time, although the latter was also getting a percentage) to play the lead in *MacArthur* (1977). At age 61, with a 33-year movie career, he could echo General Douglas MacArthur's famed 'I have returned,' since the string of duds between *Arabesque*, his last moneymaker in 1966, and *The Omen*.

This picture, about one of the giants of the Second World War, could have been Greg's run for the roses. The character had all the richness and complexity to gain Oscar attention. While he had been too young, too limited in range for Captain Ahab in *Moby Dick*, Greg was now seasoned enough by experience and tragedy to do MacArthur justice. With his voice, posture and temperament, he carried leadership with him. 'Most film stars play pretty consistently characters that are closer to their own personalities,' said Greg. The more he read about MacArthur, the more he saw himself in him. He admitted: 'As a boy I dreamed of being a great general – I think most boys do.'

Though different in many ways, Greg and the old warhorse general shared some startling similarities. Said Greg: 'MacArthur was his own man, a nonconformist, a complex man who made his own rules. He was aloof, not a clubbable man. He kept his own counsel. I think there was a shyness, a sensitive side to his nature that led him to be something of a loner. He didn't let other people get to know him very well.'

MacArthur was also brave, brilliant, flamboyant, and he loved glory. He was a military enigma who was equally capable of a strategic masterpiece like the retreat of Bataan, and the lapse that led to the destruction of his Philippine air force nine hours after the Japanese attacked Pearl Harbor. He was a 54-year-old, four-star general who trembled lest his mother learn he kept a young mistress. Also, he was a symbol of political reaction who brought civil liberties and women's rights to Japan. With all that, Greg wasn't sure he liked the guy. MacArthur was a vain, imperious showman who always had a public relations team at his elbow.

When Laurence Olivier heard Greg was going to do MacArthur, he reached over and poked Greg in the solar plexus, and asked, 'How is your breath control?' He knew that MacArthur wrote with flair and spoke in grand, rotund phrases. In that kind of speech, you have to have the breath to carry through to the end of the phrase. You can't gasp for breath in the middle. With his history of pipe smoking, Greg had most probably compromised his lungs, but he still had enough air capacity left to do the part justice.

Olivier also shared a relevant story. He told him that once, in a performance of *Richard III*, he realized he was falling flat, that the audience was just sitting there. He asked the Director, Tyrone

Guthrie, what was wrong. 'You don't love the character,' Guthrie replied. 'How can I love a character who gets to the throne by murdering his friends and relatives?' the actor demanded. 'Murder is entirely beside the point,' Guthrie counseled. 'You must love him anyway.' Peck did come to love MacArthur as a character.

Olivier had one more thing to say to Greg: 'No matter how heavy the drama, you must always look for the foibles of the character, and exploit them in tragedy.'

Greg considered Olivier the best actor in the world, so he took the advice. Greg said: 'MacArthur was absurd, pompous and egotistical. It was never any attempt to glorify him. I wanted the warts and foibles and the vanities. That's part of him.'

After spending months studying this thundering paradox of a man, Greg had to decide what physical presence he should assume. Should he make a concerted effort to look like MacArthur? 'Fortunately,' Greg reported, 'producer Frank McCarthy and director Joe Sargent and I were in complete agreement on this issue. We all felt it was more important to get inside MacArthur's skin and present him as a human being rather than doing a nightclub impersonation which would become boring after four minutes.' As a result the only concession toward a so-called 'MacArthur look' was the shaving of Peck's head to give him a bald spot in the back.

In the American Film Institute's tribute book to his father, Stephen Peck recalled the surprises in store for the kin of an actor who disappears into a role. 'Sometimes this alternate reality could be disconcerting,' he asserted. 'Dad had just finished filming MacArthur, and I hadn't seen him for a few weeks. I walked into his house and in the breakfast room came upon a tall, thin, balding man, his back to me, fiddling with the curtains. The curtain man, I thought. But he turned when he heard me and he wore my dad's face, except for a shaved hairline. Dad was completely immersed in MacArthur, and he began to recount an episode from the General's life. Then his expression softened, and he seemed to come back to earth. "So how are you?" he inquired. It was as if General MacArthur had left the room and Gregory Peck had just walked in.

'We got used to him cruising imperiously around the house, wearing a general's hat and a corncob pipe clenched between his teeth. I suppose we should be thankful that he didn't do this kind of thing while he was playing the role of Josef Mengele, the Nazi "Angel of death".

'I see him assume these personalities so enthusiastically, and sometimes think of what I've heard him say on a number of occasions – that many actors are shy people who find some comfort in hiding behind the mask of another personality. I think that could be said of him, though you wouldn't know it to look at him.'

Going into the film, Greg had high expectations. He hoped the picture would be an historical drama that would illuminate an era. His lofty goals and those of Frank McCarthy soon came into conflict with the economic projections of Universal. Staffing the production were professionals with the right credentials for making a film classic. The team of Richard Zanuck and David Brown were fresh from handling recent box-office hits: *The Sting* (1973) and *Jaws* (1975).

Alas, the studio heads at Universal started to worry the film wouldn't make a profit. They crippled the project with their paralyzing fear of financial failure. $5 million was shorn from the budget, which resulted in the film trading location shooting for local fabrications. Nearby Coronado Beach was good for the Philippines, a Japanese tea garden in Pasadena equal to Tokyo. For the House of Representatives there was an old Republic set, while the Broadway ticker tape parade scene employed documentary black-and-white footage with Peck superimposed in color. Fear made the producers hesitant about footage that might offend the British, the Japanese and the Pentagon. Fear edited the film from 144 minutes to 128.

Throughout the production, Greg became the feisty educator for the integrity of MacArthur in the film. The writers would later accuse him of betraying the script, which he and McCarthy saw as the 'fashionable '70s put-down, full of distortions, shallowness and sarcasm.' Letters flew back and forth from Greg to the producers, especially regarding MacArthur's speeches and the one scene (cut then later restored) in which MacArthur tells the Russian representative in Tokyo to keep his hands off Japan. Particularly exasperating was the rendering of MacArthur's farewell address to Congress; in 1951, the broadcast brought the country to a virtual standstill. In the film, Greg argued, the scene, 'lacks all the sweep, emotion and grandeur of an impressive setting.' Finally, resigned to the situation, he concluded: 'I fought the good fight, to get as much quality as I could in the film. They were afraid of words, even eloquent words.'

While Greg commanded US troops in the Philippines and laid waste to the Japanese on the set of *MacArthur*, Veronique went house hunting. Their place in Brentwood held so many haunting memories of Jonathan, as did their villa in Cap Ferrat. (It sold in 1977 for three times what the Pecks had paid for it.) She felt a new environment would help Greg to heal. One day she hit him with a surprise.

Greg loved to tell this house story. He recited it over and over for years until he polished it to a fine luster. 'We used to live in a house quite smaller than this one. I could have died there happily. But my wife, Veronique, called me at the set. We were filming the scenes where I'm speaking to the combined houses, during MacArthur's famous "Old Soldiers Never Die" speech. It was a 12-minute speech, and boy, I knew that sucker upside down and sideways. I mean I really had it, and I was having a good old actor's time, delivering it from all different camera angles.

'In the middle of this, my wife calls and says, "I found our dream house!"

'I said, "I didn't know we were looking for a dream house." '

Veronique went on to say somebody else was after it and Greg better hustle. Hearing this, he yelped: 'You must be crazy! I'm doing "Old Soldiers Never Die!" Nothing can tear me away from this!' She kept pleading, so Greg took a cab over to Holmby Hills in full MacArthur regalia – gold epaulettes, riding crop and hat. He strode on the property, surveyed the Norman-style house, glanced over at the swimming pool and tennis court and roared: 'Buy it!'

Veronique and the realtor ran after him and said: 'B-b-but don't you want to see the inside?'

He said, 'We'll fix it!' And left. That night, the deal was closed.

'Now, I've never been decisive,' explained Greg. 'I'm very practical. I always like to chew on things – especially things as expensive as this place. So I've always felt it was General Douglas MacArthur who bought my house.'

The mansion sat on four glorious acres in the best neighborhood in Los Angeles. Situated in the foothills of the Santa Monica mountains and slipped in between Bel Air and Beverly Hills off Sunset Boulevard, Holmby Hills is a square-mile enclave with 200-year-old eucalyptus, oak and sycamore trees shading stately Hollywood mansions, many of them built prior to the Second World War. The dwellings are some of the most extravagant in the United States. (The Pecks' road, Carolwood Drive, has also given shelter to Elvis Presley, Telly Savalas and Sonny and Cher.) Elizabeth Taylor and Michael Jackson lived near the Pecks, but 'near' is a relative term in these parts considering the size of the properties.

Residents are a cross-section of old Los Angeles from grand dames (Betsey Bloomingdale) to current industry notables (Danny DeVito). Almost none of the lots is smaller than one acre, and several overlook the Los Angeles Country Club. Except for the annoying tour buses that creep through every half-hour, Holmby Hills retains a sense of seclusion and privacy, in part because virtually every mansion is poised behind hedges and iron security gates equipped with electronic surveillance cameras. In 1982, Aaron Spelling caused raised eyebrows in this 'hood when he paid $10.5 million for the 4-acre Gordon Kaufmann-designed Bing Crosby house, which he tore down in order to build his famous mansion. The renovated structure, which cost $50 million, boasts two Olympic-sized swimming pools plus an indoor ice-skating rink. It's just a tad smaller than the White House. Rumor had it that his daughter, Tory, moved out because she couldn't find a room she liked.

Although *MacArthur* received a lukewarm reception, Greg's performance was applauded. Reviewing it in the *Los Angeles Times*, Charles Champlin noted: 'Inevitably, the riveting interest stems from the masterful performance of Gregory Peck . . . his most impressive performance since *To Kill a Mockingbird*.' Leonard Maltin also sang his praises: 'solid, absorbing, and a flamboyant military chief . . . Peck is excellent . . .' For Greg, *MacArthur* was a 'lost opportunity' that nevertheless, with each passing year, seems to be winning respect.

At the time it was released, Jack Kroll of *Newsweek* gave a balanced review that still holds up. He said *MacArthur* 'doesn't have the flair and panache of *Patton* but in many ways it cuts deeper and churns up more food for thought. This prosaic, limited, naggingly honest film finally achieves a strangely touching quality, thanks mainly to Gregory Peck, whose voice and bearing evoke exactly the "transcendent sincerity and essential rectitude" that historian Trumbull Higgins found in one of the most enigmatic heroes in American history. *MacArthur* is hardly a brilliant film, but it has a certain dogged integrity, and the figure of MacArthur as hero and bogeyman remains a crucial one.'

'Dogged integrity' was also manifest in Greg off screen. He had to force himself to get through each day still weighed down by grief over Jonathan. William Arnold, movie critic for the *Seattle Post-Intelligencer* interviewed Greg a year or so after Jonathan's death. It was at West Point, where Greg was publicizing *MacArthur*. Arnold's wife was heavily pregnant at the time and she was with him. Arnold recalled Greg was drawn to her in a curious, fatherly way: 'In fact, he soon lost all interest in hyping *MacArthur* and instead wanted to talk to us about the responsibilities of parenthood.

' "Nothing you do in your life will be as important as the time you spend with that child," I can still see that Lincolnesque figure telling me in that distinctively august voice, tears brimming in his eyes. "I learned this the hard way. Don't let it happen to you." '

Arnold realized he was thinking about Jonathan. Finally, a studio underling pulled Greg away. He paused for several awkward moments, then he put his hand on Arnold's wife's stomach and said, 'Have a good life.'

Greg had always been willing to go out of his way to play the porter for the passage, to do what he could to make things easier for people in their life's journey. Now, with the loss of Jonathan, he was making even more of an effort to extend a helping hand, especially to the young.

In the late 1970s movie critic Susan Granger's daughter, Janet, applied to Amherst in Massachusetts, a liberal arts college renowned for talented students. The girl was a good student but needed a recommendation from someone with a connection to the school. 'Unfortunately, we knew no one,' said Susan Granger, 'No one at all. Except Gregory Peck. His son Tony was an upperclassman there.'

Greg had never met the Grangers' daughter, Janet. And he made it a firm policy never to recommend anyone he didn't personally know. To complicate matters, the Grangers lived in Southern Connecticut. So he suggested they bring their daughter Janet to meet his plane on a flight that had a stopover for several hours in New York en route to Europe. While Granger and her husband sat at a table at one end of a restaurant, Greg dined with Janet at the other. He then wrote a highly enthusiastic letter. She was accepted.

A gracious gesture to be sure, but Greg didn't stop there. He asked his son Tony to act as Janet's big brother at Amherst and show her the ropes. So when the Grangers pulled up to the door with their incoming freshman Tony was waiting for them. He brought along his buddy whom he introduced as P Albert (aka Prince Albert of Monaco, who was also a student at the school). The two upperclassmen cheerfully lugged Janet's suitcases and boxes up two flights to her assigned room. Trip after trip. Back and forth. What an introduction to college!

In Greg's next film, *The Boys From Brazil* (1978), he was given the opportunity to play against type – big time. 'Villain' hardly suggests the historic treachery of Dr Josef Mengele who carried out horrifying experiments on prisoners in the Nazi death camps and sent an estimated 2.5 million Jews to their deaths at the Auschwitz-Birkenau concentration camp. Afterwards he escaped to South America (reportedly living in Paraguay).

Ira Levin's book, on which the screenplay was based, is a fictional account of Mengele's discovery of a method of cloning Hitler from samples of the Führer's blood, and his plan to establish a Fourth Reich. In addition to playing opposite Laurence Olivier, the role gave Greg a chance to forget about subtle acting and 'chew up the scenery.'

British producer Sir Lew Grade was churning out blockbuster packages with salable stories and high-profile casts. To be sure,

Greg, Olivier, James Mason, and Lilli Palmer fit that bill. Drafting the film was Franklin Schaffner, a name familiar to fans of big movies: *Planet of the Apes* (1968), *Patton* (1970), *Nicholas and Alexandra* (1971) and *Papillon* (1973).

Mengele may have been strange, interesting and flamboyant, but why would Greg, the quintessential good guy, agree to play one of the most evil, wicked, malevolent men in the world? When the question was put to him, he responded: 'One, because it was an opportunity to remind people of the Nazi holocaust, and two, because it's a plum role, a bravura role of spectacular proportions.'

Yes, but this man was a monster. How could Greg identify with a person like that? 'There is evil in all of us – resentment, jealousy, greed, hatred,' he said. 'Even though you don't commit unspeakable crimes, you can play on traits, bring them to the fore, so to speak.'

Greg further explained: 'Mengele was a loathsome rat, one of the most despicable characters in history. I really couldn't get close to him emotionally, so I resorted to a lot of technique and went after Mengele to make him as hateful as I could . . . But the great fun was working with Laurence Olivier. That's really why I did it.'

Olivier, on the other hand, was in it for the money. Between children, houses and travel, the bills were mounting. Also, his health was in jeopardy. Just before his departure from England, Olivier collapsed at his home in Brighton and was admitted to hospital in acute pain from an attack of kidney stones. When released, he felt dreadfully ill and looked awful. His gaunt and pained expression would give added poignancy to his role as Ezra Lieberman, a Viennese Jewish Nazi hunter.

Throughout the production, Olivier never complained. He saw himself as a 'physical actor,' motivated from the outside and contrary to the Method precepts of Stanislavsky or Lee Strasberg. That physicality made for memorable impressions and Olivier held to that acting style during *The Boys From Brazil*.

Greg was very conscious of Olivier's condition and altered his acting accordingly. For example, in the final climactic scene, Olivier gets into hand-to-hand combat with Greg. Wounded by Mengele's gunshot, Lieberman was to turn, stagger and collapse near a couch.

After rehearsals and several takes for various camera angles, Olivier finished the scene of the fierce wrestling match with Greg, who tried not to grasp his partner's hands or put too much of his weight on Olivier's sensitive skin. 'Nice faking,' Greg said supportively, helping him to his feet. 'Just like Tristan and Isolde,' whispered Olivier in mock flirtation.

A host of reviewers howled at Greg's Mengele. Pauline Kael's caustic review in *The New Yorker* is but one example. 'Who could accept John Wayne or James Stewart – or Gregory Peck . . . as a Nazi sadist? Peck strides into *The Boys From Brazil* with stiff black hair, beady little eyes (one squintier than the other), a chalky complexion, and a thin mustache that seems to be coming out of his nose. When an actor like Gregory Peck plays a sadistic Nazi geneticist and speaks in an arch-villain's sibilant German accent, you can't keep from laughing. Peck, in his jungle hide-away, staring into the future as he walks unconcernedly among the mutants he has created, just doesn't have it in him to inspire primitive terror; his effects are all on the surface, and he looks particularly bad because he's playing opposite Laurence Olivier, who is the aged hero, a famous Nazi-hunter (a fictional counterpart of Simon Wiesenthal).'

Greg bristled at the criticism. 'I felt, Laurence Olivier felt, friends of mine like Walter Matthau and Jack Lemmon felt, that I was good in this part. Some critics seem unwilling to accept actors when they break what they think is the mold or the image.'

Around this time journalist Steven Rubio confronted Greg with an intriguing question. 'At some point, thinking of the awful *Boys From Brazil*, I asked Mr Peck if he ever got into a movie, saw it was going to stink and decided that at least he could have some fun with his role. No, he assured me, that would be unfair to the audience. His job was to do his best, no matter what the circumstances; his audience expected no less . . . But his answer explained the problem: he was so worried about his audience that he never allowed for the possibility that in a piece of shit like *The Boys From Brazil*, we were all in on the joke, and soon he ended up looking foolish for trying to do his best. Meanwhile, in the same film, Laurence Olivier tarted up his role as if it were more fun than having a three-way with Vivien

Leigh and Danny Kaye. The result? Olivier is the only thing worth seeing in the entire film.'

As his youngest children matured, Greg tried to help them without stifling their initiative. He arranged for Tony to work on the set of *The Boys From Brazil*, as an assistant director, and for Cecilia to take photographs as an assistant to the still cameraman. He predicted that when she graduated from Princeton she would become a professional photographer. She had already done a layout for *Vogue* with Greg modeling his favorite 'best dressed man about town' clothes.

Carey and Stephen had lived with Greta while they were growing up and now Greg wanted to draw them closer to him. 'When you have a second marriage, it's not unusual for the kids from the second union to usurp the ones from the first,' said a friend of Stephen's. 'Veronique was very territorial,' explained Nancy Stesin. 'They were her kids and her house.'

When Carey decided to run for US Congress, as a Democrat against Robert K Dornan, Greg backed him 100 per cent. A graduate of Georgetown University with a degree in foreign service, he was hooked on politics while working on John Tunney's successful 1970 campaign for US Senate along with his brother Jonathan. After stints as a Voice of America announcer and two years with the Peace Corps in Senegal, Carey was hired by Senator Walter Mondale to work on the US Senate Committee on education. He then decided to return to California and run as a candidate from his home state's 27th district, a strip of beach cities that extends 37 miles down the coast. (During the campaign, Carey married Kathy Katz, the 25-year-old manager of the Westwood Art Gallery.)

Greg made it a point to stay away from the hustings, but he figured it would be equally 'ostentatious' to do nothing. So Carey found himself with a formidable pair of co-chairmen, Greg and former California governor Pat Brown. Senator Ted Kennedy and Pat Moynihan trekked more than 3,000 miles from Washington to Los Angeles to campaign for Carey. Losing the election, Carey tried unsuccessfully to defeat Dornan two years later.

Stephen had graduated from Northwestern with a degree in speech and communication. He was now working in television as one of the producers of a weekly nostalgia program, *That's Hollywood*.

Greg's personal life was beginning to reach an equilibrium. In 1978, he told an interviewer from *Women's Own* magazine: 'I don't really want to sound like a benevolent poppa, but I do get a deep joy, deep gratification, out of seeing my children growing up well and standing on their own feet, having opinions of their own and being attractive people and personalities in their own right.'

As the years went by, Greg's circle of show business intimates dwindled. Death thinned the ranks. Two people to whom he grew closer in his later years were Cary Grant and Frank Sinatra. With them, he could laugh, reminisce and play father confessor. There was no strain of presenting a public façade. And with a personality as revered by fans as Greg's, the strain was considerable. Said Stephen: 'My father has had to create and live up to a persona that matches, or at least comes close to, the worldwide perception people have of him through his films.'

Though dapper and lighthearted on screen, Cary Grant had never been truly happy. Hungry for love, he had romanced, married and broken up with a notable number of women – plus a few men. (He was reputed to have had liaisons with Howard Hughes and Randolph Scott.) Now he needed a safe harbor. So Greg took great pride in helping play cupid to Grant and his last wife, Barbara Harris.

One evening in Nice, the Pecks and the Sinatras were having dinner with Grant at the Chaumier restaurant. Grant, who was staying at the Monaco Palace with Prince Rainier said: 'I've never had such a good time, although I'm kind of lonely, seeing you four . . . '

Greg replied, 'You're Cary Grant, and you don't have a girlfriend?'

Grant said: 'Well, no, I don't.'

'Isn't there anybody?'

'Well,' sighed Grant. 'There's a woman in London. She does public relations for one of the leading hotels. I like her, but I don't know whether she likes me. I've taken her to dinner twice.'

À *la* General MacArthur, Greg insisted he fetch the woman forthwith. 'Get her down here,' Greg commanded. 'We'll come back here tomorrow night.' Grant followed orders and dispatched the plane Fabergé loaned him to fetch her. The next night Grant arrived at the Chaumier with Barbara Harris in tow. A Londoner in her 20s, she was slender and athletic, with beautifully chiseled features and intelligent, sharp eyes. The couple spent two days at the Pecks' villa in Cap Ferrat, then moved into the Hotel de Paris in Monte Carlo.

Waiving their 47-year age difference, Grant and Harris let nature take its course. They were married in 1981. Greg said: 'I think Cary's last seven or eight years were his happiest.'

Greg's friendship with Sinatra ripened in their autumn years. When Sinatra was tight with the Kennedys and raising hell with Dean Martin and Sammy Davis Jr, Greg didn't see that much of him. One day *Variety* columnist Amery Archerd ventured to ask Greg why he didn't become a member of the Rat Pack. Greg laughed, 'Bad casting!'

In actuality, the Las Vegas based clan kept round-the-clock hours as they cavorted with hookers, tossed punches at reporters, gambled excessively and knocked back booze. It was not a good scene for a middle-aged man who liked gardening and reading and was determined to stay faithful to his wife.

But as Sinatra mellowed and settled into a stable marriage with Barbara Marx (ex-wife of Zeppo Marx, the straight man in the Marx Brothers team), he began seeing himself as a humanitarian and a statesman. Although he endeared himself in many quarters by his phenomenal bequests of money, Sinatra couldn't shake his blue-collar roots. 'When he spoke to you, it was like a New Yorker did – dese, dem and dose,' said radio and TV personality Joe Franklin, a longtime Sinatra acquaintance. 'His speaking was entirely different from his singing. When he sang, it was absolute poetry.'

To compound his difficulties, there was the gangster factor. He enjoyed rubbing elbows with John Gotti's mentor, Aniello Dellacroce and Jimmy 'The Weasel' Fratinanno. Surveying the crowd at his best friend Jilly Rizzo's saloon on West 52nd Street in Manhattan, Sinatra cracked: 'There's about 43 indictments right at the bar!'

When confronted with Mafia photographs such as the one of him standing near Paul Castellano with his arm around Carlo Gambino,

Sinatra acted as if he was just being a good sport with some fans. By producing pictures of himself with a congressman, with the Prime Minister of Israel, with the President of Egypt or with Gregory Peck, he balanced out the unsavory impression.

And, in 1981 when Frank faced the five-member Gaming Control Commission, which has the final say on all casino licensing matters in Nevada, Greg stood up for him. How could somebody be a friend of pillar-of-integrity Gregory Peck and cavort with the Mafia at the same time? His support prompted *Tonight Show* host, Johnny Carson, to crack wise: 'I just got word Gregory Peck was nominated for an Oscar for his performance at the Frank Sinatra hearing.'

Syndicate men looking to chill out gravitated to Frank Sinatra's compound in Palm Springs. Headline grabbers such as Mickey Cohen, Sam Giancana, Joe Fischetti, Johnny Roselli, Johnny Formosa, Skinny D'Amato and Doc Stacher swam and played gin rummy at Sinatra's compound. The Pecks and other members of the Hollywood elite were also houseguests. Did the two crowds mesh? Imagine the small talk. Peck to Giancana: 'Sam, where'd you get those snazzy spats?'

One also wonders what Greg and Veronique thought of Sinatra's nightclub performances, which were filled with crude racial jokes and bigotry. Appearing with Count Basie and Ella Fitzgerald one night, Sinatra tried to amuse his audience: 'The Polacks are deboning the colored people and using them for wet suits.' Looking at Basie's all black band, he said, 'I'd publicly like to thank the NAACP for this chess set they gave me.' He called Johnny Mathis the 'African Queen', and used to complain about Sammy Davis Jr leaving watermelon rinds in his dressing room.

Introducing the sledgehammer set into the privileged lives of his show business friends and charity organizers was a Sinatra specialty. He brought the Establishment a touch of notoriety, a hint of the sinister. Although ordinarily they saw only the good Frank, who lavished presents upon them, sang at their benefits, and championed their causes, they occasionally glimpsed the loutish Frank.

Bruce Fessier, a journalist with the *Desert Sun* in Las Vegas, kept an eye on the two entertainers. 'Peck didn't own a home here, but he stayed often with the Sinatras, and I recall that influenced my opinion of Frank Sinatra when I moved here.

'I had heard the Kitty Kelly-type stories about Sinatra and they made me wary. But when I learned Atticus Finch, Peck's character in *To Kill a Mockingbird*, was one of Sinatra's best friends, I gained respect for him. Peck later told me he considered Sinatra a great humanitarian. And I admired Peck's devotion to humanitarian causes.

'I'll never forget attending a film tribute to Sinatra at the Palm Springs Desert Museum. Frank and Barbara were sitting with Peck and his wife, Veronique, at dinner. Then Peck stood up and people began to clap. Soon it grew into a standing ovation and Peck looked bewildered. But he composed himself and, with pure theatrical class, took a bow and made an exit. To the bathroom.'

Greg was in awe of Sinatra's talent. And of course, the two men went way back. An old friend is, by definition, irreplaceable. One year apart in age, they started out in New York about the same time. Then they both fell in love with Ava Gardner – each in his own way. But most of all, Greg liked Sinatra because he was fun. In the rarefied world in which they moved, spontaneity was hard to come by. Everything was planned. With Old Blue Eyes, you never knew what was going to happen. Greg recalled Sinatra once met his train at a deserted station near Monte Carlo and lugged his bags.

As Father Peck, pastoral counselor to the stars, Greg offered Sinatra advice. Some he didn't take. Such as when Sinatra got hopping mad at the Kennedys after they dropped him because of his mob affiliations and he started supporting Richard Nixon and Ronald Reagan. Greg did his best to bring him back to the Liberal fold.

Their relationship mystified Kirk Douglas who had known Sinatra for 40 years and felt he hardly knew him at all. At an 80th birthday party for Sinatra, hosted by George and Joleen Schlatter, Douglas recalled that as the small group sat sipping before-dinner drinks, he watched Sinatra and Greg in intense conversation. 'I don't ever remember talking with Frank for more than a minute or two at a time. Maybe Greg really knows Frank, I thought. I don't.'

Socializing with Sinatra was not without its liabilities. For example, in June 1978 Greg and Veronique and Frank and Barbara joined the star-studded guests for the wedding of Princess Caroline of Monaco to Phillippe Junot.

The bride wore white. The groom was nervous. The press corps of 200 reporters and photographers was kept at a considerable distance from the ceremony outside the security-tight palace. During the festive wedding week, the paparazzi made nuisances of themselves bribing taxi drivers, bartenders, shopkeepers, barbers, managers, hotel concierges, and anyone else who might be able to tell them anything at all about the wedding.

Grace's old friend Rupert Allen described Grace the night before preparing for 'the luncheon of the century in that part of the world.' She was up until 4 a.m. trying to figure out how to seat everybody at the celebration. There were Royals and there were heads of state and protocol was a nightmare. Tables were set up under the trees on the square and in front of the palace. The whole area had, of course, been roped off from the general public.

After the ceremony, before going to lunch, Allen was standing under the palace portico next to the Pecks and the Sinatras while Old Blue Eyes's bodyguard was dispatched to make certain that the coast was clear of photographers. When he came back to report that all was not good, Frank and Barbara decided they would not stay for lunch. So Greg and Veronique decided they wouldn't stay either. They had already attended a pre-wedding luncheon for the couple thrown by David Niven.

Allen was incensed. 'Sinatra's bodyguard gave him the wrong advice. That didn't excuse anything but it explains why he didn't stay. But how could Gregory Peck and his wife leave also? I can't understand anyone doing that to someone like Grace. How did they do that to Grace?'

It is highly unlikely Greg would want to offend Princess Grace. He bristled at the way the powers that be in Monaco treated her. From his summer home in Cap Ferrat, Greg had had an insider's view. He felt the Academy Award winning actress had too much talent to spend her days standing in reception lines shaking hands like the Princess in *Roman Holiday*.

What really rankled for him occurred later in the early 1980s when he decided to produce and star in a new movie version of

Sinclair Lewis's *Dodsworth*. It had already been written as a play and movie by Sidney Howard and filmed by William Wyler back in 1936 starring Greg's idol Walter Huston. The story concerns a middle-aged automobile manufacturer traveling in Europe in the 1920s who falls in love with a Bohemian woman living above the harbor in Naples. 'It's a glorious part,' said Greg. 'One of the few I'm not too old to play.' His dream was to have Princess Grace play opposite him.

In negotiating for the rights, Greg invested time, money, heart and soul. 'It was terribly complicated,' said Greg at the time, 'because both Sinclair Lewis and Sidney Howard have many heirs and that meant getting involved with several sets of lawyers. It took a full year just to settle the legal rights.'

In 1982, when both Greg and Princess Grace were in New York at the same time, he ran the original film for her. 'She loved it and had a little cry,' he said. 'If she were interested, I had in mind to offer a million dollars to her Monaco Red Cross to help her justify it. But she said she didn't feel the people of Monaco would understand if she made the film.' He realized her life was not her own.

Often seeing Princess Grace socially on the Riviera, Greg knew how miserable she was confined to her gilded cage. And he realized after screening *Dodsworth* for her she was not about to break the bars. After her fatal car accident, he recalled her as a sad woman, 'who got taken in by those slickers in Monaco and used.'

While the *Dodsworth* movie didn't materialize, another project came to fruition that pleased him immensely. In his first dramatic TV role, which aired in 1982, he played Abraham Lincoln in *The Blue and the Gray*. By now his collection of books on Lincoln had grown to over 1,000 and his appreciation of Lincoln had not diminished. Said Greg, 'I always wanted to play him and I finally got the chance.'

At 63, he was ten years older than Lincoln when the President was assassinated. And now that the moment had come to play him, he was determined to give the role his all: 'I must have recited the Gettysburg Address 500 times outside on the lawn, among the trees, and to anyone who would listen,' he said, laughing.

Few people looked more presidential than Greg with his silver hair, horn-rimmed glasses and courtly air, so it is understandable that at the ripe age of 71, he would again play the Chief of State. Titled *Amazing Grace and Chuck* (1987), the film is an anti-nuclear fable, the story of a young boy's crusade against atomic weapons. When producer/writer David Field and director Mike Newell approached Greg to do the low-budget film to be made for a mere $5 million, he was persuaded because the anti-nuclear theme fit with his liberal, activist politics. He swore: 'I would give up everything I do and everything I have if I could make a significant difference in getting the nuclear arms race reversed. It is the number one priority in my life. My work was the main thing in my life for a long time; now I'm beginning to think a little more about what the future will hold and what kind of world my kids will live in.'

Greg found the script of *Amazing Grace and Chuck* quite touching, yet refreshingly unsentimental. 'I choked up a little at many of those scenes.' In developing his part as the President, he decided to make him pretty much like himself. He's a Californian, he went to Berkeley, but instead of going to New York to become an actor, he runs for office. 'I thought a lot about it,' he said. 'I thought about Johnson, I thought about Kennedy, Carter, Reagan, Ford. And I threw 'em all out. To try to determine what kind of a fellow I wanted, I began to do what I almost always do – to sketch in a biography.'

Greg might just as well be speaking of himself as of the character he plays when he says: 'I knew he had some amount of steel and his backbone to get there. I knew that he had to play some politics to get that job. I knew he didn't get there by preaching disarmament constantly. I knew that he was a fellow used to authority. Didn't have to raise his voice very often to get things done.'

While most reviewers thought Greg played the US President with force and dignity, they panned the film. *Variety* went so far as to call it 'the camp classic of anti-nuke genre.'

To help the struggling picture, Greg beat the bushes – and the freeways. When a Los Angeles theater owner was shipped a defective print, Greg jumped in his 1963 Bentley, picked up a copy of the film he had loaned to his neighbor, Michael Jackson, and delivered it personally to the amazed exhibitor. On the *Tonight Show* the actor got a roaring ovation. 'It's like being with a rock star,' said one bemused reporter. 'What has this old Jasper got?'

Commanding presence. That's what. Seventy-one years old with impressive height, silver hair, broad shoulders and the stride of a born leader, Greg looked like the American ideal of the President. He dazzled the crowds in a Denver suburb when he got out of a long gray limousine. They acted as if they'd seen a ghost and then burst into startled shouts. Here was one of the last, great male stars of the Hollywood studio system, back in the limelight. As he waded through the throng, the famous smile whisking like a beacon from face to face, hands reached out to touch him. 'Oh my God, it's really him!' squealed a white-haired woman. 'I've loved him all my life!' A teenage girl gushed: 'Wow, he is really beautiful! Dumb me, I thought he was dead!'

In 1987, Greg was among the cultural and scientific luminaries invited to Moscow for then-Soviet leader Mikhail Gorbachev's forum 'For a Nuclear-Free World and the Survival of Mankind.' He was criticized for taking part in the gathering, which included Yoko Ono, Kris Kristofferson and Graham Greene as well as numerous Nobel Prize winners. In a secret dispatch, US diplomats dismissed the gathering as a stunt which 'produced little of lasting interest or value.'

While conservatives scoffed at Greg's activist activities, some Americans thought the world would be improved considerably if Greg replaced Reagan in the White House. But the problem with stars turning presidential is that they are judged by their movies. (Think of Reagan playing opposite a chimp in *Bedtime for Bonzo*, 1951.) Addressing the subject in a letter to the *Los Angeles Times Examiner*, Bob Nicholson of Northridge, California, wrote: 'March 1983 it is time to seriously consider what man in our nation is best qualified to be our next president.' He then went on to analyze Greg's role in *The Chairman* (1969). 'He exemplified perfect statesmanship, he displayed a commanding manner, blended with humility, the highest mental and athletic ability in carrying on a complex, high-level debate with the Chinese leader, while playing championship level ping pong with one hand. I kept saying to my wife, "that's our man! That's our man!"

'Paul Newman is her choice. She thinks Gregory should only be vice president. She has a weakness for blue eyes. I could go for Paul too, except that Tennessee Williams once sullied his image. Every time I have seen Gregory, he has been a good guy. Paul has a latent tendency toward ne'er-do-wellness. Even in *The Verdict* he was a reformed alcoholic. He can't get away from his past. Paul could probably best Gregory on a racetrack, but Gregory would wipe him out in ping pong.'

In imagining a competition between Charlton Heston and Greg, a columnist for *Nation* magazine decided: 'Peck has nothing to compare with Heston's Moses, although his portrayal of Douglas MacArthur cannot be taken lightly. As a negative, Peck has portrayed two certifiable lunatics: Dr Josef Mengele in *The Boys From Brazil* and Captain Ahab in *Moby Dick*. Even playing good guys, Peck shows tendencies towards mental problems, which could make some voters think he might crack in a nuclear crisis. In *Spellbound*, for example, he suffered from traumatic anxiety and amnesia and needed the help of two psychiatrists to pull him through. And in *Twelve O'Clock High*, he went to pieces under the strain of sending bombers on dangerous missions. On the other hand, moviegoers would see Peck is no patsy in the role of president. What's more, he would certainly have the black vote wrapped up with *To Kill a Mockingbird*. *Gentleman's Agreement* would win him the Jewish vote were it not for Charlton Heston who portrayed Moses with quite a bit of conviction. However, Heston is not without political liabilities. He not only failed to do as well as he might have against a group of monkeys (*Planet of the Apes*) but in the same movie bared his rear end. Nudity does not go down well with the folks from Sioux Falls.'

Bob Hope took the professional view: 'So many actors are running for president that they may put a marquee on the White House with "Now Playing" on it.'

Mellow in personal relations yet candid on issues, Greg was finally able to stop being such a pleaser. 'I find myself getting to be a little more of a truth teller,' he admitted. His willingness to speak out became apparent to Americans when he – along with Martin Sheen, Lloyd Bridges and Burt Lancaster – was approached by the People for the American Way to narrate a TV spot asking viewers to campaign against the nomination of Robert Bork for the Supreme Court. In 1987, President Reagan nominated Bork, an outspoken conservative who was widely reviled in liberal and moderate circles for his apparent opposition to advancement in civil liberties. Even a former American Bar Association president characterized Bork as 'a right-wing radical.'

The People for the American Way was a public-interest lobbying group launched by Hollywood producer Norman Lear. An enormously successful businessman, Lear is best known for creating such provocative sitcoms as *All in the Family* (1971) and *Maude* (1972) The group joined with a coalition of black, labor, environmental and feminist groups in serving up reams of analysis of Bork's judicial opinions, speeches and writing. More important, it bankrolled and created a $1.2 million advertising and direct-mail campaign that helped convert an otherwise esoteric debate into a hot political topic.

The most controversial commercial showed a young white family on the steps of the Supreme Court, while Greg's voice intoned: 'Robert Bork wants to be a Supreme Court justice. But the record shows he has a strange idea of what justice is. He defended poll taxes and literacy tests, which kept many Americans from voting. He opposed the civil rights law that ended 'whites only' signs at lunch counters. He doesn't believe the Constitution protects your privacy. Please urge your Senators to vote against the Bork nomination. Because if Robert Bork wins a seat on the Supreme Court, it will be for life. His life . . . and yours.'

Off-air Greg said: 'I came to the conclusion that having that guy on the Supreme Court would be the beginning of turning back civil rights – and I felt it was time to step up and bat.'

Bork had the support of former Chief Justice Warren E Burger, four former attorneys general, White House counsel Lloyd N Cutler and, of course, Reagan – who was supremely peeved with Greg. Not wanting to reveal himself with a public display of anger, he said simply that Greg had been 'miscast.'

Reagan left it to his White House spokesman Marlin Fitzwater to open fire. 'The liberal special interest groups are producing slick, shrill advertising campaigns that not only purposely distort the judge's record, they play on people's emotions as only propaganda campaigns can,' Fitzwater warned the public, adding, 'To say that Americans will lose their freedoms, as these ads claim, is patently outrageous and deliberately untrue. Gregory Peck ought to be ashamed.'

In screaming foul about the commercial, Bork supporters maintained it was a distortion of Bork's position. Many stations initially refused to run the anti-Bork blurb, but when Reagan reacted to it through Fitzwater, a host of news programs gave it unexpected – and free – airing. Bork's name became a household word.

After lengthy and acrimonious confirmation hearings, Bork was ultimately voted down by the Senate, 58-42. For Greg and other liberals, the defeat of Robert Bork was a major victory. At the time, Bork denied charges made by the American Civil Liberties Union (ACLU) that he opposed the very concept of a Bill of Rights that limits legislative authority and is enforced by independent federal courts. However, in his book *Slouching Towards Gomorrah*, Bork admits to the charge by actually proposing a constitutional amendment that would allow Congress, by a simple majority vote, to override any Supreme Court decision it didn't like.

'This is an extraordinary proposal,' said Ira Glasser, ACLU executive director. 'If such an amendment were to pass, every one of our basic individual rights would be in mortal danger. A woman's right to reproductive freedom, an author's right to free expression, a family's right to freedom of religion, a racial minority's right to be free of discrimination – all of these rights would be subject to Congressional vote; all could be taken away.' So Peck had been right in his initial concerns and brave in his stand.

No matter which side of the political fence an American was on, the fact remained the media war waged against Judge Bork was ugly and insulting. Reporters attempted to get a list of movies he rented from his local video store in the hope they would find some smutty titles. The store owner, quite rightly, respected Bork's privacy. So Americans will never know whether Bork rented any Gregory Peck movies – and which were his picks and pans.

CHAPTER TWENTY

Magnificent Survivor

'I realize very well now how short life is, because I've got to be considered to be in the home stretch. But I won't waste time on recriminations and regrets. And the same goes for my shortcomings and my own failures.'

Gregory Peck

Old is a dirty word in Hollywood. Not many meaty roles pop up for a man of 72, but Jane Fonda tossed Greg a good one. She asked him to play the satiric essayist Ambrose Bierce in a movie version of a Carlos Fuentes' novel, *Old Gringo* (1989).

The title of the film came from the identity of Bierce, the aged gringo in the film who journeys to Mexico in search of death. 'Bitter' Bierce was a brilliant, burnt-out Hearst newspaperman and author of *The Devil's Dictionary,* a writer of supernatural stories that have secured his place both in the weird tradition and in American literature at large. He was a celebrity when, in 1913, at the age of 71, he crossed the Rio Grande into Mexico to join Pancho Villa's revolutionaries in what some Bierce scholars speculate was an act of suicide. Bierce himself, in a letter to his niece Lora, wrote: 'Goodbye. If you hear of my being stood up against a Mexican stone wall and shot to rags please know that I think that a pretty good way to depart this life. It beats old age, disease, or falling down the cellar stairs. To be a gringo in Mexico – ah, that is euthanasia.'

Greg wasn't Fonda's first choice for Bierce. Burt Lancaster was hired for the role, then fired because he was deemed uninsurable because of his weak heart. 'A lot of the film was shot on location in the Mexican desert, 6,000 feet up,' explained Greg, 'and there was quite a bit of scrambling around, crawling and horseback riding involved.' Fonda didn't want to let Lancaster go, but her back was against the wall. 'It was one of the hardest things I've ever been through,' the actress recalled. 'I love him very much.' Rumor had it that Paul Newman then declined the part. So Greg assumed it. Lancaster subsequently filed a lawsuit in which he claimed, 'Colombia negotiated with Greg even before I was fired.' (The case was settled out of court on 15 September 1989.)

In the film, the weathered American (Greg looking lean, tanned, contours intact) walks fearlessly in the midst of battle. Harriet Winslow, the Fonda character, is an American schoolteacher, and a virgin (a challenge for 51-year-old Fonda). She encounters Bierce soon after she arrives in Mexico, and gradually comes to love his stoic acceptance and sardonic wit. She also gets involved with Villa's general, Thomas Arroyo (Jimmy Smits), and her whole life comes tumbling down.

Fonda and Greg shared the platform sometimes at liberal events, and 'Hanoi Jane,' the anti-war crusader who found salvation through exercise, had her reservations about him: 'I thought maybe he'd gotten soft. He's part Irish, and that means ups and downs. I thought, maybe the edge is gone, maybe he phones it in.'

As it turned out, Greg – after ten years away from this kind of big-budget production – was at the top of his game. His acting skills had steadily improved and he was finally breaking the stranglehold of his inhibitions. Fonda, on the other hand, was reeling from the professional and personal complications in her life. Determined to make this film perfect, yet beset by a disintegrating marriage to Tom Hayden, Fonda, the 'benevolent fanatic' as Greg called her during the shooting, finally suffered a nervous breakdown. 'The marriage was over for a long time, but Jane didn't want to admit it,' said Fonda's first husband Roger Vadim.

On screen, Fonda rallied. She made her neurosis work in service to the character. She projected the raw emotional intensity that Greg required in an acting partner to do his best work. As Pauline Kael said of her: 'Jane Fonda's motor runs a little fast. As an actor she is a special kind of smart as it takes the form of speed; she's always a little ahead of everybody, and hers is a quicker beat . . . makes her more exciting to watch.'

As death-driven Ambrose Bierce, Greg romances Jane Fonda with a gleam in his eye that says, 'I'm not dead yet.' His image as the romantic still resonates. As Bierce, he says, 'once the women sighed, I thought they'd always be there, sighing into my mustache.' When Fonda's character asks how he made them sigh, Bierce goes into a lush, seductive speech. 'I think Bierce was trying to find something that would give his life meaning,' reflected Greg, 'a moment of true passion.'

Fonda came away from the experience with an abiding respect for Greg. 'There's something about him that walks this thin line between safe and familiar and warm and welcoming, and that which is dangerous and sexual and mysterious. He has not lost the hunger to take big risks.'

Reviewers rhapsodized over Greg's performance. The *New York Times* declared his portrayal of Ambrose Bierce may have been his 'best performance.' Unfortunately, the movie died a quick death. It lacked a clear narrative line from beginning to end – and that flaw proved to be its downfall. 'There is a potentially wonderful story at the heart of *Old Gringo*,' wrote critic Roger Ebert. 'But the movie never finds it – the screenplay blasts away in every direction except the bulls-eye.'

Rolling Stone showed limited enthusiasm: 'As usual, Peck radiates dignity, intelligence and quiet strength. But he can't or won't connect with the despair that would make the character memorable. It's a star turn from an old smoothie.'

Knowing the trials and tribulations of being a producer first hand, Greg felt anguish for his colleague. 'After the many years Jane Fonda put in to get *Old Gringo* made, it's a pity to see it destroyed in 48 hours. *Old Gringo* made less than $2 million at the box office, a disastrous return for the $25 million romantic extravaganza. People didn't go right away. And by the time they wanted to go, the picture wasn't playing anymore.'

At this point in time, Greg had many blessings. Tucked away in the opulent Holmby Hills, he lived in great style in a grand but delightfully cozy Norman-style mansion. Golden retrievers romped among blazing masses of rhododendron and bougainvillea, and the house itself was a casual gallery of paintings, drawings and prints by the likes of Renoir, Matisse and Picasso. When the gardener's son admired one of the paintings, Greg lifted it off the wall and gave it to him. (One assumes it wasn't one of the masters.)

Thanks to his percentages in films such as *The Guns of Navarone* and *The Omen*, he was a wealthy man with no need to continue working.

He never stopped referring to Veronique as his soul mate. She looked after him in his dotage, serving as his life raft when the ups and downs of life became too great. 'It was very lucky for us that we met,' said Greg. 'And that after all these years of marriage we still love to be together, often for 24 hours a day. Although we do get out a bit on the social scene, we both feel happiest when we know we are going to have an evening alone together. A bottle of champagne and dinner in front of the fireplace, a stack of records on the stereo, and we are perfectly happy. We never run out of conversation, and we get along just fine.'

Often they invited close friends to an elegant, small dinner party. And when the mood struck, they traveled: Cuba for a film festival, Paris for the museums and restaurants, and Louisville for the Kentucky Derby. 'We do whatever we want whenever we want to do it. I suppose that's the ultimate freedom.'

'We still have a lot of friends here,' Greg said, referring to Los Angeles. 'But we're not in the vortex anymore. But that's the natural order of things. We travel a lot. I don't read the trade papers anymore, the little world of who's doing what and what's doing at the box-office and what pictures are moving up to the front burner.'

At the same time, he was quick to add: 'I enjoy acting. When driving to the studio, I sing in the car. I love my work and my wife and my kids and my friends. And I think, "You're a lucky man, Gregory Peck, a damn lucky man."'

'Lucky' was his mantra. For the most part, it worked. Tell yourself everything's coming up roses. Broadcast it to the world. In private, the sorrow of Jonathan's death still lingered. And, within the bosom of his family, another heartbreaking tragedy was in the making. 'I like a boy who raises a little hell,' Greg said years before. 'If a boy isn't adventurous, it isn't right.' Those words may well have haunted him. He was soon to face the prospect of another son bent on self-destruction.

Although he tried to appear sanguine about it, the fact that his career was winding down bugged the hell out of him. He loved to work. The thought of spending his golden years simply puttering around the house rankled with him. The fact remained; the parts were growing thinner and less interesting. Perhaps no one wanted to tangle with the legend of Atticus. Or perhaps no one remembered how much fun he could be.

He was a serious actor adept at career plotting and carefully choosing his roles, often opting for relevant themes over the purely commercial lot. He sought out roles that offered him an artistic challenge. 'I had a stubborn streak, the Irish in me I guess.'

'I don't want to jump out there and work just to be seen,' lamented Greg. 'And I don't want to be the darling old-grand-daddy or an old Western sourdough.' And he was determined to avoid mediocre films. He reasoned, 'It's kind of unseemly at my age to come out in a turkey.'

His spirits were lifted when he was offered a part in *Other People's Money* (1991). It starred his Holmby Hills neighbor Danny DeVito. The film was based on a successful stage play, although most critics found the film version lacking in the play's bite and complexity and slipping into a Capraesque pitting of ordinary folks against the corporate big shots.

'. . . it was just the greatest thrill of my life to work with Gregory Peck,' marveled Danny DeVito. 'I was just, like, you know, overwhelmed, blown away, flabbergasted, going to work with a legend.'

A ruthless Wall Street predator known as Larry the Liquidator (DeVito) sets his sights on acquiring – and destroying – the New England wire and cable company run in traditional and familial style by Greg.

Although his role was supportive rather than strong, Greg especially liked his speech to the stockholders. 'Every good part should have a tirade, even if the person who delivers it loses the battle.' In *Other People's Money*, Greg has an uncommonly eloquent speech, trying to persuade the stockholders to vote for his slate of directors instead of DeVito's. Greg found in DeVito, 'a wonderful fellow, a masterful actor and comedian. He puts his heart into everything.'

With a few days off during the shooting of *Other People's Money*, Greg flew to Fort Lauderdale, Florida, to do a one-day cameo appearance in Martin Scorsese's remake of the 1962 thriller *Cape Fear* (1991).

'I didn't want to do the cameo,' Greg said. 'I don't want to play little supporting parts. You can't get your teeth into it. You've got to have some horses to ride, some meat on the bones, to make it fun to do. But Scorsese and De Niro were persistent.'

In fact the two men tracked Greg to the Ritz in Paris, talked him into it and offered him a choice of cameos. 'I took the one I thought was an amusing twist – the lawyer who defends De Niro instead of prosecuting him,' Greg said. Then he added: 'I was delighted to play the southern slicker, a little pompous southern lawyer.'

Cape Fear is undeniably gripping and it certainly looks great. Shot by Freddie Francis, the imaginative use of photography is a reminder of Scorsese's encyclopedic film education that started when he was a sickly kid, besieged by asthma, pleurisy, and other physical handicaps which excluded him from sports. In the darkened theater of the local cinema house, Scorsese escaped into fantasy and thereby laid the foundation for his future career. He never forgot watching devilishly charming Greg as Lewt McCanles slink about in David O Selznick's *Duel in the Sun*. This brawling, engrossing Western had a profound effect on him, not only because his local priest warned he'd fry in hell for watching it, but also because the photography was magnificent. Now Scorsese was one of the hottest directors in Hollywood.

Because of the continuing interest in both the book and the movie *To Kill a Mockingbird*, Greg had a part-time job answering his correspondence and going out and speaking about his role in the film. Of all his movies, it was the one with which he was most associated in the public mind. Harper Lee's novel has sold 15 million copies since it was published in 1960 and it continues to sell strongly. In 1991 the Library of Congress and the Book of the Month Club asked people to name the books that had had the greatest impact on their lives. The number one book was the Bible.

Number two was *To Kill a Mockingbird*. Since the movie was such a faithful adaptation of the book, the video also continues to sell briskly. And the ranks of the devoted continue to grow. Noted John Patterson in the *Guardian* '. . . I can vouch that the fastest way to outrage a table of drunk Americans is to tell them you can't abide this movie.'

Keenly aware of donning the mantle of Atticus Finch, Greg remarked: 'I can hardly walk down the street anymore, or meet up with strangers in the parking lot or a restaurant or an elevator, but what they will say: "I've never forgotten *To Kill a Mockingbird*," or, "I became a lawyer because of you." Middle-aged men are constantly telling me that they became lawyers because they saw *To Kill a Mockingbird* when they were young.'

He was not exaggerating. Atticus Finch's professional and moral integrity, as well as Greg's extraordinary performance, has launched thousands of legal careers. One of them was Morris Dees, the eminent director of the Southern Poverty Law Center. He recalled: 'On a warm night in 1966, I saw *To Kill a Mockingbird*. When Atticus Finch walked from the courtroom and the gallery rose in his honor, tears were streaming down my face. I wanted to be that lawyer.'

For many people, Greg as Atticus Finch represented a model of parenting that is almost unattainable. Brewster Ely, headmaster of the Town School in San Francisco put it this way: 'There are few of us, man or woman, who have not at one time or another fantasized about having the wisdom of Atticus Finch, and the reassuring tones of Gregory Peck's portrayal of Atticus in the Holly-wood adaptation of the book serves only to underscore the character's appeal. What is splendid about Atticus, whether in print, or celluloid, or in our imagination, is that he is believable; this paragon of virtue is actually achievable. I have asked the middle school and upper school students what they think of Atticus Finch, and they respond with words like "awesome." I must add that when I tried to slip into Atticus's skin and walk around in my own home, there must be a few extra wrinkles, for I don't see my children, my Scout or Jem, regarding me with the Solomonesque stature accorded Atticus by his. He is, nevertheless, as fine a moral compass as we could model for navigation of our children's lives.'

In his own life, Greg had grown in relation to his children. He had deepened since the tragic death of Jonathan. He was less self-righteous, more considerate and alert to the feelings of others. He laughed easily at himself, joked now and then and did what he could to share in their lives. He realized they faced pressures that were totally alien to him growing up. 'Beverly Hills is devastating for children,' said Greg. 'There's so much peer pressure there, and so much of the talk is about nothing but movies. Our children did grow up in an atmosphere of affluence. I'm not denying that or apologizing for it. But we tried to balance it by emphasizing education.'

He thought he had all the bases covered. Pa Baxter, the character he played in *The Yearling*, uttered words of paternal love, a heart-wrenching, bone-deep anguish that Greg must have felt personally at some point. Pa Baxter tells his son: 'Every man wants life to be a fine thing, and easy. Well, it's fine, son, powerful fine, but it ain't easy . . . A man's heart aches seeing his young 'uns face the world knowing they got to have their insides tore out the way his was tore.'

In collaboration with his son Stephen, Greg produced and narrated a cassette recording of the New Testament. 'The work brought us closer,' Stephen said.

They chose to use the King James version of the Bible, as the actor says, because 'the language is the most fulsome and poetic and rich – excepting the fact that some of the passages are difficult to understand and others are full of redundancy. As an actor you find yourself at times wanting to do some editing. We didn't fool around; it's word for word.'

Carey Peck was helping to build the rapid transit system for Los Angeles. 'He's trying to get rid of the air pollution and get people around quicker,' boasted Greg. 'It'll take 20 to 25 years, but it will change LA for the better.'

In 1988, Carey got married again. This time to painter and sculptor Lita Albuquerque, California's leading female artist working in the public art arena. She developed a respect and affection for Greg. 'When I was a little girl, I was completely in love with him, of course.' Lita had two daughters from a previous marriage. Then she and Carey had a son, Christopher Jonathan Peck.

One regular on the awards circuit Greg kept bumping into was his old friend Lauren Bacall. They first met when she was a 17-year-old usher in a theater where he played on Broadway. Later they made *Designing Woman*. Now they were being given a chance to work together again. In 1993, Greg and Bacall teamed up to star in a television movie called *The Portrait*. They give an amiable loving spin to the tale of an aging couple, still very much in love, and their petulant adult daughter (well played by Greg's daughter Cecilia), who comes home to paint their portrait. It was an opened-up adaptation by Lynn Roth of Tina Howe's 1983 Off-Broadway play *Painting Churches*. Greg was the film's co-executive producer and Robert Greenwald was the producer. They completed the production in 22 days. 'It can be done,' Greg assured. Greg organized a week's rehearsal in his house in Los Angeles before they headed south to cover 16 locations around the Duke University campus in Raleigh, North Carolina.

In the movie, Greg is required to scull. The plot even alludes to rowers of the class of '39, his own from the University of California, Berkeley. With refresher lessons from UCLA's crew coach and after a few plunges into the drink, the 75-year-old Greg mastered the single shell and looks relaxed in the opening scene of the film. He also felt at home in his actor's skin. 'Some critics overlook actors who appear to be natural,' he said confidently. 'They never realize that it took a great deal of work to be that natural.'

Greg found playing opposite his daughter, 'a total unmitigated joy. She is absolutely wonderful and totally natural.' Whenever anyone asked about her, his face would beam with pleasure. (Cecilia won a Golden Globe for her supporting role.)

Cecilia – who won the genetic lottery with knockout features from both parents – had already made several movies including *Wall Street* (1987), an Oliver Stone film.

Tony was also pursuing an acting career. He was blessed with the comic gift Greg yearned to have, and was cast opposite Brooke Shields in *Brenda Star* (1989). A few years before, when he played in the movie *Pirates* (1986) Greg advised him: 'Be bold. And if you can't be bold, act bold.'

Greg was Tony's best cheerleader, but being a son and not a

daughter, comparisons were made. Tony was an actor. Greg said their styles were as different as their looks. Tony looks more like his mother. 'If he adopted all my characteristics and attitudes without branching off in his own direction, then I'd have be worried. We've been up to see him a couple of times and he's really talented. He's got a wonderful sense of comedy and moves like a rocket.'

Tony, the youngest of the boys, lost several years of his life through alcoholism. Like his half-brother Jonathan, he could not get out from under the burden of being Gregory Peck's son. And though Greg tried to give him a chance to develop his own identity by sending him to prep school abroad, four years at Aiglon in Switzerland wasn't enough, nor were the next four years at Amherst. He sought solace in alcohol. 'At first, I really liked to drink,' explained Tony. 'At the beginning, it was great, and at the end it was awful. Then, too, I guess that I was trying to hide from a life that gave me too many opportunities. I thought I was undeserving. I was given so much and didn't have to work for it.'

Tony struggled as an actor. Like Jonathan, there existed a chasm between where he was with his life and where he wanted to be. Not only was his father talented and accomplished, but so were his friends. 'I loved and revered Frank Sinatra,' explained Tony by way of example, 'who was a friend of dad's going back to the '30s when they were both struggling young entertainers. For a time, I had a musical act in Vegas called the Tony Peck Trio and wanted to swing just like Frank.' He laughed and added, 'but whenever I was going to watch Frank in concert, I would be painfully reminded that there was a big gap between his talent and mine.'

Could it have been the world he was exposed to through his parents? Supermodel Tara Shannon, a sometime girlfriend of Tony's, told an interviewer: 'I'm going out to dinner with Gregory Peck's friends, Frank Sinatra, Roger Moore, Jimmy Stewart, Billy Wilder. Gregory was a great guy, a very humble guy. I knew that I didn't like Tony, but I was digging hanging out with all these people that all the other girls were wanting to be with. That was the surprising thing for me. I got to the other side of the tracks, and I looked at these people, and they had no values, and it was bizarre.

I started seeing stars, rich people, how they treated their wives. I started hearing the gossip. How this producer's wife was a hooker, and I just got very disillusioned.'

As the 1980s progressed, Tony became a familiar sight to celebrity watchers as the companion of Cheryl Tiegs, the blonde and blue-eyed cover girl turned cosmetics guru.

Their backgrounds were markedly different. Born on her family's isolated farm in the frozen north of Minnesota, Tiegs developed grit early. There was no running water or plumbing, and she had only her older sister for a play. 'We had one pair of shoes,' she said, 'and they were for winter.'

Tiegs got a jumpstart on success because of her looks and took it from there. She was the ubiquitous cover girl for *Glamour* magazine and *Sports Illustrated*; the annual swimsuit issue was basically created as a showcase for her. She signed record-breaking deals with Sears Roebuck, Clairol and Cover Girl Cosmetics for $15 million.

In her early 20s, she married Hollywood film director, Stan Dragoti. But the relationship ended soon after he was arrested for cocaine possession and entered re-hab. Her second husband was the Kenyan wildlife photographer and adventurer Peter Beard, a scion of the East Coast establishment, who had dropped out to live in the African bush. For three years Tiegs seemed happy with him. But Beard proved to be decadent and narcissistic.

When Tony and Cheryl met, she was at the height of her fame. He took one look at her and fell in love. After a long courtship, they were married at Frank Sinatra's compound in Palm Springs. Mom and dad did not attend. Greg was filming *Other People's Money* in New England and Veronique stayed with him. Cecilia represented the family. But marriage, and the birth of his son Zackery, only exacerbated Tony's sense of unworthiness. He continued his downward spiral. It was the crackup of his marriage that made him realize he had to change. It took a while, but he did it.

There was a great fear in the Peck family that they could lose Tony as they lost Jonathan. Greg stayed close to him while he got sober and tried to make a new life for himself. He invited his son to move back home into the log cabin he had erected on the property in homage to Lincoln. He also worked with his son on a remake of Ingmar Bergman's classic *Wild Strawberries* (1957). 'My father never let me down,' Tony told Michael Sheldon of the *Telegraph*. 'I let myself down. With Dad, what you see is what you get. He is totally like the lawyer he plays in *To Kill a Mockingbird*. Gregory Peck *is* Atticus Finch.' And although the *Wild Strawberries* project didn't pan out, Tony did write a movie called *Diary of a Sex Addict* which is now available on television.

How *tempus fugit*! Before he knew it, Greg had reached the tribute stage. Just when his career was developing late life momentum, his film colleagues wanted to treat him as though he was dead and gone. Attending an awards ceremony held in your behalf is a bit like being present at your own funeral. It may be an honor but you'd just as soon put it off for another 50 years. It's particularly irksome if you are 'between engagements' and hoping for work. There was truth in jest when Greg quipped on his 80th birthday: 'If a great role comes along, I'll come charging out of the barn, snorting!' He wanted to go on acting and acting and acting because he belonged to these people of the theater and the movies and the make-believe world they created.

Still, Greg was an icon and attention must be paid. To become a legend you have to be better than your competition. Your successes have to outweigh your failures, and you have to have endurance. Greg was the stuff of legends.

Ironically, of the scores of movies Greg made, there wasn't much he really liked: *The Gunfighter, Twelve O'Clock High, Roman Holiday, The Guns of Navarone* and *To Kill a Mockingbird*. According to Harry Belafonte, Greg 'always bemoaned the fact that he never thought he quite lived up to all he expected of himself in the films he did . . . He always felt that there was someplace else he could have gone and more he could have done.'

The general feeling about Greg among his peers is that while he may not have been a great actor, he was a fine one and solidly professional. Tom Hanks, the youngest person to ever receive the American Film Institute Lifetime Achievement Award, referred to Greg in a way that must have warmed the cockles of the veteran actor's heart. 'It's too soon to tell if I will be a success or not,' said Hanks. 'To me, success is constantly getting better at your craft and performing at a high level for an extended period of time. Jimmy Stewart, Gregory Peck – those are people who have been successful. Fame is different than success. Fame does something to your head from which you may never recover.'

Starting in 1989 when he received the American Film Institute Lifetime Achievement Award, Greg was on a roll. In the following years he was fêted by the Kennedy Center and the Lincoln Center Film Society as well as receiving other accolades such as the Emmy, Golden Globe, the International Jewish Film Festival Award and the Marian Anderson Humanitarian Award. He was also honored in France – his adopted homeland thanks to Veronique – when he was made a Chevalier of the Légion d'Honneur under President Mitterand and a Commandeur under President Chirac. Of all the honors he received over his lifetime, perhaps the one that did him the most good was the Oscar. Crazy as it sounds, a study of Oscar recipients found they live an average of four years longer than those who are nominated but don't win.

While it's no fun to be treated like a Golden Oldie, awards nights are great occasions to get together with eminent friends and listen to them say wonderful things about you. At the American Film Institute Lifetime Achievement Gala, Audrey Hepburn confided to a packed house: 'The biggest disappointment of my life in making *Roman Holiday* with Greg was I didn't get to end up with him at the finish of the movie.' But she added warmly, 'What I did get out of *Roman Holiday* was 40 years of remarkable friendship.'

Isaac Stern recalled 'the time when we were together in the South of France, drinking a great deal, being rowdy, throwing plates in a restaurant and breaking them.' At that, Jane Fonda clutched her hand to her chest in awe. 'He's done it all. By God, he's even broken plates with Isaac Stern!'

Better than that, Greg had the singular distinction of becoming the subject of a zany, Marx Brothers sketch comedy titled *Hooray for Gregory Peck's Ass!* Jon Wiley, one of the troupe's principals, decided to send him a copy of their script for comments. 'We looked up his address on one of those maps of Hollywood stars' homes,' recollected Wiley.

'What can I say,' Greg replied. 'Other honors and accolades pale by comparison. *Hooray for Gregory Peck's Ass!* is the solacement of my later years.'

Now that he had achieved elder statesman status, Greg used his lofty position to act as a guide and moral touchstone to his prodigal flock. He decried the dishonest, bullying, thieving mentality of many Hollywood players. 'People don't know what to believe in, in this period of unrest and changing values, but heroic qualities – trustworthiness, courage, bravery, truthfulness, reliability – don't seem to be on the list,' he lamented. 'Tom Hanks as Forrest Gump had them all, but they couldn't play them straight – he had to be retarded.'

He sneered at 'The breast pocket executives now running the store. The old boys – Louis B Mayer, Darryl Zanuck, Jack Warner, they were dragons, but they had passion and creativity . . . I'd like to hear some glamorous talk about the quality of work,' he said. 'Imagination is the priceless resource, and it's greatly undervalued.' Another time he scoffed: 'The top production jobs at the major studios are filled by a succession of executives who skip from company to company as if they were playing musical chairs.' And still another time: 'I'm not excited by cartoon violence in outer space.'

In accepting the American Film Institute's Award, Greg gave a speech that was interrupted by applause more than a half a dozen times. In it, he questioned what movies have become. 'There has been a lot of glamorous financial news in the papers lately,' the actor said. 'Multi-media conglomerates . . . It may be that, in a few years, all pictures and all television will be made by two or three of these behemoths who happen also to own magazines, newspapers and cable stations, and to manufacture and distribute video cassettes.

'If these Mount Everests of the financial world are going to labor and bring forth still more pictures with people being blown to bits with bazookas and automatic assault rifles, with no gory detail left unexploited, if they are going to encourage anxious, ambitious actors, directors, writers and producers to continue their assault on the English language by reducing the vocabularies of their characters to half a dozen words, with one colorful but overused Anglo-Saxon verb and one unbeautiful Anglo-Saxon noun covering just about every situation, then I would like to suggest that they stop and think about this: making millions is not the whole ball game, fellows. Pride of workmanship is worth more. Artistry is worth more.'

For himself, he just wanted to get back to work as an actor. 'I don't want any more money, awards, fame or parties. My pride, if I have my vanity – and I do – is to do a good job. So I can respect myself and be respected by those actors and directors who know what acting is really all about.'

Greg's opinion counted for a lot when a heated controversy arose in the film industry over the matter of whether or not to give an award to Elia Kazan at the Oscar ceremonies. No one denied Kazan's body of work was impressive. He won Best Director Oscars for *Gentleman's Agreement* (1947) starring Greg and *On The Waterfront* (1954) starring Marlon Brando. It was a matter of the McCarthy hearings. 'Gadge' named names during the anti-Communist 'witch hunts'. He informed on eight friends who had been Communist Party members. Although more than 40 years had gone by since the hearings, Kazan's collaboration was fresh in many minds.

Walter Bernstein, a blacklisted screenwriter said of the Oscar: 'It is being given to a man who disgraced the industry. He hurt the industry and the people in it. It's being given as a lifetime achievement award. One of his achievements was that he cooperated with an infamous committee, and I don't think he should be given an award for that. Forgive him, OK – forgive him. Just don't give him an award.'

Greg held to the position that it's important to separate a man's character and actions from his creative works – otherwise you run the risk of traveling down a very slippery slope. Kazan was unquestionably one of the major influences in motion pictures in the twentieth century. So Greg felt he should be given the award. 'He's made a great contribution to American film,' asserted Greg, 'politics aside, as an artist he made a great contribution, he deserves an award.'

Pete Hamill held this position when he wrote a book about Greg's close pal called: *Why Sinatra Matters*. 'In the end, it is of minor interest that Lord Byron swam the Hellespont, that André Malraux flew in combat during the Spanish Civil War or that Ernest Hemingway shot lions in Africa. In the end, only the work matters. Sinatra's finest work was making music.'

During the 1960s, Dominick Dunne was a successful television producer and also at the epicenter of Hollywood's social scene. 'I got caught up in all that Hollywood shit,' said Dunne.

One night, while dining at a trendy Los Angeles eatery, he was tapped on the shoulder by the restaurant's captain. 'I'm sorry, Mr Dunne,' said the man, 'but Mr Sinatra made me do this.' The captain decked him in front of the A-list crowd. Old Blue Eyes watched from a nearby table with a smirk on his face. He had paid the man $50 to squelch Dunne.

Over the next decade, thanks to alcohol and cocaine, Dunne bottomed out. Then, in 1979, he left town. 'When you're down and out, there's no meaner place to live than Hollywood, said Dunne. 'You can get away with your embezzlements and your lies and your murders, but you can never get away with failing.'

Back on his feet, Dunne returned to LA in 1995 to cover the O J Simpson trial. He soon became a darling of the dinner party circuit sharing his scoop on O J. One of those nights he was invited to Greg's house where he was the center of attention – overshadowing a petulant, sulking old singer named Frank Sinatra.

'They're dying like flies in this town,' Greg said with sadness. It seemed every month he was going to a funeral and often delivering the eulogy. The list kept growing: Frank Sinatra, Ruth Gordon, Rosalind Russell, Sanford Meisner, Stanley Kramer, Jack Lemmon, Walter Matthau, Lew Wasserman, Greer Garson, Jack Benny, Fred Astaire, Billy Wilder, William Wyler, and Ingrid Bergman. He was hit especially hard by the death of Audrey Hepburn who died of colon cancer. She had been a goodwill ambassador for UNICEF for six years and toured Somali refugee camps. He had put his generation to bed, as well as some older and some younger. He had somehow successfully managed to outlive them.

A death that particularly bothered him was Ava Gardner's. She spent her last years mostly secluded in her sumptuous London flat tethered to an oxygen tank. In 1987, she came out of retirement briefly to appear on *Knots Landing* 'for the loot, Honey, for the loot.' She was strapped for money yet tried to keep up a brave front. Partially paralyzed as a legacy of her 1986 stroke, the woman with the mesmerizing looks and public life lived a harsh existence with her longtime housekeeper, Carmen Vargas, and her beloved Welsh corgi, Morgan. When her first husband, Mickey Rooney, arrived in London in the late 1980s with his smash hit musical *Sugar Babies*, he was riding high. He rang up Gardner at her flat. She told him she had had two strokes and rasped: 'Don't be surprised if someday soon you'll hear that I've blown my fuckin' brains out.' She died of natural causes on 25 January 1990.

Her graveside ceremony in a modest cemetery in Smithtown, North Carolina, mirrored the final scene of *The Barefoot Contessa* (1954): a driving rain falling on a vast canopy of umbrellas, with nearly 4,000 people showing up to say farewell. (Greg did not attend. In fact, no one from Hollywood did.)

In May 1992 Greg's mother died. He delivered the eulogy at the Cypress Lawn Chapel in San Francisco. At 97 she had really given life a run for its money. While she hadn't been a hands-on mom with Greg, Bunny was a favorite with her grandchildren. 'The one who brings us all together is my mother,' Greg said a few years before her demise. 'She's 92 and still wonderfully pretty and spirited. She goes to the races and bets like a sailor on colors and birthdays and names – and she wins!' Indeed, Bunny knew how to grab at life with both hands. That was a powerful legacy to bequeath to him.

By now, Greg wanted to make all the exciting people who had cavorted through his life live again. But how? He could write a book. Back in the 1970s, Swifty Lazar offered him a million dollars to write his memoirs. But Lazar offered every famous person he met a million dollars for their story. It was his way of saying hello.

Greg had jotted down anecdotes over the years with the idea of writing a book like David Niven's wildly popular *The Moon's a Balloon*. Like Niven, Greg had an ear for piquancy, an eye for the amusing and the absurd and the poignant, but unlike the English actor, he came up short on clear-eyed candor and refreshing frankness. He could laugh at himself, but his perfectionism acted as inner critic. It forced him to edit out unattractive aspects of himself, his friends and his family. In his desire to pretty up the picture, he missed things. And, as Hemingway said, a good writer needs a 'built-in shockproof shit detector.' If Greg had one, he kept it well hidden.

Like the words on the sundial, he was determined to count 'none but the sunny hours' – he wanted to recollect his best moments and weave them into a show. He hungered for a live audience. But he had told the same stories over and over again like lines in a play that has run too long. He knew he would have to muster his best skills as a raconteur to make it all fresh. And, he reasoned, the public in its heart of hearts loves a success story. He'd give them that. He wanted to take his production on the road getting the feel of the sawdust trail just as he did on his first tour of the United States with Katharine Cornell back in the early 1940s.

At the same time, he had his apprehensions. Appearing on stage in a one-man show is exciting because it is scary. You feel very naked up there because it is just you, telling your story, with nothing else to mediate between you and other people.

But in 1995 off he went to Calgary, Anchorage, Hartford, Atlanta, Seattle and many more cities and towns with *A Conversation with Gregory Peck*. He spent two years visiting local theaters in a kind of farewell tour to an extraordinary career. He showed clips of some of his most famous roles, paid homage to starlets and swashbucklers and evoked poignant memories of an era long gone.

'Cary Grant gave me the idea,' he admitted. (Maybe it wasn't one of Grant's best, at least not for him, since he died while trouping through the provinces on one of these gigs.)

In Greg's case, the finished product was very much Greg's own. It proved that finally, after all these years, he had expelled the stone inside him that weighed him down. Gone was the 'wooden plank' actor, the 'cigar store Indian.' There was buoyancy, a dry wit and a happy heart. And when he'd tell a story and his eyes were smiling, it took your heart away. There's no substitute for Gaelic wit and the sense of the absurd.

Through his palaver, he let his audience meet the ravishing

women and fascinating screwballs who peppered his Hollywood life. He focused on his successful movies, and the others faded into the background. He rejoiced in talking about his comedies and Westerns. His self-deprecating humor endeared him to the adoring crowds. His intelligence was fierce, assured; he always sounded smart and intellectually composed. 'I hope that my main contribution has been to entertain people over the years,' Greg reflected, 'to give them enjoyment, some pleasure, some excitement, some romance, something to think about. Something to carry away from the theater with them so that they think of me as an old friend.'

Watching her father's show, Cecilia Peck wanted to capture it on film. As it happened she was working with Barbara Kopple who is widely considered one of the finest living documentary filmmakers. She received Academy Awards for directing *Harland County, USA* (1976), about the effects of a labor strike on 180 coal-mining families, and *American Dream* (1990) about a Hormel plant strike that changed the labor movement forever.

So Cecilia asked Kopple to film Greg's one-man stage show. Kopple said: 'Well, as a gift to your dad, we'll all just go film. We'll do one show, and just give it as a gift.' But one thing led to another and Kopple and crew found they couldn't stop. So what started out as a gift, became the film *A Conversation with Gregory Peck* (1999).

Kopple traveled with Greg, capturing several of his delightful, informal talks around the country, intercut with home movies, footage of the Pecks' home life and generous clips from his films (most notably, *To Kill a Mockingbird*). Cecilia, who was pregnant at the time, co-produced, which probably accounts for how easygoing and playful Greg sometimes is.

The film version reveals the actor as a family man. He loves and argues with his daughter. He roots for his favorite basketball team with his sons. The film captures Greg's high points – as well as his darker moments, when he discusses the suicide of Jonathan. It somewhat, but not completely, catches the aura of Greg. The spiritual aspect he projected in age was more evident in person. He is frail and walks with a cane with difficulty. Yet, one senses the Lord is at his elbow. When someone asked Kopple if Greg manifested any of his famous temper during the filming of the documentary, she said 'No, never.' However, he was sensitive about his feeble gait. 'He's a tall man,' explained Kopple, 'and he was touchy about us filming him and trying to get somewhere.'

He was both modest and touching: 'I'm not as wise as I'd hoped to be. There's obviously more to remember them to look forward to. But I suppose in the end, I am a family man. I like having a 20-month-old grandchild. I like thinking about him. I like thinking about all my grandchildren. In the long term, family is what counts. The fame and the awards and the nonsense that goes with them fades away. You are left with a good family and maybe some good works.'

The continuing popularity of Greg's films on video and the success of the documentary have kept his image alive as an idol. Just as the women shrieked and swooned at the sight of him back in 1944, Greg's followers continued to be fiercely emotional about him. For example, in 1998 Rina Pertusi accompanied her husband to the play *The Beauty Queen of Leanne* in New York. As the lights dimmed, she looked down her row and spotted Greg. 'When at last the curtain fell for the intermission,' Pertusi recounted, 'I sprang out of my seat, and not caring whose kneecaps I'd be breaking, practically charged over to Mr Peck. There was a vacancy to his left and he was standing to let other people pass. I said, "Mr Peck, may I say a few words to you?" And he told me I could, and then invited me to sit beside him.'

For some of his public, Greg's advancing age put him out of the running. Columnist Meg Wood confided to her readers: '. . . I need to stress that I only love the young Gregory Peck. I mean, well, that sounds cruel, doesn't it? But he just doesn't do anything for me now. I think it's the white hair; it's a shock. Actually I think the weirdest part is that his face and body still look pretty much unchanged. But that hair! It is, well, it's a slap in the face! . . . the young Gregory – hubba hubba.'

According to a young lady who goes by the name Helen on the Internet, there's real live hope for fans dreaming of a younger Greg. Helen reports another gorgeous Peck is in the pipeline. Herewith her message: 'Gregory Peck may be nothing but an old crusty man now, but his grandson Ethan, who is in the grade below me in high school, looks just like his grandpa. Which means, in 10 years or so, you'll have a whole new Peck to drool over. Or, if you're my age, one to drool over right now. Just imagine a 16-year-old Atticus Finch in a rock band. Mmm.'

As the years added up, Greg continued paring down and shaping his life to include only those things that gave him a sense of emotional fulfillment. In the mornings, he often had thoughts of death and this motivated him to get out of bed and get rolling. He loved sitting in his garden where he grew large, juicy tomatoes. He liked devoting time to projects that meant something to him, such as the La Jolla Playhouse which he and his acting friends founded more than 50 years ago. 'He's had a huge impact on the performing arts in San Diego,' said La Jolla Playhouse artistic director Des McAnuff, 'and we at the Playhouse owe him our existence.' Greg also stayed involved with the Motion Picture and Television Fund that looks after old and sick actors, and the film department of University College in Dublin. He also produced six readings a year for the Central Los Angeles Library.

Starting in 1995, Greg asked his friends – it doesn't hurt when your friends include Morgan Freeman, Beau Bridges, James Woods, Richard Dreyfuss, Lynn Redgrave, Sally Fields, Charlton Heston and Patrick Stewart – to participate in a reading series at the central library's Mark Taper Auditorium. The events proved to be hugely popular, drawing capacity turnouts of patrons who paid $250 or more for exclusive invitations to attend.

Greg personally recruited the actors for each of the six meetings per year. He admitted: 'When I call people, mostly they say yes. Once in a while I have to go through a buffer person, or PR person.' These occasional ego bruisings didn't deter him.

With gallantry and guts, he continued to champion the cause of gun control legislation. In 1999, he accepted the Marian Anderson prize, named for the Philadelphia-born singer who broke the race barrier at the Metropolitan Opera and who advanced social progress in her humanitarian work.

However, his chumminess with America's most famous gun-slinger opened him to criticism. Charlton Heston, president of the National Rifle Association, is a zealot about an American's right to bear arms. When James Brady pinned him down about Heston, Greg didn't shilly-shally. 'We're colleagues, rather than friends,' Greg said. 'We're civil to each other when we meet. I, of course, disagree vehemently with him on gun control.'

As a board member of Handgun Control Inc. (along with Martin Sheen and Susan Sarandon), Greg was well versed on the issue. Since the 1960s, the number of guns in America has leapt from 75 million to 230 million. Still, would Greg have helped his cause more by giving Heston the treatment he'd given Robert Bork?

Perhaps. But firearms are a (forgive the pun) loaded issue in Hollywood. Why are so many celebrities reluctant to speak out? Is it because many of them pack heat themselves (Sean Penn recently reported two guns stolen from his car) or is it because they don't want to alienate their pro-gun friends? Michael Beard, president of the Coalition to Stop Gun Violence, has a quick answer: Charlton Heston. 'He has a lot of friends and a lot of respect in Hollywood,' Beard says. 'He and [wife] Lydia are liked personally.' According to Beard, even Greg kept a relatively low profile to avoid butting heads with the NRA's most outspoken point man. 'They are friends, and he doesn't want to take on that.'

Out of the public arena, Greg could drop the heavy weight of his gravitas. In his tight circle, he could let his gray lion's-mane hair down. Roger Moore provided a glimpse of the more relaxed Greg when he talked about him to a dinner of Great Britain's Variety on 24 July 2001. 'This was from my great friend Gregory Peck, who said to me one day, and you know the way Gregory Peck speaks, you don't really think of him as being long on humor – Frank Sinatra used to say about Gregory he is like Mount Rushmore, every time he laughs dust comes out. Anyway, Greg said [Moore put on a very sincere voice]: When things go wrong, and they usually will, when your daily role seems all up hill, when your funds are low and your debts are high, when you would like to laugh but you can only cry, when you really feel you will have to quit, don't come to me. I don't give a shit.'

One of Greg's favorite drinks was Guinness stout – Ireland's mother's milk. This preference came to the attention of his cousin Thomas Ashe, a direct descendent of Greg's ancestral hero whose photograph hung on the wall of his study. Realizing his cousin's fondness for a pint of plain, Ashe used his contacts in Guinness to make a dream of Peck's come true. 'We were having a few pints one night and he mentioned that he would love to have a tap back in his place in California. I got in contact with Guinness in Dublin and they got on to their reps in California and the tap was installed. He was delighted. His neighbors, Jack Nicholson and Frank Sinatra's wife, would meet in Peck's house regularly to play cards and drink pints, they all loved the stuff, he told me.' Greg's other poker buddies included Angie Dickinson, Larry Gelbart, who wrote *M*A*S*H**, and Jack Lemmon, who was a lousy player but liked to sit at the piano and toss in some rollicking tunes while his more adventurous friends won and lost money. Beats playing bingo at the Beverly Hills senior citizen center.

As Greg moved up in his 80s, he looked thin and frail. He quipped: 'I'm on a first-name basis with three or four doctors.'

With the loss of weight and the resultant definition of his features, he bore a resemblance to the lean and bony young man he was when he played Father Chisholm in *The Keys of the Kingdom* back in 1944.There was also the same spiritual aspect that he exhibited in that film of an ecclesiastical father. Kathleen Murphy in *Film Comment* in 1992 wrote that he represented a 'father for all seasons. His visage, voice and frame came to signal home ground, to shelter whole litters of lost sons and daughters, and to foster faith in just, though sometimes controversial, causes.'

In public, Greg leaned on a cane. Sometimes that wasn't enough and he relied on Veronique or Cecilia to support him. His memory was failing. But offered a part, and he was up and at 'em. In 1998, he played Orson Welles' role of Father Mapple in *Moby Dick*, a made-for-TV version also starring Patrick Stewart. Though it was only one day's work, it garnered him a Golden Globe for Best Supporting Actor in a Series, Miniseries or Movie Made for Television.

'It all started in Berkeley with *Moby Dick*,' Greg reminisced with his agent Monroe Friedman. 'Then I came to Hollywood and it was *Moby Dick*. And now I'm retiring and I'm in *Moby Dick* again.'

Most of the time, Greg stayed on the grounds of his home on

Carolwood Drive, sheltered from the world. Just beyond the double wrought-iron gates, the squat tour-buses, stuffed with avid fans, clutching their 'Map to the Stars' Homes,' craned their necks to get a glimpse of him. At the same time, he welcomed the precious few visitors fortunate enough to penetrate his private world.

Lisa Krohn of Minneapolis developed a special friendship with Greg. It sprang up quickly when he blew through town with his one-man show in the mid 1990s. After his return to Los Angeles, they wrote to each other and sent each other Christmas cards and small gifts. When she traveled to the West Coast, he invited her into his home for an afternoon.

As he showed her around the grounds of his 4-acre estate, he spoke eloquently about his trees and flowers in a slow, deliberate manner. 'He had a kumquat tree near the house,' said Krohn, 'and took great delight in convincing me to try one and then watching my face curl up in a grimace with the tart taste. I'll never forget that laugh and look of glee on his face after I bit into it.'

Greg had difficulty walking and his stamina started to flag. Struggling with the steps on his terraced property, he confided to Krohn that Ava Gardner – afflicted with serious emphysema and unable to go far without her oxygen tank in the later stage of her life – taught him how to navigate stairs. 'Step one, rest one,' he uttered. 'He seemed to like that and we laughed and went up the steps just that way.'

'I'm lucky to have you as a friend,' Greg said at the end of her visit. 'I almost laughed,' recalled Lisa, 'but as I look back, that was the nicest thing he could have said to me.'

On any given day, one or two, or all six of his grandchildren romped about. And he took great joy in participating vicariously in his children's lives. Now in middle age, the four of them had each accomplished the difficult task of carving out their own identities.

Stephen is a respected leader in US VETS, the largest organization in the country dedicated to helping homeless veterans. Once having given Greg so many sleepless nights during his tour of duty as a combat marine in Vietnam, he now directs a program for homeless veterans at March Air Force Base property in Long Beach, California. 'There has always been a feeling among veterans, born out of battle, that we take care of those who fight side by side with us,' said Stephen. Greg frequently attended Homeless Veterans Coalition events and lent his name to the cause. Asked about the wellspring of his altruism, Stephen said, 'That certainly came right from Dad.'

Carey, still casual and youthful, works in real estate in Los Angeles. His true passion, however, is skydiving. While Greg's athletic accomplishment of sweep rowing is often cited as the ultimate team sport, Carey has probably done one better. He was the dive leader and choreographer of the 'weed whacker' formation that a group of skydivers – 24 cancer survivors from nine states – attempted to make in the sky. The purpose was to show that having cancer does not necessarily rule out strenuous activities. In Carey's case, he has skin cancer. 'It's my repayment for my boyhood spent on the beach in California.'

Tony successfully made the switch from acting to screenwriting. In 1998, he co-wrote the made-for-television comedy *Free Money* with Joseph Brutsman and acted as executive producer. It starred Charlie Sheen, Marlon Brando and Donald Sutherland. In 2001, he wrote *Diary of a Sex Addict,* starring Michael Des Barres, Rosanna Arquette and Natasha Kinski, of which he was the producer. Since his divorce from Cheryl Tiegs, he has forged a viable friendship with her as they partner in raising their son Zackery.

On 8 September 2001 Greg finally had the honor of giving away his only daughter in marriage. Cecilia, 45, wed Daniel Voll in a ceremony performed at the Peck home. Guests arrived from as far away as Bali. Most of those who gathered were close friends of Cecilia and Daniel's, but Greg's old buddies included Lauren Bacall, Jennifer Jones, Barbara Sinatra, Felicia Farr Lemmon, Angie Dickinson and Pat and Larry Gelbart. The ring bearer was Cecilia and Daniel's two-year-old son Harper (named for Harper Lee). Then on 2 April 2002 Ondine Alexandra Peck-Voll was born.

At the beginning of 2003, Greg went into dramatic decline. His system was finally starting to break down. He suffered from a flare-up of his old back injury originally incurred by Martha Graham at the Neighborhood Playhouse and then exacerbated when he fell off a horse while preparing for his role in *Yellow Sky.* Now, hunched over, he needed help just to walk a few feet. In fact, according to Greta, he was bedridden much of the time.

In contemplating his passage to eternity, Greg said: 'The lead line for my obituary is sure to be 'Academy Award Winner for *To Kill a Mockingbird*.' In early June 2003, an announcement by the American Film Institute set the stage for lots of publicity on that score. In a poll they conducted, Atticus Finch was voted the most admired hero in American cinema. Imagine that. Gentle Atticus, not a slam-bang, fists-ready, guns-blazing action hero, but a thoroughly decent human being.

In a welcome kindness of fate, Greg was alive to hear the news. A week after the media trumpeted Atticus's title, and just days before Father's Day, Greg neared the end. On the night of 12 June he told Veronique he didn't feel well. So she sat with him and held his hand. What must have passed through her mind in these final hours? Here was a man who won the applause, devotion, admiration, and respect of the world. Yet, for all his renown, she knew him in his private moments. In fact, she played a large part in helping him to realize his remarkable depth and breadth as a human being. Now 71, she had been married to him for 48 years. And they had rarely been apart – even for a day at a time.

'They leaned on each other,' said Angie Dickinson, a close friend of the couple. 'They helped each other. They worshipped each other.' Added Harry Belafonte: 'I've never seen a couple that was so persistently in a honeymoon . . . I thought it was fake for a while.'

Around 4 a.m. Greg looked at Veronique, dozed off and died quietly.

His life, as Shakespeare would say, was 'rounded in a sleep.' And, indeed, he was the stuff that dreams are made of. No particular cause of death was given. He had simply expired from old age.

'He had such a remarkable career and life and had so many people who admired him,' said James Woods, 'and genuinely liked him, that if you have to go you couldn't do better than to have been Gregory Peck for all those years.'

Michael Jackson was one Greg's steadfast friends. The day following Greg's death, the pop star visited Veronique and helped her plan the memorial service. The two men had been close for 25 years. Surprising to some, Greg was an outspoken defender of Jackson as a parent.

The bond was forged when 'The Gloved One' rang him up one day and asked to pay a visit. 'He had actually memorized all the dialogue in *To Kill a Mockingbird*,' Greg recalled, 'and he was full of questions about it.' As their friendship deepened, Greg accompanied Jackson on horseback rides at Neverland, the superstar's 2,600-acre ranch in the Santa Ynez Valley.

While Greg was all but canonized as a model parent, Jackson has drawn the world's wrath as an accused child molester. When accusations against the singer surfaced several years ago, Greg and Veronique praised the star in an open letter carried on Jackson's website.

Telling of the happy times the Pecks had spent with Jackson as well as with Prince Michael I and Paris (from his three-year marriage to his dermatology nurse Debbie Rowe) and Prince Michael II (by a surrogate mother), the Pecks said: 'We and our children, who are of your generation, have always admired you as a loving and caring father.' Greg also gave a glowing video tribute to Jackson at the singer's 30th Anniversary Celebration held at Madison Square Gardens in 2001.

*   *   *

The news of Greg's death shot round the world. It was greeted with sadness but also with recognition that Greg wouldn't be replaced any time soon. Recalling the actor was one of those 'people who come into a room and change the room,' Larry King said he couldn't think of anybody in Greg's league. 'I mean,' he said, 'there's some extraordinary actors today – Jack Nicholson and De Niro and Pacino. These are extraordinary figures, and they would have been major stars in the '40s or '50s or anywhere. But there's no one quite – you know, Peck was one of those guys that you – he was unique.'

Much of the sadness was the realization that America, and even the world, had lost a father figure. Greg and Atticus had seemed to meld into one.

To Kill a Mockingbird, the book and film, has been studied for so many years and has left such a deep impression that people now in their mid-20s, born long after Greg was in his acting prime, still felt a twinge of sadness when they heard about his passing.

There was also an American everyman aspect to Greg that his fans would sorely miss. 'We might have wanted to be Cary Grant or Clark Gable,' wrote a reporter for the *Washington Post,* 'but we knew we weren't smooth enough. We might have wanted to be Burt Lancaster or Kirk Douglas but they were too flashy and athletic. Jimmy Stewart was a bit too aw shucks, and Charlton Heston too granite-jawed handsome. But Gregory Peck made us feel we *were* him. And when he made us into Atticus Finch he helped all of us see what was possible.'

Greg's passing unleashed a flood of memories from people out of the spotlight whose lives he touched. Like a Greek god who swooped down to earth for brief visits with a mortal, Greg extended himself in a way few stars do. An English woman remembered that as a gangly girl of 13 with her hair in plaits, she danced with Gregory Peck. It was at the Grand National ball at the Adelphi hotel in Liverpool. Greg had a horse running and he was taking part in the festivities.

A man recalled that when he was a student, Greg presented him with a rowing medal and some sage advice. Another recalled how he stayed in the alumni tent at a Berkeley crew race because he didn't want his celebrity to take away from the glory of the rowers.

In the week following Greg's death, television channels broadcast instant Gregory Peck film festivals, running one movie of his after another. With 53 films to his credit, they had a large selection to choose from. In life, Greg had often been called inscrutable. But anyone interested in plumbing his depths need only visit their local video store. As we know by now, he hid behind his roles. Yet in bringing his screen characters so vividly to life, he exposed his innermost self.

In *The Big Country*, he displayed moral grit by refusing all manner of provocation, yet in *The Paradine Case*, he showed refreshing signs of moral frailty as a British barrister whose judgment is seriously flawed. In the original *Cape Fear*, he portrayed a peculiar masculine hysteria as a lawyer obliterating legal scruples to defend his family. In his scenery-chewing rendition of Josef Mengele in *The Boys From Brazil*, we see the normally inhibited Greg seizing the opportunity to bust loose. 'The no-goods make things happen,' said Greg who wished he had the opportunity to play more of them. 'They make people react.' In *Yellow Sky*, as the leader of a gang of robbers who are chased into a salt flat after robbing a bank, Greg prevails. Though tortured with fatigue and thirst, he remains every inch the man in charge.

Greg captured the brilliant but insecure Horatio Hornblower and, in doing so, exposed his own vulnerability. In *Duel in the Sun*, we see Greg the sexy rascal, the leering and sardonic seducer of Jennifer Jones. As Joe Bradley in *Roman Holiday*, we get to know Greg at his breezy best as the wised-up, cosmopolitan reporter. In *Twelve O'Clock High*, he reveals some of his core personality as the commander of an American bomber unit who dithers traumatically when he is obliged to send crews to their deaths over Nazi Germany. More than most of his films, we see a great deal of Greg in General Douglas MacArthur. He not only looked and sounded like MacArthur, but the two men shared vanity, stubbornness and intransigence.

In the course of his life, Greg sought out the company of eccentrics, law benders, chandelier swingers, midnight ramblers and misbegotten souls. It's safe to assume there were elements of Greg in these incorrigible mischief-makers.

Because he was such a meticulous planner, it is quite likely that Greg talked at some length with Veronique and his children about his funeral. What better setting for a Catholic who loved a good show than the new modernistic Our Lady of the Angels Cathedral situated in the heart of LA.

But was Greg a practicing Catholic? Some years before, while Greg was attending a film festival in Tokyo, Andrew Urban of *Weekend Australian,* put the question to him. 'I am a Roman Catholic,' Greg answered. 'Not a fanatic, but I practice enough to keep the franchise.' He laughed. Then he became more serious. 'I don't always agree with the Pope . . . there are issues that concern me, like abortion, contraception, the ordination of women . . . and others. I think the Church should open up.' Certainly, Greg's unequivocal support of Gay Rights pitted him in direct opposition to the Pope. In 1997, as a presenter at the Gay and Lesbian Alliance Against Defamation (GLAAD) awards ceremony, he said: 'It just seems silly to me that something so right and simple has to be fought for at all.'

Our Lady of the Angels Cathedral is the seat of the largest US Catholic diocese. It rests on an elevated section of downtown Los Angeles called Bunker Hill, where it can be seen by millions of people each year as they travel the busy Hollywood Freeway. In its size, proportions and beauty both within and without, it is exquisite. With a total of 27,000 square feet of windows, it is the biggest installation of its kind in America. Lita Albuquerque, Greg's daughter-in-law who is married to Carey, designed the Gateway Pool and Water Wall on the grounds of the Cathedral.

On Monday, 16 June 2003 Greg was laid to rest in a quiet family funeral in the crypt mausoleum beneath the Cathedral. Located across from St Vibiana's Chapel, it contains 6,000 crypts and niches for burials.

Crypts were believed to have been developed from the catacombs used by early Christians as hiding places from persecution, as shrines to saints and martyrs, as funeral memorials. Early churches often were constructed over the tombs of martyrs. At the entrance to the crypt mausoleum are two beautifully etched windows depicting guardian angels holding torches.

Mourners for the public service held after his burial beheld huge black-and-white portraits of Greg as they approached the Cathedral, designed by Robert Graham, husband of Anjelica Huston. They then passed through the Great Bronze Doors. Church officials estimated almost 3,000 people attended. Seats were reserved for Greg's friends, a sizeable number of whom were celebrities – they were instructed to whisper the secret password 'Atticus' to the red-coated ushers who escorted them to the reserved section – Harry Belafonte, Anjelica Huston, Michael York, Louise Fletcher, Tony Danza, Piper Laurie, Harrison Ford, Calista Flockhart. Michael Jackson, wearing a red jacket, caused a stir when he arrived 20 minutes late. Decked out in a bright blue pants suit and clutching a program with Greg's picture on it, Greta, at 92, was present looking hale and hearty.

Cardinal Roger Michael Mahoney, Archbishop of Los Angeles, presided over the service. The program included bible readings by Carey, Cecilia and Tony. Mahoney said: 'He lived his life authentically, as God called and willed him and placed him in his room, with gifts and talents.'

Seventy-five-year-old Brock Peters, who co-starred with Greg in *Mockingbird* delivered the eulogy. The film spawned a close friendship between Greg and Peters that lasted more than 40 years. 'In art there is compassion,' said Peters, 'in compassion there is humanity, with humanity there is generosity and love. Gregory Peck gave us these attributes in full measure.'

The crowd visibly warmed to a videotape performance of Greg featuring a lecture he gave several years before. In that rich baritone voice, which sounded like no other he said he hoped to be remembered first as a good husband, father and grandfather. Then, with quiet strength and unforgettable presence, he added: 'I'd like to be thought of as a good storyteller.' He will be. For many years to come. All in all, it was a glorious sendoff.

Filmography

1944
Days of Glory
Gregory Peck (Vladimir), Tamara Toumanova, Alan Reed, Maria Palmer, Lowell Gilmore, Hugo Haas, Dena Penn.
RKO
Producer: Casey Robinson.
Director: Jacques Tourneur.
Screenplay: Casey Robinson, from the story by Melchior Lengyel. Cinematography by Tony Gaudio.
86 minutes. Black and white.

1944
The Keys of the Kingdom
Gregory Peck (Father Francis Chisholm), Thomas Mitchell, Vincent Price, Rosa Stradner, Roddy McDowell, Edmund Gwenn, Sir Cedric Hardwicke.
Twentieth Century Fox
Producer: Joseph L Mankiewicz.
Director: John M Stahl.
Screenplay: Joseph L Mankiewicz and Nunnally Johnson, from the novel by A J Cronin. Cinematography by Arthur Miller.
137 minutes. Black and white.

1945
The Valley of Decision
Gregory Peck (Paul Scott), Greer Garson, Donald Crisp, Lionel Barrymore, Preston Foster, Gladys Cooper, Dean Stockwell, Jessica Tandy, Dan Duryea.
MGM
Producer: Edwin J Knopf.
Director: Tay Garnett.
Screenplay: John Meehan and Sonya Levien, from the novel by Marcia Davenport. Cinematography by Joseph Ruttenberg.
111 minutes. Black and white.

1945
Spellbound
Gregory Peck (Dr Anthony Edwardes/John Ballantine), Ingrid Bergman, Leo G Carroll, Michael Chekhov, Rhonda Fleming, Donald Curtis.
Selznick International/Vanguard Films/United Artists
Producer: David O Selznick.
Director: Alfred Hitchcock.
Screenplay: Ben Hecht, from the novel *The House of Dr. Edwardes* by Francis Beeding. Cinematography by George Barnes. Dream sequence designed by Salvador Dalí.
111 minutes. Black and white.

1946
The Yearling
Gregory Peck (Penny Baxter), Jane Wyman, Claude Jarman Jr, Chill Wills, Clem Bevans, Margaret Wycherly.
MGM
Producer: Sidney Franklin.
Director: Clarence Brown.
Screenplay: Paul Osborn, from the novel by Marjorie Kinnan Rawlings. Cinematography by Charles Rosher, Leonard Smith, and Arnold Arling.
134 minutes. Black and white.

1946
Duel in the Sun
Narrated by Orson Welles. Gregory Peck (Lewt McCanles), Joseph Cotton, Jennifer Jones, Lionel Barrymore, Lillian Gish, Walter Huston.
Vanguard/Selznick Releasing Organization
Producer: David O Selznick.
Director: King Vidor.
Screenplay: David O Selznick. Suggested by the novel by Niven Busch. Cinematography by Lee Garmes, Hal Rosson and Ray Rennahan.
138 minutes. Color.

1947
The Macomber Affair
Gregory Peck (Robert Wilson), Robert Preston, Joan Bennett, Reginald Denny, Earl Smith, Jean Gillie.
United Artists
Producers: Benedict Bogeaus and Casey Robinson.
Director: Zoltan Korda.
Screenplay: Casey Robinson and Seymour Bennett from the story 'The Short Happy Life of Francis Macomber' by Ernest Hemingway. Adaptation:

Seymour Bennett, Frank Arnold. Cinematography by Karl Strauss.
89 minutes. Black and white.

1947
Gentleman's Agreement
Gregory Peck (Phil Green), Dorothy McGuire, John Garfield, Celeste
Holm, Anne Revere, June Havoc, Albert Dekker, Jane Wyatt, Dean
Stockwell, Nicholas Joy, Sam Jaffe.
Twentieth Century Fox
Producer: Darryl F Zanuck.
Director: Elia Kazan.
Screenplay: Moss Hart, from the novel by Laura Z Hobson.
Cinematography by Arthur Miller.
118 minutes. Black and white.

1947
The Paradine Case
Gregory Peck (Anthony Keane), Charles Laughton, Charles Coburn, Ann
Todd, Ethel Barrymore, Louis Jourdan, Alida Valli, Leo G Carroll.
Vanguard/Selznick Releasing Organization
Producer: David O Selznick.
Director: Alfred Hitchcock.
Screenplay: David O Selznick, from the novel by Robert Hichens.
Cinematography by Lee Garmes.
132 minutes. Black and white.

1949
Yellow Sky
Gregory Peck (Stretch), John Russell, Richard Widmark, Charles Kemper,
Henry Morgan, Robert Adler, Anne Baxter.
Twentieth Century Fox
Producer: Lamar Trotti.
Director: William A Wellman.
Screenplay: Lamar Trotti. Based on a story by W R Burnett.
Cinematography by Joe MacDonald.
98 minutes. Black and white.

1949
The Great Sinner
Gregory Peck (Feodor 'Fedja' Dostoyevsky), Ava Gardner, Melvyn
Douglas, Walter Huston, Ethel Barrymore, Frank Morgan.
MGM
Producer: Gottfried Reinhardt.

Director: Robert Siodmak.
Screenplay: Ladislas Fudor and Christopher Isherwood, from a story by Fodor and Rene Fulop-Miller. Cinematography by George Foley.
110 minutes. Black and white.

1950
Twelve O'Clock High
Gregory Peck (General Frank Savage), Hugh Marlowe, Gary Merrill, Dean Jagger, Millard Mitchell, Robert Arthur.
Twentieth Century Fox
Producer: Darryl F Zanuck.
Director: Henry King.
Screenplay: Sy Bartlett and Beirne Lay Jr, from their novel. Cinematography by Leon Shamroy.
132 minutes. Black and white.

1950
The Gunfighter
Gregory Peck (Jimmie Ringo), Helen Westcott, Millard Mitchell, Jean Parker, Karl Malden, Skip Homeier, Richard Jaeckel.
Twentieth Century Fox
Producer: Nunnally Johnson.
Director: Henry King.
Screenplay: William Bowers and William Sellers, from a story by William Bowers and Andre de Toth. Cinematography by Arthur Miller.
84 minutes. Black and white.

1951
Only the Valiant
Gregory Peck (Captain Richard Lance), Barbara Payton, Ward Bond, Gig Young, Lon Chaney Jr, Neville Brand, Jeff Corey, Steve Brodie, Warner Anderson, Michael Ansara.
Warner Bros
Producer: William Cagney.
Director: Gordon Douglas.
Screenplay: Edmund H North and Harry Brown, from the novel by Charles Marquis Warren. Cinematography by Lionel Linden.
105 minutes. Black and white.

1951
David and Bathsheba
Gregory Peck (King David), Susan Hayward, Raymond Massey, Kieron Moore, James Robertson Justice, Jayne Meadows.

Twentieth Century Fox
Producer: Darryl F Zanuck.
Director: Henry King.
Screenplay: Philip Dunne. Cinematography by Leon Shamroy.
116 minutes. Color.

1951
Captain Horatio Hornblower
Gregory Peck (Captain Horatio Hornblower), Virginia Mayo, Robert Beatty, James Robertson Justice, Moultrie Kelsall, Terrence Morgan, Richard Hearne, James Kenney, Ingeborg Wells.
Warner Bros
Producer: Gerry Mitchell.
Director: Raoul Walsh.
Screenplay: Ivan Goff, Ben Roberts and Aeneas MacKenzie from the novels *Ship of the Line*, *Beat to Quarters*, and *Flying Colors* by C S Forester. Cinematography by Guy Green.
117 minutes. Color.

1952
The Snows of Kilimanjaro
Gregory Peck (Harry Street), Susan Hayward, Ava Gardner, Hildegard Knef, Leo G Carroll, Torin Thatcher, Ava Norring, Helene Stanley.
Twentieth Century Fox
Producer: Darryl F Zanuck.
Director: Henry King.
Screenplay: Casey Robinson, from a story by Ernest Hemingway. Cinematography by Leon Shamroy.
117 minutes. Color.

1952
The World in His Arms
Gregory Peck (Jonathan Clark), Ann Blyth, Anthony Quinn, John McIntire, Andrea King, Carl Esmond, Eugenie Leontovich.
Universal-International
Producer: Aaron Rosenberg.
Director: Raoul Walsh.
Screenplay: Borden Chase, from the novel by Rex Beach. Cinematography by Russell Metty.
104 minutes. Color.

1953
Roman Holiday

Gregory Peck (Joe Bradley), Audrey Hepburn, Eddie Albert, Hartley Power, Laura Solari, Harcourt Williams.
Paramount
Producer: William Wyler.
Director: William Wyler.
Screenplay: Dalton Trumbo, Ian McLellan Hunter and John Dighton, from a story by Ian McLellan Hunter. Cinematography by Franz F Planer and Henri Alekan.
119 minutes. Black and white.

1954
Night People
Gregory Peck (Colonel Steve Van Dyke), Broderick Crawford, Anita Bjork, Rita Gam, Walter Abel, Buddy Ebsen, Hugh McDermott.
Twentieth Century Fox
Producer: Nunnally Johnson.
Director: Nunnally Johnson.
Screenplay: Nunnally Johnson, from a story by Jed Harris and Thomas Reed. Cinematography by Charles G Clarke.
93 minutes. Color.

1954
Man with a Million (*The Million Pound Note* in the UK)
Gregory Peck (Henry Adams), Jane Griffiths, Ronald Squire, Joyce Grenfell, Reginald Beckwith, Hartley Power, A E Matthews, Wilfred Hyde-White.
J Arthur Rank Organization/United Artists
Producer: John Bryan.
Director: Ronald Neame.
Screenplay: Jill Craigie, from the story 'The Million Pound Bank Note' by Mark Twain. Cinematography by Geoffrey Unsworth.
92 minutes. Color.

1955
The Purple Plain
Gregory Peck (Squadron Leader Bill Forrester), Win Min Than, Bernard Lee, Maurice Denham, Ram Gopal, Brenda De Banzie, Lyndon Brook, Anthony Bushell.
J Arthur Rank Organization/United Artists
Producer: John Bryan.
Director: Robert Parrish.
Screenplay: Eric Ambler, from the novel by H E Bates. Cinematography by Geoffrey Unsworth.
100 minutes. Color.

1956
The Man in the Gray Flannel Suit
Gregory Peck (Tom Rath), Jennifer Jones, Fredric March, Marisa Pavan, Lee J Cobb, Ann Harding, Keenan Wynn, Gene Lockhart, Gigi Perreau, Arthur O'Connell.
Twentieth Century Fox
Producer: Darryl F Zanuck.
Director: Nunnally Johnson.
Screenplay: Nunnally Johnson, from the novel by Sloan Wilson. Cinematography by Charles G Clarke.
153 minutes. Color.

1956
Moby Dick
Gregory Peck (Captain Ahab), Richard Basehart, Leo Genn, Orson Welles, James Robertson Justice, Harry Andrews, Bernard Miles, Noel Purcell, Fredrich Ledebur.
Moulin/Warner Bros
Producer: John Huston.
Director: John Huston.
Screenplay: Ray Bradbury and John Huston, from the novel by Herman Melville. Cinematography by Oswald Morris.
116 minutes. Color.

1957
Designing Woman
Gregory Peck (Mike Hagen), Lauren Bacall, Dolores Gray, Sam Levene, Tom Helmore, Mickey Shaughnessy, Jesse White, Chuck Connors.
MGM
Producer: Dore Schary.
Director: Vincente Minnelli.
Screenplay: George Wells, from a suggestion by Helen Rose. Cinematography by John Alton.
117 minutes. Color.

1958
The Bravados
Gregory Peck (Jim Douglas), Joan Collins, Stephen Boyd, Albert Salmi, Henry Silva, Kathleen Gallant, Barry Coe, Lee Van Cleef.
Twentieth Century Fox
Producer: Herbert B Swope Jr.
Director: Henry King.
Screenplay: Screenplay by Philip Yordan, from the novel by Frank

O'Rourke. Cinematography by Leon Shamroy.
99 minutes. Color.

1958
The Big Country
Gregory Peck (James McKay), Jean Simmons, Carroll Baker, Charlton Heston, Burl Ives, Charles Bickford, Alfonso Bedoya, Chuck Connors, Chuck Hayward, Buff Brady.
United Artists
Producers: William Wyler and Gregory Peck.
Director: William Wyler.
Screenplay: James R Webb, Sy Bartlett, and Robert Wyler, from the novel by Donald Hamilton. Cinematography by Franz Planer.
166 minutes. Color.

1959
Pork Chop Hill
Gregory Peck (Lieutenant Joe Clemons), Harry Guardino, Rip Torn, George Peppard, James Edwards, Bob Steele, George Shibata, Woody Strode, Norman Fell, Robert Blake, Biff Elliot, Barry Atwater.
Melville/United Artists
Producer: Sy Bartlett.
Director: Lewis Milestone.
Screenplay: James R Webb, from the book *Pork Chop Hill: The American Fighting Man in Korea, Spring 1953* by Brigadier General S L A Marshall. Cinematography by Sam Leavitt.
97 minutes. Black and white.

1959
Beloved Infidel
Gregory Peck (F Scott Fitzgerald), Deborah Kerr, Eddie Albert, Philip Ober, Herbert Rudley, John Sutton, Karin Booth, Ken Scott, Buck Class.
Twentieth Century Fox
Producer: Jerry Wald.
Director: Henry King.
Screenplay: Sy Bartlett, from the book by Sheilah Graham and Gerald Frank. Cinematography by Leon Shamroy.
123 minutes. Color.

1959
On the Beach
Gregory Peck (Dwight Towers), Ava Gardner, Fred Astaire, Anthony

Perkins, Donna Anderson, John Tate, Lola Brooks, Guy Doleman, John Meillon, Harp McGuire, Lou Vernon.
United Artists
Producer: Stanley Kramer.
Director: Stanley Kramer.
Screenplay: John Paxton, from the novel by Nevil Shute. Cinematography by Giuseppe Rotunno.
134 minutes. Black and white.

1961
The Guns of Navarone
Gregory Peck (Captain Keith Mallory), David Niven, Anthony Quinn, Stanley Baker, James Darren, Anthony Quayle, Irene Papas, Gia Scala.
Highroad/Columbia
Producer: Carl Foreman.
Director: J Lee Thompson.
Screenplay: Carl Foreman, from the novel by Alistair MacLean. Cinematography by Oswald Morris.
157 minutes. Color.

1962
Cape Fear
Gregory Peck (Sam Bowden), Robert Mitchum, Polly Bergen, Lori Martin, Martin Balsam, Jack Kruschen, Telly Savalas, Barrie Chase.
Melville/Talbot/Universal-International
Producer: Sy Bartlett.
Director: J Lee Thompson.
Screenplay: James R Webb, from the novel *The Executioners* by John D MacDonald. Cinematography by Sam Leavitt.
105 minutes. Black and white.

1962
To Kill a Mockingbird
Gregory Peck (Atticus Finch), Mary Badham, Philip Alford, John Megna, Frank Overton, Rosemary Murphy, Ruth White, Brock Peters, Estelle Evans, Paul Fix.
Pakula-Mulligan/Brentwood/Universal
Producer: Alan J Pakula.
Director: Robert Mulligan.
Screenplay: Horton Foote, from the novel by Harper Lee. Cinematography by Russell Harlan.
129 minutes. Black and white.

1963
How the West Was Won
Gregory Peck (Cleve Van Valen), [same episode] Debbie Reynolds, Robert Preston, Thelma Ritter. Narrated by Spencer Tracy.
MGM/Cinerama
Producer: Bernard Smith.
Directors: Henry Hathaway ('The River', 'The Plains', 'The Outlaws'), John Ford ('The Civil War'), and George Marshall ('The Railroad').
Screenplay: James R Webb and (uncredited) John Gay. From the *Life* magazine series *How the West Was Won*. Cinematography by William H Daniels, Milton Krasner, Charles Lang Jr, and Joseph La Shelle.
155 minutes. Color.

1963
Captain Newman, M.D.
Gregory Peck (Captain Josiah Newman), Tony Curtis, Angie Dickinson, Eddie Albert, Bobby Darin, James Gregory, Robert Duvall, Bethel Leslie, Larry Storch, Dick Sargent.
Brentwood/Reynard/Universal
Producer: Robert Arthur.
Director: David Miller.
Screenplay: Richard L Breen, Phoebe Ephron, and Henry Ephron, from the novel by Leo Rosten. Cinematography by Russell Metty.
126 minutes. Color.

1964
Behold a Pale Horse
Gregory Peck (Manuel Artiguez), Anthony Quinn, Omar Sharif, Mildred Dunnock, Raymond Pellegrin, Paolo Stoppa.
Brentwood/Highland/Columbia
Producer: Fred Zinnemann.
Director: Fred Zinnemann.
Screenplay: J P Miller, from the novel *Killing a Mouse on Sunday* by Emeric Pressburger. Cinematography by Jean Badal.
112 minutes. Black and white.

1965
Mirage
Gregory Peck (David Stillwell), Diane Baker, Walter Matthau, Leif Erikson, Kevin McCarthy, Jack Weston, George Kennedy, Walter Abel.
Universal
Producer: Harry Keller.
Director: Edward Dmytryk.

Screenplay: Peter Stone, from the novel *Fallen Angel* by Walter Ericson. Cinematography by Joseph MacDonald.

108 minutes. Black and white.

1966
Arabesque

Gregory Peck (David Pollock), Sophia Loren, Alan Badel, Kieron Moore, John Merivale, Carl Duering.

Universal

Producer: Stanley Donen.

Director: Stanley Donen.

Screenplay: Julian Mitchell, Stanley Price, and Pierre Marton, from the novel *The Cipher* by Gordon Colter. Cinematography by Christopher Challis.

105 minutes. Black and white.

1969
The Stalking Moon

Gregory Peck (Sam Varner), Eva Marie Saint, Robert Forster, Noland Clay, Russell Thorson, Frank Silvera, Lonny Chapman.

Pakula-Mulligan/National General

Producer: Alan J Pakula.

Director: Robert Mulligan.

Screenplay: Alvin Sargent, from the novel by Theodore V Olsen. Cinematography by Charles Lang.

111 minutes. Color.

1969
MacKenna's Gold

Gregory Peck (MacKenna), Omar Sharif, Camilla Sparv, Telly Savalas, Keenan Wynn, Julie Newmar, Ted Cassidy, Lee J Cobb, Raymond Massey, Burgess Meredith, Anthony Quayle, Edward G Robinson, Eli Wallach.

Highroad/Columbia

Producers: Carl Foreman and Dimitri Tiomkin.

Director: J Lee Thompson.

Screenplay: Carl Foreman, from the novel by Will Henry. Cinematography by Joseph MacDonald.

128 minutes. Color.

1969
The Chairman (*The Most Dangerous Man in the World* in the UK)

Gregory Peck (John Hathaway), Anne Heywood, Arthur Hill, Alan Dobie, Conrad Yama, Zienia Merton.

Apjac/Twentieth Century Fox
Producer: Mort Abrahams.
Director: J Lee Thompson.
Screenplay: Ben Maddow, from the novel by Jay Richard Kennedy.
Cinematography by John Wilcox.
104 minutes. Color.

1969
Marooned
Gregory Peck (Charles Keith), Richard Crenna, David Janssen, James
Franciscus, Gene Hackman, Lee Grant, Nancy Pruett, Mariette Hartley,
Scott Brady.
Columbia
Producer: M J Frankovich.
Director: John Sturges.
Screenplay: Mayo Simon, from the novel by Martin Caidin. Cinematography by Daniel Fapp.
133 minutes. Color.

1970
I Walk the Line
Gregory Peck (Sheriff Henry Tawes), Tuesday Weld, Estelle Parsons,
Ralph Meeker, Lonny Chapman, Charles Durning.
John Frankenheimer Productions/Edward Lewis Productions/
Halcyon Productions/Columbia
Producers: Edward Lewis and Harold D Cohen.
Director: John Frankenheimer.
Screenplay: Alvin Sargent, from the novel *The Exile* by Madison Jones.
Cinematography by David M Walsh.
95 minutes. Color.

1971
Shootout
Gregory Peck (Clay Lomax), Pat Quinn, Robert F Lyons, Susan Tyrell,
Jeff Corey, James Gregory, Rita Gam, Dawn Lyn.
Hal B Wallis Productions/Universal
Producer: Hal B Wallis.
Director: Henry Hathaway.
Screenplay: Marguerite Roberts, from the novel *The Lone Cowboy* by Will
James. Cinematography by Earl Rath.
95 minutes. Color.

1972
The Trial of the Catonsville Nine
Gwen Arner, Ed Flanders, Barton Hayman, Mary Jackson, Richard Jordan, Nancy Malone, Donald Moffat, Davis Roberts, Leon Russom, William Schallert, David Speilberg, Peter Strauss, Douglas Watson.
VHS – Axon Video
Producer: Gregory Peck.
Director: Gordon Davidson.
Screenplay: Father Daniel Berrigan. Saul Levitt. Based on the play *The Catonsville Nine* (1970) by Daniel Berrigan. Cinematography by Haskell Wexler.
85 minutes. Color.

1973
Billy Two Hats
Gregory Peck (Arch Deans), Desi Arnaz Jr, Jack Warden, David Huddleston, Sian Barbara Allen, John Pearce.
Algonquin/United Artists
Producer: Norman Jewison and Patrick Palmer.
Director: Ted Kotcheff.
Screenplay: Alan Sharp. Cinematography by Brian West.
80 minutes. Color.

1976
The Omen
Gregory Peck (Robert Thorn), Lee Remick, David Warner, Billie Whitelaw, Leo McKern, Harvey Stephens, Patrick Troughton.
Harvey Bernhard-Mace Neufeld Productions/Twentieth Century Fox
Producers: Mace Neufeld and Harvey Bernhard.
Director: Richard Donner.
Screenplay: David Seltzer. Cinematography by Gil Taylor.
111 minutes. Color.

1977
MacArthur
Gregory Peck (General Douglas MacArthur), Ed Flaners, Dan O'Herlihy, Ivan Boner, Ward Costello, Marj Dusay.
A Richard D. Zanuck-David Brown Production/Universal
Producer: Frank McCarthy.
Director: Joseph Sargent.
Screenplay: Hal Barwood and Matthew Robbins. Cinematography by Mario Tosi.
128 minutes. Color.

1978
The Boys From Brazil
Gregory Peck (Dr Josef Mengele), Laurence Olivier, James Mason, Lilli Palmer, Uta Hagen, Steven Guttenberg, Denholm Elliott, Rosemary Harris, John Dehner, John Rubinstein, Anne Meara, Jeremy Black.
Producers Circle/Twentieth Century Fox
Producers: Robert Fryer, Martin Richards, Stanley O'Toole.
Director: Franklin J Schaffner.
Screenplay: Heywood Gould, from the novel by Ira Levin. Cinematography by Henri Decae.
182 minutes. Color.

1981
The Sea Wolves
Gregory Peck (Colonel Lewis Pugh), Roger Moore, David Niven, Trevor Howard, Barbara Kellerman, Patrick Macnee.
Lorimar/United Artists
Producers: Chris Chrisafis and Euan Lloyd.
Director: Andrew V McLaglen.
Screenplay: Reginald Rose, from the book *The Boarding Party* by James Leasor. Cinematography by Toni Imi.
120 minutes. Color.

1987
Amazing Grace and Chuck
Gregory Peck (President), Jamie Lee Curtis, Alex English, William L Peterson, Joshua Zuehlke, Lee Richardson, Alan Autry, Dennis Lipscomb, Frances Conroy.
Turnstar/David Field/TriStar/Rastar
Producer: David Field.
Director: Mike Newell.
Screenplay: David Field. Cinematography by Robert Elawit.
115 minutes. Color.

1989
Old Gringo
Gregory Peck (Ambrose Bierce), Jane Fonda, Jimmy Smits, Patricio Conteras, Jenny Gago, Gabriel Roel, Sergio Calderon.
Fonda Films/Columbia
Producer: Lois Bonfiglio.
Director: Luis Puenzo.
Screenplay: Aida Bortnik and Luis Puenzo, from the novel *Gringo Viejo* by Carlos Fuentes. Cinematography by Felix Monti.
119 minutes. Color.

1991
Other People's Money
Gregory Peck (Andrew 'Jorgy' Jorgenson), Danny DeVito, Penelope Ann Miller, Piper Laurie, Dean Jones.
Yorktown/Warner Bros.
Producer: Norman Jewison, Ric Kidney.
Director: Norman Jewison.
Screenplay: Alvin Sargent, from the play by Jerry Sterner. Cinematography by Haskell Wexler.
101 minutes. Color.

1991
Cape Fear
Robert De Niro, Nick Nolte, Jessica Lange, Juliette Lewis, Joe Don Baker, Robert Mitchum, Gregory Peck (Lee Heller).
Amblin/Cappa/Tribeca/Universal
Producer: Barbara DeFina.
Director: Martin Scorsese.
Screenplay: Wesley Strick, from the screenplay by James R Webb and the novel *The Executioners* by John D MacDonald. Cinematography by Freddie Francis.
123 minutes. Color.

Major Television Appearances

1982
The Blue and the Gray
Gregory Peck (Abraham Lincoln), John Hammond, Stacy Keach, Colleen Dewhurst, Lloyd Bridges, Diane Baker, Kathleen Beller, Penny Peyser, Michael Horton, Cooper Huckabee, Dan Shor, Julia Duffy, Robin Gammell, Davis S Haroer.
Producers: Hugh Benson, Harry Thomason.
Executive Producers: Larry White, Lou Reda.
Director: Andrew V McLaglen.
Teleplay: Ian McLellan Hunter, from a story by John Leekley and Bruce Catton, based on the writings of Bruce Catton. Cinematography by Al Francis.
Eight hours. Color.

1983
The Scarlet and the Black
Gregory Peck (Monsignor Hugh O'Flaherty), Christopher Plummer,

John Gielgud, Raf Vallone, Kenneth Colley, Walter Gottell, Barbara Bouchet, Julian Holloway.
ITC Productions/CBS-TV
Producer: Bill McCutchen.
Director: Jerry London.
Teleplay: David Butler, from the book *The Scarlet Pimpernel of the Vatican* by J P Gallagher. Cinematography by Giuseppe Rotunno.
180 minutes. Color.

1993
The Portrait
Gregory Peck (Gardner Church), Lauren Bacall, Cecilia Peck, Paul McCrane, Donna Mitchell, Joyce O'Connor, Mitchell Lawrence, William Prince.
Robert Greenwald Productions/Atticus/TNT
Producer: Philip Keinbart.
Executive Producers: Robert Greenwald, Gregory Peck, Carla Singer.
Director: Arthur Penn.
Teleplay: Lynn Roth, from the play *Painted Churches* by Tina Howe. Cinematography by Dick Quinlan.
120 minutes. Color.

1998
Moby Dick
Gregory Peck (Father Mapple), Patrick Stewart, Henry Thomas, Ted Levine, Piripi Warentini, Hugh Keays-Byrne, Shane Feeney, Michael Edward-Stevens.
A Whale/Nine Network Australian Production and United Kingdom/Australia coproduction in association with USA Pictures
Producer: Franc Roddam, Kris Noble, Steve McGlothen.
Executive Producers: Robert Halmi Sr, Francis Ford Coppola, Fred Fuchs.
Director: Franc Roddam.
Teleplay: Anton Diether and Franc Roddam, from the novel by Herman Melville. Cinematography by Anton Diether. Cinematography by David Connell.
240 minutes. Color.

Broadway Productions

The Morning Star
Gregory Peck (Cliff Parrilow), Brenda Forbes, Gladys Cooper, Jill Esmond, Cecil Humphreys, Rhys Williams, Wendy Barrie, Nicolas Joy.

Morosco Theater
Producer: Guthrie McClintic.
Director: Guthrie McClintic.
Playwright: Emlyn Williams.
14 September 1942. 24 performances.

The Willow and I
Gregory Peck (Robin Todd and Kirkland Todd), Martha Scott, Barbara O'Neil, Amanda Randolph, R Davis Williams, Edward Pawley, Cora Witherspoon, Robert Harrison
The Windsor Theater
Producer: Donald Blackwell, Raymond Curtis and David Merrick.
Director: Donald Blackwell.
Playwright: John Patrick.
10 December 1942. 28 performances.

Sons and Soldiers
Gregory Peck (Andrew Tadlock), Geraldine Fitzgerald, Herbert Rudley, Millard Mitchell, Jack Willet, Joan Sweeney, Ted Donaldson, Karl Malden, Stella Adler, Jesse White.
The Morosco Theater
Producers: Max Reinhardt, Norman Bel-Geddes and Richard Meyers.
Director: Max Reinhardt.
Playwright: Irwin Shaw.
4 March 1943. 22 performances.

The Will Rogers Follies
Keith Carradine, Dee Hoty, Dick Latessa, Cady Huffman (only Greg's voice was featured in the production).
Producers: Pierre Cossette, Martin Richards, Sam Crowthers, James M Nederlander, Stewart F Lane, Max Weitzenhoffer in association with Japan Satellite Broadcasting, Inc.
Director: Tommy Tune.
Book by Peter Stone. Music by Cy Coleman. Lyrics by Betty Comden and Adolph Green.
1991. 983 performances.

Awards and Honors

Academy Awards

1968 – Jean Hersholt Humanitarian Award

1963 – Won Oscar – Best Actor in Leading Role for *To Kill a Mockingbird* (1962)

1950 – Nominated for Oscar, Best Actor in Leading Role for *Twelve O'Clock High* (1950)

1948 – Nominated for Oscar, Best Actor in Leading Role for *Gentleman's Agreement* (1947)

1947 – Nominated for Oscar, Best Actor in Leading Role for *The Yearling* (1946)

1946 – Nominated for Oscar, Best Actor in Leading Role for *The Keys of the Kingdom* (1944)

American Civil Liberties Union

1991 – Bills of Rights Award

American Film Institute

1989 – Life Achievement Award

American Society of Cinematographers, USA

1990 – Board of Governors Award

Angelus Awards Student Film Festival

2003 – Spirit of Angelus Award (Bestowed posthumously)

British Academy of Film and Television Arts Awards

1964 – Nominated for BAFTA Film Award, Best Foreign Actor for *To Kill a Mockingbird* (1962)

1954 – Nominated for BAFTA Film Award, Best Foreign Actor for
Roman Holiday (1953)

Banff Television Festival
1983 – Award of Excellence

Berlin International Film Festival
1993 – Honorary Golden Berlin Bear

Cannes Film Festival
1989 – Palme d'Or Award

César Awards, France
1995 – César, Honorary Award

David di Donatello Awards
2003 – Special David

Emmy Awards
1998 – Nominated, Emmy, Outstanding Supporting Actor in a
Miniseries or a Movie for *Moby Dick* (1998) (TV)

Film Society of Lincoln Center
1992 – Gala Tribute

Franklin and Marshal College
1977 – Honorary Doctor of Humane Letters

George Eastman Award
1987 – For Distinguished Contribution to the Art of Film

Golden Apple Award
1998 – Golden Apple, Male Star of the Year
1947 – Golden Apple, Most Cooperative Actor
1945 – Golden Apple, Most Cooperative Actor

Golden Globes, USA

1999 – Won, Golden Globe, Best Performance by an Actor in a Supporting Role in a Series, Mini-Series or Motion Picture for *Moby Dick* (1998) TV. Tied with Don Cheadle for *The Rat Pack* (1998) TV

1979 – Nominated, Golden Globe, Best Motion Picture Actor – Drama, for *The Boys From Brazil* (1978)

1978 – Nominated, Golden Globe, Best Motion Picture Actor – Drama for *MacArthur* (1977)

1969 – Won, Cecil B DeMille Award

1964 – Nominated, Golden Globe, Best Motion Picture Actor – Drama for *Captain Newman, MD* (1963)

1963 – Won, Golden Globe, Best Motion Picture Actor – Drama for *To Kill a Mockingbird* (1962)

1955 – Won, Golden Globe, World Film Favorite – Male

1951 – Won, Golden Globe, World Film Favorite – Male (Henrietta)

1947 – Won, Golden Globe, Best Motion Picture Actor for *The Yearling* (1946)

Golden Scroll Award

1977 – Best actor in a horror film in 1976 for *The Omen* (1976)

Hearst Award

Presented to Veronique and Gregory Peck for outstanding humanitarian service

International Jewish Film Festival

1999 – Humanitarian Award

Karlovy Vary International Film Festival

1996 – Special Prize for Outstanding Contribution to World Cinema

Kennedy Center Honors

1991 – Lifetime contribution to the Performing Arts

Laurel Awards

1970 – Nominated, Golden Laurel, Male Star, 12th place

1967 – Won, Golden Laurel, Special Award
> Nominated, Golden Laurel, Action Performance for *Arabesque* (1966)

1966 – Nominated, Golden Laurel, Male Star, 5th place

1965 – Nominated, Golden Laurel, Male Star, 14th place

1964 – Nominated, Golden Laurel, Top Male Star, 5th place

1963 – 2nd place, Golden Laurel, Top Male Dramatic Performance for *To Kill a Mockingbird* (1962)
> 3rd place, Golden Laurel, Top Male Star

1962 – 3rd place, Golden Laurel, Top Male Dramatic Performance for *The Guns of Navarone* (1961)

1960 – Nominated, Golden Laurel, Top Male Star, 13th place

1959 – 3rd place, Golden Laurel, Top Action Performance for *The Bravados* (1958)

Légion d'honneur

1993 – Award for Outstanding Contribution to Arts, France's highest national honor

Look Magazine

1947 – Best Actor for the year 1947

1946 – Outstanding Actor of 1946

Marion Anderson Award

1999 – Humanitarian Award

National Board of Review

1983 – Career Achievement Award

New York Film Critics Circle Award

1950 – NYFCC Award, Best Actor for *Twelve O'Clock High* (1949)

Paris Film Festival

1949 – Best Foreign Actor of 1949 for *Paradine Case* (1947)

Photoplay **Magazine**
1946 – Gold Medal Award for Best Actor for *The Keys of the Kingdom* (1944)

Reno Chamber of Commerce
1950 – Silver Spurs Award, Top Western Star

San Sebastian International Film Festival
1986 – Donostia Lifetime Achievement Award

Screen Actors Guild Awards
1971 – Life Achievement Award

White House
1969 – Medal of Freedom Award

Sources

Books

Andersen, Christopher. *Citizen Jane: The Turbulent Life of Jane Fonda*. New York: Dell Publishing, 1990.

Arce, Hector. *Gary Cooper: An Intimate Biography*. New York: William Morrow & Company, 1979.

Astaire, Fred. *Steps in Time*. New York: Harper & Brothers, 1959.

Aumont, Jean-Pierre. *Sun and Shadow*. New York: W.W. Norton & Company, 1977.

Bacall, Lauren. *By Myself*. New York: Alfred A. Knopf, 1979.

Baker, Russell. *The Good Times*. New York: William Morrow and Company, 1989.

Basinger, Jeanine. *Silent Stars*. New York: Alfred A. Knopf, 1999.

Baxter, Anne. *Intermission*. New York: G.P. Putnam's, 1976.

Behlmer, Rudy, ed. *Memo from David O. Selznick*. New York: Viking, 1972.

Benny, Jack and Joan Benny. *Sunday Nights at Seven*. New York: Warner Books, 1990.

Bergman, Ingrid. With Alan Burges. *Ingrid Bergman: My Story*. New York: Delacourte, 1980.

Berlin, Joey (editor). *Toxic Fame: Celebrities Speak on Stardom*. Simi Valley, CA: Visible Ink, 1996.

Berrigan, Daniel, S.J. *The Trial of the Catonsville Nine*. New York: Bantam Books, 1971.

No Bars to Manhood. New York: Doubleday & Company, 1970.

Biskind, Peter. *Seeing is Believing: How Hollywood Taught Us to Stop Worrying and Love the Fifties*. New York: Henry Holt and Company, 1983.

Boller, Jr., Paul F. and Davis, Ronald L. *Hollywood Anecdotes*. New York: William Morrow and Company, 1987.

Brown, David. *Let Me Entertain You*. New York: William Morrow, 1990.

Buchwald, Ann and Buchwald, Art. *Seems Like Yesterday: A Fond Memoir*. New York: G.P. Putnam's Sons, 1980.

Buchwald, Art. *I'll Always Have Paris!: A Memoir*. New York: G.P. Putnam's Sons, 1996.

Carey, Harry, Jr. *My Life as an Actor in the John Ford Stock Company*. Lanham, MD, Rowman & Littlefield, 1996.

Chase, Chris. *How To Be a Movie Star: Or, a Terrible Beauty is Born*. New York: HarperCollins, 1974.

Collins, Joan. *Past Imperfect: An Autobiography*. New York: Berkley Books, 1978.

Collier, Peter. *The Fondas: A Hollywood Dynasty*. New York: G.P.Putnam's Sons, 1991.

Coppedge, Walter. *Henry King's America*. Metuchen, NJ: Scarecrow, 1986.

Cowley, Malcolm. *-And I Worked at the Writer's Trade: Chapters of Literary History, 1918-1978*. New York: The Viking Press, 1978.

Crowther, Bosley. *Hollywood Rajah: The Life and Times of Louis B. Mayer*. New York: Dell Publishing, 1960.

Crivello, Kirk. *Fallen Angels: And Tragic Deaths of Hollywood's Doomed Beauties*. New York: Berkley Books, 1988.

Curtis, Tony, and Paris, Barry. *Tony Curtis: The Autobiography*.

Custon, George F. *Twentieth Century's Fox: Darryl F. Zanuck and the Culture of Hollywood*. New York: Basic Books, 1997.

Dally-Watkins, June. *The Secrets Behind My Smile*. Camberwell, Victoria: Penguin Books Australia, 2002.

Dardis, Tom. *Some Time in the Sun*. New York: Charles Scribner's Sons, 1976.

Davidson, Bill. *Jane Fonda: An Intimate Biography*. London: Sidgewick & Jackson.

DeMille, Agnes. *Martha: The Life and Work of Martha Graham*. New York: Random House, 1956.

Dmytryk, Edward. *Odd Man Out: A Memoir of the Hollywood Ten*. Carbondale, Il: Southern Illinois University Press, 1996.

Douglas, Kirk. *Climbing the Mountain: My Search for Meaning*. New York: Simon & Schuster, 1997.

The Ragman's Son: An Autobiography. Pocket Books, 1988.

Dunne, Philip. *Take Two: A Life in Movies and Politics*. New York: McGraw-Hill, 1980.

Durgnat, Raymond & Simmon, Scott. *King Vidor, American*. University of California Press, 1988.

Eells, George. *Hedda and Louella*. New York: Warner Paperback, 1973.

Farber, Stephen and Green, Marc. *Hollywood on the Couch: A Candid Look at the Overheated Love Affair Between Psychiatrists and Moviemakers*. New York: William Morrow and Company, 1993.

Feinman, Jeffrey. *Hollywood Confidential*. Chicago: Playboy Press, 1976.

Fishgall, Gary. *Gregory Peck: A Biography*. New York: Scribner, 2002.

Flamini, Roland, *Ava*. New York: Coward, McCann & Geohegan, 1983.

Fonda, Henry and Teichmann, Howard. *Fonda: My Life*. New York: New American Library, 1981.

Fowler, Gene. *Good Night, Sweet Prince*. New York: The Viking Press, 1943.

Freedland, Michael. *All the Way: A Biography of Frank Sinatra*. London: Weidenfeld & Nicholson, 1997.

Gregory Peck. New York: William Morrow, 1980.

Freidrich, Otto. *City of Nets: A Portrait of Hollywood in the 1940s*. New York: Harper & Row, 1986.

Gabler, Neal. *An Empire of Their Own: How the Jews Invented Hollywood*. New York: Crown, 1988.

Gam, Rita. *Actors: A Celebration*. New York: St. Martin's Press, 1988.

Geist, Kenneth. *Pictures Will Talk*. New York: Da Capo Press, 1978.

Gardner, Ava. *Ava: My Story*. New York: Bantam, 1990.

Gill, Brendan. *Tallulah*. New York: Holt, Rinehart & Winston, 1972.

Graham, Sheilah. *A State of Heat*. Grosset & Dunlop, 1971.

Hollywood Revisited. New York: St. Martin's Press, 1984.

The Gregory Peck Tribute Book. American Film Institute Life Achievement Award Program. Los Angeles: John Johns and Associates, 1989.

Griggs, John. *The Films of Gregory Peck.* Secaucus, N.J.: Citadel Press, 1984.

Grobel, Lawrence. *The Hustons.* New York: Charles Scribner's Sons, 1989.

Gross, Michael. *Model.* New York: William Morrow, 1995.

Gussow, Mel. *Don't Say Yes Until I Finish Talking: The Biography of Darryl F. Zanuck.* New York: Doubleday, 1971.

Halberstam, David. *The Amateurs: The Story of Four Young Men and Their Quest for an Olympic Gold Medal.* New York: Fawcett Columbine, 1985.

The Fifties. New York: Villard Books, 1993.

Halliwell, Leslie. *The filmgoer's Book of Quotes.* London: Granada Publishing, 1973.

Harmetz, Aljean. *Rolling Breaks and Other Movie Business.* New York: Alfred A. Knopf, 1983.

Harris, Marlys J. *The Zanucks of Hollywood: The Dark Legacy of an American Dynasty.* New York: Crown Publishers, 1989.

Harris,Warren G. *Audrey Hepburn: A Biography.* New York: Simon & Schuster, 1994.

Sophia Loren: A Biography. New York: Simon & Schuster, 1998.

Harvery, James. *Movie Love in the Fifties.* New York: Da Capo Press 2001.

Hemmingway, Mary. *How it Was.* New York: Ballantine Books, 1977.

Hyams, Joe. *Bogie: The Biography of Humphrey Bogart.* New York: Signet, 1966.

Hay, Peter. *Movie Anecdotes.* New York: Oxford University. 1991.

Hayward, Brooke. *Haywire.* New York: Alfred A. Knopf, 1977.

Hecht, Ben. *A Child of the Century.* New York, Simon & Schuster, 1954.

Herman, Jan. *A Talent for Trouble: The Life of Hollywood's Most Acclaimed Director, William Wyler.* New York: Putnam, 1995.

Heston, Charlton with Isbouts, Jean-Pierre. New York GT Publishing, 1998.

In the Arena: An Autobiography. New York: Simon & Schuster, 1995.

Higham, Charles and Mosley, Roy. *Carey Grant: The Lonely Heart.* New York: Harcourt Brace Janovanovich, 1989.

Higham, Charles and Wallis, Hal. *Starmaker: TheAutobiography of Hal Wallis.* New York: MacMillan. 1980.

Hopper, Hedda. *From Under My Hat.* New York: Doubleday & Company, 1952.

Hotchner, A.E. *Sophia: Living and Loving.* New York: Bantam Book, 1979.

Hower, Barbara. *Laughing All the Way.* New York: Fawcett Books, 1976.

Huston, John. *An Open Book* New York: Alfred A. Knopf, 1980.

Johnson, Nora. *Flashback: Nora Johnson on Nunnally Johnson.* New York: Doubleday, 1979.

Kael, Pauline. *Deeper Into Movies.* Boston: Little, Brown and Company, 1973.

Going Steady: Film Writings 1968-1969. London: Marion Boyars Publishers, 1968.

I Lost it at the Movies: Film Writings 1954-1965. New York: Marion Boyars Publishers, 1994.

5001 Nights at the Movies. New York: Henry Holt and Company, 1982.

Kanin, Garson. *Hollywood.* New York: Viking, 1974.

Katz, Ephraim. *The Film Encyclopedia.* New York: HarperPerennial, 1994.

Kazan, Elia. *A Life.* New York: Alfred A. Knopf, 1988.

Kelly, Kitty. *His Way: The Unauthorized Biography of Frank Sinatra.* New York: Bantam Books, 1987.

Kent, Nicolas. *Naked Hollywood: Money and Power in the Movies Today.* New York: St. Martin's Press, 1991.

Keyes, Ralph. *Is There Life After High School?.* New York: Warner Books, 1976.

Koppes, Clayton R. and Black, Gregory D. *Hollywood Goes to War.* London: Collier MacMillan, 1987.

Korda, Michael. *Charmed Lives: A Family Romance.* New York: Random House, 1979.

La Jolla Historical Society. *Inside La Jolla.* La Jolla, CA.

LaSalle, Mick. *Complicated Women: Sex and Power in Pre-Code Hollywood*. New York: St. Martin's Press, 2000.

Lawrence, Gabriel. *The Hustons*. New York: Avon, 1989.

Lee, Harper. *To Kill a Mockingbird*. New York: July 11, 1960.

Leamer, Laurence. *As Time Goes By: The Life of Ingrid Bergman*. New York: Harper & Row, 1986.

Leaming, Barbara. *Katharine Hepburn*. New York: Avon Books, 1995.

Marilyn Monroe. New York: Three Rivers Press, 1998.

Orson Welles. New York: Viking, 1985.

Leff, Leonard J. *Hitchcock & Selznick: The Rich and Strange Collaboration of Alfred Hitchcock and David O. Selznick in Hollywood*. New York: Weidenfeld & Nicolson, 1987.

Levine, Robert. *Joan Collins: Superstar*. New York: Dell Publishing Co, 1985.

Linet, Beverly. *Star-Crossed: The Story of Robert Walker and Jennifer Jones*. New York, G.P. Putnam's Sons, 1986.

Loos, Anita. *Kiss Hollywood Goodbye*. New York: The Viking Press, 1974.

MacLaine, Shirley. *My Lucky Stars: A Hollywood Memoir*. New York: Bantam Books, 1995.

Malton, Leonard. *TV Movies and Video Guide*. New York: Signet, 1994.

Malvern, Gladys. *Curtain Going Up!: The Story of Katherine Cornell*. New York: Julian Messner, 1943.

Manchester, William. *American Caesar: Douglas MacArthur 1880-1964*. New York: Dell Publishing, 1978.

Manners, Dorothy. *Los Angeles Herald-Examiner*. November 20, 1970.

Marx, Arthur. *The Secret Life of Bob Hope*. Barricade Books.

McClelland, Doug. *StarSpeak: Hollywood on Everything*. London: Faber & Faber, 1987.

McGillan, Buhle, Paul. *Tender Comrades: A Backstory of the Hollywood Blacklist*. New York, St. Martin's Press, 1997.

Milland, Ray. *Wide-Eyed in Babylon: An Autobiography*. New York: Ballantine Books, 1974.

Minnelli, Vincente, with Hector Arce. *I Remember It Well*. Garden

City, New York: Doubleday, 1974.

Miller, Arthur. *Timebends: A Life*. New York: Grove Press, 1987.

Morley, Sheridan. *The Other Side of the Moon: The Life of David Niven*. New York: Harper & Row, 1985.

Tales From the Hollywood Raj: The British, the Movies, and Tinseltown. New York: The Viking Press, 1983.

Molyneaux, Gerard, *Gregory Peck: A Bio-Bibliography*. Westport, Connecticut: Greenwood Press, 1995.

Mordden, Ethan. *The Hollywood Studios: House Style in the Golden Age of the Movies*. New York: Alfred A. Knopf, 1988.

Mosley, Leonard. *Zanuck: The Rise and Fall of Hollywood's Last Tycoon*. Boston: Little, Brown, 1984.

Munn, Michael. *Gregory Peck*. London: Robert Hale, Ltd, 1999.

Neal, Patricia. *As I Am: An Autobiography*. New York: Simon & Schuster, 1988.

Nelson, Nancy. *Evenings with Cary Grant: Recollections in His Own Words and by Those Who Knew Him Best*. New York: William Morrow, 1991.

Nevasky, Victor. *Naming Names*. New York: Viking Press, 1980.

Knef, Hildegard. *The Gift Horse: Report on a Life*. New York: Dell Publishing Co, 1972.

Newquist, Roy. *Counterpoint*. Chicago: Rank McNally, 1964.

Niven, David. *The Moon's a Balloon*. New York: Dell Publishing Co, 1973.

Bring on the Empty Horses. New York: Dell Publishing Co, 1975.

Paris, Barry. *Audrey Hepburn*. New York: Putnam, 1996.

Parrish, Robert. *Hollywood Doesn't Live Here Anymore*. Boston: Little, Brown, 1988.

Peary, Danny. *Close Ups: The Movie Star Book*. New York: Workman, 1978.

Quinn, Anthony, with Paisner, Daniel. *One Man Tango*. New York: HarperCollins, 1995.

The Original Sin. Little, Brown and Company, 1972.

Quirk, Lawrence. *Bob Hope: The Road Well-Traveled*. Applause Books, 2001.

Randall, Tony and Mindlin, Michael. *Which Reminds Me*. New York: Delacorte Press, 1989.

Randolph, Howard. *La Jolla Year by Year*. La Jolla: Library Association of La Jolla, 1955.

Reed, Rex. *Valentines & Vitriol*. New York: Dell Publishing Co, 1977.

Robinson, Jeffrey. *Rainier and Grace*. London: Simon & Schuster Ltd, 1989.

Rodgers, Richard. *Musical Stages: An Autobiography*. New York: Random House, 1975.

Rosen, Marjorie. *Popcorn Venus: Women, Movies and the American Dream*. New York: Avon Books, 1973.

Rosenfield, Paul. *The Club Rules: Power, Money, Sex, and Fear – How It Works in Hollywood*. New York: Warner Books, 1992.

Power, Money, Sex, and Fear – How it Works in Hollywood. New York: Warner Books, 1992.

Ross, Lillian. *Picture*. New York: Avon Books, 1952.

Schaelchlin, Patricia A. *La Jolla: The Story of a Community 1887-1987*. La Jolla, Calif.: Friends of the La Jolla Library, 1988.

Schatz, Thomas. *The Genius of the System: Hollywood Filmmaking in the Studio Era*. New York: Pantheon Books, 1988.

Schickel, Richard. *The Men Who Made the Movies*. New York: Atheneum, 1975.

Server, Lee. *Robert Mitchum: "Baby, I Don't Care"*. New York: St. Martin's Press, 2001.

Signoret, Simone. *Nostalgia Isn't What it Used to Be*. New York: Harper & Row, 1978.

Silverman, Stephen M. *Dancing on the Celing: Stanley Donen and His Movies*. Alfred A. Knopf, New York, 1996.

Sinatra, Tina with Copton, Jeff. *My Father's Daughter*. New York: Simon & Schuster, 2000.

Speck, Gregory. *Hollywood Royalty: Hepburn, Davis, Stewart and Friends at the Dinner Party of the Century*. New York: Birch Lane Press, 1992.

Spoto, Donald. *The Dark Side of Genius: The Life of Alfred Hitchcock*. Boston: Little, Brown, 1983.

Laurence Olivier: A Biography. New York: HarperCollins, 1992.

Taylor, John Russel. *Hitch: The Life and Times of Alfred Hitchcock*. New York: Pantheon Books, 1978.

Strangers in Paradise: The Hollywood Emigres, 1933-1950. New York: Holt, Rinehart and Winston, 1983.

Taylor, Robert Lewis. *W.C. Fields: His Follies and Fortunes.* New York, Signet Books, 1949.

Thomas, Bob. *Astaire: the Man, the Dancer.* New York: St. Martin's Press, 1987.

Clown Prince of Hollywood: The Antic Life and Times of Jack L. Warner. New York: McGraw-Hill 1990.

Selznick. Garden City, N.Y. Doubleday, 1970.

Thomas, Tony. *Errol Flynn: the Spy Who Never Was.* South Yarmouth, Ma: Curley Publishing, 1990.

Thomson, David. *Showman: The Life of David O. Selznick.* New York: Alfred A. Knopf, 1992.

Truffaut, Francois.

Turnbull, Andrew. *Scott Fitzgerald.* New York: Ballantine Books, 1962.

Tyler, Parker. *Magic and Myth of the Movies.* New York: Simon and Schuster, 1947.

Vidor, King, *A Tree Is a Tree.* New York: Harcourt, Brace and Company, 1953.

Wagner, Walter. *Inside the Golden Ghetto.* New York: Grosset and Dunlap, 1975.

Wallis, Hal, and Higham, Charles. *Starmaker: The Autobiography of Hal Wallis.* New York: Macmillan, 1980.

Wilk, Max, *The Wit and Wisdom of Hollywood.* London: Cassell, 1971.

Wilkerson, Tichi and Borie, Marcia. *The Hollywood Reporter.* New York: Arlington House, 1984.

Williams, Esther with Diehl, Digby. *Million Dollar Mermaid.* New York: Simon & Schuster, 1999.

Wilson, Earl. *The Show Business Nobody Knows.* Chicago: Cowles Book Company, 1971.

Winters, Shelley. *Shelly Also Known as Shirley.* New York: Ballantine Books, 1989.

Shelley II. New York: Simon & Schuster, 1989.

Woodward, Ian. *Audrey Hepburn.* New York: St. Martin's Press, 1986.

Zierold, Norman, *The Moguls: The Power Princes of Hollywood's Golden Age*. New York: Avon Books, 1969.

Periodicals

Archerd, Armand. *Los Angeles Herald Express*. August 4, 1951.

Archerd, Army. *Variety*. September, 17, 2001.

Alpert, Hollis. *Saturday Review*. May 16, 1959.

Amory, Cleveland. *Parade*. December 4, 1988.

Architectural Digest. April, 1996.

TV Guide. November 11, 1969.

Armstrong, Lois. *People*. August 8, 1977.

Barrios, Greg. *Los Angeles Times*. April 24, 1988.

Battelle, Phyllis. *Los Angeles Herald-Examiner*, January 14, 1962.

Beck, Marilyn.

Philadelphia Evening Bulletin. December 5, 1977.

Philadelphia Evening Bulletin. November 17, 1976.

Benson, Sheila. *Los Angeles Times*. October 6, 1989.

Philadelphia Evening Bulletin. January 8, 1978.

Bell, Joseph N. *San Jose Mercury News*. December 7, 1969.

Benson, N.E. *Confidential*. ca. 1955-56.

Berg, Louis. *This Week*. February 19, 1950.

Berges, Marshall. *Los Angeles Times: Homes Magazine*. July 21, 1974.

Berkvist, Robert. *New York Times*. May 21, 1972.

Bernstein, Matthew. *Film Quarterly*. Summer, 1999.

Billington, Michael. *The Times Saturday Review*. November 9, 1968.

Blair, Ian. *Chicago Tribune*. October 1, 1989.

Blair, Ian. *Chicago Tribune*. July 6, 2003.

Block, Jean Libman. *Good Housekeeping*. May 1966.

Blowen, Michael. *Boston Sunday Globe*. February 23, 1997.

Boston Post. April 2, 1944.

Bovsun, Mara. *New York Daily News*. June 8, 2003.

Brenson, Michael. *New York Times*. February 18, 1983.

Burdin, Martin. *New York Post*. May 14, 1987: 29.

Burr, Ty. *Entertainment Weekly*. May 7, 1993.

Champlin, Charles. *Los Angeles Times: May 3, 1973*.

 October 20, 1991.

 May 19, 1997.

Christy, George. *Hollywood Reporter.* February 13, 1981.

Collins, Nancy. *Washington Post.* September 13, 1978.

Coronet. July, 1961.

Cosmopolitan. February 1955.

Creelman, Eileen. *New York Sun.* December 27, 1944.

Crotta, Carol A. *Los Angeles Herald-Examiner.* February 2, 1983.

Crist, Judith. *New York Herald-Tribune.* October 12, 1955.

Cullen, Jenny. *Ladies' Home Journal.* November 1988.

Cunningham, Laura. *Cosmopolitan.* January 1977.

Darrach, Brad. *People Weekly.* June 15, 1987.

Dean, Samantha. *Newsday.* September 4, 1977.

Deutsch, Linda. *Associated Press.* May 15, 1998.

Delehanty, Thorton. *New York Herald-Tribune.* October 10, 1943.

Dreifus, Claudia. *New York Times.* May 4, 1998.

Dunne, Philip. *New York Herald-Tribune.* August 12, 1951.

Evening Times. April 27, 1953. Evans, Hal. *National Enquirer.* October 7, 1973.

Farley, Ellen. *Los Angeles Times.* October 22, 1978.

Fessier, Bruce. *The Desert Sun.* July 6, 2003.

Gallo, Hank. New York *Daily News.* October 13, 1991.

Gardell, Kay. New York *Daily News.* August 24, 1988.

Gittleson, Natalie. *McCalls.* September 1984: 108.

Grant, James. *Los Angeles Times.* June 2, 1994.

Green, Ann. *Los Angeles Times: TV Times.* February 7, 1993.

Hale, Wanda. New York *Daily News.* August 31, 1964.

Hall, William. *New York Post.* December 17, 1977.

Harmetz, Aljean. *New York Times: Art/Entertainment.* March 11, 1989.

Haun, Harry. New York *Daily News.* May 17, 1987.

Hirsch, James S. *The Wall Street Journal.* June, 18, 1997.

Healy, Michael. *Denver Post.* April 5, 1987.

Holland, Jack. *Silver Screen.* February 1950.

Hopper, Hedda. *Chicago Sunday Tribune.* November 24, 1946.

Modern Screen. May 1949.

Harris, Leonard. *New York World-Telegram and Sun.* August 17, 1964.

Harris, Radie. *Photoplay.* September 1955.
People. February 12, 1990.
Hodges, Sam. *Mobile Register.* June 13, 2003.
Hopper, Hedda. *Chicago Tribune.* October 15, 1944.
Modern Screen. May 1949.
Huebler, Richard G. *Coronet.* March 1956.
Ito, Robert. *Los Angeles Magazine.* August, 1999.
Jacobs, Tom. *Long Beach Press-Telegram.* October 8, 1989.
James, Caryn. *New York Times.* March 13, 1998.
New York Times. April 12, 1992.
Jory, Tom. *New York Post.* December 12, 1978.
Karp, Josh. *January Magazine.* December, 2001.
King, Andrea. *Hollywood Reporter.* March 14, 1989.
King, Susan. *Los Angeles Times.* May 26, 1990.
Los Angeles Times, October 18, 1999.
Knight, Leonard. *Journal of San Diego History.* Spring, 1966.
Koski, Richard. *Finger Lakes Finns Newsletter.* May, 2001.
Krause, Betsy. *Columbia Daily Tribune.* May 10, 1987.
Lardine, Bob. New York *Daily News.* October 31, 1976.
Las Vegas Sun. November 5, 1978.
Leclair, J.E. *Confidential.* c 1955-56.
London Times. December 16, 1959.
Long Beach Press Telegram. June 28, 1998.
Los Angeles Examiner. May 7, 1948.
Los Angeles Examiner. May 10, 1959.
Los Angeles Herald-Examiner. January 9, 1972.
  June 27, 1975.
  July 22, 1971.
  April 5, 1946.
  February 2, 1983.
Los Angeles Times. April 22, 1948.
  November 9, 1978
  December 30, 1954.
  September 28, 1980.
Luce, William P. *New York Times.* July 11, 1977.
Lowrance, Dee. *Photoplay.* July 1947.
Macinnis, Craig. *Toronto Star.* October 11, 1991.

Mann, Roderick. *Los Angeles Times*, June 26, 1983.

Manners, Dorothy. *Los Angeles Herald-Examiner*. August 16, 1964.

Markfield, Alan. *National Enquirer*. August 19, 1975.

Marshman, Donald. *Life*. February 10, 1947.

Martin, Pete. *Saturday Evening Post*. September 22, 1945.

Matheson, Whitney. *USA Today*. October 17, 2000.

McCalls, July 1958.

McElwaine, Sandra. *New York Daily News*. October 22, 1989.

McIntyre, David. *San Diego Evening Tribune*. March 13, 1963.

Melton, Mary. *Los Angeles Times Magazine*. January 17, 1999.

Merina, Victor. *Los Angeles Times*. November 9, 1978.

Miles, Cynthia Wilkerson. *The Hollywood Reporter*. July 11, 1977.

Mills, Bart. *Chicago Tribune Magazine*. June 9, 1974.

Morris, Mary. *PM*. January 31, 1944.

Life. January 15, 1945.

   August 5, 1946.

   February 10, 1947.

Look. July 24, 1956.

Muir, Florabel. *New York Daily News*, December 30, 1954.

Murphy, Kathleen. *Film Comment*. March 4, 1992.

National Enquirer. July 23, 1974.

National Enquirer. Sept 15, 1974.

Nesselson, Lisa. *Variety*. November 15, 1999.

Newman, Larry. *The American Weekly*. November 9, 1952.

Newman, Randy. *Los Angeles Examiner: American Weekly*. November 9, 1952.

New Republic. May 19, 1947.

Newsweek. October 21, 1957.

Newsweek. March 3, 1947.

   June 8, 1999.

New York Daily News. May 2, 1958.

New York Times. January 7, 1945.

   January 11, 1978.

   July 7, 1977.

   April 12, 1992.

   June 11, 1973.

New Yorker. May 17, 1947.
New Yorker. April 20, 1992.
   April, 20, 1992.
O'Dowd, John. *Crime Magazine.* April, 29, 2003.
O'Hare, Kate. *Orange County Register.* October 17, 1999.
Coronet, July, 1970.
Oram, Hugh. *The Irish Times.* July 26, 2003.
Osbourne, Robert. *Hollywood Reporter.* April 15, 1992.
Parsons, Louella O. *Photoplay.* May 1949.
International New Service. October 8, 1950.
International News Service. June 9, 1946.
Los Angeles Examiner. November 8, 1959
Peck, Gregory. *Photoplay.* December 1945.
Morris, J. *Parents.* July 1951.
Saturday Evening Post. March 22, 1947.
Hollywood Citizen News. August 7, 1964.
Peck, Greta. *Photoplay.* May 1946
Newsweek. October 21, 1957.
Peck, Veronique. *Family Weekly.* June 3, 1961.
Hollywood Citizen-News. June 3, 1961.
Penfield III, Wilder. *Toronto Sun.* September 5, 1996.
People. October 9, 1995.
   August 8, 1977.
Philadelphia Inquirer. April 5, 1977.
Photoplay. c 1949-1950.
Pittsburgh Post-Gazette. July 11, 2003.
Price, Michael H. *Fort Worth Star-Telegram.* April 26, 1987.
Providence Journal. May 9, 1947.
Quick. June 26, 1950.
Ringle, Ken. *Washington Post.* June 13, 2003.
Regelings, Lowell E. *Hollywood Citizen-News.* August 5, 1958.
Rickey, Carrie. *Philadelphia Inquirer.* June 27, 1999.
Ridgely, Roberta. *San Diego Magazine.* June 1987.
Robbins, Fred. *Celebrity.* March 1976.
Rochlen, Kendis *Los Angeles Mirror News. May 23, 1958.*
Rogers, John G. *Los Angeles Times.* March 15, 1964.
Rosenfield, Paul. 'Gregory Peck Accepts AFI Life Award.' *Los*

Angeles Times. March 11, 1989.

Russell, Bruce. *Reuters.* July, 6, 1977.

Ryan, Desmond. *Philadelphia Inquirer.* October 8, 1978.

Saturday Review. June 9, 1956.

Saunders, Marsha. *Modern Screen.* May 1953.

Savoy, Maggie. *Los Angeles Times.* December 18, 1967.

Scheer, Robert. *Los Angeles Times.* November 19, 2000.

Schallert, Edwin. *Los Angeles Times.* January 10, 1954.

Scheuer, Philip K. *Los Angeles Times.* December 14, 1947.
    December 16, 1962.

Schier, Ernest. *Philadelphia Evening Bulletin.* May 9, 1972.

Scott, Vernon. *McCalls.* September 1963.

Schuller, Robert. *Hour of Power.* June 22, 2003.

Screen Guide. October 1946.

Seidelman, Arthur A. *After Dark.* January, 1970.

Shalit, Gene. *Look.* August 12, 1969.

Shearer, Lloyd. *Toronto Star Weekly.* July 14, 1956.

Shelden, Michael. Telegraph.co.uk. June 22, 2003.

Silver Screen. February 1950.

Skow, John. *People.* November 22, 1982.

Slater, Leonard. July 1958.

Smith, Cecil. *Los Angeles Times.* November 27, 1982.

Smith, Donna. *Photoplay.* April 1945.

Smith, J.Y. *Washington Post.* June 12, 2003.

Smith, Robert. *National Enquirer.* May 10, 1977.

The Star. December 13, 1988.

Stein, Herb. *New York Morning-Telegraph.* March 13, 1963.

Stein, Jeanne. *Films in Review.* March 1967.

New Yorker. April 20, 1992.

Strick, Anne. *Negro Digest.* July 1948.

Stratthaus, Mary Ellen. *American Jewish History.* 1996.

Suillivan, William. *San Diego Magazine.* May 1978.

Tacoma News Tribune. May 24, 1987.

Taylor, John. *Variety Weekly.* July, 7, 1966.

Thomas, Bob. *New York Post.* April 2, 1982 (excerpted from Thomas' book, *Heartbreak Kids: The Tragedy of Hollywood's Children*).

Associated Press. June 13, 2003.

Time. March 17, 1947.
   January 12, 1948.

Tobey, Kenneth. *Photoplay.* April 1947.

Tornabene, Lyn. *Cosmopolitan.* October 1961.

TV Guide. November 13, 1982.
   January 29, 1983.

Toronto Star Weekly. July 14, 1956.

Turegano, Preston. *San Diego Union Tribune.* June 8, 2003.

Valery, Bernard. *Daily News.* January 25, 1955.

Van Wyk. *Calgary Sun.* May 10, 1996.

Warga, Wayne. *Los Angeles Times.* May 30, 1971.

Waterbury, Ruth. *Photoplay.* September 1945 and October 1945.

Los Angeles Examiner. September 27, 1959.

Weiler, A.H. *New York Times.* August 6, 1972.

Whitcomb, Jan. *Cosmopolitan Magazine.* January 1961.

White, Betty. *Saturday Evening Post.* January/February 1977.

Williams, Pharrell. *Interview.* August, 2003.

Wilson, Earl. *New York Post.* November 18, 1959.

Woolfenden, john. *New York Times.* July 7, 1963.

Zeitling, Ida. *Photoplay.* April 1952.

Zinsser, William K. *New York Herald-Tribune.* July 1, 1956.

Libraries and Research Centers

Academy of Motion Picture Arts and Sciences Los Angeles –
   Margaret Herrick Library

American Film Institute – Louis B. Mayer Library

Brooksville Public Library

Clinton Public Library

District of Columbia Public Library

Jersey City Public Library

La Jolla Historical Society

Library of Congress – Motion Picture Collection

Lincoln Center Library of the Performing Arts – Billy Rose Theatre
   Collection

Los Angeles Public Library

Lyndon B. Johnson Library

Madison Public Library
Pasadina Public Library
Philadelphia Free Library Theatre Collection
University of California, Berkeley – Bancroft Library
Rochester Public Library
San Diego Historical Society
San Diego Public Library
University of California, Los Angeles Theatre Arts Collection
University of Southern California – Doheny Library
Wesleyan University Cinema Library
Yale University – Sterling Library

Websites
www.canoe.ca
www.bigpond.com
www.megwood.com
www.Nevilshute.org
www.thecolumnists.com/kinneylittlefield
www.waka.com

Acknowledgements

First, I'm grateful to Gregory Peck for being such a bloody marvelous biography subject. The very mention of his name around inbred show business folk caused doors to swing open that would otherwise have remained shut.

Next, a rousing cheer for the research staffs of theatre and film libraries from coast to coast. It reinforced my conviction that librarians are the smartest people on earth. Special thanks to the specialists at: the Academy of Motion Picture Arts and Sciences Margaret Herrick Library, The American Film Institute, the Bancroft Library at the University of California at Berkeley, the University of Southern California's Dohney Library, The UCLA Theatre Arts Collection, the New York City Public Library for the Performing Arts Billy Rose Theatre Collection at Lincoln Center and the film archives at the Museum of Modern Art.

In the approximately 200 interviews for the book, I had the opportunity to meet all kinds of people who knew Gregory Peck. Both the famous and obscure were kind enough to share their reminiscences with me. I am particularly indebted to June Dally-Watkins of Australia who confided in me about her whirlwind romance with Greg during 1952 when he was just coming off the filming of *Roman Holiday*. Similarly, I'd like to say thanks to Tommy Henkkanen who helped me create a vivid portrait of Greg's first wife Greta, a woman who has been given short shrift in previous accounts of Greg's life. Also, I'm appreciative of the wry observations of Leslie Epstein, Greg's neighbor in the Pacific Palisades who had a chance to observe the star out of the spotlight. For relating poignant moments in Greg's later years, I want to say thank you to Lisa Krohn. I am also indebted to my close friends Donna and Art

Wolff who contributed their canny insights about the Hollywood scene as well as supplying me with plenty of out-loud laughs.

There's a special group of individuals I'd like to acknowledge. These were friends of Greg's firstborn son Jonathan who took his own life in 1975. Among those who supplied me with information never before brought to light were: Nancy Stesin, John Bell, Carter Black, Paul Sack, Blair Bolles, Jamie Auchincloss, and Susan and Tom Casey.

At Robson Books, I had the good fortune to work with Jane Donovan. If Oscars were passed out to editors, she'd be first in line. Her sharp-eyed attention to the text and her posing of critical questions enable me to sort through the chaff and select the wheat. The manuscript also benefited greatly from the scrupulous copyreading of Alison Moss and Sarah Barlow. For first-rate picture research, I am indebted to Louise Daubeny and Aline Morely. And for creating an exquisite book jacket, my thanks go to Richard Mason. Last, but not least, a toast to publisher Jeremy Robson. Now, there's a charmer.

The publisher wishes to thank the following for kindly providing the photographs that appear in this book:

Page 1 (main) courtesy of © John Springer Collection/CORBIS
Pages 1 (inset), 3 (bottom right), 5 and 13 (top) courtesy of © Bettmann/CORBIS/© CinemaPhoto/CORBIS
Page 2 (top) courtesy of Getty Images/Hulton Archive
Page 2 (bottom) courtesy of Rex Features/Crollalanza
Page 3 (top) courtesy of the Kobal Collection
Page 3 (bottom left) courtesy of © Tommy Hinkkanen
Page 4 (top and middle) courtesy of June Dally-Watkins
Page 4 (bottom) by kind permission of Jeff and Carol Lang
Page 6–7 (left) courtesy of Selznick/United Artists/The Kobal Collection
Page 7 (bottom right) courtesy of Selznick/RKO/The Kobal Collection
Page 8–9 courtesy of Warner Bros/The Kobal Collection
Page 10 courtesy of Rex Features/SNAP

Page 11 (top) courtesy of Rex Features/PHA
Page 11 (bottom) courtesy of United Artists/The Kobal Collection
Page 12 courtesy of Rex Features/LUC
Page 13 (bottom) courtesy of Associated Press
Page 14 (top and bottom) courtesy of Chrysalis Images
Page 15 courtesy of Rex Features/ADC
Page 16 courtesy of Paramount/The Kobal Collection

Front cover photograph courtesy of © CinemaPhoto/CORBIS

Index

Bell, John 319–21, 323, 337, 361, 364
Bell, Judy 337
The Bells of Hell Go Ting-a-Ling-a-Ling
  327–8
Beloved Infidel (1959) 28, 192, 287–91
Bennett, Joan 15–16, 143, 144–5
Bennett, Seymour 143
Benny, Jack 351
Bergen, Polly 301
Bergman, Ingrid 22–6, 116, 119–23, 182
Berkeley 3, 61–70
Berlin 237–41
Berlin, Joey 363–4
Bernstein, Elmer 308–9, 339
Bernstein, Henri 87, 89
Bernstein, Walter 404
Berrigan, Daniel 355, 357
Berrigan, Philip 355
Bickford, Charles 126, 129, 272
Bierce, Ambrose 390–2
The Big Country (1958) 269–75, 301, 418
The Billionaire (later *Let's Make Love*)
  291–4
Billy Two Hats (1973) 357–8
Binford, Lloyd T 135
Birch, Ruth 169
Bird, Dorothy 74–5
Bishop, Joey 324
Black, Carter 342, 343
blacklist 163–7, 202, 404
Blake, Robert 278
The Blue and the Gray (1982) 384
Boccalandro, Iginia 26
Bogart, Humphrey
  alcohol 20
  Ava Gardner 284
  death of 268
  fights 193
  HUAC 164, 165
  Lauren Bacall 264–6
  Method 77
  privacy 26
  smoking 170
Bogart, Leslie 266
Bogart, Stephen Humphrey 266, 352
Bogeaus, Benedict 144–5
Bohan, Mark 331
Bolles, Blair 341–2, 343
Boochester, Buck 71, 72–3
Bork, Robert 388–9, 411
Bow, Clara 53, 110
Bowden, Dorris 240
Bowers, William 194
The Boys From Brazil (1978) 375–8, 387,
  418
Bradbury, Ray 246, 256
Brady, James 411
Brand, Harry 239–40

Brand, Phoebe 165
Brando, Marlon 15, 209–10, 349, 363
The Bravados (1958) 192, 276–7
Brecht, Bertolt 164
Breen, Joseph 149, 169
Brentwood 262, 337
Brentwood Productions 306, 323, 325
Bridges, Lloyd 388
Broadway
  leaving for Hollywood 93–4
  Leland Hayward 17–18
  The Morning Star 6, 91–2
  move to 72
  moving to 70
  The Willow and I 8, 92, 93
Bromley, Hunt 196
Brookes, Sir Norman 280
Brooks, Richard 111
Brown, Clarence 139
Brown, David 371
Brown, James Mason 92
Brown, Kay 9, 100
Brown, Pat 344, 378
Bruce, Nigel 102
Brutsman, Joseph 414
Bruzzi, Stella 315–16
Buchanan, Johnny 44
Buchwald, Ann 227–8
Buchwald, Art 227–8, 229, 249–50
Buckley, William F 313
Bud (pet dog) 43, 45–6, 77
Burns, George 267
Burns, Gracie 9
Busch, Niven 125
Button Button (play 1940) 83–4

Cabanne, Christy 205
Cagney, James 77, 165, 199
California, Fact Finding Committee 166–7
Canary Islands 250–1
Cap Ferrat, France 297, 299–300, 318,
  360, 372
Capa, Robert 122–3
Cape Fear (1962) 300–3, 418
Cape Fear (1991) 303, 395
Cape Playhouse, Massachusetts 90, 140–1
Capote, Truman 309
Captain Horatio Hornblower (1951)
  158–9, 205–8, 418
Captain Jinks (play 1941) 86
Captain Newman, M.D. (1963) 323–5
Carey, Harry, Jr 106, 126, 189
Carlini, Paolo 221
Caroline of Monaco, Princess 383
Carroll, Leo G 168
Carroll, Madeleine 165
Carson, Johnny 381
Carter, Jimmy 366